D1565946

Enlisting Faith

Enlisting Faith

HOW THE MILITARY CHAPLAINCY SHAPED RELIGION AND STATE IN MODERN AMERICA

Ronit Y. Stahl

 Harvard University Press

Cambridge, Massachusetts
London, England 2017

Library of Congress Cataloging-in-Publication Data

Names: Stahl, Ronit Y., 1980– author.
Title: Enlisting faith : how the military chaplaincy shaped religion and
    state in modern America / Ronit Y. Stahl.
Description: Cambridge, Massachusetts : Harvard University Press, 2017. |
    Includes bibliographical references and index.
Identifiers: LCCN 2017009230 | ISBN 9780674972155 (alk. paper)
Subjects: LCSH: Military chaplains—United States—History—20th century. |
    Religion and state—United States—History—20th century.
Classification: LCC UH23 .S73 2017 | DDC 355.34/70973—dc23
    LC record available at https://lccn.loc.gov/2017009230

For my mother, Sharyn W. Stahl,

and in memory of my father, Richard J. Stahl z"l

Contents

Illustrations follow page 164

A Note on Terminology

In the United States, chaplains enter the military as First Lieutenants and can receive promotions. However, unlike other officers, they are always addressed as "Chaplain" rather than by their rank ("First Lieutenant," "Colonel," "Rear Admiral," etc.). As a result, I refer to chaplains as "Chaplain" and include their rank only if it is relevant.

Although chaplains are charged with serving all personnel no matter their religious background, military clergy come from specific denominational traditions. To quickly illustrate this, I include, upon first reference, their faith tradition in parentheses after their names—for example, Chief of Chaplains William Arnold (Catholic). To the extent possible, I use the religious nomenclature found in military rosters from the time; as a result, some of these labels may seem anachronistic (e.g., Northern Baptist) or obsolete (Presbyterian U.S.), but they reflect how the military viewed religious groups and historically accurate affiliations. Occasionally, chaplains appear fleetingly in the archives without much additional data, in which case I used information found by searching for them in unit histories, seminary rosters, newspaper articles, census records, and obituaries. Religious identifications are, therefore, less systematic than ideal, but nevertheless impart a reasonable sense of military classification.

Finally, throughout the book I use "religion" and "faith" interchangeably—not because they are the same, but because the government, including the military, employed them as synonyms. "Faith" and its corollary, "belief," reflect Protestant ideas about the root or core feature of religion, whereas other traditions often center on rituals or communal practices. The use of faith as a stand-in for religion underscores the often unlabeled Protestant religion that anchors American law and society. Yet as this book shows, equating faith and religion both enabled the military to open the chaplaincy to multiple faith groups and structured the struggles it faced in trying to accommodate a wide range of religious needs.

Enlisting Faith

Prologue

The Mixed-Up Dog Tags of
Private Leonard Shapiro

THE NEWS WAS incomprehensible. The letter was hard to read. Her son had been killed in France on August 20, 1944? Was that really true? But it was the condolence note that shattered the mother. If her child's body "received respectful and reverential care," why did "a modest Christian cross" adorn his grave? How was it possible that "last rites of the Church were held, his grave was blessed, and Masses were being said regularly for him and the others who have made the supreme sacrifices for their country"?[1] Rose Shapiro's son was a Jewish soldier from Chicago. Why was he buried as a Catholic?

For Rose Shapiro, this moment was a trial of faith—in her country, not God. It prompted a personal odyssey to uncover what happened to her twenty-two-year-old son, killed in action as the 80th Infantry Division liberated Argentan, France, from the Nazis. Like millions of other Gold Star mothers, she had to live with her son's death.[2] But his burial compounded her personal grief. She had entrusted the military to care for her son, yet a chaplain stationed "somewhere in France" challenged her confidence in her country, in its promise to honor the religious choices of its citizens. Solving this riddle turned Rose Shapiro's private anguish into a state concern. Army Chief of Chaplains William Arnold (Catholic) thus labored to ascertain where military knowledge of and procedures for religion went wrong.

To Rose Shapiro and her supporters, her son and his family were "obviously Jewish." Arnold agreed, noting in his letter of inquiry to

Chaplain Kenneth C. Martin (Catholic) that "Mrs. Shapiro is, as the name so strongly suggests, Jewish."[3] Moreover, while the state did not track the religion of its citizens, starting in World War I, men in uniform wore military identification (dog) tags. During World War II, religious affiliation joined name, serial number, and blood type on the small metal discs. When bullets and bombs silenced soldiers, the stamped ovals spoke for them. Dog tags distinguished one American from another, verified religious identities, and informed chaplains which death and funeral rites they should perform or oversee. When Private Shapiro entered the army, he could have selected one of three initials to indicate his religion: P for Protestant, C for Catholic, or H for Hebrew.

Of course, not everyone followed regulations. Chaplain Lyman Berrett (LDS), who was stationed at Okinawa, recalled that "when we would bury men . . . we would not always go by the name on the dog tags" because superstitious soldiers believed that their dog tags marked them as targets for bullets. They exchanged dog tags with one another, which led chaplains to develop additional means of corroboration.[4] In addition, during World War II, Jewish soldiers often deliberated whether or not to include their religion at all, fearing that if they were captured in Germany, they might be singled out for punishment as Jews rather than treated as prisoners of war. Chaplain Charles S. Freedman (Jewish) understood the risk-benefit calculations many soldiers considered: on the one hand, "for many men and their families back home, it would be of the greatest importance that, should death come on the field of battle, a Jewish burial be given the deceased." On the other hand, he acknowledged, in practice, it is better to be "a live dog rather than a dead lion."[5] So, reasonably, the chief of chaplains launched his investigation by asking what was marked on Leonard Shapiro's dog tag. Then, he wondered, had the young man converted overseas? Was his religious preference unclear, but if so, "could not his buddies have supplied the necessary information?" Finally, was this incident merely a mix-up, a letter sent in error?[6]

Chaplain Martin meant no harm. He was likely flustered when he opened the letter from his superior officer, learning that he had made a potent mistake in the midst of combat. He had done what all chaplains were supposed to do. To show that deaths were more than serial numbers on a list, military clergy wrote personalized condolence letters to comfort the kin of those killed in action. Families on the home front often appreciated this gesture, one that bridged the distant war and their immediate loss.[7] But as Chaplain Berrett experienced in the Pacific, confusion also reigned on the European battlefront. In the absence of a clearly designated religious preference, Chaplain Martin reported that he had "selected names that I thought were of a Catholic faith. Inadvertently I selected the name Shapiro to be an Italian name, and one that was a Catholic."[8]

For Chaplain Martin, this episode exemplified a process of religious encounter. Religions differ, and war brought Americans into contact with other and sometimes unfamiliar faiths. Prior to military service, most clergy had limited interaction with other religious groups.[9] Although Catholics and Jews shared experiences as religious outsiders in a predominantly Protestant nation and often lived in close proximity in urban spaces, these commonalities did not necessarily familiarize groups with one another. Thus arose the predicament of a chaplain who did not know Shapiro was a Jewish name. He saw a surname that ended with a vowel and guessed it was Italian—and thus Catholic. In contrast, over several decades of military service, Chief of Chaplains Arnold had developed a keen sense of discrete religious communities and dedicated his office to meeting their needs. He apologized to Rose Shapiro. Then he instructed his men to replace the grave's cross with a Star of David and locate a Jewish chaplain to "conduct a proper memorial service."[10]

The eight-month exchange between Rose Shapiro, the chief of chaplains, and Chaplain Martin was both anomalous and routine. For the Shapiro family, the effort to trace the circumstances of Leonard's burial was a one-time crisis that brought them into close contact with authorized representatives of the state. For the chief of chaplains, enforcing regulations and interacting with the public constituted his daily work. Crafting and implementing government policies meant navigating military and civilian spheres and negotiating religious disjunctures. For Chaplain Martin, it highlighted a significant challenge faced by chaplains: learning how to effectively minister to men of different faiths.

The interlocking threads of religious encounter, state regulation, and trials of faith that explain the interaction between a mother, a deployed chaplain, and the army chief of chaplains during World War II also reveal how the military chaplaincy functioned in—and shaped—modern

America. First, the history of the twentieth-century chaplaincy demonstrates how the state encouraged religious engagement and struggled to manage the tension between faiths inherent in a pluralist environment. When the United States entered World War I, its chaplaincy corps consisted of mainline Protestants (including African Americans) and Catholics. Midwar congressional legislation enabled Christian Scientists, the Eastern Orthodox, Jews, Mormons, and the Salvation Army to accept chaplain commissions. Over the twentieth century, the diversity of religious affiliations represented in the chaplaincy continued to increase, propelled by Americans who wanted the state to recognize their clergy as legitimate religious representatives of the nation. During World War II, the military set quotas for chaplains by denomination, allocating one spot for every 100,000 members enumerated in the 1936 Census of Religious Bodies. By the end of the war, chaplains represented almost seventy religious groups. Although the armed forces did not acquire its first Muslim, Buddhist, and Hindu chaplains until the late twentieth and early twenty-first centuries, the chaplaincies nevertheless grappled with how to serve personnel from these faiths beginning in World War II. Over the twentieth century, then, the military served as a crucible for religious change.

Second, the chaplaincy unveils the processes of state regulation in an arena rarely considered within government purview: religion.[11] Exposing how bureaucracy worked in modern America shows that the regulatory state could operate directly and indirectly, and the military afforded the opportunity to do both. The state set parameters for religion in the armed forces through standards, policies, and procedures that framed chaplains' work. In turn, these regulations exerted oblique pressure on religions and denominations to conform to guidelines—or, at times, to bend and stretch to meet them while advocating changing them. Minority faiths, for example, bristled at the limited categories the state allowed on dog tags. Mormons protested regulations that labeled them "Protestant," for example, by pointing out that they—like Buddhists and many others—"are in no sense Protestants."[12] It took years of advocacy and argument, but eventually the military relented, first by offering an "other" category and then by allowing individuals to spell out their religious identities on dog tags. In this sense, the military managed religions through both carrot and stick. It beckoned with possibilities—to serve one's country, to reach young men, to be recognized as legitimate, to imprint God on the nation, and to access state power. (And, in the case of proselytizing faiths, to win souls.)[13] For many denominations and religions, the military represented an irresistible opportunity. But as a coercive institution, the military also demanded adherence to specific norms—by soldiers, by officers, by chaplains, and, ultimately, by religious groups too. And over the twentieth century, each new inclusion, whether religious, racial, or gendered, produced additional exclusions. The military acted with force, it took with force, claimed with force, and ruled with force. But it could not force faith. It could, however, strongly encourage and build structures to fortify and deploy faith, and that it did.

Finally, an account of the chaplaincy makes American trials of faith visible: the challenges of adhering to religious faith in secular spaces, of retaining faith in inconsistent institutions, and of equitably managing multiple faiths. Strains of resistance were common, but rarely uniform in voice or goal. Some families resisted the idea of Catholic chaplains ministering to Protestant sons, while some chaplains struggled to embrace pluralism. Some soldiers requested religiously sanctioned food, while others bridled at the presence of religion in their midst. Similarly, some religious groups, like Seventh-day Adventists, objected to any valence of state religion, while others, such as evangelical Protestants, became frustrated by insufficiently bellicose faith. At the same time, war could challenge faith. During the Vietnam War, for example, liberal Protestants, Catholics, and Jews—onetime stalwarts of the chaplaincy—reconsidered the commingling of the sword and the spirit. And while some women chafed at restrictions on female chaplains, some African American clergy resented the assumption that they would serve a racist state. Braided together, these stories— of religious encounter, the regulatory state, and the trials of faith— underscore the centrality of religion in modern America.

Examining how the state mobilized for war demonstrates that religion was rarely separate from the workings of the state. Despite assumed secularism, the military built a massive infrastructure to instill religion in its men. As one of the most important, if sometimes underappreciated, institutions of the American state, the military functions as an administrative agency with the power to define, construct, and enforce norms of believing in, behaving under, and belonging to the American nation.[14] *Enlisting Faith* therefore describes how the military chaplaincy evolved from World War I through the late 1980s to demonstrate how a state institution worked hard—sometimes succeeding and sometimes failing—to build a religiously diverse and pluralist nation.

The story of the modern American military chaplaincy unmasks the bidirectional influence of religion and state.[15] The chaplaincy connected the military, a federal entity that regulated the lives of millions of Americans across the globe, to religion, that elixir of belief and rituals that, theoretically, existed entirely outside the framework of the state.[16] In fact, arming men with the faith to die fighting opened a vast arena of military ministry. Across the twentieth century, the nation's consistent engagement in armed conflict along with its increasing religious diversity generated new tasks for the chaplaincy and invigorated tensions between religion and the state. Just as the state relied on religion to sanctify war death and sanction military missions, so too did religious groups seek validation as recognized American faiths. At times the military co-opted religion to advance its imperial goals. But religious believers pushed back, challenging the state to live up to the constitutional promises and moral standards it claimed to uphold.

Chaplains became commonplace fixtures in a multitude of twentieth-century public and private settings, ranging from universities and hospitals to prisons and businesses.[17] But in no other realm did the federal state acquire such significant oversight of religion as the military chaplaincy, which structured the relationship between soldiers and God on behalf of the government.[18] The military can be an all-encompassing environment—especially on the battlefield and in enclosed spaces like Fort Knox—and it was one of very few domains in which the federal government formally employed and managed clergy.[19] Through the chaplaincy, the state mediated military necessity and religious obligations, public ceremonies and private faith. Yet chaplains who volunteered to serve their nation at war frequently returned to civilian pulpits or to institutions like universities and hospitals, which made the military chaplaincy a porous military-civilian space. Lessons learned marching in combat boots spread to American society by former chaplains preaching in wing tips.

The work of the military chaplaincy in the twentieth century underscores both the evolving religious commitments of the state and the ways religious leaders brokered relationships between the military and civilian society. The military marketplace of religion offered a selection of government-preferred choices, and the rhetoric of religious pluralism often outpaced reality. Nevertheless, in the military, religion operated as a public interest—overseen by public officials, staffed by publicly funded clergy, and aware of (if not always responsive to) public concerns expressed by individual taxpayers, soldiers' families, and religious groups—all while carefully toeing the line of the First Amendment's establishment and free-exercise clauses. The Constitution forbids privileging one religion over others and requires accommodating individuals' exercise of religion, a particularly tricky balance to strike in a controlled environment like the military. Thus, there were rules and regulations, but there could also be sympathy and kindness. Rose Shapiro brushed up against the state in many venues over the course of her lifetime—immigration inspectors who let her into the country from Russia, census takers who knocked on her door to count her household, the city clerk who registered her marriage, Home Owners Loan Corporation officials who redlined her neighborhood, public school teachers who monitored her children's attendance, mail carriers who delivered condolence letters—but those were fleeting, if noticed at all.[20] Her pursuit to correct her son's errant burial took her out of her Chicago tenement apartment all the way to the top of the military chaplaincy brass, to Chief of Chaplains William Arnold, who intervened on her behalf. War formed a triangle between the individual, the state, and God. Just as religion structured relationships between God and the individual, soldiering blurred the distinctions between the individual and the state, and the chaplaincy bridged the state to God.

The American century was a century of war, and "wartime brings the ideal of the State out into very clear relief." As journalist Randolph Bourne observed during World War I, "government is the idea of the State put into practical operation in the hands of definite, concrete, fallible men."[21] It is not the word, but acts of governance that reveal state interests. Its values, priorities, and blind spots emerge through the millions of quotidian decisions made by its agents. On a day-to-day basis, administrators, officers, and commissioners interpreted, implemented, and sometimes even created state policy.[22] Integrating Chaplain School but maintaining a Jim Crow system of black chaplains serving only black units, or fashioning a dog tag taxonomy that included

Catholics and Jews but cast everyone else as Protestant, discloses the racial order and religious sensibilities prized by the military at specific moments in time.

The military is as much a social and cultural space as a martial one. Focusing on the granular details of discretionary decision-making within the military chaplaincy, such as determinations about what insignia chaplains wore, which faiths could endorse chaplains, or whose Sabbath rituals were accommodated, makes the religious interests, anxieties, and preferences of government detectable. The army, as the largest branch of the military and the most responsive to civilian input, serves as the foundation for assessing how political concerns, social contexts, and legal constraints shaped religious duties in the armed forces. The experiences of navy and air force chaplains generally reinforce, but occasionally counter, how the army saw, understood, and managed religious friction.

Chaplains, as clergy serving as military officers, exemplified diffuse state power. Like immigration examiners, Border Patrol agents, public health inspectors, Social Security administrators, tax assessors, FBI operatives, and marriage clerks, military chaplains operated autonomously within the rules set by an administrative bureaucracy.[23] Attending to the ways in which the armed forces contracted or expanded religious options—for example, the decision to suppress access to female preachers or to hold a memorial service for Malcolm X—helps calibrate the religious latitude afforded to American military personnel. As chaplains brokered religious accommodations within military space, they molded and challenged religious, racial, and gender norms. Their official duties centered on leading public worship and conducting funerals, but the reach of their work extended far beyond those tasks. By commissioning chaplains from various faiths and requiring them to address all religious needs, the state quietly legitimized multiple claims to truth. The chaplaincy thus shaped religion in the military into an entity different than a single totalizing faith, but nevertheless contingent on believing in one God, behaving morally, and partaking in religious practices that accorded with military decorum. Theologically vague, ethically simplistic, and ritually pliant standards could be precarious, but they created a remarkably resilient foundation for striving to achieve the chaplaincy mottos "unity without uniformity" and "cooperation without compromise."[24]

Enlisting Faith is a history of religion, the state, and society from World War I through the 1980s. It offers a new perspective on the military, which is often viewed as an authoritarian and conservative institution. The military's religious division was, like the rest of the armed forces, hierarchical and often coercive, but the chaplaincy could also be progressive, innovative, and pragmatic. Frequently, chaplains pressed for more equitable treatment of religious and racial minorities. And because the military, like religion itself, is at once local and global, compulsory military service produced encounters between Americans and less familiar religions abroad. In these ways, religion was bound up with the rights and responsibilities of citizenship within the modern state.[25] Because the military could enforce its norms, because millions of Americans served, and because the military, though distinct, was not insulated from civilian society, changes wrought through the chaplaincy traveled back home and permeated American life. Religious friction was inescapable, but managing—and sometimes succumbing to—such tension often paved the way for American politics, culture, and society to follow.[26]

The chaplaincy was not new in 1917, but it was on the brink of a radical overhaul. European colonialists in the seventeenth and eighteenth centuries toted clergy with them on their expeditions across the Atlantic and early settlements appointed chaplains to serve in residence and out on military campaigns. During the American Revolution, ministers accompanied loyalists and patriots alike into battle, and Congress sanctioned legislative and military chaplains beginning in 1775. Then as now, they led worship, delivered sermons, boosted morale, and buried the dead. But, more often than not, they were expected to occupy ancillary roles on an ad hoc and as-necessary basis. James Madison tried to eliminate chaplains, but George Washington convinced the fledgling republic's lawmakers that chaplains served the public good. Nevertheless, the military chaplaincy remained rudimentary and makeshift. During the Civil War, parsons and priests trudged alongside soldiers of the Confederate and Union Armies and pastored the wounded in hospitals but generally operated as self-sufficient individuals, with little communication or supervision from either church or state. By the late nineteenth century, as the military became more professionalized, chaplains, though few in number, organized to improve their status and increase their authority. Organizationally, World War I created the opening that transformed a muddled and middling chaplaincy into a professional officer corps with rank, autonomy, and a clear chain of command.[27]

As this infrastructure grew alongside the wartime expansion of the chaplaincy, it generated its own bureaucratic logic. Citizenship required men to defend the nation, and military service demanded that Americans live, fight, and worship with men from a variety of backgrounds and faiths.[28] The obligations of military service thus compelled men to experience religious difference within the nation. But the draft exempted clergy, which made the chaplaincy an all-volunteer organization even during times of conscription. As the chaplaincy developed to meet the needs of American military personnel, the state had to sift through a variety of constitutionally protected religious commitments, a task that was often more befuddling than clarifying.[29] Religious accommodations developed inconsistently, as religious practices vary significantly and chaplains tended to address specific requests rather than overhauling military conventions. Likewise, the chaplaincy incorporated religious groups unevenly, especially because blurred religious and racial categories confounded a military tied to racist classification of manpower.[30] When the military placed white clergy into three religious groups—Protestant, Catholic, and Jewish—it leapfrogged American society, which did not necessarily see Catholics and Jews as white in 1917. But in uniform, immigrant priests and rabbis became white, for Catholic and Jewish chaplains could, like white Protestants, serve any units. In contrast, the military restricted the assignment of black chaplains, no matter their religious background, to black units until after the desegregation of the armed forces. Ethnic, racial, and religious identities that did not conform to a white/black binary challenged the chaplaincy as well. For decades, neither Filipino Catholics nor Japanese American Buddhists could serve as chaplains, though other Catholics and Japanese American Christians could. Over the course of the twentieth century, these restrictions diminished as the military responded to religious and racial minorities advocating for inclusion.

Until 1973, the chaplaincy was an entirely male organization serving a predominantly male military. Women stood on the periphery—recognized primarily as mothers concerned for their sons, wives worried about their husbands, or innocent victims of venereal disease transmitted by promiscuous male soldiers. While the conservative gender politics may not be surprising, the idea that men could, on their own, embrace religion astonished quite a few civilians. Women sustained American religious life, dominating the pews and cultivating religion in domestic spaces.[31] Given this, some asked, how could men nurture religious life in the armed forces? In the late 1930s, Chief of Chaplains Alva Brasted (Northern Baptist) answered this question directly, insisting that when men could not depend on women to preserve religion, they took on the responsibility themselves.[32] Displacing men from the home, transplanting them into all-male spaces, could turn religious indifference into religious devotion, or so the military hoped. Thus, the chaplaincy's gaze focused on men, and on the simultaneous power and danger of homosocial spaces.[33] As Chaplain Morris Lazaron (Jewish) put it in 1923, "there is no intimacy like the intimacy of the barracks." In bivouacs and billets, men bonded as "brothers" who "come instinctively to feel that the big human aspirations are the same in all races, nations and creeds."[34] Lazaron's optimism relied on masculinity as a binding agent, a glue that rendered other differences moot (even as the military viewed homosexuality as a menace).

Yet the task of managing difference dominated the work of military chaplains. After Congress opened the chaplaincy to some religious minorities in World War I, the federal government spent the rest of the century tweaking protocols to grant American military personnel access to religion in neutral and fair ways. Legal scholars have trawled the thicket of religious neutrality, showing that law can be formally neutral (not making overt distinctions between faith groups) without being substantively neutral (producing equal outcomes for different religions).[35] For decades before the courts weighed in, however, Americans intuited and experienced these differences through their interactions with the military. Thus, evangelical Protestants seethed when God replaced Jesus in interdenominational settings, Mormons decried ordination requirements for chaplains, the Eastern Orthodox chafed at dog tag categories that erased their existence, Jews confronted pork in the mess hall, Seventh-day Adventists blanched at Saturday guard duty, Muslims contended with bans on beards, and Sikhs contested prohibitions on turbans. None of these general policies—about prayer, credentials, identification, food, Sabbath, or uniforms—intentionally targeted any faith groups, but it was impossible to craft procedures that did not have disparate impacts. Some religious groups weathered these obstacles more easily than others through negotiation, avoidance, or indifference, but all reckoned with ignorance, marginalization, and exclusion.

Federal judges provided little formal guidance on how the military should balance its delicate embrace of pluralist religious practice. When the Supreme Court briefly meditated on the military chaplaincy, it did so indirectly, not because minority religions faced imperfect accommodations but as a foil for religion in public schools. In *Abington v. Schempp* (1963), a sharply divided court held public school Bible readings unconstitutional, an unauthorized mixing of religion and state. The justices on both sides of the case agreed on one thing, however: that military chaplains, unlike Bible readings, represented a constitutionally acceptable synergy between religion and state. In his dissent, Justice Potter Stewart hailed the military chaplaincy as "a single obvious example" that demonstrated how "religion and government must necessarily interact in countless ways." To counter those who might claim that the military chaplaincy was itself an Establishment Clause violation, he pictured "a lonely soldier stationed at some faraway outpost [who] could surely complain that a government which did not provide him the opportunity for pastoral guidance was affirmatively prohibiting the free exercise of his religion."[36] The "lonely soldier" in need of "pastoral guidance" may have been close in age to the public school student, but he was distant from his home community and potentially on the brink of death. This trope, no matter how imprecise, sustained federal supervision and regulation of religious activity in the military.

As a vast environment controlled by the federal government, the military proved to be an ideal laboratory for the state to experiment with religion. Military management of religion began in earnest during World War I and continued to evolve over the twentieth century. For the next half century, restrictive immigration policies limited the arrival of outsiders while the draft brought together Americans from an array of class, ethnic, religious, and, after 1948, racial backgrounds. This era witnessed two significant debates about pacifism and religion, in the 1930s and the 1960s, both of which challenged the validity of military interventions abroad and, with it, the legitimacy of clergy in uniform. Mid-twentieth-century Americans also confronted two major ideologies—Nazism and Communism—in conflict with democracy and

opposed to some or all religion. In the postwar period, the militarization of American society through the domestic defense industry and
war abroad led the state to begin to see—and occasionally recognize—
additional faiths, recalibrating the work of the chaplaincy anew.[37] The
military operated simultaneously on local, national, and global scales,
and chaplains presided over faith in tight quarters continually influenced by defensive and imperial contact with religious difference.

Through the military chaplaincy, the state articulated and offered
religious citizenship to American soldiers who, in response, made claims
for their rights and, in so doing, transformed religion and state anew.
Each major twentieth-century war forged a new sensibility about religion within the military that percolated through civilian American
society. First, in World War I and the interwar years, the chaplaincy
consolidated a panoply of white immigrant and native-born Americans
into three more manageable religious groups: Protestants, Catholics,
and Jews. While Protestants stigmatized white ethnic groups through
Prohibition and restrictive immigration policies, the military recognized Catholics and Jews as equals, successfully building a tri-faith
model that, though more fictive than real, would permeate midcentury
American political culture. Second, during World War II and the early
Cold War, the chaplaincy promoted a pluralistic and universalizing
religious vision domestically and globally, celebrating the common
threads among religions and insisting on religion as a fundamental element of democracy. Implanting religious consensus in political culture
invited religious and racial minorities—such as Japanese American
Buddhists and African American Seventh-day Adventists—to lobby
for inclusion and leverage faith to agitate for full citizenship rights. It
also enticed white Protestant evangelicals and fundamentalists, often
understood as hostile to government, to enter the military in order
to engage with the American state. Third, during Vietnam and its aftermath, religious Americans used their faith to critique the state's
moral, religious, and racial blind spots. When some liberal religious
groups withdrew from the chaplaincy to protest the Vietnam War,
conservative evangelicals seized the opportunity to insert sectarian
ideas in state space. At the same time, the military encouraged racial
minorities and women to enter the chaplaincy and began reconsid-
ering the needs of religious minorities such as Muslims and Sikhs. As
political and religious fissures polarized the nation, the chaplaincy

struggled to reconcile its longstanding but imperfect commitment to pluralism with new iterations of American diversity.

Over the twentieth century, then, chaplains built—in concrete policy and as figurative symbols—state-sponsored American religion. Whether anchoring the "band of brothers" or sidestepping the My Lai massacre, chaplains deployed religion to achieve American military goals and sanction imperial aims. Overseas, chaplains often embodied the soft side of American intervention, but at home, they signaled an irresistible opportunity to access state power. In constructing a state religious institution, the military dangled an appealing opportunity for many American clergy to shape government ideas about religion by advancing pluralism or advocating particularity. Undoubtedly a state religious project, the military chaplaincy was also a political project, invested and intertwined with domestic life and foreign affairs. From a legal perspective, the constitutional mandate to separate church and state hovered over the chaplaincy, yet the greater challenge lay in the more quotidian effort to enable daily free exercise. The ability of the chaplaincy to adjudicate norms of public life and set the terms of American self-understanding gave it great power and commensurate responsibility. This interaction between religion and the state was regular, dynamic, and powerful, if sometimes concealed and often overlooked. *Enlisting Faith* renders these interactions visible, probing the processes, conflicts, and exchanges between the federal government and faith groups to relay how the military chaplaincy evolved and forged the possibility of remaking American society in its image.

1

Mobilizing Faith

JOSEPH ODELL'S career took many turns. He was a minister by training, an education reformer by conviction, and a writer by trade. In 1917, these roles merged. The former army chaplain traversed the United States to investigate War Department outposts, stopping by a number of camps and forts. By the time he reached Atlanta in November 1917, he was generally impressed by the activity he encountered. This was a surprise, because Odell expected to be disappointed in the South. Fort McPherson and Camp Gordon housed high percentages of foreign-born men, black men, and illiterate southern white men. The combination appeared combustible. Yet when Odell spoke with soldiers and attended the weekly meeting of the executive board of the local Commission on Training Camp Activities (CTCA), he was taken aback.[1]

As he reported to readers of *The Outlook*, a liberal religious weekly that supported the war effort, and then to other papers that reprinted his column, in Atlanta he unexpectedly discovered "a unique spirit of cooperation." Women mended soldiers' clothing, the Transportation Committee furnished automobiles for the sick, and the Entertainment Committee arranged concerts. The Federated Women's Club taught men how to sew and the Daughters of the American Revolution taught black women to knit. The Hebrew Association and the Knights of Columbus thanked the Young Men's Christian Association (YMCA) for lending them space for worship, dances, and lectures. As a booster for the moral, religious, and educational work of the War Department, Odell was far from objective. He appreciated the quotidian integration of religion into military procedures, remarking that "there is nothing remote or separate or esoteric about this religion; it fits into the order of the day as naturally as the meals in the mess-room." His reportage indicated that supporting the religious and moral welfare of soldiers could be coercive and patronizing. But his wonder at the "common sense" efforts to deemphasize difference among Protestants, Catholics, and Jews was real.[2]

Early twentieth-century Atlanta was not the most obvious place to witness interreligious coordination and fledgling, if condescending, multiethnic and multiracial discussions. Eleven years before Odell's visit, racial violence erupted in the southern boomtown as the gubernatorial candidates debated how to disenfranchise black men and newspaper headlines alleged black violence against white women. Four days of street violence destroyed black bodies and black businesses. The city remained heavily segregated, and overtly racist legislation entrenched Jim Crow policies. By late 1915, an opportunistic organizer revived the Ku Klux Klan with a march up a ridge outside Atlanta, and capacity crowds broke attendance records at the opening of the bigoted movie *The Birth of a Nation*. Religious minorities faced less hostility, but Atlanta did not welcome Jews and Catholics. The 1915 lynching of Leo Frank weighed heavily on the city's Jewish population. Catholics, a small population in a largely Protestant city, also faced the Klan's wrath. Despite the racial and religious tensions plaguing Atlanta, the war years provided an opportunity to gather together to meet the needs of conscripted soldiers.[3]

Listening to the reports of Atlantans' service compelled Odell to volunteer a war story of his own. The setting was the June 1917 Battle of Messines Ridge, a British offensive that recaptured a strategic outlook from German hands at the cost of 25,000 Allied lives. About three miles from the French border, he told the Atlanta volunteers, "a Catholic soldier lay dying, blown almost to pieces by a bomb. No Catholic chaplain happened to be near, and no Protestant chaplain was available; but a Hebrew rabbi, acting as a chaplain to the Jewish troops, bent over the dying Catholic and held the crucifix to his lips while he breathed his last." The committee members listened to Odell in captivated silence, then applauded in unison. They too valued "religious comity." That only a trickle of Americans had arrived in Europe in June mattered little. The tale reflected American values and priorities. As Odell reassured his readers, "some of the by-products of this war may be worth all the sacrifices of men, money, and strength."[4]

Odell joined a small but growing chorus of chaplains and military officers who viewed religious cooperation as an important and positive consequence of the United States' participation in World War I. Chaplain Lee Levinger (Jewish) returned from Europe extolling the virtues of an ecumenical chaplain corps. "Religious unity," he insisted, "is more than a far-off ideal." In his final report on the war, General John Pershing agreed. "Chaplains, as never before, became the moral and spiritual leaders of their organizations, and established a high standard of active usefulness in religious work that made for patriotism, discipline, and unselfish devotion to duty." Pershing's casual intermingling of religious and moral work was typical, for the separation between them was blurry, in civilian and military realms alike. By war's end, Pershing affirmed, religion had become a crucial weapon in the U.S. military's arsenal. But at war's beginning, this conclusion could not be anticipated. In spring 1917, the chaplaincy was small and consisted only of mainline Protestants and Catholics. To serve millions of newly conscripted men, the military intensified its efforts to expand the chaplaincy while continuing to regulate the appointments and activities of military clergy. Together, military needs, civilian agitation, and Congressional legislation irrevocably altered the institution of the chaplaincy, making it more religiously diverse and laying the foundation of tri-faith America.[5]

Over eighteen months of active American participation in the Great War, the state mobilized faith to sustain its martial goals. The state used religion to streamline its diverse and ethnically fragmented citizenry into more manageable groups. Regardless of birthplace, native tongue, or ethnicity, in the military, American soldiers were Protestants, Catholics, and Jews. This tri-faith architecture, expressed in tacit but significant ways during World War I, facilitated religious decision-making and set boundaries for inclusion. The military began cultivating an ethos of moral monotheism, an imprecise yet productive religious worldview that stressed belief in one God, respectable conduct, and belonging to the American nation.[6] Building a religious institution suitable to the new American fighting forces demanded altering the contours of the chaplaincy itself—opening it to more faiths while holding fast to educational standards and enunciating the duty to serve all men. Yet even as the state attempted to distance itself from sectarianism, it could not remain isolated from religious schism and

racial strife. Clergy volunteered to enlist as chaplains, and minority religious groups—Christian and Jewish, white and black—lobbied to participate in the chaplaincy. Through its responses to wartime exigencies
and requests for religious accommodations, the military chaplaincy
slowly constructed a new but unarticulated American religious ideal.

The United States waited as the world went to war in 1914. The army
numbered soldiers in the hundreds of thousands and attended only to
matters close to home. The Colorado National Guard massacred
striking coal miners, U.S. Marines occupied Haiti, and General John J.
Pershing led a failed pursuit of Pancho Villa in Mexico. In 1916,
Woodrow Wilson was reelected on the campaign slogan "He Kept
Us Out of War," and Americans settled into encountering bloody
battles in newsprint. The nation remained neutral while German submarines trolled the Atlantic; British intelligence cracked the Zimmerman Telegram, which planned for unrestricted submarine warfare
against commercial vessels and proposed a military alliance between
Germany and Mexico; and the Russian Revolution toppled the czar.
Finally, with public outrage against Germany mounting, President
Wilson asked Congress to declare war in order to "make the world
safe for democracy." Within days, Congress complied, and in a matter
of weeks, the federal government became responsible for the millions
of young men it conscripted to fight and die for the nation.

The unprecedented scale of the Great War and the mass mobilization required to fulfill American commitments to allies raised daunting
questions. How would the army and navy manage the adolescents who
would swell their ranks, swarm domestic posts, spill out of ships onto
European shores, march into combat, lie in trenches, and possibly die
for Uncle Sam? How would the military command masses of American immigrants who could barely croak a few phrases in English and
recruits who had never read words on a page? And how would the state
unify men whose only shared experience was the draft notice that arrived in their mailboxes?

President Woodrow Wilson capitulated to mandatory military service mere days before entering the United States into war, and on
June 5, 1917, 10 million young men arrived at city halls, post offices,
high schools, and public libraries to register for the draft. Passed barely
a month earlier, the Selective Service Act of 1917 required men between

twenty-one and thirty-one to present themselves to local draft boards. This new ritual meant ticking boxes on Form 1001 to provide the government with the data used to sort men into categories that separated the conscript from the exempt. In addition to names and addresses, the state collected vital statistics and background information about schooling, employment, military experience, language abilities, criminal history, physical fitness, and citizenship. This information distinguished those who would be called to serve and those who would stay home. Clergy earned automatic exemptions, husbands and fathers acquired temporary deferrals, and single men without dependents garnered trips to newly created army camps and naval stations, and, in 2 million cases, overseas. Men employed in essential war work could keep their jobs, and conscientious objectors could—with the right convictions and religious ties—abstain from combat. Immigrants and resident aliens, technically eligible for military service only if they intended to make the United States their permanent home, endured further scrutiny about their loyalty. "Few programs," John Chambers has written, "could coincide better with the progressive era's emphasis upon social efficiency than this idea of classifying much of the nation's manpower." This categorization of more than 24 million young men determined who, where, and how Americans served their nation in war. A small but significant number resisted, but most reluctantly accepted this new relationship between state and society, between Washington and local communities, between coercion and obligation.[7]

The men who donned army khakis or navy blues for a war "over there" were a varied lot. They were white and black. They hailed from Alabama and New York, California and Illinois. They were born in Cleveland and Kielce, Salt Lake City and Salerno. Some had graduated from high school; others could barely write their names. Some spoke only in English while others conversed in Polish, Italian, Russian, Yiddish, German, Czech, Norwegian, Spanish, or Japanese. Some felt at home on farms; others forged their way in cities. They were rowdy and quiet, skilled with rifles and scared of shotguns. They were restless and excited, worried about death and determined to return as heroes.[8]

But most of all, they were young—sheltered and inexperienced, unaccustomed to discipline and susceptible to vice. Or so the military assumed. As Secretary of War Newton Baker asked, "What are those soldiers going to do in the towns, and what are the towns going to do to the soldiers?" His question encapsulated the torrent of letters received from concerned citizens troubled by the immoral temptations—alcohol, prostitution, gambling—and the scourge of impure behavior reputed to fester in military camps. The lure of worldly desires was not exclusive to the military, but the net of the American armed forces was large, geographically expansive, and tied to the federal government. Neither a local ordinance nor a city vice court would suffice to harness the energies of virile young soldiers.[9]

The federal government addressed these concerns through two programs: the CTCA, which directed men's eyes away from liquor, ladies of the night, and card games by organizing recreation and clean entertainment, and the military chaplaincy, which offered religious programs and promoted moral behavior. Chaplains often shared the moral commitments of Progressive Era reformers dedicated to eradicating vice, stimulating health, educating youth, promoting temperance, and Americanizing immigrants through a blend of civic leadership and government regulation. If schools, factories, courts, hospitals, and libraries could merge state authority and civil society to better social welfare, surely chaplains could foster the public good through moral uplift and religious succor. And as state-sponsored clergy, they could eschew pernicious sectarianism in favor of religious unity—a war goal unto itself.

The millions of men who made their way to army camps and naval installations in 1917 and 1918 arrived with their own moral and religious standards. They may have liked a nightcap or a dance with the ladies, but more often than not, they also knew the hard edge of a church pew and the rhythm of a Sabbath hymn. The Selective Service never asked their religious affiliation except as it pertained to conscientious objection. But the military knew its ranks consisted of men with diverse religious identities—far more diverse than in previous wars due to immigration, new American religions, and the splintering of various Protestant denominations.[10]

Chaplains therefore conducted a very particular type of religious work. As clergy vetted and approved by the state, they would transcend religious differences to buoy the spirits, discipline the bodies, and yoke together the hearts of doughboys. The government assigned them three specific duties: to lead worship "for the benefit of the commands," to bury the dead according to appropriate religious rites, and to teach. While Congress had not specifically delegated moral instruction to chaplains, it permeated much of their work. To be successful, Chaplain Clinton Wunder (Northern Baptist) argued, the modern chaplain "must be a social worker, lawyer, doctor, teacher, business man, officer, preacher—all combined into one. He baptizes, marries, and buries people." As members of the Senate's Committee on Military Affairs heard in September 1917, the size of the wartime military demanded more chaplains to support "the character—the moral character, as well as the religious sentiment—of the men." In particular, chaplains advocated "clean living" and stood as a bulwark against the sexual depravity and venereal disease the military feared would infect its corps. Chaplain John Frazier (Southern Methodist), who became the navy's first chief of chaplains, advised his fellow clergy that men from rural areas and small towns "have not been exposed to the pitfalls of seaport cities and consequently are unaware of the dangers, physical and moral, that attend association with lewd women." Being a chaplain entailed more than saving souls or blessing the dead; it required teaching as well as preaching, inspiring as well as inhibiting.[11]

Yet in April 1917, the chaplaincy mustered fewer than 200 clergy and was ill prepared to serve the millions of Americans on the brink of service. Over the course of the war, the army's total population increased from a little over 200,000 soldiers to more than 3.5 million, while the navy expanded from about 95,000 sailors to 533,000. Chaplains multiplied as well, with the army growing from 146 to 2,230 military ministers and the navy quintupling from 40 to 201. More than numerical proliferation, these changes indicated the state's commitment to providing soldiers with regular, effortless access to religion. To ensure that the men dispatched as chaplains were capable of serving men across religious faiths and instilling moral principles, Congress set qualifications for chaplains. An applicant had to be (1) a "regularly ordained minister of some religious denomination," (2) a minister "in good standing" endorsed by an "authorized ecclesiastical body," and (3) under forty-five years old. In sum, to be commissioned as chaplains, clergy had to be young professionals approved by denominational authorities.[12]

These standards represented more than bureaucratic measuring sticks. They epitomized the Progressive Era push toward professionalization, which in turn signified the development of the American military as a modern institution and heralded the government's effort to enlist religion as an instrument of statecraft. The clamor for a well-trained military chaplaincy began in the early twentieth century when navy chaplains sought to improve their status by establishing clear standards for the military's religious officers. Army chaplains quickly followed suit, advocating stiff credentials as well.[13] This impetus toward a professionally trained officers' corps echoed the late-nineteenth-century drive toward standardization, legitimization, and certification in occupations such as medicine, law, education, and social work.[14] Yet squabbles abounded over the best preparation for clergy. The University of Chicago's William Rainey Harper, a biblical scholar turned college president, argued that nonsectarian (Protestant) divinity schools best equipped ministers to influence modern society, while Princeton Theological Seminary's Charles Hodge favored charisma, calling, and denominational training.[15] If not all religious leaders wanted the sanction of school, degrees nevertheless signaled authority and legitimacy to the government. Starting in World War I, chaplains had to burnish professional credentials: bachelor's degrees and seminary ordination.[16]

Mandating professional standing, education credentials, and civilian endorsement appeared objective: a rigid checklist of competencies that candidates either achieved or missed. Reality, however, was different. What, for example, did it mean to be a "regularly ordained minister"? Congressional legislation about chaplains did not define the phrase, and ordination standards varied wildly. The Selective Service excused both "duly ordained ministers of religion" and "regular ministers of religion" from the draft. Formal education distinguished the two, with the draft making allowances for all clergy, regardless of whether they earned degrees. In contrast to this leniency, the military chaplaincy enforced a more rigorous standard, demanding both formal education and career ministry. When applicants indicated that they also stood on an assembly line or taught in high school, they received rejections. Although the required civilian endorsement ensured that denominational bodies—not the military—determined spiritual aptitude, the education and professional standing requirements nonetheless meant that the state preferred and sanctioned some forms of religious leadership over others.[17]

In practice, then, these requirements forced civilian religious organizations to sift through candidates using metrics chosen by the state. If the physical served as a proxy for fitness, the diploma became a surro-

gate for tolerance. Just as "nonsectarianism became a point of orthodoxy among education reformers" in the late nineteenth century, so too
did it become the mantra of the chaplaincy in the early twentieth
century. Chaplain George Waring (Catholic), the author of a War Department chaplain manual, noted, "While a Chaplain could not be expected to hold services successfully for denominations other than his
own, he could always hold a general service . . . and he should preach
such sermons as would be spiritually helpful to every one, without discussing dogmatic or controversial doctrines." Not everyone could or
would abide by this worldview. Framing religion as a common good
required setting aside doctrinal and ritual differences, and the military
wanted only those clergy dedicated to religious inclusivity.[18]

The military thus imported ethos of liberal Protestantism through
the recruitment of well-educated chaplains. Nondogmatic religion
was best, voluntary prayer encouraged spiritual development, and
ethics could unify disparate theologies.[19] As Episcopalian Bishop Charles
Brent described it, "'interdenominationalism' will be the watchword, so
that no one will be subjected to the proselyting spirit." Some disliked
this ecumenical effort. When Monsignor James Connolly, the military
vicar of the Catholic Church, disparaged General Headquarters (GHQ)
chaplain Francis Doherty (Catholic) as "altogether too military and
YMCA and not enough sacerdotal to suit me," he illuminated the tension between the nonspecific religion favored by the military and the
distinctive religion preferred by many faiths. Both Doherty and
Connolly were Catholic, but the military expressed a clear preference
for Doherty's catholic Catholicism, much to the dismay of more parochial churchmen.[20] Through expectations and education requirements,
the military lodged liberal Protestant assumptions in the chaplaincy's
infrastructure, a decision that would continue to reverberate—in creating possibilities and incurring resistance—in the decades to follow.

The chaplain selection process relied on the cooperation of nongovern-
mental civilian religious organizations, such as the Protestant Federal
Council of Churches (FCC), the Catholic Military Ordinariate, and the
Jewish Welfare Board (JWB), to screen and endorse clergy. This delegated authority granted these religious organizations the opportunity for
sustained engagement with government policies. The FCC emerged
in 1908 to promote ecumenical Christian fellowship to transform

American society and became the most significant (though not exclusive) vehicle for Protestant engagement with the military chaplaincy during World War I. Initially focused on social ills such as the working conditions of industrial laborers, it expanded its reach over the next decade. In 1917, the FCC joined other interdenominational groups like the YMCA and the American Bible Society to form the General War-Time Commission of the Churches as a "temporary and emergency body" devoted to religious war work for the men and women "suddenly taken from their accustomed surroundings and plunged into an unfamiliar life." The Commission also hoped to "Christianize the ideals of the nation and so to promote that consciousness of the worldwide brotherhood without which true democracy is impossible." This lofty rhetoric, which meshed well with Wilsonian ideals of making the world safe for democracy, translated into routine activities such as circulating pamphlets, building chapels, and repairing automobiles. If the work was mundane, it nevertheless opened access to state power. FCC secretaries met with War Department officials, its subcommittees studied servicemen's morals and morale, and its leaders assessed applications from clergy interested in ministering to the armed forces.[21]

Civilian religious groups sometimes altered the military more than either anticipated. Six months after the United States entered the war, the FCC's Committee on Negro Churches turned its attention to black chaplains. The question was not whether the military would commission African American clergy as chaplains—for unlike Jews, Mormons, and Christian Scientists, it already did—but how many spots black chaplains could secure. Pursuing this task made sense for the FCC because it had incorporated African American churches into its membership at its inception. While the arrangement was fraught, as African American representatives operated under the aegis of white organizational executives, it nevertheless enabled black churches to leverage the power of the FCC when negotiating with the military. By October 1917, it was clear that war would not diminish the segregationist policies of the state. The African Americans who battled for their country could not serve as equals to white soldiers, in either the status accorded or the opportunities afforded to them. Prewar military preparedness efforts explicitly prohibited black officers from the Reserve Officer Training School in Plattsburgh, New York. Much to the consternation of African Americans, who chafed at supporting segre-

gation, the army sent black officer candidates to Fort Des Moines,
Iowa—over 1,100 miles away from the white training school. And this
unsatisfactory arrangement emerged only after Joel Spingarn, the white
Jewish chairman of the NAACP, lobbied to build a training camp for
black officers on the promise that he would find 200 willing and able
candidates. Cognizant of the harsh realities of the Jim Crow military,
the FCC committee focused on molding the segregated system to its
ends: increasing black religious leadership within the armed forces
because "negro soldiers can be managed most successfully by negroes."
In contrast to the army and navy, both of which remained skeptical of
black leadership, the FCC's Committee on Negro Churches championed the appointments of black officers as the best men for the job, especially in a military opposed to integration.[22]

With regard to black chaplains, then, the Committee resolved "that
there be negro chaplains appointed at once to serve . . . in the same proportion to the number of troops as in the case of white chaplains."
Their resolution could only go so far. The War Department employed
complementary racial and religious logics to limit the presence of minority chaplains. The approximately 300,000 African American soldiers
in service by the spring of 1918 should have merited several hundred
chaplains. But because the men often served in small groups of fifty to
one hundred, the War Department found it easy to dodge employing
black chaplains. And the FCC's General War-Time Commission did
not complain, even if the Committee on Negro Churches advocated for
equal treatment.[23]

Instead, the group focused on increasing numbers. Charles H. Williams, the Committee's field secretary, appealed to the military's
consistent interest in promoting morale to advocate for more black
chaplains. He portrayed white chaplains as "sincere, conscientious,"
but ultimately impotent men who could not "influence . . . the colored
soldiers in a religious sort of way." In contrast, he asserted, "the negro
units, particularly the service battalions, that have gone to France with
the clearest conception of their mission and with the finest spirit, have
been those accompanied by colored chaplains." The strength of black
chaplains rested not only in their ability to rouse and motivate their
men but also in their mastery of chaplain training. Indeed, the FCC's
Clyde Armitage confided that in contrast to white ministers, one-fifth
of whom flunked out of Chaplain School—the training school that

turned civilian clergy into military officers—all the black ministers succeeded and became chaplains.[24]

The 100 percent success rate of African American chaplain candidates was intentional. While the FCC clamored to send African American ministers to the military, it insisted on scouring the nation for "suitable" clergy, "those who could handle men well." This proved challenging, for the age limits and education requirements set by the War Department eliminated many pastors. Furthermore, the War Department preferred chaplains from "the regular negro denominations, especially the National Baptists." Thus, black chaplain candidates successfully completed training courses at rates higher than white candidates for one very clear reason: the FCC would offer only "the very best" applicants to the nation's armed forces. Despite the high financial and human cost, Clyde Armitage insisted that the organization "[could] not afford" any other course of action, even, he acknowledged, "if it does mean a drain on the ministry and on the faculty of some of the better educational institutions." Black chaplains comprised an aristocracy of sorts—they represented African American sociologist W. E. B. Du Bois's "talented tenth." With the appropriate education and comportment, they could and would succeed amidst white elites. But military criteria and FCC perceptions of excellence conspired to keep the number of black chaplains low. By February 1918, only about a dozen African American chaplains, out of a quota of seventy, made it into the service. The number expanded to twenty-six by June 1918 and ultimately to sixty-three by November 1918, a miniscule proportion of the thousands of chaplains commissioned to serve the American fighting forces.[25]

Even as the army accepted the presence of black chaplains, the color line pervaded policy decisions. Hence, when African American soldiers served under white officers, the War Department elected to fulfill the predilections of those officers rather than the men they commanded, soberly stating that "they [did] not desire to place negro chaplains with these [white-led] regiments." This policy did not go unnoticed, but it remained unchallenged by Protestant leaders. Multiple FCC subcommittees agitated for more black chaplains but refused to insist on their placement in units led by white officers. However, insubstantial numbers did not equate to inconsequential experiences.[26]

Unacknowledged and perhaps unrecognized at the time, the FCC's advocacy of African American chaplains tested the War Department's commitment to segregation and radically altered a tiny sliver of the Jim Crow military. Chaplain School was quietly integrated. Whether stateside or in France, black clergy trained aside white clergy. Moving from Fort Monroe, Virginia, to Fort Hamilton, New York, and ultimately to Camp Zachary Taylor, Kentucky, the domestic school brought together recently commissioned chaplains as well as approved but not-yet-commissioned applicants to introduce ministers to military life. Passing the course meant appointments as First Lieutenants, while failing the course sent men back to civilian pulpits. Ignominious dismissals occurred. One white Catholic nominee, for example, earned his dismissal for "not being a good mixer and . . . being a poor preacher." Chaplains who made it to Europe received further training in a ten-day course intended to ready clergy for battle conditions and life on the Western Front. No matter the location, in the north and the south, at home and in France, black and white clergy learned how to be chaplains together.[27]

The tiny quotient of black chaplains thus exerted an outsized impact on the army as an institution by initiating the glacial, decades-long process of desegregating the U.S. military. The constrained conditions of emergency, the status of religious leaders in American society, and the relatively peripheral role chaplains occupied within the military command structure created the opening through which African American clergy began to slowly dissolve segregationist policies within the military. Like Heman Sweatt and George McLaurin, whose efforts to attend law and graduate school paved the way for the *Brown* decision and the desegregation of public secondary and elementary schools, chaplains played a strategic role that anticipated the NAACP's legal strategy. Charles Houston and Thurgood Marshall started their quest to dismantle segregated schools by integrating small numbers of educated and mature students into graduate and professional schools. So too did black chaplains—few in number and representative of the well-educated black religious elite—model successful integration of Chaplain School as a first step toward desegregation of the armed forces. While the military as a whole was, like Southern graduate schools, hostile to ending a white supremacist regime, the chaplaincy included white liberal religious ministers who were invested in religious and racial pluralism. When field-ready chaplains became essential, building a separate school for a few black chaplains was impractical. A pragmatic wartime decision driven by limited resources that made segregated training unfeasible, the integration of the Chaplain School signaled a slow start. It did not follow black chaplains into the army after they completed training, but it demonstrated that integration was possible.[28]

Other groups joined the FCC in lobbying the military to diversify its chaplain corps in 1917, though they focused on religion rather than race. The War Department's embrace of nonsectarianism meant that all religions theoretically stood equal in the eyes of the military as well as the Constitution. Yet many religions and denominations stood in the shadows, neither invisible to the state nor formally recognized by it. The chaplaincy was hardly a representative institution, in composition or credentials, and that made it a target for those seeking state validation and accommodation. Among the items on the Jewish Welfare Board's (JWB) agenda in the summer of 1917 was an appeal the War Department was reluctant to settle: a request to appoint Jewish chaplains. Representative Isaac Siegel (R-NY) lobbied both the army and the navy to support commissioning Jewish chaplains. A brisk July 1917 correspondence between Siegel and Cyrus Adler, the head of the JWB, highlights the effort made by the Jewish politician on behalf of Jewish soldiers. Secretary of the Navy Josephus Daniels agreed that one Jewish chaplain could serve, while Secretary of War Newton Baker was amenable to more than one Jewish chaplain. War Department officials disagreed over the necessity of special legislation and suggested that Siegel forward two to three applications "forthwith" to test the issue.[29]

The impasse reflected a tension between military custom and military needs. Earlier in the summer, Baker had informed the Committee on Military Affairs that he supported "the principle" of Senate Bill 2527, which proposed appointing chaplains "representing religious sects not recognized in the apportionment of chaplains now provided by law." This was a misnomer. The law had never enumerated a list of acceptable religion groups for the chaplaincy. In practice, however, chaplains came from a few mainline Protestant denominations and the Catholic Church. The proposed statute, which would not be signed into law until October 6, 1917, rectified this problem by creating a new type of chaplain, one tied not to regiments but to a religious group (even if ultimately assigned to a particular unit). Baker expressed some qualms about this development and cautioned that "a maximum of 10 rather than 20 is a fair proportion of chaplains who should be appointed under this authority, which number will fully meet all the requirements of military service." In its final form, the law stated that "division commanders may apply to the Adjutant General of the Army for the services of chaplains-at-large of the Jewish, Christian Science, Eastern Catholic, Mormon, and Salvation Army denominations if they deem that there are sufficient numbers of the adherents of such faiths in their divisions to render chaplains-at-large necessary."[30] The emphasis on "sufficient numbers" reflected the World War I–era distribution of manpower in which drafted men usually received assignments to domestic bases and ports close to their hometown region.

Chaplains posted to stations with large clusters of religious minorities often sought extra religious assistance as the military tarried in staffing a more religiously diverse chaplaincy. Majority-LDS units existed at Camp Kearney (California) and Fort Lewis (Washington), while significant numbers of Jews lived together at Camp Upton (New York) and the Philadelphia Navy Yard. From Cape May, New Jersey, navy chaplain Ernest L. Paugh (Presbyterian) wrote to the JWB's Cyrus Adler to ask "if the Jewish Church could send us an assistant to work on my staff." He recognized that "there are quite a few of the men of your faith" among the 3,500 men in his care, though "this work would not be exclusively among the Jewish boys." Siegel's summer effort to cultivate a pool of possible applicants proved useful, as the JWB could supply rabbis to the armed forces as soon as legislation made it acceptable. Ten months later, General Pershing himself requested twenty-five additional Jewish chaplains so long as they were naturalized citizens.[31]

To review and endorse the best applicants to the military, the JWB created a Committee on Chaplains, which consisted of representatives from the Orthodox, Conservative, and Reform Jewish movements. Representative Siegel fretted that such a group, dedicated as it was to deciding "the qualifications of Jewish chaplains[,] would bring about a lot of unnecessary controversy." Once he received assurances that the military would "take my word in that the man presented by us is qualified both by learning, education, and character to be a chaplain," he claimed he should control the process in the best interest of time and community. His concerns, if not his hubris, had some validity, but the JWB stood firm. The committee received 149 applications for Jewish chaplains and endorsed thirty-four, of which the military commissioned twenty-five, all of whom represented the Reform and Conservative movements. Despite allegations of discrimination against Orthodox rabbis, deference to Reform and Conservative rabbis stemmed from military regulations. Only the Reform and Conservative seminaries required college degrees. Orthodox rabbis, many of whom were not U.S. citizens and received ordination from nonaccredited European seminaries, could not meet the basic citizenship and education requirements. Just as state policy had enabled the inclusion of only some black clergy, so too did it privilege some rabbis over others.[32]

Although American Jews played a significant role in lobbying for the chaplains-at-large bill, which formally opened the chaplaincy to members of minority faiths, the other faiths added were Christian. Though Christian Scientists, Mormons, and the Eastern Orthodox varied considerably, the military classified all of them as "Protestant." Christian Scientists and Mormons, eager to embrace the chaplaincy, accepted the opportunity to appoint chaplains without questioning the label. Yet few Americans viewed Mormon or Christian Science chaplains as merely another shade of Protestant or equipped to lead general Protestant worship. Mormonism and Christian Science represented American-made faiths, traditions born of nineteenth-century religious revivals and charismatic leaders that derived, but nonetheless stood apart, from Protestantism. In 1830, Joseph Smith Jr. published the *Book of Mormon*, an epic saga translated by Smith into English after he received instructions revealing the location of buried golden tablets in Palmyra, New York, from the angel Moroni. Whether viewed as fantastic or fraudulent, Smith heralded a religion with America as its historic and contemporary epicenter. In text, church structure, worship, ritual, and—most famously—the (brief) embrace of plural marriage, the Saints made themselves distinctive, all the while asserting that they embodied America. Christian Science emerged about a half century after Mormonism from the experiences and teachings of Mary Baker Eddy in the urbane environs of Boston. Like Joseph Smith, Eddy created an updated canon by offering her followers a new scripture—*Science and Health with Key to the Scriptures* (1875). Eddy's emphasis on faith healing and spiritual practice distinguished Christian Science from more common Protestant denominations. Christian Science generally appealed to a small subset of white, middle-class Americans in the Northeast and neither attracted the level of wrath Mormonism faced nor claimed to be archetypically American. But it too incurred suspicion and lingered at the periphery of acceptable American religions.[33]

For both Mormons and Christian Scientists, entering the chaplaincy meant determining how their men could meet the established standards for chaplains, or absent that, how flexible the military would be about different training. In particular, both groups needed to work around the requirement for ordination as neither formally educated professional clergy. Rather than issue an open call for potential chaplains, Mormon leaders hand-selected the men they forwarded to the army. Herbert Brown Maw, one of the three Mormon chaplains to serve in World War I, recalled that he had enlisted in the Air Corps when he received a message to call the church—leaders had decided he represented one of their best options and instructed him to complete the application. The exigencies of war overtook scrutiny of credentials, and the army accepted the men appointed by the the LDS Church and Christian Science Board of Directors without recorded discussion.[34]

Christian Scientists felt that their chaplains' "willingness to conduct undenominational services in addition to their own created a very favorable impression." At least some Christian Science chaplains earned the aplomb of higher-ranking officers for their efforts. Martin Jackson's senior chaplain, for example, wrote, "Your task is peculiarly difficult because of the fact that your men are scattered and you cannot throw yourself into the little group in which you live, and feel justified in forgetting the rest of the division." Civilians also discerned the ramifications of the inclusion of chaplains from these minority religious groups. When the navy appointed a Christian Science chaplain in February 1918, the *New York World* editorialized that this decision reflected a new attitude toward the long-marginalized faith: "Christian Science then and long after was an anathema to the regular religious denominations. . . . Now the Government gives it full recognition and accords its readers an equal status with the ministers of other creeds."[35]

While the equal status of Christian Scientists remained uncertain, Mormons faced the most enmity. Fifteen years earlier, the nation erupted over the election of Senator Reed Smoot, a Utahan who also served as an apostle of the LDS Church. If Americans resisted seating elected Mormon members of Congress—successfully in the 1898 case of B. H. Roberts and unsuccessfully in the 1902 case of Smoot—how would they respond to the appointment of Mormons in a state-sanctioned religious role? The YMCA was displeased, alleging that the LDS Church was "unChristian" and thus unfit for the chaplaincy. Mormon leaders were dismayed to find that the army allotted them only three chaplains, believing that the government had provided for "'not less than twenty chaplains.'" Perhaps the Church misunderstood the legislation as allowing for twenty LDS chaplains or misconstrued the rejection of educationally unqualified candidates. But Mormons faced significantly more scrutiny than others, in part because allegations of polygamy persisted and in part because the Mormon emphasis on proselytization unsettled Americans.[36] Anxiety about new religious groups filtered into the military. Despite the paucity of available clergy, one report announced that "it is not felt that more Christian Science or Mormon Chaplains are needed." These religions flustered the U.S. military for the same reason: they did not fit easily into the new Protestant-Catholic-Jewish schema used to organize chaplains.

Yet demarcating space for "chaplains-at-large" instigated what would become a decades-long project to redefine American religion—to untether American religion from Christianity, from mainstream groups, and from large percentages of the American population. As the service of twenty-five Jewish chaplains during the war highlights, the quota of twenty chaplains from "religious sects not recognized" did not hold. Over the course of the war, one Salvation Army, three Mormon, eleven Christian Science, and twenty-five Jewish chaplains served in the U.S. military. Immediate induction of Mormon, Christian Science, and Jewish chaplains did not mean that the process was smooth. Bureaucratic norms bred discontent, and the nation did not automatically accept or fulfill the needs of less common or conventional religions. But on an instrumental level, the chaplains-at-large bill created opportunities for minority faiths to present themselves as American. Indeed, the decisions to include Jewish, Mormon, and Christian Science chaplains and to classify the latter two as Protestant marked the beginning of the rhetoric of tri-faith America, a descriptive norm that simultaneously embraced pluralism and elevated administrative ease over religious complexity.[37]

The bill's consequences extended beyond new chaplains; it also pushed religious groups to develop the infrastructure to work with the military. The Jewish Welfare Board faced a different set of challenges than the hierarchical LDS Church or the centrally organized Christian Scientists. It was new, formed in spring 1917 to partner with the Commission on Training Camp Activities to aid Jewish soldiers. It was unofficial, not yet sanctioned by the government as the authorized agency for Jewish welfare work. It was unstable, challenged by existing communal institutions such as the Young Men's Hebrew Association and opposed by immigrant leaders chafing at the authority of New York Jewish elites. While it had but a tenuous hold on American Jewry, war enabled the JWB to justify itself as the religious community's representative to the government and pursue its work on behalf of Jewish soldiers. As the civilian interface between the military and American Jews, the JWB planned to secure the rights of Jewish servicemen and shield impressionable men from the influence of Christianity. It shepherded American Jews through war as patriotic Americans and committed Jews, thus demonstrating the consonance between Judaism and Americanism.[38]

These incompatible goals, of advocating particularity and championing universality, sometimes clashed overtly, as in the case of seeking kosher food for military personnel. Jewish law demanded separating milk and meat and forbade eating pork or shellfish. The regular presence of pork presented the biggest difficulty in a military that understood meat as a dietary mainstay. One sensitive officer notified Chaplain Louis Egelson (Jewish) that "he would order the substitution of other food for me on the occasions when pork or ham was served. This he did voluntarily without the slightest intimation of my part." Case-by-case improvisation helped individuals but not Jews writ large. Religious leaders within the community acknowledged that combat conditions constituted abnormal circumstances. Rabbi Bernard Levinthal, a leader of Philadelphia's Orthodox Jewish community, wrote, "Jewish law is lenient with the soldier who goes to war. He may eat the food that is given to him." Not all Jews were as sanguine. Albert Lucas, of the Union of Orthodox Jewish Congregations, sought military-provided kosher rations "which we feel the Orthodox Jews of this country are entitled to" because "it is an absolute requisite to the peace of mind and spiritual content" of many Jewish soldiers. Despite Levinthal's dispensation, then, many Jews found food inseparable from identity and expected a more "vigorous" effort to acquire kosher food for observant Jews.[39]

To make the case for kosher food provisions to the military, the JWB focused on the potential benefits to the armed forces. It was true, the

JWB conceded, that not all Jews observed dietary laws, that feasibility "in the actual line of battle" presented a challenge, and that Jewish law "declared for many hundreds of years that religious laws may be set aside in defense of one's country." But the military's interest in strengthening morale dictated "that men should [not] be furnished with food which is abhorrent on conscientious or religious grounds." Lest the appeal to national interest be insufficient, the JWB justified its stance with a nod to military practices worldwide. "We have evidence that in the British Army, Mohammedans and Hindoos [sic] have their special dietaries arranged for them according to their religious practices . . . [also] this has been done in the French Army for the Mohammedans and in the German and Austrian Armies for the Jewish soldiers." If American allies in the British and French militaries could meet the needs of its imperial volunteers and conscripts, surely the United States could match the standard set by its enemies—Germany and Austria—in disbursing cans of kosher meat to Jewish soldiers. The Hebrew National Sausage Factory agreed to sell kosher items to the government at a loss by matching the prices of nonkosher meat. But the military remained unswayed. One general worried about "the dangers of such a step and the undesirability of permitting" kosher food, lest it generate "further demand elsewhere and abroad." The solution sought by the JWB was exactly the sort of precedent the military resisted: altering protocol to suit distinct religious practices. The military would not prevent the JWB from distributing kosher goods, but it would not tweak its dining procedures either. Reciprocal obligation had its limits, and compromise was necessary—but not by the government.[40]

Advocacy from the margins illuminated blind spots in the military's desire for nonsectarian religion and accentuated tensions between universal religious commitments and particular ritual needs. As the largest new group to enter the chaplaincy during the war, American Jews occupied an odd position. On the whole, the military actively welcomed rabbis into the ranks of the chaplaincy, and Jewish chaplains often exalted their inclusion. In their eagerness to serve their country, however, rabbis could not help but literally flag their difference: they would not wear the Latin cross, the symbol of the chaplaincy, as their insignia. The JWB's Cyrus Adler reported being "startled" to see the cross on navy chaplain David Goldberg's collar and thought, "Jewish men will also be a little surprised." Chaplain Harry Davidowitz (Jewish)

concurred, divulging that "whenever I approach any soldier who cor-
roborates my estimate of him as Jewish, I have to begin by explaining
away my insignia." The War Department looked at the situation rather
differently. According to Adler, it feared "that various minor sects will
each ask for some special form of recognition. I have replied with the
argument that no Christian sect could set up a valid objection to the
Cross whereas Jews or Mohammedans could. I daresay the matter will
ultimately be adjusted."[41]

Adler's prognostication proved accurate, but the process was somewhat unwieldy. The War Department wavered as it grappled with religious difference. It allowed Jewish chaplains to remove the cross from
their uniforms but dallied over a replacement. It rejected the options
proffered by the JWB, deeming a six-pointed Jewish star too similar
to a five-pointed general's star. By late spring General Henry Jerver,
acting assistant chief of staff, proposed a new plan. Rather than visually separate chaplains by faith, he suggested that all chaplains wear the
shepherd's crook, the insignia of the nineteenth-century army chaplaincy. While more Christological than Jerver realized, the shepherd's
crook offended American Christians who found it insufficiently Christian, not Jews. Here, finally, religious Americans could unite. The
Committee of Six, an ecumenical advisory group composed of Protestant, Catholic, and Jewish representatives, appealed to the War Department to revoke this insignia change. The Six spoke as one, affirming
Harry Cutler's statement on behalf of the JWB: "We are decidedly in
favor of the Christian chaplains wearing the cross as the insignia of
their office. We would consider it a national calamity particularly in
these critical days to eliminate a symbol which to millions of men is
the greatest inspiration and sign of salvation." At the same time, the
group asserted, "We are equally concerned in the welfare of non-Jews
as well as the Jews in a broadminded way . . . [these] chaplains may not
in conscience wear the cross, nor should they be asked to do so." The
Committee of Six prevailed, and Jewish chaplains began wearing a tablet
(representing the Ten Commandments) with a Star of David affixed to
the top. Where the War Department sought sameness, the tri-faith
Committee of Six recognized difference. It insisted that collaboration
rested on validating literal marks of distinction. A tolerant, "broadminded" nation could encompass (some) variety without relinquishing
unity.[42]

World War I precipitated the rapid development and religious restructuring of the military chaplaincy, but quick growth and effective management did not come together. The number of chaplains commissioned surged, yet the military still lacked an organized approach to wartime religion. When civilian organizations vetted applicants to the chaplaincy, distributed Bibles and holiday food to soldiers, and funneled money to chaplains through discretionary funds, they participated in a burgeoning government-industry-citizen operational matrix. As the war began in earnest for Americans, soldiers in the United States encountered official military chaplains, CTCA war workers, and civilian camp pastors. For spiritual comfort abroad, American Expeditionary Force (AEF) soldiers could turn to a commissioned military chaplain or to any number of civilian religious clergy—Red Cross chaplains, YMCA ministers, Knights of Columbus priests, Salvation Army "lassies," or JWB war workers—who made their way to France to assist American troops. Access to religious services abounded, but inefficiency and insufficient oversight troubled military leaders who preferred more control.[43]

In response to the sprawling, decentralized, and uncoordinated religious services in France, General John Pershing asked Episcopalian bishop Charles Brent to devise a more systematic approach to the military chaplaincy. Like many Pershing appointees, Brent was a friend. In the early twentieth century, he had served as a trusted confidante to President Theodore Roosevelt and then–Secretary of War William Howard Taft, which secured his status as the most politically influential bishop of the period. As "one of the outstanding pioneers in the modern ecumenical movement," Brent's commitment to Christianity devoid of division extended beyond rhetoric into practice. Canadian by birth, American by naturalization, and worldly by inclination, Brent prohibited his missionaries from proselytizing Catholics, whom he saw as part of the unified church, in the Philippines. In Brent, nepotism and merit merged, and the well-connected minister committed to theological variety became the architect of a new American chaplaincy.[44]

But first he had to accept the job. Pershing first spoke with Brent about managing chaplains in April 1917. Brent resisted the call but continued to promote ecumenism while shuttling between London, Manila, and Washington. As the leaves changed color and American troops settled into trench warfare in 1917, the bishop arrived in France as a representative of the YMCA. Like Brent, the "Y" embodied a particularly ecumenical approach to religion. Central to Progressive Era religious life on college campuses, the YMCA emphasized muscular Christianity, which fused manliness and morality, and work rather than piety to mute doctrinal differences and erase "hard boundary lines between religious groups." Just as the YMCA encouraged everyone, including nonbelievers, to participate in their activities, so too did Brent believe that "while the varieties of religious faith are great[,] the . . . purpose is one."[45]

When he agreed to aid the military chaplaincy, Brent folded his interest in religious ecumenism into the military's organizational regime. He was an optimist, but not starry-eyed or naïve. As he surveyed the conditions in France in December 1917, he discerned "the prospect of a Glorious death pro patria at a distance is far more glorious than when it is near at hand." But the proximity of death also magnified the gravity of crafting a sturdy religious program, and in that, he was undeterred. Military rank eased his work, and Major Brent maintained a single-minded focus, to "put the Chaplain's office and function, as an important military asset, in its right relation to the Army." By early January 1918, he began sketching a plan for AEF chaplains, one intended to fix the problem of "no co-ordination between all these moral and spiritual agencies." Drawing on the British and Canadian chaplaincies, Brent suggested a new model of pluralist and hierarchical leadership. A GHQ Staff Chaplains' Office, comprised of three chaplains from different religious traditions, would administratively oversee division chaplains, who would, in turn, manage unit chaplains in Europe. The first trio of GHQ chaplains consisted of Brent, representing liturgical Protestants; Paul Moody, a National Guard chaplain and son of famed evangelist Dwight Moody, representing congregational Protestants; and Francis Doherty, a regular army chaplain, representing Catholics. This configuration ensured that multiple streams of Christianity would be present at the highest levels of authority and that decisions would have the imprimatur, if not the full agreement, of a confederation of clergy.[46]

The GHQ Chaplains' Office, approved by General Pershing on April 30, 1918, and established the next day, managed AEF chaplains and synchronized the work of external religious organizations for the duration of the war—in Europe. Even within this limited scope, the task was formidable. The men started from scratch, since they did not know even the most rudimentary information, such as the number of chaplains in France, was unknown. As one report declared, "no list existed, and owing to the fact that Chaplains were frequently carried on rosters by their rank (First Lieutenant), it was not always immediately possible to find them on the records." Determining the number, location, and denomination of chaplains allowed the GHQ to better allocate their most prized resource: clergy. Even as the war progressed and Congress passed legislation to increase the number of chaplains, the GHQ suffered from an insufficient number of military ministers. In October 1918, 866 chaplains were available to serve 2 million American men in France. Instead of one chaplain for every 1,200 men, as the new legislation called for, or even the higher existing ratio of one chaplain for 1,800 men, each chaplain served about 2,300 men. The GHQ Chaplains groused that 604 Protestant, 255 Catholic, and 7 Jewish chaplains had to suffice when there should have been 1,080, 566, and 30, respectively. The quantity of clergy always lagged, but the tri-faith taxonomy of the American chaplaincy was set.[47]

While the GHQ worked furiously to dispatch chaplains fairly across units, some Americans found the military's willingness to blur religious lines disturbing. Minnie Brown was one such citizen. She wrote Father John Burke, the head of the National Catholic War Council, on behalf of her son, a soldier serving in the 7th Regiment. Like the other Catholics in his unit, he had access only to a Protestant chaplain, who could not lead Mass or administer sacraments. Burke suggested that a soldier-led petition might produce a remedy, but only if the request did not denigrate the chaplain as a person and merely highlighted "his inability, as a Protestant, to give them what they want." Burke harbored no ill will toward Protestant chaplains, but Protestant chaplains could not save Catholic souls. Despite his advice to Minnie Brown, Burke knew that these circumstances were unlikely to change.[48]

Two related problems stymied Burke and other religious leaders trying to assuage concerns about the religious background of chaplains assigned to particular units. First, while a particular religion could predominate in geographically determined regiments, the Selective Service did not collect information about religious identity. As a result, a Catholic chaplain could be attached to a unit stationed at Camp

Beauregard, Louisiana, in which only 1 percent of the men were Catholic. As the local bishop reminded Father Burke, "this is of course discouraging and altogether wrong. . . . If no attention is paid to the religious make-up of the Regiments, our chaplains will in many cases not be assigned where they can do the most good, and many regiments that are largely Catholic may be left without a priest." The bishop correctly observed that many regiments consisting of largely Catholic soldiers lacked priests. But his assessment of this condition as "altogether wrong" mistook the military's openness to religiously varied clergy for a desire to parcel out chaplains according to the religious composition of units. In fact, the decision to distribute chaplains without matching the faith of the minister to the faith of men accentuated the military's interest in encouraging moral monotheism—religious identity and moral behavior unfettered by doctrinal specificity.[49]

Second, the military never procured the necessary number of chaplains to fulfill the 1-to-1,200 ratio it sought. For many Christians, the truly problematic ratio was that of Catholics to Protestants. If Mormons, Christian Scientists, and Jews fought to be represented in the chaplaincy during World War I, Protestants and Catholics fought over the number of chaplains allotted to them. The military used data from the 1916 World Almanac to earmark slots for Protestant and Catholic chaplains according to their respective percentages of the population of the United States. Protestants alleged that this ostensibly fair method miscalculated the religious breakdown of the nation. They claimed that any statistics based on church membership unjustly elevated the Catholic population because Catholics baptized infants while most Protestant denominations did not. As a result, they argued, the military needed to adjust Catholic numbers downward. The American Catholic leadership, in contrast, agonized over not receiving enough spots. Father Lewis O'Hern, who supervised the appointment of Catholic chaplains to the military, carped that the FCC had "convinced the War Department that since we count children in our Church membership, we cannot be given Chaplains based on our numerical strength at all." Cognizant of the politics of perception, he asked John Burke to intervene with the secretary of war, noting that instead of requesting 40 percent of the chaplaincy quota, "it does not sound quite so big to say Thirty-Nine percent." A month later Baker pleased O'Hern by adjusting the Catholic chaplain quota to 38 percent, "practically what we felt we were entitled to." Though the truce would prove temporary, Baker's shrewd move tempered the heated exchanges between Catholics and Protestants.[50]

In the midst of war, the trio of Protestant and Catholic chaplains managing the AEF chaplaincy focused on developing appropriate administrative procedures through which to manage military needs. As men prepared for battle, chaplains prayed, preached, and counseled the soldiers in their units. As they followed their men into battle, however, their duties changed. "I aimed to be near the center of activity," Chaplain Homer C. Stuntz (Northern Methodist) explained. That way he could "carry wounded, cheer dying, bind up wounds, make coffee, roll cigarettes, write letters, anything, in fact, that anybody could do for men under such abnormal conditions." While "the work of burial was one of the most arduous tasks," taking the pain and bloodshed of war in stride helped boost flagging spirits. "If he could smile as he crawled out of a shell hole where he had been forced to jump to escape an incoming shell," then, like the "really recklessly brave" Catholic chaplain with whom Stuntz served, a chaplain could improve morale. No matter the specific duty, all of this work needed to be documented and reviewed, accounted for and appraised.[51]

Bureaucracy could be burdensome, and few chaplains relished writing weekly reports, but these procedures contributed to improving the stature of the chaplaincy. In September 1918, Brent emphasized that the army chaplaincy was a work in progress, with only 700 chaplains performing the work of 1,200. "Owing to the low rank of Chaplains they have not that official recognition which is given to other officers with analogous responsibilities," Brent stated. "I am very far from stressing rank for a Chaplain, except so far as it enables him to fit into the Army system." Brent's friendship with Pershing played a key role in facilitating respect for chaplains. The general, after all, could issue orders, and that he did, informing his subordinates that " 'a sympathetic recognition of the chaplain's duties and responsibilities is expected of every officer. It is only through their ready cooperation that he can reach the entire army.' "[52]

To earn the respect of others, army chaplains often emphasized the demands of military ministry. Chaplain G. W. Weldon reported, "We used tallow candles when we could get them, carried our own water, waded through mud, held services in a leaky tent, taught Bible classes . . .

with the sky for shelter, played volley ball with both officers and enlisted men, boxed with them, rode horse back with and without a saddle
with them, sang with them around the piano in the evenings when the
days work was done and a lot of other things that might seem too trivial
to mention." If preaching under the sun and the stars strengthened
God's presence, it also heightened the risks of war. Another chaplain
disclosed, "We have been bombed nearly every night and on Sunday
last while reading the service out in the open field to five boys, an air
fight took place directly over our heads." Chaplain Patrick J. Lydon
(Catholic) could worship anywhere—"a wrecked chapel, or an old barn
or a shed, or maybe an old box in the woods"—which led him to conclude, " 'what chaplains need more than a chapel is a small Ford truck.' "[53]

Rustic conditions and trench warfare created a distinct atmosphere
for religious work, but the military differed significantly from their
home churches in another way: unlike civilian clergy, military chaplains were responsible for men beyond their own denominations. As
Chaplain C. C. Bateman (Northern Baptist) described it, "the chaplain
[was] a spiritual sportsman [who] could use fishing tackle or exercise
his use of the Gospel gun as a wing shot." While chaplains did not carry
weapons, Bateman's martial metaphor bespoke dexterity and adapt-
ability. Soldiers' needs varied over the course of the war and in different locales, but the value of fulfilling obligations to all men in novel
ways consistently appeared in reports. In France, Chaplain S. Arthur
Devan (Northern Baptist) helped arrange Saturday services for the
Jewish soldiers in his regiment. At the end of services, "I always (at their
request) preached a sermon to them from the [O]ld Testament. It was
probably an unusual combination for a Protestant clergyman to administer communion from a Catholic Altar after preaching at a Jewish
synagogue service—which I often did however, at St. Leonard." In his
civilian life as a Protestant minister, Devan would have had little reason
to address Jews. As a military chaplain, however, he saw his flock in
tri-faith terms and regularly delivered sermons to Jewish soldiers.
Similarly, Chaplain James Howard reported that Catholics attended
his Protestant services and, in contrast to dicta from the Church to
avoid interfaith activities, would "take communion at my hands [and]
in a Bible class, which we kept going for several months, first in
training camp and later at the front, there were both Catholics and
Jews—studying the New Testament!" For chaplains and soldiers alike,

war produced encounters between men of different faiths. It also acquainted men with unfamiliar religions, created opportunities to experience new rituals, and encouraged a tri-faith outlook.[54]

Ecumenical religious service to American soldiers on the Western Front had its limits, however. Chaplain Arthur C. Whitney (Christian Science), who earned a Croix de Guerre from the French government for his service at the front lines, received "a request or warning from one of the Chaplains at General Headquarters Chaplains' Office not to set my religious views before others than Christian Scientists." Classified by the military as a Protestant, Whitney remained constrained by his minority Christian Science background, unable—by dint of implied threat—to engage religiously with all the soldiers of his division. In place of spiritual ministration, Whitney turned to sports and recreation—setting up a canteen, running a barbershop, and organizing a library. As much as Brent and his fellow GHQ chaplains sought to professionalize the chaplaincy, concerns about perceived parochial or provincial religious groups restrained the reach of some new chaplains.[55]

The army developed a feasible training regimen through which to instill the spirit of cooperation but, Brent lamented, it ceased with war's end. The GHQ Chaplains' Office had used the Chaplain School in Chateau d'Aux to teach fresh arrivals about "the conditions of the Army and of life in France," including the military's distinctively ecumenical religious work. And as soldiers returned to the United States, Brent reported, "a chaplain either Protestant or Catholic is to be assigned to every transport. If the naval chaplain already assigned to a ship is a Catholic—the Army chaplain will be a Protestant and vice versa. This gives us a Protestant and a Catholic chaplain on every transport." Lessons gleaned "over there" could, quite literally, travel home.[56]

Chaplain Charles Bruton (Catholic) kept busy in the fall of 1918. Every Sunday the priest led two masses, each week he conducted nonsectarian services, and during Rosh Hashanah, the Jewish New Year, he arranged for Jews to attend synagogue on military orders. As he remarked to *The Rochester Post*, "I am resolved to be as good a rabbi to them as I possibly can be." Chaplain Frank Wilson (Episcopalian) would not have been surprised by Bruton's work or commentary. He too flourished in the multireligious milieu of war. Reminiscing about his work in Europe, he wrote about his interfaith endeavors, concluding, "So there you have it—the *Jewish* Feast of Purim, celebrated by *American* soldiers in *Italy*, in a Young Men's *Christian* Association hut, addressed by an *Episcopalian* chaplain, refreshments being furnished by the *Red Cross* society, and cigarettes donated by the *Roman Catholic* Knights of Columbus." Over and over again, the chaplains who served among the American Expeditionary Forces repeated tales of ecumenical accomplishment in the wilderness of war. As Joseph Odell reported to his Atlanta audience in 1917, the chaplains worshipped in novel venues, embraced the customs and rituals of other faiths, and fulfilled their duty to all men in their units.[57]

Their stories were real, but they belied the tension undergirding the U.S. military's experiment in religious inclusion and concealed the role of the state in cultivating their unorthodox congregations. Interfaith engagement occurred over eighteen months of war, but the perception of these cooperative tri-faith endeavors as valuable would not linger for long. It did not disappear, however, because the National Defense Act of 1920 codified structural and organizational changes informally crafted during the war. For chaplains, it legislated the ratio of one chaplain per 1,200 soldiers, permanently granted chaplains military rank, and fortified the position of the Chief of Chaplains. In this leadership role, the chief of chaplains oversaw "general coordination and supervision of the work of chaplains." Having spent eighteen months of war puzzling its way toward a tri-faith model, the chaplaincy acquired the power to implement this religious ideal in 1920. How the chaplaincy ought to manage American religion became the organization's peacetime task.[58]

2

"Christ Is the Melting Pot
for All Our Differences"

As THE NEW army chief of chaplains, John Axton's insignia remained a cross, rather than a Colonel's silver eagle. When the Congregationalist minister and eighteen-year veteran of the armed forces accepted his promotion in 1920, he acquired the responsibility of addressing the nation's religious concerns. Soon after, he began receiving a lot of mail. Samuel Cavert, the secretary of the Federal Council of Churches (FCC), requested the appointment of a Protestant chaplain to complement the existing Catholic chaplain at Fort Slocum, New York. Axton responded immediately: No. "Chaplain Campbell," Axton replied, "is one of our finest and constantly on the alert to see that the religious needs of all of the men are cared for." Axton consistently reiterated that any chaplain could serve all men. To Cyrus Adler, the head of the Jewish Welfare Board (JWB), he confirmed that the War Department had already solicited materials about Jewish holidays and that chaplains would convey "the wishes of the War Department concerning religious observances for men of all shades of religious belief." After Christian Scientist representative Judge Clifford Smith endorsed two candidates as potential chaplains, Axton reminded him that too few Christian Scientists remained in the army to warrant regular appointments. Nevertheless, he directed chaplains to "call in upon occasion representatives of sects not represented in their post" and concluded, "The experiment is working very well."[1]

The same could not be said for religion in civilian American life. The citizens writing to the military chaplaincy lived amidst religious discord. Had William Joseph Simmons been privy to Axton's correspondence, he surely would have used it to recruit members to his burgeoning reincarnation of the Ku Klux Klan (KKK). The white Southern Methodist preacher and first Imperial Wizard of the second KKK leveraged any racial or religious mixing as fodder for his white supremacist and conservative Protestant fraternal organization. The KKK recruited as many as 5 million white men in 4,000 chapters across all forty-eight states into its "'army of Protestant Americans.'"[2] Whether burning towering crosses, firebombing homes, or lynching people, the KKK terrorized African Americans, Jews, and Catholics. About 700 miles north of the second KKK's Atlanta origins, Simmons had an ally in Detroit industrialist and auto-making titan, Henry Ford. The press, rather than vigilante violence, represented Ford's weapon of choice. After buying the *Dearborn Independent* in 1918, he used the paper to print the inflammatory forgery, *The Protocols of the Elders of Zion*, in 1921 and continued to peddle his antisemitic views to its national readership. Although this blatant antisemitism led to its downfall in 1927, the *Dearborn Independent* fomented and nourished anti-labor, anti-immigrant, and antisemitic sentiments of the 1920s.[3]

While organizations like the FCC protested the KKK and the *Dearborn Independent*, nativism and racism percolated in more genteel realms of American life as well. In the early 1920s, elite universities such as Harvard, Yale, and Princeton identified the rising number of Jewish students as a problem. Quotas—both stated and secret—became their preferred tools for maintaining Protestant hegemony in higher education.[4] The first Red Scare's anxiety about Bolshevic infiltration of American life intensified enmity toward Eastern European Jewish immigrants, some of whom identified as socialists, communists, or anarchists, but all of whom became potential agents of social and political upheaval in the eyes of nativists and scientific racists.[5] Successive restrictive immigration acts culminated in the 1924 Johnson-Reed Act, which limited new arrivals to a yearly cap of 2 percent of the national-origin group's population in 1890. This severely curtailed immigration from Southern and Eastern Europe, the origin of most Catholic and Jewish migrants.[6] Anti-Catholicism, which had occasionally quieted but never abated, flared anew with the nomination of Catholic Al Smith as the Democratic candidate for President in 1928. Theological and social furor convulsed Protestants as well. The stewing modernist-fundamentalist divide erupted in the Scopes trial and ripped apart Protestant denominations whose liberal and conservative wings had previously united over Prohibition. If interwar American society "reeked of religion," conflict was its dominant stench.[7]

John Axton and John Frazier, the respective army and navy chiefs of chaplains, ignored the religious tension whirling around them. Revival was their focus. True, the Great War was over, the National Defense Act of 1920 passed, the troops demobilized.[8] The military rushed to decommission its resources and disperse its personnel, but the chaplaincies began to mobilize and create. As other religious Americans fought one another, Axton and Frazier set their sights on larger goals: How could, should, and would military clergy serve soldiers? Answering these questions enabled the military's religious branch to initiate a state-sanctioned campaign to alter the contours of religious belonging in the United States. In the 1920s, the chaplaincy voiced its religious outlook through a series of conferences that brought together military chaplains and civilian religious leaders and tangibly reinforced it by writing manuals and publishing a tri-faith hymnal. Military chaplains also contributed to interfaith organizations such as the National Conference of Christians and Jews (NCCJ), taking their positive experiences with religious pluralism out of the barracks and into civilian society. Ideas batted about in the 1920s became live experiments in the 1930s when the New Deal's Civilian Conservation Corps (CCC) Camps provided the army chaplaincy with an opportunity to intentionally implement its religious convictions. By construing American religion as moral monotheism, the chaplaincy endorsed an idea of faith that was simultaneously inclusive and exclusive. The military vacillated between pluralism and white mainline Protestantism as the central feature of a religious worldview that turned American men into strong, masculine, God-fearing, and morally upstanding citizens. By the 1930s, the peacetime military began to enact its deliberately constructed vision for American religious life and, in so doing, fostered the use of tri-faith metrics as signs of religious pluralism.

Three weeks before Congress passed the National Defense Act of 1920, more than fifty navy chaplains mustered in Washington, DC, for a three-day conference. Ordered to the leafy nation's capital for professional development, the men needed their overcoats and umbrellas as they traipsed between several downtown churches and tourist attractions for worship, socializing, education, and sightseeing. At the Mt.

Vernon Place Methodist Church South, Protestants and Catholics recited "All Hail the Power of Jesus' Name" together before the latter walked four blocks northeast to St. Patrick's Church for Mass. Most of the daytime sessions occurred further south, at the Navy Building on the edge of the National Mall, where participants could watch the final stages of the Lincoln Memorial being built. The mixture of sacred and secular space established the tone for the conference, in which chaplains offered lectures and participated in discussions of topics ranging from "The Personal Religious Work of the Chaplain" to "How We May Enlist the Sympathies and Cooperation of Our Superior Officers in Our Work."[9]

Talks ranged from the pastoral to the administrative, but most of all, these meetings seeded ideas, giving clergy the space to refine the mission of the chaplaincy. During "The Place of Preaching in a Chaplain's Work," chaplains heard about the importance and difficulty of proclaiming the Gospel to military personnel. Amidst his clarion call to bring sailors to Jesus, Chaplain Carroll Q. Wright (Northern Presbyterian) admonished those who relied on "propaganda, which impresses the people as being of a sectarian spirit," and therefore loses listeners. By 1920, military clergy deemed the denominationalism that permeated civilian life unacceptable. Protestant and Catholic chaplains may have prayed separately, but they needed to preach holistically. More explicitly, Wright declared, "Christ is the melting pot for all our differences." He explained, "He is the only hope of unification, of harmony and success, and just now is a great opportunity to emphasize Him as the *one means* of bringing men together and holding them together."[10] Wright's message emphasized Christianity as the religion of the United States military—which matched his audience of Protestant and Catholic chaplains—and hailed Christ as the great harmonizer of Americans from different backgrounds. But the language of "the melting pot" reflected the larger task the American military faced: unifying diverse Americans. Although Wright focused on Christianity, he borrowed a phrase and an idea popularized by Jewish thinkers. The melting-pot discourse of white cultural and religious pluralism was articulated in the 1910s by the British Jewish playwright Israel Zangwill and contested in 1915 by the American Jewish philosopher Horace Kallen.[11] Whether Wright consciously adapted Zangwill's assimilatory melting pot or Kallen's nonassimilatory harmonizing orchestra—or merely borrowed a common refrain of the time—the career chaplain understood the military's religious program as a project that fused native-born and immigrant Americans into several distinct but manageable faith groups.

In so doing, the military intended to organize, rather than erase, religious diversity, Chaplain Charles M. Charlton (Northern Methodist) explained. He described surveying the religious needs of sailors, subscribing to forty-eight religious periodicals (including Catholic and Jewish ones), and maintaining a library of "doctrinal or ritualistic or manual books" that covered faith traditions beyond his own. Stationed at Newport, Rhode Island, he brought in a different "denominational shepherd" each week. This allowed "an evangelical Christian minister" to aid "soul-hungry Hebrews" with the aid of a local rabbi. Charlton's practices were necessary because the smaller peacetime military scattered personnel across the country without access to chaplains of their faith. Too few Jews remained in the standing army to warrant dedicated Jewish chaplains, so civilian rabbis supplemented the work of Christian chaplains. As legislators learned at a Congressional hearing, even when a rabbi was delayed over an hour because "the automobile which was sent for him was wrecked," a large group waited patiently to meet with him.[12]

Coordinating with civilian clergy, Chaplain Charlton reflected, maximized the "power of united impact" and made it possible "to be 'all things to all men.'" Derived from Paul's message in I Corinthians, the injunction to be "all things to all men" emerged in World War I as the mission of chaplains. Like Paul, chaplains could evangelize. But unlike Paul, they could evangelize only religion in general, offering nondenominational spiritual succor that transcended sectarian differences. This emphasis embodied the military's view of religion as a stabilizing social force, a public good shared by all. Acknowledging different faiths but downplaying distinctions between them allowed the military to advance personal piety over creedal superiority. Even as he relied on distinctly Christian language to make his point, Charlton's inclusion of Jews, Christian Scientists, and Mormons in his lecture alluded to a vision of American religion that moved beyond Protestant-Catholic categories.[13]

The effort to bridge denominational differences took a more concrete form in the development of the *Army and Navy Hymnal*. If chaplains devised worship services from the same text, the military reasoned, they could pick and choose among a set of options that mobile personnel would find familiar and, hopefully, a comfort in new places. Initially, Chaplain Julian Yates (Northern Baptist), who would become army chief of chaplains in 1929, and Navy Chief of Chaplains John Frazier (Southern Methodist) sketched a two-part, Protestant and Catholic, text. By including liturgy popular in multiple denominations, the hymnal represented many traditions and still granted chaplains autonomy over their services. They distributed a draft for feedback, and the responses—which included prayers to cut as well as to add—guided the revisions. With a vetted copy in hand, Frazier and Yates looked for a publisher. Their efforts attracted the attention of Caroline Parker, music editor of the New York–based Century Publishing Company, and she agreed to take their project. The publishing company assumed some risk, for the military left purchasing decisions up to individual chaplains. Parker, who maintained a robust correspondence with the chaplains in Washington, heavily marketed the hymnal and developed band and orchestral versions to enhance its use.[14]

After Century acquired the rights to publish the hymnal, the JWB learned of the endeavor and sought to add a Jewish section as well. The JWB offered to pay for the additional pages, and the military accepted. Parker worked assiduously to accommodate everyone and became a voluble proponent of the hymnal's chief innovation: its tri-faith character. When Louis Marshall, the president of the American Jewish Committee, objected to the forward's claim that "the ideal officer is a Christian gentleman," Parker advocated on his behalf. She was the vanguard of educated and ambitious women entering the publishing industry and, with a mixture of delicacy and force, asked Frazier to omit "Christian" to ensure the hymnal would be acceptable to all. Whether Parker's motivation stemmed from her marketing needs or sympathy for Marshall's claim that many "'possess all the qualifications mentioned by the authors except that they are [not] Christians,'" she convinced Frazier to construct a nonsectarian hymnal.[15]

Dedicated to praising "the glory of God and upbuilding patriotic citizenship," the tri-faith hymnal was, like military chaplaincy, both religiously innovative and religiously lopsided. The compilation, which spanned over 300 pages, included about 250 hymns and songs divided into categories by time of day, theme, and holiday (including a "Patriotism and Democracy" section with options such as the "Battle

Hymn of the Republic" and "the Star-Spangled Banner"). The Catholic section encompassed twenty-six hymns, ritual texts such as the Apostle's Creed and the General Confession, a ritual calendar, and the Catholic version of the Ten Commandments. The Jewish section offered twenty-six transliterated and translated Hebrew prayers—some for daily prayers, some for the Sabbath, and some for the holidays—as well as several psalms in English. The final twelve pages offered nine responsive readings from the American Standard Version of the Bible selected by Harry Emerson Fosdick, one of the leading liberal Protestant ministers of the era. Dominated in form and substance by mainline Protestantism but covering Catholicism and Judaism as well, the hymnal was undoubtedly uneven. But it was also inventive: a curious soldier or a bored sailor could flip through the pages and discover other faiths.[16]

If fashioning a tri-faith hymnal was unplanned, branding it as such was not. As Yates wrote in his brief history of the hymnal in 1923, it "is unique in one particular [way] if in no others. It is believed to be the only publication extant containing Protestant, Catholic and Jewish hymnology under one cover, and as such it is the confident hope of the compilers that it may be a factor in drawing more closely together the three grand divisions of the fraternity of God serving Americans." Yates correctly identified the tri-faith hymnal as new and, though he did not state it explicitly, the state's coordination of such a prayerbook was unprecedented. Contending that the compilers intentionally included "the three grand divisions" of American religion elided the active efforts made on behalf of and by American Jews. Yet this erasure signified acceptance as well. In ignoring the input of the JWB and taking credit for including Catholics and Jews alongside Protestants, Yates normalized all three religious groups as standard-bearers of American religion.[17]

Yates's 1923 proclamation reflected his own recollection and, perhaps, redrafting of the past. But it did not stand alone. Rather, it bespoke the military's concurrent effort to define its religious worldview. In 1923, the War Department convened a Conference on Moral and Religious Work in the Army. Unlike the navy's 1920 chaplains conference, the army did not limit its conference to chaplains. It brought together chaplains and military officials with "certain prominent citizens of the country" to improve religious and moral training. When ninety-three white and one black "distinguished clergymen, educators, laymen, line officers, and chaplains of the Army of the United States" escaped the muggy summer thunderstorm and gathered inside the New National Museum (later the Natural History Museum) on June 6, 1923, they carried the prestige of rank and position. Famous World War I chaplains, including Paul Moody (president of Middlebury College), Charles MacFarland (general secretary of the Federal Council of Churches), and Father Francis Duffy (the most highly decorated clergyman in the army) sat with the leaders of organizations such as the FCC, the National Catholic Welfare Council, the National Baptist Church, the JWB, the Red Cross, and the American Bible Society as well as university presidents and local ministers. Secretary of War John Weeks and General John Pershing headlined the military officials in attendance.[18]

The conference explicitly connected military training, religion, and citizenship, asserting that the War Department prioritized transforming the "finest type of young men" into exemplary citizen-soldiers. To do this, the Secretary of War claimed, the military needed its chaplains because "nothing will hold mankind better together or be of as much benefit to men of all nations as religion." Why? Because, General Pershing observed, it offered the tincture of tolerance: soldiers "have little time or sympathy for those who indulge in unbrotherly denunciation of others who seek the same God through different forms of faith, expression, and relationship." Religion, or the good religion that the military promoted, meant moral monotheism—"clean living" and belief in one God, regardless of specific rituals, traditions, or prayers. Pershing, who instigated the first recorded chaplains conference among the Eighth Brigade in Texas in 1915, again emphasized that successful chaplains ministered to all men.[19]

Indeed, gender linked the officers and enlistees, immigrants and native born, Christians and Jews, who constituted America's fighting forces. Masculinity defined the military, as the conference's plenary address, "Religion for American Manhood," reminded the audience. Given by Morris Lazaron, the speech outlined how chaplains could inculcate manliness while demonstrating the state's commitment to nonsectarian religion. Lazaron was a pragmatic choice. Ordained as a rabbi in 1915, he served as chaplain in the Reserve Corps in World War I, earned the rank of major, and remained in the service until 1953.

Moreover, he lived nearby and had grown accustomed to making the forty-mile trek between his pulpit at Baltimore Hebrew Congregation and ceremonies in Washington, DC. Two years earlier, in 1921, he had joined Charles Brent, John Axton, and John Frazier at the November 11 ceremony dedicating the Tomb of the Unknown Soldier at Arlington National Cemetery. But Lazaron was also an inspired choice, for he dedicated much of his career to interfaith dialogue.[20]

Lazaron claimed to "speak for no denomination or group." He reflected on "the manhood of America, and particularly the soldiers of America, not so much as Protestant or Catholic or Jew, but rather as related to those moral and religious truths which we all of us hold in common." Like Weeks and Pershing before him, Lazaron emphasized that the military rendered denominational divisions irrelevant; common "moral and religious truths"—even if limited to a belief in God— could bridge differences. All men, Lazaron argued, recognized a sense of awe, loyalty to larger causes, and the importance of brotherhood. By foregrounding these attributes, chaplains could help develop religious sensibilities and masculine tendencies. Hailing God as the majestic creator would help make religion accessible to young soldiers enthralled by adventure. Similarly, comradeship and duty—two elements of the soldier's life—deserved emphasis because fighting "over differences in ceremon[y] and liturgy and doctrine let the hearts of our youth go hungry." Lazaron's emphasis on moral spirituality rather than doctrinal particularity meshed well with the military's larger goal of influencing a broad range of young men. However, his message stemmed from genuine conviction as well. As a Reform rabbi, he accepted the 1885 Pittsburgh Platform, which stressed the sanctity of God and ethics while repudiating law and ritual. In his address, then, he spoke as a military chaplain and a Reform rabbi, roles that he and the military saw as complementary.[21]

Moral monotheism, the religion of one God and upstanding behavior, could melt difference. The conditions of the army, Lazaron argued, presented an optimal situation for feeding the souls of soldiers. In war, "the crown of heroism rested alike on brow of Catholic Protestant and Jew." Living together turned denominationalism into a petty irritant. Sectarianism dissolved because the soldier "feels that fundamentally all religions are based upon a belief in God." The American soldier, Lazaron asserted, considered denominations merely "the way different groups attempt to describe and interpret the God-idea." Although Lazaron's portrait of the mind of the young American soldier was more ideal than real, it nevertheless highlighted the military's aspiration for American religion in a world gnawed by nativism, anti-Catholicism, and antisemitism. If Lazaron captured the military's vision well, he did not speak as a puppet of the state. He simply buried his most partisan claim deep in his rendering of American faith. The American soldier, he contended, "believes that neither Synagogue nor Church can declare itself to be the sole and final representative of God on earth . . . He believes that all men of all creeds shall have a portion in the world to come, if they have led lives of goodness and service." Lazaron's appeal to religious unity was standard, but his rejection of Christ's power of salvation stood out. In ethics, not in Christ, he alleged, Americans could find common ground. Through the military, Americans of many faiths could unite into one nation.[22]

With a triumphant call to religious arms, to shame those who "sow seeds of strife among us," and to "declare the truth that we are all of us alike sons of the living God, the loving Father," Lazaron turned the podium over to Brigadier General Charles Martin, the assistant chief of staff, who asked the assembled audience to transform Lazaron's preaching into action. How should the army enhance military-civilian communities, strengthen American manhood, and encourage cooperation among faiths? Attendees emphasized that the chaplain, "conscientiously respectful of the faith of others," would stress morals and religion as the lifeblood of male citizenship and the nation. To best live this role, the chaplain needed the benefits of regular visits from the chief of chaplains, consistent contact with his denomination, and periodic conferences with other chaplains. The military would boost this work by developing a chaplains' manual, hosting Chaplain School, codifying regulations, building chapels, and petitioning Congress to fill the Chaplain Corps to guarantee all men access to a chaplain.[23]

With the backing of the state and the sanction of faiths to attain these objectives, the military chaplaincy could and would promote pluralism as American religion. When Acting Secretary of War Dwight Davis dutifully filed a report about the conference, he informed President Warren G. Harding that there was "absolute unanimity in all pronouncements and findings." And this unanimity was notable for "it was pansectarian." The chaplaincy emerged as a national asset because it granted citizens "a better appreciation of all religions. We know that each expresses the common impulses of reverence for and belief in God." With an increasing awareness of religious diversity, the army clarified that the chaplain exemplified both religious faith and religious liberty. "Chaplains are commissioned to work for all men without distinction of creed." But "to interpret this as meaning that all creeds are alike, or that creed is of no value, is to impose one's own religious beliefs upon others. This is to offend religious liberty, because religious liberty postulates religious differences. To wipe out all religious differences, and then claim to be tolerant, has no meaning." The report enunciated the military's view that serving all faiths did not quash religious difference. Rather, the War Department offered an innovative way of thinking about religion, one in which embracing diversity enhanced liberty.[24]

Implementing the recommendations advanced by the conference ranged from easy to onerous. Army Chief of Chaplains Axton had already started visiting chaplains and requested more descriptive reports from the field. But some tasks required outside resources. In 1924, the Congressional Subcommittee on Military Affairs discussed increasing the number of chaplains, and most legislators were skeptics. Congressman John McKenzie (R-IL) questioned the efficacy of chaplains. He wondered whether military men of cloth could reach the young men he knew back home who regularly abandoned church for a lazy Sunday at the fishing hole or to cruise around in an automobile. Reverend S. Z. Batten, a spokesperson for the Northern Baptist Convention, attempted to allay McKenzie's fears. He testified that a military chaplain ought to be "a man of ability . . . a man of initiative." But McKenzie interrupted him to ask, "Do you draw the line between ministers who belong to the new school of evolution, as against those who do not believe in it?" Batten deflected this query, asserting that evolution lay beyond the scope of chaplains: "A man who would go in as a chaplain and would harp on that question in one way or another is just the type of man we do not want as a chaplain. We want men there who represent the larger religious life and who will avoid all purely trifling questions." Construing evolution, which would become a national controversy in the Scopes Trial a year later, as a mere "trifling" matter illustrates the degree to which military and civilian supporters of the chaplaincy committed themselves to avoiding religious quarrels. If they could duck the most vexing religious issue of the day, then chaplains could certainly dodge deep but less publicly fraught theological debates.[25]

For instructions on how to embody the military's religious ideals, chaplains could finally turn to a handbook. During the first week of work in January 1926, Major General John Hines ordered the printing of the army's first official training manual for chaplains, *The Chaplain: His Place and Duties*. The seventy-three-page guide offered a range of philosophical and practical advice. It defined the role of the chaplain, outlined qualifications, and delineated duties. The four overlapping main tasks of the chaplain consisted of (1) providing opportunities for public worship; (2) offering "spiritual ministration, moral counsel, and religious guidance"; (3) championing ethical behavior; and (4) promoting character.[26] Effective religious and moral leadership, the guide instructed, rested on being scrupulous, tactful, judicious, motivated, and intelligent. Chaplains must possess "the ability to put oneself into another man's place" and hold "that much-to-be-coveted reputation for square dealing." Struggling to find appropriate language, the section on leadership suggested an "indefinable quality which makes people follow him" as crucial to the chaplain's personality. Dismissing "magnetism" as a "misnomer," the manual insisted that the chaplain "be able to attract and hold and permanently influence for good the personnel within his pastoral charge." Flamboyant preachers, whether emulating the dazzlingly real Aimee Semple McPherson or the fictional notoriety of Elmer Gantry, need not apply. The manual conveyed the government's clear stance that the ideal chaplain would persuade soldiers to commit to religion *and* conform to military procedures, thereby encoding a narrow definition of acceptable behavior under the guise of broadmindedness.[27]

Barreling down on the claims made at the 1923 Conference on Morals and Religion, the manual promoted a capacious understanding of ritual and the divine. Section five, "Religious Observances," trumpeted, "Officers and soldiers in the Army represent all forms of faith and hold every known religious view." An exaggeration to be sure, it nevertheless evinced a dedication to religion writ large. Even without representatives from the full spectrum of world religions, the military positioned itself as a reflection of religious diversity and an incubator of religious pluralism. Indeed, for worship, funerals, weddings, and other ritual occasions, "the United States Government clearly expects each chaplain to be conscientious in the performance of his sacred duties and to maintain a high ideal of his obligations to *all* religious needs of his military family." The guide cautioned that soldiers' religious commitments could vary and chaplains therefore should prepare to address mixed audiences—those ready to receive his words and those ready to reject the word. Particular beliefs, provided they fell within the monotheistic theological orbit recognized by the military—primarily but not exclusively mainline Protestant, Catholic, and Jewish traditions—mattered little. An ability to imbue morality and spark spirituality while working with the many, not the few, mattered most.[28]

There were, however, tangible limits to the army's rhetorically capacious religious outlook. The mandate to hold two Sabbath services every Sunday, for example, applied regardless of whether the chaplain's denomination would regularly schedule services that day. Most Jews, for example, would have prayed together on Friday nights and Saturday mornings. And when the War Department convened another military-civilian gathering on religion and morals, the 1926 Pan-Denominational Conference, the boundaries of inclusion became even more apparent. Secretary of War Dwight Davis announced, "We have invited representatives from every religious body in the country. You have assembled here without distinction of creed, dogma, race, or color." As in 1923, the list of over 140 attendees included clergy and laity from an array of Protestant, Catholic, and Jewish denominational bodies, endorsing agencies, and welfare organizations. Unlike in 1923, more African American church leaders, women, and Congressional chaplains attended as well.[29]

But atheists were not invited. If, as Davis, pronounced, "we have a united Church—united in the love of God and the love of country," nonbelievers stood outside the communal doors. And the American Association for the Advancement of Atheism (AAAA) protested this barricade. When Davis informed them that he had summoned only those who had already demonstrated an interest in moral and religious training, Dr. Charles Smith, who founded the AAAA in 1925, insisted that atheists were committed to those goals. Chief of Chaplains Axton was unimpressed and shooed away the atheists, noting, "It is not a gathering for the discussion of questions which are in controversy." Given that the AAAA had been agitating for the military to cease paying chaplains' salaries, Axton's emphasis on avoiding controversy was not unwarranted. Nevertheless, the exchange underscored that a belief in God circumscribed the chaplaincy's openness to religious diversity.[30]

Atheists stood apart because, as Secretary of War Davis insisted from the conference podium, the military made men into citizens and citizenship hinged on religion—conceptually, if not constitutionally. The future of the nation, he argued, depended on "an educated citizenry in which love of country, veneration of its institutions, and love of God predominate." Though this gathering was larger than the 1923 conference, most of the individuals who assembled in the auditorium of the Interior Department on May 4, 1926, would have recognized one another. Familiar faces beckoned from the podium, but three years had intensified the stakes of religious and moral training: "Without a virile, honest and Godfearing youth, as strong in moral courage as in physical makeup, a nation is doomed to early oblivion." Fear loomed over the conference. The speakers dwelled less on pluralism and more on the creeping threat posed by certain strains emerging within religion.[31]

By the mid-1920s, an unmistakable air of pacifism floated through almost all major American faiths, and the military perceived these ideas as perilous, threatening citizen and soldier alike. As religious organizations debated whether their clergy ought to serve as military chaplains, the military attacked what it saw as narrow-minded, pacifist religion. Chaplain Lazaron argued that opposition to national defense was shortsighted and, more importantly, that the chaplain served the individual soldier, not militarism. Thus, clergy who resisted the uniform unfairly denied men "ministry and inspiration of religion." Three years after his address on "Religion for American Manhood," Lazaron could assume that disparate faith traditions would work together. He could no longer assume, however, that they would support the state. He celebrated those who understood that citizenship incorporated responsibilities as well as rights. Religious denominations, Lazaron insisted, retained the duty to reach the souls of soldiers, to endorse clergy as chaplains, to provide fighting men with pathways to God. The conference affirmed dual commitments to peace and to the military. Chaplains characterized their work as "essentially . . . peaceful" and rejected "even the inference" that uniforms turned clergy into weapons of war. Because "war is caused by the failure of men to obey the laws of God," they insisted, "it is our function and high calling to lead them to observe these laws more fully." Religion, the 1926 Pan-Denominational Conference declared, hungered for peace and yearned for justice, at home and abroad.[32]

If chaplains dedicated themselves to the causes of peace and justice, the former was more attainable than the latter in the relatively halcyon days of the 1920s. In a military far more comfortable with religious heterogeneity than racial diversity, justice signaled the edge of impossibility.

Inasmuch as Axton repeatedly reminded his chaplains and other correspondents that a chaplain of one religious background could serve soldiers of different religious beliefs, the same commitment did not cross racial lines. Three black chaplains—or three-fifths of the total population of black officers in the army (the navy had none)—served during the interwar years. A single African American chaplain, Alexander Thomas (CME), coordinated religious life for 850 black soldiers at Fort Benning, Georgia. Axton characterized Thomas as "an exceptionally capable colored man [who] yields tremendous influence," but—unlike white chaplains—his authority extended only to men who shared his skin color. Leaders of the National Baptist, African Methodist Episcopal (AME), and African Methodist Episcopal Zion (AMEZ) churches attended the major conferences in the 1920s. Yet while the War Department deliberately encouraged a podium of Protestant, Catholic, and Jewish speakers, it did not ask African American clergy to sit on the dais.[33]

The navy prided itself on an even more elite officer corps than the army, and this conceit mixed with racism to exclude nonwhite chaplains. In 1930, Chaplain George Waring (Catholic) wrote to Navy Chief of Chaplains Sydney Evans (Episcopalian) to inquire about a potential applicant. He enclosed a photograph of the Filipino priest and explained that he wanted to discern "the attitude of the Department regarding such an appointment, before replying to Father Rodriquez's letter." Evans replied the next day, advising Waring of the priest's incompatibility. "I regret to inform you that the Navy Department does not deem it advisable to consider the question of Father Rodriquez's appointment at this time. All Navy Chaplains must be able to officiate anywhere, and as ministers must be acceptable, in theory at any rate, to all officers and men in the Navy," he wrote. "This would not be true in the case of a Chaplain who was a Filipino." The navy insisted that Protestant and Catholic chaplains could tend to one another's flocks, but deemed a Filipino Catholic, like an African American Protestant, a preposterous addition to the corps. Religious toleration did not beget racial equality, and the navy would not order its men to accept a Filipino priest as their chaplain. In 1930s America, Christ was a melting pot for some, but not all; interfaith cooperation ceased at the intractable color line.[34]

By the mid-1930s, voluntary religious associations began to map the military's pluralist religious ethos onto civilian life. Under the vaulted ceilings of Washington's National Cathedral during the depths of the Depression, a handful of leading DC clergy invited all local religious leaders to join them in strengthening religious life in the city. They possessed an expansive view of religion and included Christian Scientists, Latter-day Saints, Quakers, the Russian Orthodox, and Seventh-day Adventists in addition to the more typical assemblage of mainline Protestants, Catholics, and Jews. Even in the segregated city, the committee sought out African American clergy. Despite prevailing racial and religious intolerance of the 1930s, Washington, DC's, clergy championed a citywide program of cooperative religious outreach and uplift through the Committee on Religious Life in the Nation's Capital (CRLNC).

In January 1935, the CRLNC resolved to gather "ministers of all communions . . . in some neutral place that is appropriate and central, with four speakers representing the Protestant, Catholic, and Jewish faiths and a high officer of the government." The latter addition was no accident, for the committee had determined it would "naturally give special attention to the needs of government employees." In its effort to lead the District's citizenry to embrace religion as a pillar of American democracy, this nascent interfaith and interracial group recognized Washington as a unique city, one built upon and fortified by the business of government. Four of the nation's state-supported clergy, the army and navy chiefs of chaplain and the Senate and House chaplains, served on the CRLNC. They helped the fledgling organization access confidential civil service and military address lists. In FDR's Washington, civilian branches of government began opening high-level positions to religious minorities while remaining racially segregated—much like the military chaplaincy had been doing for almost two decades. The Committee's emphasis on a robust religious life strengthened by diversity echoed the War Department's perspective articulated a dozen years earlier.[35]

The military anticipated and modeled interwar interfaith cooperation. The rank intolerance of the 1920s generated a countermovement, a cascade of "goodwill" efforts that attempted to build religious coalitions. In 1928, the most enduring organization, the National Conference of Christians and Jews (NCCJ), began promoting tolerance in a bid to transform American society. The NCCJ was more than a "wary collaboration" among Protestants, Catholics, and Jews. Rather, under the leadership of Presbyterian minister Everett Clinchy, the group strove to "make Protestants better Protestants, Catholics better Catholics, and Jews better Jews" while allying to diminish conflict, animosity, and prejudice. Most importantly—and quite differently than earlier iterations of goodwill organizations—the NCCJ started as a tri-faith union, embedding the idea into its administrative structure by insisting on Protestant, Catholic, and Jewish cochairs. When Clinchy needed a Protestant cochairman, he immediately thought of Newton Baker. To appeal to the former secretary of war, Clinchy opted for flattery, remarking, "We need you because of what your name stands for in American life." But he also pointed out what made Baker distinctive. "I happen to know," Clinchy divulged, "that the Jews of America trust you and respect you as only a few of our nation's leaders have gained their confidence." Baker's war work, and effort at religious inclusion as a politician in Cleveland, made him enticing. The NCCJ benefited from the military in other ways as well, for many former military chaplains contributed their experiences and multifaith networks.[36]

Drawing on his War Department experiences, Baker pressed the group to maintain a multidenominational outlook. On a draft of Sunday School material, he rejected hedging as feeble and ineffective. "A Christian ought to believe in Christianity, just as a Mohammedan should believe in Mohammedanism and a Jew in Judaism," he wrote. Much like Secretary of War Dwight Davis asserted that religious liberty depended on religious difference, so too did former Secretary of War Newton Baker link religious toleration to religious distinction. The War Department proved a viable training ground for the interfaith work of the NCCJ, teaching its leadership the value of recognizing, rather than excising, religious variety and bracing the organization for criticism. When personally attacked by those who disdained his cooperative approach, Baker mischievously replied, "I propose that you pray for me and I will pray for you and the God in whom we both believe will probably then give the greater influence to that one of us whose spirit is most in accord with His divine will."[37]

In an effort to bring Baker's calm resilience to the nation, the NCCJ initiated its first signature activity: the tolerance trio. As Clinchy described it, the NCCJ demonstrated that "a Roman Catholic priest, a rabbi of a synagogue, and [a] Protestant cleric can live together harmoniously in a suitcase for seven weeks." The rabbi was Morris Lazaron, the military's interfaith exemplar, while the priest, Father John Elliott Ross, joined the group from the University of Iowa. Together, Clinchy, Lazaron, and Ross modeled civil discussion of religious ideas, stereotypes, and fears while promoting the common ground shared by Protestants, Catholics, and Jews. In this way, the NCCJ carried the views and messages the military discussed at conferences in the 1920s to national audience in the 1930s. Over time, the NCCJ broadened its reach through seminars, pamphlets (including "One God—One World: True Stories of US Army Chaplains"), films, and Brotherhood Weeks, all of which swept into military environs over the next decade through the NCCJ's Armed Services Program. Thus the NCCJ built on the tri-faith work instigated by the military and the military disseminated the tri-faith message broadcast by the NCCJ.[38]

As an early adopter and a receptive host of interfaith ventures, the chaplaincy linked grassroots organizing to the state. The CRLNC, one of many local NCCJ offshoots, underscored the importance of the military's religious program in creating access to power. When the CRLNC needed names and addresses of government employees, it turned to chaplains. The navy promptly supplied a list of DC newcomers. In contrast, the commissioner of the U.S. Civil Service notified the group that official policy instructed the office "not to furnish lists of federal employees to outside organizations or agencies." But he would make an exception "in view of the purpose sought by the Committee on Religious Life in the Nation's Capital." When the CRLNC hosted annual mass meetings in Constitution Hall, it likewise asked the army and navy chiefs of chaplains to participate. Collaborative efforts like the CRLNC underscored the vitality of Washington connections in promoting religious pluralism. Military chaplains often participated in more symbolic than substantive roles, yet even minor contributions helped cement military–civilian alliances. Cultivating these partnerships enabled the chaplaincy to expand its reach beyond military personnel to the broader American public. During the 1930s, then, civilian organizations and state institutions began to prime Americans to accept the pluralistic worldview and moral monotheism rooted in the military chaplaincy.[39]

The chaplaincy's work proceeded in fits and starts during the 1920s and early 1930s, but the state's vision of a tri-faith religious order would, like other sectors of American society, get a boost from the New Deal. Saving the banks was a priority for the president-elect as he journeyed to the nation's capital days before his inauguration in March 1933. America had experienced depressions before, but none had so thoroughly shaken the economic and social foundations of the United States. Rampant speculation decimated corporations; farmers wrung their hands as prices plummeted and credit froze; unemployed workers lost their homes. Calamity supplanted panic as swelling poverty overwhelmed local benevolent institutions. Franklin Delano Roosevelt's inauguration harkened a national rescue effort, one ultimately defined as much by intransigence and failure as by compromise and success. But before Roosevelt uttered the oath of office with his hand resting on a 1686 Dutch Bible, the patrician Episcopalian told his Catholic campaign advisor that religious faith would buoy the American people. That sentiment sustained him as he rallied Congress to open the banks, secure farms, create jobs, and resuscitate the country.[40]

For Roosevelt in 1933, faith was private, religion a personal matter best left to man and his maker. But when he ad-libbed the language of his inaugural address, changing "this is a day of consecration" to "this is a day of national consecration," he shifted from a personal sense of the sacred to the sanctification of secular politics. Thanking the divine and asking for providential blessings was part and parcel of the presidential repertoire. Lincoln, the only formally unchurched president, used the same rhetoric of consecration at Gettysburg, recognizing the role of dead Civil War soldiers in ushering in new freedoms. Roosevelt needed faith to forestall fear long enough to bring about a national economic recovery. Little did the military chaplaincy know on that cold and gray inauguration day that it would become a significant engine of spiritual solace.[41]

The chaplaincy, constrained like the rest of the military by the moribund economy and isolationist politics, was about to embark on a grand experiment. Less than a month after he took office, Roosevelt signed legislation creating the Civilian Conservation Corps (CCC). Officially intended to protect forests, counter soil erosion, and control flooding, the public works program hired and housed young men. As Roosevelt predicted, by July, over 250,000 men were employed and deployed to over 1,300 camps around the country. Over its decade-long existence,

2.5 million American men would participate in the CCC. Managing this effort required the cooperation of multiple federal agencies, including the Departments of Labor, Agriculture, the Interior, and War. Only the army had the capacity to handle the required personnel needs—screening, transporting, housing, feeding, and clothing men. Sixteen years after the United States mobilized its army for World War I, the War Department mobilized FDR's Tree Army. And by midspring 1933, the military's religious leaders began to implement the much-discussed ecumenical vision of the 1920s.[42]

The CCC camps attempted to address two issues simultaneously: unemployment and natural resource preservation. But the program, focused as it was on unmarried men between the ages of eighteen and twenty-five, also engaged in character-building and citizenship training. CCC camps were "state-created enclaves of male intimacy," and as such, they provided an opportunity to impress particular state-sanctioned ideas—including religion—upon single men. Roosevelt promised Congress that the benefits of the CCC included "moral and spiritual value" because creating work for the unemployed masses would lessen "the threat that enforced idleness brings to spiritual and moral stability."[43]

As the army took on camp administration, chaplains became stewards of religion and morality in the CCC. The chaplain's primary purpose, one FCC funding appeal stated, was "to instill true religion into the hearts of the men he serves. This will be evidenced in strengthened character, right relation with God, and fitness for individual and social obligations." Like the soldiers who served in World War I, the millions of Americans who fulfilled stints in the CCC camps came from many backgrounds. James McEntee, the CCC's second director, described the camp population in terms that would become familiar during World War II. "They are from farms and cities, from Catholic, Protestant, and Jewish homes, from English, German, Irish, Italian, Polish, Swedish, French, and Indian ancestries. Some are illiterates, some college students." No matter their origins, "they have a new experience when they are all thrown together in the CCC. They must learn to live with other men of all faiths and backgrounds. They must learn to be tolerant of the opinions and respectful of the rights of others." These embedded pluralist religious assumptions generally escaped notice; even conservative religious critics who found plenty to condemn about other New Deal efforts silenced their opprobrium when it came to the CCC.[44]

Chaplains modeled tolerance through their own behavior, though occasionally some needed reminders about government expectations. Early in the CCC experiment, Army Chief of Chaplains Julian Yates received a message that a Lutheran lad alleged that " 'the services of a Protestant Chaplain or minister in that camp are not to be had. He furthermore states that the only spiritual ministration is given by a Catholic Priest who in his zeal, it is claimed, endeavors to have some of the boys turn Catholic.' " Proselytization was unacceptable, and Yates ordered the chaplain to conduct himself with proper neutrality. "Possibly the accusation of proselytizing efforts are wholly imaginary," Yates acknowledged, "but the Chaplaincy of the U.S. Army has always steered a safe distance from even the appearance of such a practice and I am sure you will not be the exception." Four years later, then–Army Chief of Chaplains Alva Brasted explained, the chaplain's "work is not denominational . . . he must not fail to minister spiritually to all groups."[45]

For the three Chiefs of Chaplains who served during the duration of the CCC—Julian Yates (Northern Baptist), Alva Brasted (Northern Baptist), and William Arnold (Catholic)—encouraging interfaith work proved easier than harnessing a robust supply of chaplains. In 1933, the army chief of chaplains had 125 Regular Army chaplains at his disposal, not enough for the expanding CCC system. Chaplains in the Reserve Corps numbered 1,200, but their availability varied because they usually held civilian pulpits. A September 1933 report from the FCC announced, for example, that "the continuation of the Conservation Camps through the winter makes it important that the places of Reserve Chaplains who have been carrying on the work during the summer months, but who will need to return to their pastorates in the fall, shall be filled by other Chaplains not otherwise employed."[46]

As the primary source of Protestant chaplains, the FCC proposed using civilian clergymen to augment the work of military chaplains. In fact, Roy B. Guild, the organization's executive secretary, thought the CCC camps could provide relief for unemployed and destitute clergy. He encouraged the army to pay seventy-five to one hundred "very capable" jobless ministers as "temporary chaplains" to fortify religion in the CCC. To Guild's probable dismay, Yates apologetically replied, "there is no authority for the employment of civilians for welfare work (including religious activities) in the Conservation Camps." Although some civilian pastors ably assisted chaplains as volunteers, the government restricted paid work to commissioned chaplains. Notably, the FCC saw a "decided increase" in applicants to the army reserve chaplaincy after the CCC camps opened. Over the first seven months of 1933, 122 prospective military ministers contacted them, 66 percent of whom responded to the opening of Camp Roosevelt in mid-April 1933. Five years later, by April 1938, reserve chaplains presided over five times the number of worship services as regular chaplains.[47]

Outfitting the army with additional reserve chaplains did not resolve all the logistical problems associated with the CCC. The biggest obstacle was distance. The CCC divided the country into nine Corps Areas, and many chaplains received assignments to serve up to twenty camps within broad geographic territories. The problem was particularly acute in the American West. In California, David Greenberg—a rabbi turned part-time reserve chaplain—described the conditions he confronted in the Fresno area: "The roads, for the most part, were one lane, unpaved, generally gravel and, in some places, just hard-packed dirt." In April 1935, he found the mountain roads impassable "due to flood and road conditions . . . I would be traveling on a one lane mountain road with a drop of several hundred feet at the edge into a valley. The column of flash flood waters would start racing down the road ahead of me and I would have to back up the road for a quarter of a mile to a place where I could turn around and head for home." CCC terrain lacked the bullets of the battlefield, but weather remained "a great handicap" and transportation "very vexing."[48]

Precarious roads and hazardous weather played significant roles because the government assigned chaplains to so many camps. As one report recounted, many chaplains routinely covered eight camps that required traveling upwards of "607 miles over roads that often are not roads." Before moving to Washington, Alva Brasted oversaw the work of chaplains in sixty-two camps in Minnesota, while William Arnold presided over chaplains strewn across Texas, Arizona, and New Mexico in addition to personally serving twenty camps. Chaplain Richard Braunstien (Methodist) aptly characterized this work of tending to men scattered in the wilderness through his own denominational tradition. In "The Circuit Rider Returns," he wrote, "the soul of Francis Asbury marches on" in the form of the CCC chaplain. In automobiles rather than astride horses, CCC chaplains traversed the country, demonstrating the state's faith in faith.[49]

The limited number of clergy available to care for men flung across the country created opportunities for creative use of technology. David Greenberg, the Fresno rabbi, teamed up with a Catholic priest and Episcopalian minister to develop a weekly radio program, the Radio Forum of Better Understanding. Despite the clunky name, the show lasted seventeen years. The religious triad—much like the NCCJ's traveling trios—offered commentary on the "religious understanding of the three faiths" and encouraged men to share their religious experiences. Whether CCC listeners found the show stimulating for its content or simply because "men stationed in lonely outposts" appreciated company in the wilderness, the CCC demonstrated the viability of interfaith cooperation on a larger military scale. The Chaplains Association encouraged its members to lead "non-sectarian" services: "Catholics, Protestants, and Jews should be made welcome, and the service should be sufficiently broad in its scope as to allow all to attend without embarrassment." What exactly that service entailed remained shrouded in mystery, but circulars, bulletins, and articles consistently encouraged inclusive pastoral care.[50]

The prominence of character-building among the CCC's goals seemed to make ecumenical activities more attainable, though streaks of religious specificity remained. Because CCC enrollees dwelled "in most unusual and unnatural circumstances, living together for the first time in new social units" away from home and family, the CCC and its chaplains often viewed the men as ripe for training and at risk for delinquency. As young men, "their minds are plastic and approachable," which meant "they are willing to learn and to understand the responsibilities of citizenship." When Chief of Chaplains Brasted reconfigured the fours Cs of the Civilian Conservation Corps Camps to refer to "counsel, consecration, cooperation, [and] character," he highlighted work all chaplains could perform. More specifically, he enumerated the values he expected chaplains to inculcate. "Our task is to help men build into their personalities faith, courage, honesty, reliability, self-control, unselfishness, love, and all the essential parts of our highest character," he wrote. The attributes he prized, much like Benjamin Franklin's list of personal virtues, reflected the ecumenical orientation of moral monotheism. Trained at the University of Chicago's Divinity School, Brasted disavowed denominationalism and bigotry to focus on a collaborative effort "with all my comrades of all Churches in the work of the Kingdom." Tinged with Christianity's worldview of building a Kingdom of God, Brasted could not escape his own mainline Protestant mores.[51]

The rhetoric of nondenominationalism often masked Protestant assumptions. Brasted allowed that "not all Army officers are professing Christians," but, he continued, "I have never found a commanding officer who did not profess to be a believer in God." That these believers might pray differently or perform distinct rituals escaped his consideration. On the matter of worship services, he instructed, "The proper time for the formal service of worship is on Sunday morning. There can be no good substitute for this." This ostensibly nonsectarian view belied the fact that not all religions or denominations held Sunday morning sacred. Protestant Christianity could likewise stand in for morality, even when the intent was the broader pursuit of "orderliness, justice, and brotherhood," as in the case of Chaplain Louis C. LaMotte's (Presbyterian USA) club, the "Civilian Conservation Corps Christian Code Comrades." The group asked men to pledge, "As a Christian man, enrolled in the CCC, I promise, trusting in God for help, to endeavor to live an upright life." Men needed to "strive to be true to [their] religious convictions," but the language apprehended that faith in Protestant terms, as personal and unmarked, consisting of only "private devotions and public worship." The standards for entry were actually rather broad—avoid "carelessness and evil," preserve morale in the camps, play fair, and act as "a good comrade with my fellows"—but the cloak of liberal Protestantism was inescapable. Supposedly predicated on universal qualities, character tested the promise of pluralist citizenship.[52]

For some Christian Americans, the equation of character with justice and brotherhood rang hollow. Despite the intentional geographic, ethnic, and religious mixing of men in camps away from their home communities, the CCC remained racially segregated, with opportunities for African American men scarce and underdeveloped.[53] In line with standard army policy, black chaplains could minister only to black men, and chaplains, along with educational advisors and medical officers, represented the few leadership positions granted to African Americans. In 1933, the Regular Army included three black chaplains, and by 1935, eight African American chaplains had been appointed to CCC camps. When the number dwindled to four in 1938, Edgar Brown, a CCC administrator and founder of the National Negro Council, complained to the War Department. A ratio of one chaplain to twenty-five African American CCC camps was inadequate and definitely unequal.[54]

The FCC tried to leverage its standing to alter racist assumptions embedded in CCC policies. After conducting an interview with Loyd Hickman, a black minister who had served as an educational advisor in a CCC camp, the organization alerted Chief of Chaplains Alva Brasted to problems Hickman had identified. First, when Hickman replaced a white educational advisor, he was not quartered with the other officers but sent to the infirmary to sleep and to the enrollees' bathroom to shower. The prevailing racial and racist logic meant that his race trumped his officer status. Second, he quickly learned that white officers held "too many assumptions relative to the dispositions, temperament, and desires of Negroes." One report claimed they "were lazy and would not read," and the officers therefore blocked access to the temporary traveling library. "The expressed fear was that the young men would take the books and never return them and not read them, of course." But Hickman opened the library, and "the books were always returned promptly. He found, therefore, that the boys would read."[55]

Brasted's response, more hackneyed than substantive, highlighted the difficulty African Americans faced in trying to change the separate and unequal CCC facilities. The chief of chaplains allowed that "the race question is a delicate one" and that "we don't need anything to happen in the CCC which will make for ill feeling between the races." He advised pursuing the issue with the regional chaplain, but little was "delicate" about the hurdles faced by African Americans aside from the government's desire to ignore racial discrimination. Brasted acknowledged as much when he stated, "There is dynamite in reports of this kind. All that is needed to set it off is certain publicity." Seeking to avoid an uncontainable explosion but "at a loss to know what to suggest regarding the solution of this old and vexing problem," all he could offer was "the key to the solution of all social problems . . . *Christ*." Unwilling to prioritize the well-being of black CCC members over potentially inflammatory publicity, Brasted opted instead to stall, tagging God with a responsibility he and other white moderates wanted to evade. Eager to quickly dispose the problem of discrimination, the chief of chaplains assured the FCC that CCC leaders "desire that both the white and colored enrollees shall receive all the benefits to which they are entitled." Such assurances meant little to the men who lacked fair access to the material advantages the CCC gave white men. Christ was not "the melting pot for all our differences," at least not racial ones, in the 1930s. Yet even when unsuccessful, civilian religious organizations could poke and prod the state through the chaplaincy, hoping that with enough advocacy, results might eventually follow.[56]

While the chief of chaplains quivered when tested by racial inequality, he was unequivocal when addressing what he considered a bigger and more intractable problem: a turn to antimilitarism and pacifism among many churches and, with it, a critique of the chaplaincy itself. The outcry began three years before the CCC legislation arrived on FDR's desk. During a Lenten sermon at Washington's First Congregational Church, Reverend Peter Ainslie of Baltimore spoke bitingly against war. His were fighting words to an audience that included Chief of Chaplains Julian Yates. "There is no more justification for being a chaplain in the army or navy," the minister fulminated, "than there is for being a chaplain in a speakeasy." His host, Jason Noble Pierce—a World War I chaplain and pastor to Calvin Coolidge—glowered, publicly disavowing Ainslie's claims as insulting and inaccurate. But "the venom of his pseudo-pacifist passion" was merely an opening shot. As the CCC camps magnified the role of military chaplains, charges of immoral militarism followed.[57]

Military leaders sought to sideline peace activists as radicals unmoored from mainstream American politics, but pacifists treaded dangerously close to military operations. Like those dedicated to the military chaplaincy, pacifists spent the 1920s reshaping their vision for the nation and the world. Secular and religious groups, ranging from the War Resisters League and the Women's International League for Peace and Freedom to Dorothy Day's Catholic Worker movement and the interfaith Fellowship of Reconciliation, all advocated resistance to war.[58] Peter Ainslie campaigned to dissolve the relationship between the chaplaincy and the churches. At the 1933 meeting of the Church Peace Union, he proposed that denominations forbid their ministers from serving in the chaplaincy in war or in peace—which made the CCC a target too. Among the civilian endorsing agencies, the FCC felt the influence of pacifism most keenly. In the mid-1930s, the Newark Conference of the Methodist Episcopal Church, the Disciples of Christ, and the Evangelical and Reformed Churches of Christ all voted to withdraw their clergy from the chaplaincy or to disband the FCC's General Committee. In 1934, the FCC itself wondered how to address "a situation in which large numbers of men are separated from the usual civilian forms of religious ministration. We have *de facto* a military parish." How to serve military men "consistently with the Church's teaching about war and peace" remained unclear.[59]

Within months of the CCC's formation, then, antiwar religious leaders began broadcasting their skepticism. When Thomas G. Speers, former army chaplain and FCC liaison to CCC camps in the mid-Atlantic, criticized the military from the pulpit, he made Julian Yates wonder if he could serve the CCC enthusiastically. "Candidly," the chief of chaplains said, "his usefulness will be considerably diluted and our cause handicapped." Even on assignment to popular CCC camps, chaplains could not escape religious and political conflict. The FCC's internal debates often spilled from private correspondence into the public sphere, leading Chief of Chaplains Alva Brasted to warn the organization about the deleterious effects of this debate. "As a result of sensational publicity," he wrote in 1936, "many good Christian people in the military service . . . have come to feel that the hand of the church is against them because they are in the military service, and against the country."[60]

Although Brasted recognized that the rabble-rousers did not necessarily represent the majority of churchgoers, the insurgency from within troubled the army's top minister. When he argued that "the radical in the churches does our cause more harm than many realize" and instructed the FCC to contain "the ultra-pacifists" lest they corrupt the organization's otherwise good work, he signaled a new concern. Since World War I, the chaplaincy and the FCC had operated in sync, but pacifism introduced a wedge into the relationship between the chaplaincy and the churches it depended on to supply clergy to the military. In the context of the New Deal, this church–state tension emerged as a pesky annoyance, as support for the CCC was strong, but in the shadow of war, this friction presaged a major vulnerability. The government could not staff the chaplaincy without the voluntary support of religious groups and, as chief of chaplains, Brasted tried to fend off this worst-case scenario.[61]

Thus, by the late 1930s, the military chaplaincy challenged pacifists publicly. Almost every issue of the quarterly *Army Chaplain* discussed pacifism in some form, frequently in direct opposition to voices on the pages of *The Christian Century*, the major mainline Protestant periodical. To emphasize their service to the nation, the chaplains' journal changed its standard cover image, swapping out the image of the chaplains' insignia for an American flag to visually reinforce its patriotic commitment.[62] Amidst growing tremors of war in Europe, Brasted embarked on his own publicity campaign, publishing opinion pieces in denominational periodicals to make his case for the chaplaincy. In the *Lutheran Herald*, he offered a "Defense of Chaplains: Plain Philosophy of a Practical Pacifist." To those who opposed war as sinful, he presented a litany of precedents for acceptable uses of force, from Joshua commanding an army of Israelites to Patrick Henry leading the American Revolution. Since "no sane person wants war more than he wants disease or flood," Brasted viewed the American military only as a tool of defense. World peace, he concluded, rested on the ability to wage war, for "better a righteous war than an unrighteous peace."[63]

Little had changed a year later when FCC General Committee Chairman Joseph Sizoo attempted to allay the "great anxiety . . . that the Protestant Church has no longer loyal love and regard for those who are ministers of our faith in the Services." But Brasted no longer accepted platitudes. The "sensational anti-chaplaincy statements made by certain religious leaders" was "unfortunate," and so long as the "hostile barrage against the chaplaincy" continued, he could see little productive coming from it. With fighting in Spain and Manchuria in the daily news, the rancor toward both the chaplaincy specifically and the military generally harmed church and country. The chief of chaplains dedicated ten pages to defending the chaplaincy, outlining his understanding of chaplains' roles and asserting the importance of maintaining good relationships between the military and American churches.[64]

In 1938, reserve chaplain William Hughes (Catholic) submitted a thesis in support of his application for promotion in rank. The study's premise assumed a "major emergency" in which a reserve chaplain was ordered to active duty as a division chaplain. Local recruits came from a hotbed of pacifism "due to the activities of clerical and lay propagandists." Sixty percent were religiously affiliated, 25 percent were "indifferent to all religion," and 15 percent were "avowed atheists." Given these constraints, the thesis asked, how could the chaplain provide moral and religious instruction that engendered enthusiasm and limited the subversive influence of local activists? Hughes was confident that chaplains could mold the men into faithful, loyal citizens. To address the men who appeared agnostic toward religion, he suggested making sermons attractive and energetic, tapping the mind as well as stirring the heart. Certain that "peacetime lethargy . . . gives way in war time in many cases to serious thoughts" on God, religion, and death, he deemed music desirable and philosophical discussions essential to reaching the atheistically inclined. Worship conducted by ministers, priests, and rabbis interchangeably offered an ideal opportunity to bring together the community. The chaplain would have to incapacitate pacifism, in part by bringing in outside speakers whose personal conversion experiences led them to forsake their pacifist pasts. Aiming for the "fraternal correction of [the] recalcitrant" required vigilance as well as an eagerness to "find the cure and the tonic in love of God and country and fellowman."[65]

Hughes exaggerated the atheist-pacifist threat to spiritual and physical preparedness. But it was also fitting, for it illuminated the state of the chaplaincy in a world on the brink of war. While many Americans sought to distance themselves from the rapidly approaching European conflagration, the likelihood of a "major emergency" had increased. As chaplains read Hughes's plans in the fall of 1938, newspapers carried word of a night of broken glass in Germany, where synagogues went up in flames in coordinated attacks on Jews. A year earlier, Japan had invaded China and less than a year later, Germany would occupy Poland. This much was clear: after two decades of crafting an ecumenical vision for the American military chaplaincy, chaplains understood that their responsibilities included ministering to Protestants, Catholics, and Jews alike. They recognized that the religion and patriotism could be linked, with God, country, and brotherhood coalescing into a state-supported religious adhesive critical to national defense. And so it was in April 1941, with much of the world at war and the United States at peace, that a Catholic priest reflected on his time

in the military. "When I came into the Army, the Chaplains' organization was a scooter outfit; and now it is more like a streamlined high-
powered vehicle," Army Chief of Chaplains William R. Arnold opined.
Eight months later, his revved-up religious machine would be tested
on an uncharted and unprecedented track.[66]

3

The Boundaries of Religious Citizenship

THERE WAS A LOT to discuss in early November 1943. First, the Army Air Corps stood twenty-four men short of its quota of 1,831 chaplains, and eleven ministers still needed to attend Chaplain School. Colonel A. S. Goodyear, the army chaplaincy's legal advisor, wanted to know how the group looked, denominationally speaking. Of the 1,214 chaplains stateside, Chaplain Harry Fraser (Northern Methodist) reported an acceptable breakdown: 70 percent Protestant, 25 percent Catholic, 3 percent Jewish, and 2 percent black. The army had filled 91 percent of its 7,500-chaplain allocation, but finding additional clergy presented a problem. In particular, the Catholics lagged, but the Military Ordinariate promised to quickly appraise 120 waiting applications. As far as denominational quotas went, Mormons, Christian Scientists, and the Salvation Army were straggling, but chaplains from such small denominations were also hard to place because not everyone viewed these chaplains as Protestant. The five chaplains in the room surmised that Army Chief of Chaplains William Arnold (Catholic) would still encourage their appointments, but, Colonel Goodyear cautioned, "you have to have a need along with a quota."[1]

The November 12 meeting represented a typical week's work as William Arnold's staff developed strategies to sustain and promote the wartime chaplaincy. There were other administrative topics to tackle as well. Chaplain Aryeh Lev (Jewish) was busy preparing for his upcoming assignment as a military aide to Rabbi Barnett Brickner's mission to Jewish troops. Colonel Goodyear instructed Lev to leave local civilian concerns to the State Department. While away, Chaplain Emil Weber (Lutheran) would take over Lev's duties as the fiscal officer, and in turn, Chaplain Clarence Hagan (Catholic) would assume Weber's oversight of literature distribution, prison camps, and personal difficulties. There were some hymn-related copyright issues to work out before mailing Christmas packages overseas. By the end of the month, a draft of the new chaplains' manual would be ready for review and editing. The office's best typist had resigned due to a long commute, but they hoped to retain her with a promotion and a raise. Complaints about snags in transportation, equipment, and promotions landed on the desk of Senator Robert Reynolds (D-NC), who forwarded the list to the secretary of war, who passed it along to the chief of staff, who relayed it to the chief of chaplains. The office was responsible for writing a reply ready for the secretary of war's signature, which was done "in the usual manner not indicating the full implications of the problem." Finally, there were some publicity matters deserving attention. The office cleared "The Power of the Gospel" for publication in *The Christian Digest*. The chief approved the 167th episode of the radio show *Chaplain Jim*, based on Chaplain Terence Finnegan's (Catholic) experiences, for the air. Local Washington listeners, the chaplains lamented, would have to tune in to a Baltimore or New York station since the local channel would be broadcasting a football game.[2]

The American entrance into World War II amplified the need for chaplains and for policies to manage the work of a massive and diffuse religious operation. The Office of the Army Chief of Chaplains skyrocketed from three chaplains and three civilian clerks to twenty-six chaplains and 125 civilian clerks.[3] Still, it clamored to keep pace, as commissioning, training, and supervising the 9,000 army chaplains who served during World War II required communication and administration across military and civilian channels. Pragmatic policy-making shaped and was shaped by diffuse implementation efforts. The intense and uncertain war years helped naturalize religious unity against enemies abroad, but the act of categorizing Protestantism, Catholicism, and Judaism as American religions central to the war effort inevitably placed other faiths outside its bounds.

World War II marked the culmination, not the beginning, of tri-faith America. Because the army chaplaincy connected religion to the obligations of citizenship, it beckoned Americans to use religion to fight for inclusion, equality, and full citizenship rights. (The navy actively resisted these burgeoning controversies by isolating itself from the

efforts of religious and racial minorities to access the chaplaincy.)[4]
The public prominence of tri-faith language notwithstanding, the
World War II army operated according to a "Protestant-Catholic-
Jewish-Negro" logic, which cast African Americans as a separate but
not quite equal religious group.[5] Ecumenism could not overthrow the
restrictive realities of Jim Crow. However, through the chaplaincy, religious and racial minorities forced the state to reconsider and tinker
with purportedly innate and fixed classifications. Those excluded from
representation in the military chaplaincy advocated recognition and
acceptance. If religious freedom signaled democracy, as the state alleged, then religious Americans ranging from Christian Science women
and Japanese American Buddhists to the Greek Orthodox and white
evangelicals reasoned they belonged in the military chaplaincy too.
The military considered their claims without necessarily fulfilling
them. Religion undergirded the state's wartime project, but the rhetoric of democracy and pluralism collided with the reality of its clear
racial, gendered, and religious limits.[6]

"War is a dastardly business," remarked Rabbi Moritz Gottlieb in a report from the Southwest Pacific in 1943. But even amidst the most
hellish conditions, signs of sacred forbearance materialized. While traveling with Chaplain Ivan Bennett (Baptist), a colonel and the highest-
ranking chaplain in General MacArthur's Pacific Command, Gottlieb
witnessed "millions of men [who] have learned not to judge each other
as Catholic, Protestant, or Jew." Chaplains set the standard, including
a Catholic chaplain who arranged services for his Jewish men in a local
Methodist Church and an Episcopalian chaplain who searched for lost
Passover matzah by going "from island base to island base on small
boats," pausing only to conduct funeral services. On visits to military
posts, Archbishop Francis Spellman noticed this cooperation as well,
assessing "relations with non-Catholic chaplains" as "excellent." In
1944, Chaplain Edward Larsen (Lutheran) found himself drawn to
midnight mass on Christmas Eve and celebrated the combined
Protestant-Catholic choir's successful service the next day. Later, the
navy minister confided to his wife, "I am afraid that the constricted
thinking of our synod is a little too stifling. . . . There are so many congregations where it would be hard to fall in line especially after serving
men of all faiths."[7] Larsen typified the chaplains Gottlieb and Spellman

observed in his openness to thinking outside the strictures of his own faith to reach a diverse array of Americans.

The military generally reported the work of the chaplaincy through a Protestant-Catholic-Jewish lens. A midwar press release, for example, noted that 180 chaplains had recently completed Navy Chaplain School at the College of William & Mary—"139 were Protestant, representing 18 denominations, 34 were Roman Catholic, and 7 were Jewish." Reports used the same metrics. Chaplain Robert Sassaman (Lutheran) enumerated the enlisted men of his battalion as "658 Protestants, 318 Roman Catholics, and 31 Hebrews" and found that "of the 29 officers, 18 are Protestant, 7 are Roman Catholic, and 3 are Hebrew, and 1 is an atheist." Even visits to Civilian Public Service camps for conscientious objectors classified men into these religious categories, leading one chaplain to describe the space as an "experiment of a medley of religious males trying to live together." Whether measuring those fighting the war or objecting to it, the army and navy chaplaincies publicly imprinted a tri-faith worldview, their interpretation, in other words, of regulations instructing chaplains to "serve the moral and religious needs of the entire personnel of the command," at least "so far as practicable."[8]

Fidelity to this ideal began with the recruitment of chaplains. While each denomination corralled its own men for the military, the application process sought to ferret out the "fair-minded" from the sectarian. As in World War I, the military commissioned chaplains who met the age, physical, and educational standards and received the endorsement of a sanctioned civilian religious organization. The Federal Council of Church's General Commission on Army and Navy Chaplains (Protestant), the Military Ordinariate (Catholic), and the Jewish Welfare Board remained the largest endorsers. While the exact application process varied from group to group, all applicants had to complete forms, write personal essays, and supply reference letters. The Jewish Welfare Board's Committee on Army and Navy Religious Affairs (CANRA) insisted on interviewing prospective chaplains, in part to assess appearance and speech and in part to determine "the religious integrity of the candidate and the flexibility of his views in terms of the needs of the service." Protestants applying through the General Commission had to secure references that ensured that "only the right men" would be chosen. To glean a better sense of how the ministers might interact with military parishioners, the rating form pressed for information about attitudes on "a) democracy, b) interdenominational cooperation, c) social problems, d) economic order, e) people of different racial or religious background, f) pacifism and militarism." The ideal chaplain could wrestle angels like the biblical Jacob and make decisions like Solomon. To be "fit for service" meant living a morally upright life while showing brains and brawn, sensitivity and charisma, wisdom and wit—preferably with a good voice to boot. It also meant holding correct opinions: acclaiming democracy, applauding ecumenism, praising capitalism, tolerating difference, and accepting military force as necessary.[9]

Chaplain School, which was reinvigorated after a period of interwar dormancy, reinforced the reality of a multi-faith military. Initially located at Fort Benjamin Harrison, Indiana, the Army Chaplain School moved to the grounds of Harvard University in August 1942 (and the navy to William & Mary) to accommodate the ever-increasing cohorts, which grew from 75 to 450 men. The stated purpose of the five- to six-week sessions, in military parlance, was indoctrination. Not of religion, which the state presumed chaplains possessed via seminary training, but in military life. Dorm rooms provided indoctrination of another sort: the school intentionally assigned clergy of different denominations to room together to cultivate an ethos of religious cooperation. By talking to clergy of other faiths, a chaplain would learn "what *in conscience* he can do for men of other faiths in pastoral, educational, and cultural work." Chaplain Harold Saperstein (Jewish) bunked with two Catholic priests and one Protestant minister. "They are all very fine fellows," he recorded, "and we get along splendidly." Saperstein learned the lesson the Army hoped he would, finding that uniform-clad clergy made it "difficult to tell the difference between the faiths."[10]

Not all incoming chaplains interpreted the interfaith lodging experiment glowingly. Lyman Berrett (LDS) traveled from Salt Lake City to Cambridge, where he noticed that "the six in the room were all six different religious denominations." The Mormon chaplain was surprised by their habits—they drank coffee, tea, and liquor, they smoked, they caroused in the evenings, and they seemed sexually libertine. But most strangely to him, "I was the only one of six of us who actually believed that Jesus Christ was the Son of God and divine." He spurned the behavior of and was disappointed in the "philosophies" espoused by his fellow chaplains, but Berrett showed that he graduated from Chaplain School having accomplished its aims. Despite his disdain for their ideas and conduct, he still talked to his roommates and learned from them. He shipped out as a Graves Registration Chaplain in Okinawa where, he later reminisced, "I enjoyed my association with Latter-day Saint men and Protestant, Catholic, and Jewish men."[11] He absorbed the message of Chaplain School even as he resisted its carriers.

The military enacted its commitment to a tri-faith ideal in numerous ways. It encouraged the National Conference of Christians and Jews (NCCJ) to present "Trialogues on National Unity" on military bases across the country. During the NCCJ's Brotherhood Weeks, Protestant, Catholic, and Jewish chaplains hosted joint "Brotherhood Services" and participated in "Brotherhood Programs" on local radio stations. More tangibly, recruits selected one of three options for their dog tags: P (Protestant), C (Catholic), or H (Hebrew). As in World War I, the military distributed pocket-sized Armed Forces Hymnals and, following the prompting of an Iowa woman, Bibles. The military-distributed Protestant (King James), Catholic (Douay), and Jewish (Jewish Publication Society) scriptures contained a greeting from Commander-in-Chief Roosevelt and advocated contact with chaplains.[12]

Military chapel construction soared in the early 1940s and concretely reinforced religious toleration. Congress allocated almost 13 million dollars for chapels in March 1941, and over the course of the war, the army spent about 32 million dollars on approximately 1,300 chapels in the United States and abroad. Designed, according to William Arnold, "by a government which declares that man shall be free to worship God as seems best to himself," the extensive construction campaign assumed Protestant, Catholic, and Jewish worship would occur in the same building. While the standardized blueprint for a clapboard-framed building with a high steeple that could seat 350 may have resembled a New England meetinghouse, the nondenominational interior offered a variety of setups for different forms of worship. At the dedication ceremony for the first chapel built as part of the 1941 expansion project, the quartermaster general lauded the structure as "distinctively American . . . because only in a free country could you find a church built to be used for worship by Catholic, Protestant, and Jew alike." Wooden pews included folding kneeling benches, the balcony could seat a choir, and an electric organ could provide musical accompaniment. The cloth draped across the altar declared "Holy, Holy, Holy," one of few phrases accepted (though interpreted differently) by Christians and Jews. No art, crosses, or figures permanently adorned the exterior or interior walls because, Arnold wrote, "if the display of religious appointments in the chapel is such that men do not feel free to come into the chapel to meditate or worship when no specific service is being held by a Chaplain then we are breaking faith with the government that made these chapels possible." When asked about the display of overtly sectarian literature, Arnold offered a general principle: "Controversial writings may have their value, but an Army chapel is a poor place to distribute them." Religious debates had their place, but not in army space.[13]

From the top down, the army chaplaincy tried to acknowledge distinctions while abating tension. On a local level, however, respecting difference and tempering friction depended on specific chaplains, as the recommendations by Arnold had not yet been fully codified in army regulations. In some places, the religious opportunities were vast and space easily shared. The Church Services Bulletin at Fort McClellan, Alabama, listed 106 activities across twelve regimental chapels, ranging from worship services, Bible studies, and devotionals to Confession, Vespers, and choir practices. On Sundays, the Second Regiment Chapel started with Mass at 9 a.m. and proceeded with Protestant and Jewish services in the morning and additional Christian Science and Protestant services in the evening. Chaplains carried the sequential use of chapels abroad. Samuel Faircloth (American Baptist) recalled sharing a chapel near Florence with a Catholic chaplain: "We wouldn't clash with each other . . . The Catholic would have his service ahead of me."[14]

In contrast, difficulties arose at Fort Meade, Maryland, a mere thirty miles from Arnold's DC headquarters, where a built-in Catholic-style altar and image of the crucifixion bothered the new Jewish chaplain. The inspector general confirmed both the prohibition on affixing permanent symbols in the chapels and the violation of the policy. The Jewish chaplain refused to conduct services until the army installed a curtain to cover the picture and the altar. The problematic display of crucifixes extended beyond Fort Meade, but as Chaplain Aryeh Lev (Jewish) understood, when "gifts of a Christological nature are made, little can be done to deter the authorities from accepting these gifts."[15]

Personal relationships, rather than policy directives, often determined the degree to which wartime chapels remained neutral religious spaces.

The presence of multiple chapels could foment rather than alleviate tension. Reverend Bratcher, a member of the American Baptist Home Mission Society, found the presence of a Catholic chapel at Camp Grant, Illinois, troublesome. Arnold pointed out that Protestants and Catholics were free to "make separate use of two chapels" as long as everyone agreed and it caused no "inconvenience." In reality, Camp Grant had four chapels, but Baptists resented the allocation of one to Catholics. Their complaint deflected attention away from potentially parochial Protestant–Catholic clashes by commenting, "Obviously, the Jewish group would feel quite embarrassed to use that chapel." The rhetoric of tolerance allowed civilian visitors to appeal for changes without relying on their own preferences; after all, ecumenism, not Protestant sectarianism, demanded neutral buildings.[16]

Tri-faith reasoning pervaded many denominationally rooted appeals for accommodations. When Chaplain Otho Sullivan (Catholic) addressed his inquiry to Monsignor Arnold, he probably expected a sympathetic response. After all, he was a Catholic priest asking his superior cleric for a meatless menu on Good Friday. He noted that it would ease the observance of Holy Week, and "fish are kosher, and usually acceptable to Protestants too." Chief of Chaplains Arnold, however, saw the situation rather differently. "The law of abstinence," he replied, "is a disciplinary regulation binding only on those who voluntarily profess belief in Catholic doctrines." In his experiences, moreover, not all Catholics followed the regulation, especially those in the Southwest where parishes "had turkey suppers on Fridays, though I limited myself to the oyster stuffing." The military expected a certain degree of flexibility in religious practice, and William Arnold had an ally in Archbishop Francis Spellman. In his role as military vicar, Spellman informed all Catholic chaplains in 1942 that war required relaxing certain sacramental rules and obligations. Mass, for example, could be said in the evening if morning services were impossible.[17]

For American Jews, too, inclusion required ritual accommodations. If a meatless Good Friday menu was impossible, so too was kosher food in the mess hall. Saturday morning Torah reading most often occurred on Friday nights, and one Passover Seder generally sufficed instead of the usual two. Because the military wanted a single interface with

American Jewry, the Jewish Welfare Board had to present a united front
even though American Judaism consisted of multiple movements with
differing perspectives on theology, law, and ritual. The state's need for
one Jewish voice combined with wartime exigency to produce the Responsa Committee, which required rabbis from the Reform, Conservative, and Orthodox Jewish movements to render legal decisions
together—unheard of in civilian life. Although *Responsa in Wartime* cautioned that its answers to Jewish legal questions, which were notably
supple, applied only to Jews serving the nation, it revealed how engagement with the state propelled shifts within religious groups and doctrine.[18] The military prescription of tri-faith religion moved Catholics
and Jews from the margins to the mainstream, but the government still
insisted on concessions to military order.

War renewed attention to the religious opportunities provided by the
military, but some civilian faith leaders struggled to gain coveted access to military bases. The chief of chaplains delegated decision-making
authority about "where and when, and by whom those services are
to be conducted" to local commanding officers. Hempstead Lyons, a
civilian Christian Science practitioner, wanted to hold services at
Chanute Field, Illinois, but since the military defined Christian Scientists as Protestants and Protestant services occurred as scheduled,
local authorities excluded Lyons as unnecessary. "They have classed
me along with the Methodist and Baptist ministers," he fumed. "They
evidently feel that the Army Protestant Services suffice in a general
way for men interested in Christian Science." Christian Science leaders
appealed to the chief of chaplains to intervene, but that proved futile.
If soldiers of the denomination made a request, "in general, it would
seem proper for Army chapels to be made available" so long as they did
not interfere with others. But without an invitation, civilian ministers
could not offer their services. Lyons felt frustrated by the military's
failure to distinguish Christian Science from other groups, assuming
that blurred denominational lines prevented him from reaching Christian Science soldiers. His interpretation was likely correct: granting
local commanders discretion and requiring soldiers to request services
kept meddling outsiders at bay and allowed the military to assert its
vision of religious fellowship.[19]

That vision often encompassed unwritten standards of respectability.
Joseph Gredler (Catholic) was the only chaplain on his post and there-

fore responsible for finding local ministers to lead Protestant worship. He found several willing to oblige, but, he wrote, "one of them put on a rather sensational service, with a woman preacher. It lacked dignity." He wondered whether there were guidelines he could use to bar that type of service and asked whether he could differentiate between reputable ministers and "free lancers." The answer he received was perhaps less precise than he expected but otherwise quite clear. He ought to ensure that "in religious matters all things should be done decently and in order" and should invite only those "clergymen who belong to recognized religious bodies."[20]

The emphasis on men was deliberate. After enlisting in the Women's Auxiliary Army Corps (later, the Women's Army Corps or WAC), Mary Elizabeth Dibble wrote to the Christian Science Board of Directors noting the "need of spiritual aid" and "divine guidance" among her fellow servicewomen. Wanting to be "of the greatest service possible," she asked "if I might not be of greater use to the Christian Science movement as a chaplain." Dibble was probably disappointed by the response she received. Arthur Eckman, manager of the Christian Science Committee on Publication, suspected she had been misinformed about the possibility of female chaplains but nonetheless investigated. As a committed Christian Scientist, he knew female religious leaders and had received letters from other Christian Science women who thought they would make capable chaplains—at least for WACs and Women Accepted for Voluntary Emergency Service (WAVES). But Chaplain George Rixey (Southern Methodist) confirmed Eckman's hunch: women could not serve as chaplains. To Rixey and the other men in the Office of the Chief of Chaplains, Dibble's query was preposterous. The men running the military chaplaincy could scarcely imagine how women could serve as chaplains. Although no policy explicitly banned civilian women clergy from visiting military bases, they were not welcomed either. By delegating power to local authorities, the military permitted personal preferences and social convention to regulate access to religious worship.[21]

While the military fended off undesirable civilian clergy, it vacillated on how to handle pleas from religious groups who slipped through the cracks of the tri-faith taxonomy. The Eastern Orthodox churches presented a particularly vexing case. The 1936 Census of Religious Bodies had revealed a "considerable" number of Greek and

Russian Orthodox in the United States, enough to merit several chaplains. But neither group received a chaplain, even though the army
anticipated that a "sufficient . . . though necessarily scattered" group
of Orthodox Americans would serve. In fact, Eastern Orthodox men
were hard to detect because bureaucrats indiscriminately translated
their professed religious identities as either Catholic or Protestant.
There were those who self-identified as Catholics—which, technically, they were, albeit not Roman Catholics—while others self-selected
as Protestants—which, under the military's classification scheme
that designated everyone not Catholic or Jewish as Protestant, they
were too. In an attempt to coax the state to see his flock, Metropolitan
Antony Bashir reminded the president, "We are not Roman Catholic,
nor are we any form of Protestant," which meant forgoing "Spiritual
guidance and Religious Worship."[22] The problem persisted, however,
as extant religious categories continued to camouflage the Eastern
Orthodox.

But the White House had other plans. In January 1943, the commander-in-chief issued an executive order to create a Greek Battalion
with one purpose: to liberate Greece. Its commandoes were almost all
Greek Orthodox, which prompted the chief of chaplains to contact the
Greek Orthodox Archbishop and request one of his best priests. With
a Greek Orthodox chaplain in the ranks, the Russian Orthodox thought
it was their turn and campaigned for a chaplain at Fort Jackson, South
Carolina, where a 500-man-strong Russian Orthodox group clustered.
Much to his dismay, the chief of chaplains had unintentionally waded
into internal disagreements among the Orthodox churches in America. "It is not the function of this office to enter into the denominational
differences," he warned Ralph Montgomery Arkush, the attorney representing a faction of the Russian Orthodox Church. "Therefore, the
differences among the churches of the Orthodox group should be
worked out among themselves." Although Arkush contended that allowing the Greek Orthodox to pick a Russian Orthodox chaplain was
akin to Protestants selecting Catholics, his rejoinder fell flat. From
the military's perspective, the Eastern Orthodox needed to behave
like the Protestant denominations consolidated under the FCC or the
multiple movements of American Judaism under the JWB.[23]

The Eastern Orthodox effort to reason from military religious categories reflected the state's robust effort to advertise its tri-faith com-

mitments beyond military gates. Letters, circulars, and bulletins often referenced the work of Protestant, Catholic, and Jewish chaplains—not as an unusual event but as part of everyday army life. John G. Lambrides (Baptist), a regimental chaplain, briefed families and friends of soldiers about the schedule of events at Camp Maxey, Texas, provided by Chaplain Robert J. Baldauf (Evangelical & Reformed), Chaplain Edward C. Henry (Catholic), Chaplain Abraham Klausner (Jewish), and himself. Together they tendered "spiritual support to all men, irrespective of religious affiliation." When Chaplain Oakley Lee (Southern Methodist) wrote for *The Christian Advocate*, a Methodist weekly, he lauded military pluralism. After Jewish violinist Yehudi Menuhin played for his troops, he remarked, "The Stradivarius was playing a tune of tolerance, of freedom from want of religious liberty and all the thousand and one things that go to make democracy . . . it mattered not that the 'Ave Maria' is usually associated with Catholic literature, it mattered not that we were in the Methodist Church, or that we were Protestants, Catholics, and Jews, allied forces from all the Nations, somehow it symbolized the whole thing we were fighting for."[24]

Chaplain Roland Gittelsohn (Jewish) agreed that the United States was fighting for these democratic and religiously expansive ideals. At a service dedicating the Fifth Marine Division Cemetery for those who had "paid the ghastly price of freedom," he intoned, "Here lie officers and men, Negroes and Whites, rich men and poor—together. Here are Protestants, Catholics, and Jews—together." Yet when the fighting ceased, so too could this ideal, as Gittelsohn himself learned on the rocky soil of Iwo Jima. He believed that "among these men there is no discrimination, no prejudice, no hatred," but found himself in the midst of an imbroglio over who could consecrate the graves of the American war dead. After his Protestant supervisor invited him to preach at the joint interdenominational memorial service, several other Protestant chaplains complained about a "Jewish chaplain preaching over graves which were predominantly those of Christians." The division chaplain resisted this concern, reinforcing that "the right of the Jewish chaplain to preach such a sermon was precisely one of the things for which we were fighting the war." Despite this support, Gittelsohn withdrew to spare his superior officer and spoke instead at an alternative service. It remained, however, his "saddest experience of brotherhood in arms," for "Protestants, Catholics, and Jews had lived together, fought together, died together, and now lay buried together. But we the living could not unite to pray together!"[25]

If freedom of religion encompassed a variety of faith traditions, however unevenly experienced, it also allowed freedom from religion. William Arnold sometimes had to remind chaplains that they could not, in fact, compel worship. As he wrote, "the service is there; and if any man fails to attend the burden of responsibility rests upon the man and not the chaplain." Sometimes pressure came from others, however. Colonel L. G. Fritz of the North Atlantic Wing Air Transport Command issued a memo to all personnel invoking his authority as their commanding officer "to bring to your attention the importance of divine worship." Attending "the service of your choice, whenever your duties permit" would not only grant "spiritual strength and insight" but also "give support to a very important phase of the North American Wing program." Fritz's logic presumed that the availability of "the service of your choice" mitigated his injunction to show up at such services. Religious effort and military success, according to some leaders, went hand in hand. If cajoling was not exactly the same as compelling, it came perilously close when slated into the missive of a military superior.[26]

Objections to required participation could arise from religious quarters too. At the Field Artillery School at Fort Sill, Oklahoma, the commanding officer invited Protestant, Catholic, and Jewish chaplains to lead an interfaith Sunday service and designated a different commissioned officer to formally greet worshippers each week. His ecumenical program backfired for Catholic chaplains and officers who, according to canon law and papal directive, were restricted to Catholic services. They attended uncomfortably, uncertain about whether they could disobey the chain of command. When asked, the chief of chaplains office reiterated that attendance at religious services, even in the military, was always optional. "The advice of this office," Chaplain Frederick Hagan (Congregationalist) counseled, "is to let each individual worship God in his own way in accordance with his training and conscience. Commanding officers and chaplains should so plan the religious activities to give each soldier that privilege." Prescribing tri-faith experiences exceeded the bounds of military authority, but not everyone recognized the limits of forced ecumenism.

Identifying the edges of religious toleration was challenging in part because the state knit religion into the fabric of the warfare state. When someone like Colonel Fritz referenced "Freedom of Worship" in his missive, he explicitly drew on President Roosevelt's classification of "Freedom of Worship" as one of the "Four Freedoms" for which the United States was fighting. Eleven months before the bombing of Pearl Harbor, Roosevelt devoted his State of the Union address to a rationale for war readiness. Along with ramping up war manufacturing, increasing munitions production, and stimulating patriotism, Americans needed to position themselves as guardians of "four essential human freedoms"—freedom of speech and worship, freedom from want and fear. The viability of domestic religious freedom rested, in part, on the military chaplaincy's ability to adequately provide for the religious needs of all Americans, an effort that proved uneven at best.[27]

Despite the prevalence of the Protestant-Catholic-Jew triptych in American wartime rhetoric, the army chaplaincy actually operated through a Protestant-Catholic-Jew-Negro lens. The military was segregated, but the army—unlike the navy—actively recruited and promoted black chaplains, and the presence of black chaplains increased black soldiers' chances of encountering black officers. And, on occasion, the inclusion of African American chaplains in predominantly white spaces pressured the military to impede segregation. When a black chaplain ordered to Omaha's Paxton Hotel was refused a room, for example, the Seventh Service Command decided to restrict its conference sites to integrated businesses.[28] While race added another variable to categorical religious thinking, religion similarly disturbed the racial order by making African American ministers equal to white Protestant, Catholic, and Jewish clergy. When the army compiled internal statistics of worship attendance and chaplain numbers, it sorted data in rows marked Protestant, Catholic, Jewish, and Negro. When the military dispatched civilian religious leaders overseas to boost morale, it sent Protestant, Catholic, Jewish, and African American delegations. And when the military designated chapel space for different services, it set aside time for Protestant, Catholic, Jewish, and African American worship.[29] While some integrated worship occurred, it almost always adhered to policies of strictly segregated seating.[30]

The racial architecture of the Jim Crow military enabled white chaplains to serve any units while restricting nonwhite chaplains to same-race units.[31] This raised the question of how predominantly white ministers would and could serve nonwhite troops. By 1944, a pamphlet, "The Chaplain and the Negro in the Armed Services," provided some answers. It cautioned chaplains that lack of experience with African Americans would not preclude assignments to black units, and furthermore, all chaplains bore responsibility for improving race relations. "There is no reason in religion," the thirty-page booklet announced, "why any chaplain should not minister to men of any race. Thus the chaplain who at the moment is at a distance from Negroes in the service should bear in mind that tomorrow he may be assigned to a Negro unit." While the logic did not run in reverse, white chaplains had to be prepared to serve black and other nonwhite units because, as the pamphlet expounded, "the good of our Nation is involved." In the spirit of wartime patriotism, then, white clergy needed to understand African American soldiers. The military informed white chaplains that African Americans, like whites, remained individuals with particular concerns; that units consisted of men from a variety of faith traditions, albeit most commonly Baptists and Methodists; that the segregated military "irritat[ed]" them and that African Americans posted to the South faced discrimination "ranging from simple inhospitality to brutal abuse."[32]

The instructions downplayed structural discrimination while supplying pithy advice—avoid assumptions about faith, refrain from stereotypes and distasteful jokes, eschew minstrelsy as entertainment, and empathize with the difficulties of civilian racism. The military admonished white chaplains to spurn racist language like " 'nigger,' 'darkey,' [and] 'coon,' " but ignored the Double V campaign's push for freedom and equality for African Americans. Ever conscious of the fragility of perceptions abroad, "The Chaplain and the Negro" pressed chaplains to sway opinions and encourage acceptance of African American soldiers: "The American uniform, no matter by whom it is worn, must be respected by all other Americans if our armed forces are not to suffer a dangerous loss of prestige in the eyes of foreign peoples."[33]

Yet the biggest problem, from the perspective of the army chief of chaplains, was how to fill the African American chaplain quota. In early 1943, the army chief of chaplains reached out to the five principal African American churches—National Baptists, Methodists, African Methodist Episcopal (AME), Colored Methodist Episcopal (CME), and

African Methodist Episcopal Zion (AMEZ)—and requested their assistance in filling 445 slots available for black chaplains.[34] He fretted that only 116 chaplains—a quarter of the quota—were on duty, and should the churches not be able to fill the remainder, the chaplaincy would turn to other denominations. Working under the World War I assumption that "the religious leaders of Negro churches consider it advisable to have Negro Chaplains for Negro troops," Arnold wanted to "cooperate fully" to meet the "chaplain procurement objective." Within six months, the army had doubled the number of black chaplains to 247, but they were sprinting after a goal increasing by ten chaplains a month.[35]

Some African American chaplains felt their own denominations dallied recruiting clergy. Chaplain S. A. Owen (National Baptist) informed the chief of chaplains that the National Baptist Convention, USA, "has not been the most diligent" in sending ministers to the chaplaincy. He admitted that the scarcity of "well trained men" was a "handicap." Much as he wanted to dedicate his postwar life to helping develop better educational pathways to grant more "Negro ministers . . . the advantage of liberal training," there was little he could do to alter the present.[36] Of the typically white denominations, the Congregationalists funneled more African American clergy to the military than most and harnessed their religious influence to lambaste segregation. When a hotel forced a black chaplain to use a service elevator at a meeting or denied food service at a group meal, the Congregationalists protested. Even as the army vacillated between seeking out more African American chaplains and ignoring the racism they experienced, a few religious groups seized opportunities to challenge unequal treatment.[37]

For the chief of chaplains, the lack of African American chaplains was a numbers game, an equation to be solved. But for black ministers, the chaplaincy was a vortex of variables, a space governed by the uncertainty principle. Some, like Chaplain Harold Charles (AME), spoke fondly of baptizing black and white men together in the warm Mediterranean waters off the coast of Tunisia, delighted in serving "1500 men of all creeds" on the shores of Anzio, and "described his finest lesson of war: that colored and white men could not only fight together, but could make a place for each other in the world." Yet there were scores more clergy embittered and scarred by their experiences. During the sixteen months Chaplain Jackson B. Dove (AME) spent tending to soldiers stateside, he observed "the humiliation of colored soldiers" and watched as the military "hinder[ed] the work of chaplains to aid them." Three months at Camp Shelby, Mississippi, proved worst and convinced him that " 'I could not carry on my work as a morale builder while white officers consistently beat colored soldiers in the stockade and insulted them openly by calling them "n----rs." ' " *The Baltimore Afro-American*'s Saturday readership encountered the profile of Chaplain Charles and the exclusive interview with Chaplain Dove a mere three pages apart. And if neither of their stories—the heroism of the minister dubbed "Chappie" by his grateful troops in Italy or the aggressive racism reported by Chaplain Dove—entered the homes of the nation's white families, this more capricious and fickle Uncle Sam was a familiar face to the country's black clergy.[38]

In the summer of 1943, as the Allies bombed Rome and American B-24 Liberators pounded Wake Island, William Arnold relaxed the qualifications for black ministers. In a letter sent to every denomination that had endorsed African American clergy, the chief of chaplains declared, "We have an urgent need for Negro chaplains." Hence, the military would accept ministers with only two years of college or seminary, if combined with three years in a pulpit. Despite consenting to adjusted guidelines, the army equivocated, noting, "Of course, the full educational and professional training is most desirable but hand-picked men with the qualifications indicated will be given consideration as the need of the service requires." Moreover, the letter concluded, "we are not announcing any lowering of standards for Negroes and each applicant will be considered on his merits." When the supply dwindled and pragmatism demanded change, the army chaplaincy hesitantly acceded to trimming the formal education requirements. But this did not mean churches could easily provide more black clergy. Willard Wickizer of the Disciples of Christ pointed out that the paucity of African American ministers afflicted their churches as well. It was a "problem we have been working on." Tellingly, he was also uncertain about the capacity of black ministers and feared losing "the few able men we do have," as they held "such key positions in the Negro brotherhood that if they were to give up their present work things would almost collapse."[39]

That same summer, as Arnold loosened qualifications for black chaplains, Chaplain Luther Fuller (AMEZ) found himself standing before an Army Reclassification Board, uncertain of his future in the armed forces. His sin, for which he would not ask for forgiveness but for justice, was lashing out against Jim Crow. A year earlier, in the summer of 1942, he set sail for the South Pacific with troops beginning the long and vicious fight for control of Guadalcanal. As the ship left port in San Francisco, he learned that neither he nor his superior could sleep on the white officers' deck. Instead, the white men scrambled about, finally depositing them "down in the hold of the vessel in what is known as 'the glory hole.'" As the journey continued, Fuller witnessed white officers' brutish treatment of black soldiers, including a colonel kicking "'a colored soldier who had his lifebelt over his shoulder. He called the man a black s-- of a b----, and said these d--- n----- just would not do right, although I saw white officers walking around without their lifebelts.'" Arriving in the South Pacific did little to subdue the chaplain's rancor, for it was no tropical paradise. There he encountered indigenous people laboring under colonial masters, African American soldiers starving from one meal a day, casualties resulting from inadequate medical care, and officers contesting these appalling conditions as too good. One white Southern officer, Chaplain Fuller reported, told him, "'If it was left to me, you d-- n------ wouldn't get that. You're not worth anything.'"[40]

Segregation was bad enough. But having to "fight Japs and race hate" together was too much. When reporting incidents to the inspector general elicited no aid, the minister turned to his most valuable weapon: preaching. In late September, Chaplain Fuller castigated the military from the pulpit, "'telling the men that it had been left to the chaplains to build army morale, but we were fighting for brotherhood and democracy, and it was impossible to build morale when the men were being beaten over the head by their superior officers and were half-starved.'" His sermon, though presumably given to an all-black audience, incensed his superiors. He created an uproar. For this, Fuller was reprimanded and ordered to submit his sermons to censors. Even worse, "'the handkerchief headed Uncle Toms had let the word slip that the white officers were planning to lynch me on the night after I made this sermon.'" His men protected him, sleeping by his side and accompanying him with loaded rifles until the military sent him home. He returned to Fort Dix, New Jersey, physically unscathed but emotionally drained. Before long, he was ordered to plead his case.[41]

Chaplain Fuller had encountered Jim Crow before he experienced "race hate" in the South Pacific. In 1941, he used his leave to attend a Baptist convention, but waiters refused to serve him in the train's dining car. Then, he invoked his status as a military chaplain, informing the rail officials that he would discuss this discrimination with the War Department. After a lengthy conversation, the train authorities conceded and allowed the dining car staff to serve him in a crowded car full of whites. The army was less conciliatory than the railway, however, and the uniformed officers at the 1943 hearing concluded that his work as a chaplain was "detrimental to the service." It took several months, but military leaders labeled Fuller "lacking in cooperation and leadership," a minister who "exercised poor judgment, has distorted viewpoints concerning the unfairness of his associates and the continual discrimination against colored soldiers," finally concluding, his "personal integrity is questionable."[42] When the state equated rule-following with right, justice could hardly roll down military waters.

The state, Chaplain Fuller learned quickly, could both fail to protect your rights and eject you from its service. Indeed, despite glowing commendations from commanding officers, one of whom described him as "a god-send" to his unit at Fort Dix, Fuller found no sympathy when he invoked the military's own arguments for brotherhood and democracy against its treatment of African Americans. While one of his superiors characterized him as "courteous, conscientious, a very hard worker, a thorough gentleman, and a real soldier," the army board claimed he "abused his position as a chaplain" by encouraging his men to protest maltreatment. Blaming black chaplains—at best nuisances and at worst agitators—was common. An intelligence report from India, for example, judged African American chaplains the "cause of much dissension among Negro troops" due to their "inflammatory speeches." Fuller's case surfaced publicly, but even well-connected civilians could do little to help. William Jernagin, a National Baptist minister well versed in the ways of Washington and the War Department through his leadership of the Fraternal Council of Negro Churches, convinced Judge W. C. Hueston, former president of baseball's National Negro League, to stand at Fuller's side during the hearings. While Hueston could offer moral support and legal advice, there was little he could do to change the outcome.[43]

However, Fuller's case changed the reaction of black clergy to the military's pleas to serve their people and their nation. As Hueston told the press, "the only thing that Fuller did was to speak out against wrongs. If they kick him out of the army for that, then there is very little good that a chaplain can do in the army." Unlike most American rabbis, who saw military service during World War II as an opportunity to uplift American Judaism and rescue Jews in Europe, African American clergy doubted the value of military service. By 1945, this was public—at least in the black press. As one newspaper story opened, "colored ministers avoid the Chaplains' Corps because they dislike the manner in which members of their race are jim-crowed, censorship of their sermons and small pay." Although leaders of the AME, AMEZ, and National Baptist churches understood that "colored troops want colored chaplains," they asserted that the military's poor racial climate combined with publicity about the Fuller case made it nearly impossible to entice black preachers into the army. What the *Pittsburgh Courier*, one of the nation's most widely circulated black newspaper and the leader of the Double V campaign, deemed the "strange justice" of Chaplain Fuller's case resembled the strange fruit with which Billie Holiday chilled American ears and the American soul. When the army ousted Chaplain Fuller, it informed African Americans that Jim Crow was alive and well in the U.S. military. Without tempering that white supremacy, there was little William Arnold and his staff could do to recruit the hundreds of black chaplains they needed.[44]

Among the black clergy who volunteered as chaplains, experiences varied considerably, but that bothered white officials only so much as negative treatment potentially affected the military, not African Americans. The army chief of chaplains strenuously claimed that "race discrimination is not practiced" and that "chaplains use their influence as far as possible to prevent racial disturbances." At the same time, however, the administration also worried that this work of pacifying black troops was insecure, constantly influenced by external "agitators of the race question" and diminished by "prejudiced white men bungling their jobs by improper speech and action." This dangerous combination of outside pressure and internal discrimination sometimes "got hold of some chaplains and stir[red] them up . . . sometimes they lose their sense of loyalty to the large interests of their country and people."[45]

Racial inequality, in other words, could run afoul of patriotic commitments, but the solution, as Chaplain Benny Jones found out, rarely rested on dismantling discrimination. What exactly he said one muggy September night over the chapel's public address system remained in dispute. Did he encourage the men to stand up for their rights as American citizens, suggesting they stop sitting in the back of buses or cease entering local restaurants anywhere except the front door? Did he tell them war at home loomed, a battle for the rights and dignity of black men? Did he goad racial turbulence? Or did he simply affirm his unit's prowess as fighters and their rights as Americans in order to boost their morale? The military intelligence officer who filed the complaint never interviewed Chaplain Jones. But sent through proper channels, the memo eventually landed on the desk of the army chief of chaplains, whose staff instructed Jones's superior to remind his clergymen of their proper role. The command chaplain ought to advise his "colored chaplains that they are definitely not to promulgate racial hatred," as if their oratory, not white action, created the problem. Instead, their task was only to "furnish religious ministration, preach the word of God, and to counsel men in the right direction."[46]

In the Jim Crow army, the boundaries of religion ended at the door to civil rights; the Gospel, it seemed, had little to say about segregation. Although the military recognized that race-related "disaffection . . . continues to constitute an immediately serious problem," the "urgent necessity" to prevent discrimination and stem "inflammatory gossip" required "positive preventive measures" rather than systemic critique from the pulpit.[47] From this perspective, race relations stood separate from the military's project of promoting religious toleration. But the admonition to focus on religious work and sideline racial matters was actually impossible. In the administrative headquarters of the army chaplaincy, race and religion regularly commingled, often bedeviling bureaucrats but never wholly separating from one another.

Two and a half months after the bombing of Pearl Harbor, President Roosevelt issued Executive Order 9066, which permitted the incarceration of about 120,000 Japanese Americans. With the notable exceptions of left-leaning public intellectuals such as journalist Carey McWilliams, photographer Dorothea Lange, Socialist Party leader Norman Thomas, and civil rights activist Bayard Rustin and groups such as the pacifist

Fellowship of Reconciliation, the Quaker American Friends Service Committee, and the American Civil Liberties Union (ACLU), most whites accepted the detention of Japanese Americans as an acceptable cost of war. Most whites, of course, were not directed to pack up their possessions, forced to leave their homes, and required to begin new, uncertain lives in barracks upon the order of the benign-sounding but hostile War Relocation Authority.[48]

Some in the War Department took a slightly different tack. Although the Selective Service classified all Japanese Americans as enemy aliens after Pearl Harbor, the military realized it could benefit from Japanese American loyalty and skills. Both the army and navy provided opportunities to serve as translators, journalists, cartographers, interrogators, and spies. When members of the Hawaiian Territorial Guard petitioned to serve, the army transformed it into the 100th Infantry Battalion, which included future U.S. senator Daniel Inouye. After the 100th proved its mettle in Europe, the army created the 442nd Regimental Combat Team, which consisted primarily of mainland men whose families were interned. The patriotic bait did not entice all Japanese Americans, but some *Nisei* (children of Japanese immigrants)— especially those from the territory of Hawaii—wanted to enlist. While over 10,000 men from Hawaii were willing to sign up and complete loyalty questionnaires, mainland *Nisei* hesitated, and the 442nd could not subsist on volunteers alone. To fill its ranks, the Selective Service reclassified Japanese Americans as eligible for service in November 1943 and drafted about 14,000 Japanese Americans.[49]

For the chaplaincy, the inclusion of Japanese Americans in the army posed three related questions: first, what chaplains would serve the 100th and the 442nd; second, could Japanese Americans serve as chaplains; and third, how would the military handle Buddhism, the faith of many *Nisei* as well as the enemy Japanese? Technically, the racial and religious composition of units was irrelevant, since chaplains were commissioned to serve all men. But as in the case of African Americans, rhetoric and reality diverged. Nevertheless, when Chaplain Israel Yost presented himself to Lieutenant Colonel Farrant L. Turner in October 1943, the Hawaii-born commanding officer of the 100th wondered whether the military had sent a rabbi to minister to Buddhists and Christians. Yost, a pastor from Pennsylvania, quickly realized that he would find few fellow Lutherans in the seats of his chapel. Instead, for

the next two years he learned how to counsel, address, and lead or arrange services for an array of Protestants, some Catholics, a core
group of Mormons, and many Buddhists. Although Yost lacked any experience with Japanese Americans, he committed himself to the men
in his care. He maintained Lutheran standards for Communion and
"never attempted to conduct a Roman Catholic or a Mormon or a
Buddhist religious rite," but also "prayed with soldier who wanted a
prayer . . . witnessing to my own faith but also explaining how others
taught differently." He relished baptizing those who chose to become
Christians while also advocating on behalf of a soldier's stepfather, an
imprisoned Shinto priest.[50]

Yost crafted an imperfect but viable path through a religious
canvas stretched to encompass faiths, traditions, and rituals beyond
his previously known and preferred religious worldview. By the time
the War Department approved the 442nd Battalion, however, Yost
no longer represented the ideal chaplain for a Japanese American unit.
By then, the army had commissioned several Japanese American
Christian chaplains and began discussing the possibility of a Buddhist
chaplain. The request for a Buddhist chaplain came not from Buddhist
soldiers, but—at least officially—from Colonel C. W. Pierce, the commanding officer of the newly formed regiment. With the permission
of the commanding general of the Third Army, which oversaw the
442nd's training at Camp Shelby, Mississippi, he solicited a Buddhist
chaplain. This was not the first time the army handled an inquiry about
serving Buddhists. In December 1942, Chaplain Wilfred Munday
(Episcopalian) received a response to his query for someone to serve
Buddhists at Camp Grant, Illinois: "Our impression would be that
probably the nearest Buddhist priests to Camp Grant would be found
in Chicago. . . . If our impression is correct, that should be close enough
to secure the occasional services of one of them in ministering to those
of his faith." Neither omniscient nor well versed in Buddhism, the
army chaplaincy could merely hazard a guess as to where Buddhist
leaders might live. A few months later, with a large cadre of Japanese
American soldiers on base in Mississippi, "impressions" about Buddhists no longer sufficed. The chief of chaplains needed to find a Buddhist chaplain.[51]

And William Arnold tried. With the adjutant general peering over
his shoulder, Arnold looked for a Buddhist priest who could meet the

requirements. He informed Bishop Matsukahe, the leader of the Buddhist Mission of North America, that the army would "be pleased to consider a clergyman of your faith who meets the eligibility standards" and noted that "a clergyman appointed from your faith will be assigned to a unit the majority of whose members are Buddhists." This was unusual. Most clergy seeking appointments contended with the unknown and some, like Israel Yost, found themselves with unexpected assignments. But a Buddhist priest was different. He, like the Greek Orthodox priest, would join the chaplaincy knowing his future, in demographic if not geographic terms, because the chaplaincy was both flexible and rigid: elastic enough to consider a Buddhist but stiff enough to assume there was only one appropriate spot for him.[52]

Matsukahe furnished Arnold with one name, Reverend Masara Kumata, then incarcerated in Topaz, Utah. Based on advice from the Japanese American Citizens League, Kumata had already written to the secretary of war looking for a spot in the chaplaincy. At the same time, Reverend Newton Ishuira, then living in the Gila River Relocation Center in Arizona, offered his services. To Kumata, Arnold sent an application form and requested he apply, pointedly observing, "If you are appointed, you will be the first Buddhist chaplain in the army." In response to Ishuira, Arnold equivocated. He thanked him for his interest, wondered whether Bishop Matsukahe would endorse him, and allowed him to apply while cautioning that the response was not "an offer or a guarantee of appointment, as appointments from your faith are made as the requirements of the service justify." Arnold's wary tone may have reflected impatience with Ishuira's unsolicited letter or concern about his background. But Arnold was open to a Buddhist chaplain, as his letter to Kumata suggested, and the army had commissioned several Japanese American Christians. Although Arnold may have sounded sharp, he used stock phrasing. "Appointments from your faith" was generic, a standard line used in most responses to potential chaplains, letters usually sent by Arnold's subordinates and not the chief himself.[53]

By April 1943, pressure mounted. If Arnold accepted the notion of Japanese American Buddhist chaplains, he also knew that the appointment process would be difficult. The commanding general of the Hawaiian Department recommended two Buddhist ministers who had participated in the Reserve Officer Training Corps (ROTC) program

at the University of Hawaii, while several civilian women furnished
names too. But Colonel William Scobey from the assistant secretary
of war's office reminded the chief of chaplains that Military Intelligence would have to frisk and authorize Kumata, a standard applied to
no other chaplains. The impediment to Kumata's appointment turned
out to be a cataract, not loyalty. When he failed the military physical,
Arnold requested another option from Bishop Matsukahe, but the Buddhist bishop informed him he lacked suitable alternatives. Thus, "at
the present time," Arnold reported to his superiors, "it does not seem
possible that there will be an appointment of a Buddhist chaplain."[54]

The present time was June 1943, and by then, another factor mitigated against the appointment of a Buddhist chaplain: tension between
Christians and Buddhists, inside and outside the Japanese American
community. From Pasadena came a message from relocated Episcopal
priest Reverend John M. Yamazaki, who implored his California contact to "make [a] 'confidential' report to Army not to take [a] Buddhist
Priest" on the grounds that Buddhism inhibited Americanization. Based
on this information, the correspondent concluded, "Personally, I think
it is most important if a Japanese Chaplain or Chaplains are to be appointed for the Japanese Combat Unit, that they should be Christian
ministers, whether the majority of the Unit are Buddhist or not." Internally, the two chaplains assigned to the 442nd, a Baptist and a Methodist, agreed. They insisted that worship attendance was good, Bible
class turnout consistent, and morale fine. Moreover, according to the
inspection report filed with the War Department's general staff, "'both
chaplains had heard that a Buddhist priest might be assigned to the
combat team and recommended against such action.'" With the needs
of the new trainees apparently met, a Buddhist chaplain became unnecessary. By early July, William Arnold acknowledged that his office had
not commissioned a Buddhist chaplain, but "because of advice from
various sources it seems best that none should be."[55]

A month later, when Newton Ishuira alleged religious prejudice
against Buddhist priests, the army chaplaincy denied the accusation.
Tellingly, Arnold's office argued that the composition of the 442nd was
insufficiently Buddhist to warrant a Buddhist chaplain. "The prepon-
derance of religious adherents are Christians," the reply stated, although
no formal census was taken and no set threshold existed. Outside the
Japanese American battalion, the religious composition of units did not

determine chaplain assignments. But, the letter continued, "the unit now has its full complement of chaplains," thereby negating the need to consider Ishuira or any other Buddhist candidates. Yet Ishuira was correct. Discriminatory religious logic pervaded the decision to exclude Buddhist priests from the chaplaincy. Despite Arnold's initial willingness to open the chaplaincy to Buddhist priests, the inadequate supply of ready-to-endorse Buddhist clergy combined with resistance to placing a Buddhist in the corps enabled Arnold to dismiss Buddhism as unnecessary to the chaplaincy.[56]

This decision did not extend to Japanese Americans writ large, for the blessing of the Congregational Church enabled four Japanese American ministers to serve as chaplains. Some Japanese Americans questioned the choice of men like Chaplain George Aki (Congregationalist) to enlist. He signed up specifically to "be with my 'church in exile,' the volunteers from the relocation camps and Hawaii and willing to go wherever they were sent." It was a confined and controlled military service, limited to Japanese American units, heavily scrutinized by military intelligence, and bound by tiny numbers. Aki complained to his liberal colleagues about his Chaplain School roommate, "who was from the fundamental tradition" and threatened to report him to the FBI for "dissension." But, as Aki reminded the fundamentalist, he had already been the target of a comprehensive investigation in order to enlist. The two remained "quietly cordial" thereafter. Chaplains like Aki served both Japanese American Christians and Buddhists. He understood that there were Buddhist men who self-described as Christian, "for to put down Buddhism might not be acceptable since Japan and Buddhism signified the enemy." For Japanese Americans, Christianity opened the door to inclusion in the chaplaincy, while race restricted their ministry to the men of the 100th Battalion and 442nd Regimental Combat Team.[57]

For white Christians, the wartime chaplaincy could be a temptress, luring and rejecting them simultaneously. Some conservative Protestants, especially those wary of ecumenism and pluralism, wanted to enter the chaplaincy in order to serve soldiers and shift the military's religious orientation. But the education requirements for chaplains stymied a number of groups whose ministers lacked formal credentials. Out of about 23,300 Southern Baptist ministers, for example, only

13.4 percent (or a little over 3,000) had BAs and seminary training, while 32.2 percent (or about 7,500) had never attended either college or seminary. Some denominations responded to the military by trying to fashion acceptable schooling options. The experience of the Pentecostal Assemblies of God is instructive. Although encouraged to champion the chaplaincy to their clergy, J. Roswell Flower, the general secretary, conceded that the Assemblies of God "is not so strict in the matter of educational requirements as are some other denominational bodies." As a "spontaneous, aggressively evangelical movement," college graduation was unnecessary, and "ordination to the ministry is dependent upon ability and success in the ministry," not seminary. Flower acknowledged that the qualities prized by Pentecostals—a conversion experience, religious fervor, and enthusiastic preaching—contrasted with the formal education demanded by the military. Six months later, though, Roswell's position changed. He forwarded the course catalog of the Central Bible Institute and argued for accepting its graduates, since, he asserted, it "compares favorably with the Moody Bible School of Chicago." Eager to send Assemblies of God preachers to the military, the denomination legitimated education. But the military was unconvinced and continued to stress the importance of accredited colleges and seminaries.[58]

For other conservative Christians, the educational ballyhoo distracted from more diabolical military decisions. The American Council of Churches of Christ (ACCC), led by fundamentalist Carl McIntire, viewed the military chaplaincy as a great opportunity, albeit one bedeviled by both the Federal Council of Churches and the 1936 Census of Religious Bodies. While the military had decided the Federal Council of Churches "truly represent[ed] a cross-section of the so-called Protestant element in our national life," McIntire—and other evangelicals and fundamentalists—disagreed. On its own, the census was descriptive, if imperfectly so. But in the hands of the military, it became prescriptive. It had identified 256 different religious bodies with almost 56 million members, most of whom were Protestant, and the chaplaincy used it to legitimate which religious groups deserved chaplains and which did not. The army's loose threshold of 100,000 members for inclusion in the chaplaincy rankled many smaller denominations.[59] While McIntire was a separatist who resisted cooperation with nonfundamentalists and saw little positive value in interfaith efforts, he was also politically aware, if not always savvy. The census, he asserted, operated as "a perfect gerrymander against independent fundamentalists, against small denominations not in the Federal Council plan, and against fundamentalists who have been contending against modernistic Federal Council tendencies." Staff chaplains found these claims bewildering, filling the margins with an assortment of question marks, exclamation points, and comments such as "impractical," "inaccurate," and "mistaken."[60]

But McIntire's news release did not merely critique. It proposed a "simple action" as remedy: the military needed to rid itself of denominational quotas, thereby ending the discrimination against "Protestant non-ritualistic evangelicals" that resulted from the "monopolistic hold of the Federal Council." As the FCC was, to their mind, "pacifistic, non-evangelical, and un-American," nothing less than the future of the nation was at stake: "In this emergency Bible-believing Christians must exert themselves to see to it that a proper percentage of fundamentalist and true American chaplains are appointed." The ACCC advanced an alternative vision of operationally efficient quotas. J. Oliver Buswell, the president of the ACCC's Commission on Army and Navy Chaplains, assured the chief of chaplains that he could simplify the process of chaplain appointments by reducing the number of categories to five: Catholic, Jewish, Ritualistic/Sacramentarian (e.g., Episcopalians and Lutherans), Evangelical Protestant, and miscellaneous. While his office remained unfailingly polite, Arnold found the ACCC's effort to reshape his command exasperating. As for the suggested denominational allotment, the chief retorted, "On the contrary it will complicate matters and increase dissatisfaction and friction." This did not please Buswell, who continued to badger Arnold for more spots. The ACCC intuited that military procedures were imperfectly neutral, substituting the authority of census categories for individual professions of faith.[61]

But the organization—and the fundamentalists it represented—was also grasping for power, a move the army chaplains recognized and rebuffed. As one interoffice memo fumed, the ACCC wanted "to tell us who cannot be chaplains." The organization persisted, and, after months of regular correspondence, Chaplain Harry Lee Virden (Episcopalian) was fed up. He was quite sure of several things. First, the ACCC "would welcome a battle-royal" with the FCC; second, it "has a chip on its shoulder—and makes it sound as though they are against all

other Christians—and that they are the only believers in the Bible";
third, "they are more interested in using the chaplaincy for the spread
of their propaganda than in self-sacrificing ministry." If Virden was
frustrated, Arnold was stuck. Virden's contentions were apt, and his
latter concern presented a significant philosophical and administrative
hurdle. A willingness to offer nonsectarian worship and counsel represented the finely calibrated balance between avoiding the establishment
of religion while facilitating individual free-exercise rights in the military. Were the ACCC to use the chaplaincy to impose its religious
ideals, it would almost certainly violate individual freedoms. But pre-
venting the ACCC from nominating chaplains would likewise signal a
restriction of religion verging on the establishment of an alternative,
but exclusionary, religious worldview.[62]

Arnold put his faith in the military bureaucracy. In the winter of 1943,
he asked his staff to figure out how to reapportion denominational
quotas to offer slots to the Independent Fundamentalists. His staff puzzled over who, exactly, the "Independent Fundamentalists" were: "They
seem to be a group of Congregationalists, Methodists, [and] Baptists out
of line with their denominations, probably on the question of Fundamentalism." Whoever they were, "the Chief feels that they should be
represented," and their task was to determine a number. They placed the
Independent Fundamentalists in the Miscellaneous group and granted
them .003 of the total. Since the War Department sought to add 4,300
chaplains in 1943, this meant about twelve Independent Fundamentalist
ministers. Neither the ACCC nor the Independent Fundamentalists
ever felt satisfied with their quota, but Arnold was confident he did the
best he could under trying circumstances.[63]

For the chief of chaplains, additional relief came from another up-
start organization, the conservative but conciliatory National Association of Evangelicals (NAE). Founded in 1942, the organization sought
to promote a positive evangelical alternative to the FCC. While Carl
McIntire grumbled about being characterized as one of the "'extreme
evangelicals," the NAE approached the military with more deference
and less bluster. Prominent evangelicals like Bob Jones certified that
the NAE was "not the radical crowd," and by 1944, it was ready to endorse chaplains. Less than two weeks later, Arnold informed the NAE
that it could serve as an endorsing agency, provided it conformed to
basic rules such as representing denominations not already committed
to other groups.[64]

The NAE was generally more cordial than the ACCC, but it presented some of the same administrative complications. It also received ten to twelve chaplain slots for its scattered membership, and the staff chaplains debated whether they should "throw the entire block at them and let them fight it out among themselves" or try to carefully subdivide the allocation. In a preemptive effort to fend off complaints, one chaplain quipped that allowing the NAE to make decisions was best because it "seems much nicer for the other fellow to have the headache." Moreover, competition between the NAE and the ACCC to challenge the FCC did not escape the attention of the army. Deputy Chief of Chaplains George Rixey attempted to maintain an unofficial truce between the organizations by recommending that War Department staff refuse to meet with the leadership of either organization. V-E Day was five weeks away, but Rixey's diplomacy did little to relax unrelenting internecine Protestant conflict.[65]

Exactly what happened as the ship listed and finally slunk beneath the frigid North Atlantic waters on that cold winter night will never be certain. This much is clear: soon after midnight on February 3, 1943, a German U-boat torpedoed the *Dorchester*, one of six ships in a convoy headed from Newfoundland to the U.S. Army Command Base in Greenland. At dinner, the day's gale-force winds had calmed and most men could again stomach food. But the sea still churned with danger as the *Dorchester* entered Torpedo Junction. Less than 100 miles from safe harbor, the ship's captain received word that submarines had been detected and ordered all 900 men aboard—soldiers, merchant marines, and civilians—to sleep in life jackets. Not even thirty minutes elapsed between the torpedo blast and the disappearance of the luxury-liner-turned-military-transport ship into the iceberg-laden ocean. Two of the convoy's escort ships rescued frozen survivors—226 in all. Despite sufficient lifejackets, panic combined with hypothermia to kill most of the men. Among the 674 men who died that night were four chaplains: George L. Fox (Methodist), Clark V. Poling (Dutch Reformed), John P. Washington (Catholic), and Alexander B. Goode (Jewish).

The chaplains, unlike some of their charges, understood the chaos. They knew most men were scared, cold, and ill prepared as they clambered into lifeboats and tipped into the water. They encouraged terrified soldiers to act like sailors and get into the boats—by climbing over railings, sliding down ropes, or hoisting themselves overboard. Chaplain

Washington fastened a life preserver onto an unprotected young man. Chaplain Goode gave away his gloves and then his boots. Chaplain Poling pushed men into the sea. Chaplain Fox waved and wished men luck. All four tossed their lifejackets to others before linking arms, praying in English, Latin, and Hebrew, and going down together, having abandoned neither ship nor soldier nor spirit.[66]

News of the deaths filtered out slowly. The chaplains' families received notice that they were missing in action about ten days after the *Dorchester* went down. Almost two months later, the press began publishing articles about the calamitous night. Despite the lag, the American reaction was swift and unambiguous. Newspaper coverage dubbed the four chaplains heroes, and the men were quickly honored for their heroic sacrifice. For those who survived the bitter night tossing in the bone-chilling sea, the chaplains' cooperative last stand was courageous and uplifting. First-person accounts of the chaplains' dedication quickly spurred commemoration of the "immortal chaplains." Within five years, a three-cent postage stamp brought the image of the four chaplains who exemplified "interfaith in action" to American mailboxes. Stained-glass windows, chapels, and awards quickly followed. The symbolic power of the chaplains aboard the *Dorchester* was unmistakable. It highlighted ecumenical generosity in its highest form and the promise of American faith in its darkest hour.[67]

But the oft-used and much-lauded emblem of American religious unity was far more complicated than four men of different faiths praying together in the face of imminent death. The state played roles both obvious and invisible. The particular chaplain assignments were accidental—indeed, two chaplains were switched at the last minute—but their interfaith commitments probable. The military committed to staffing transport ships with Protestant and Catholic chaplains; it happened that a Jewish chaplain was already assigned to this voyage. Deliberate policy-making also ensured that the chaplains would be white, well educated, and ecumenically inclined. The application process and Chaplain School prepared these clergymen to make the decision to link together as one. Twenty-five years of military vision and indoctrination coalesced in the image of four wise men, praying aloud, each to his own maker, each in his own way, each to his own end.[68]

The Office of War Information, in collaboration with private ventures, also crafted a political culture that trained Americans to understand the *Dorchester* in richly figurative and vividly momentous terms. The press coached listeners to understand religion as vital to the war effort and to view faith as an adhesive of unity rather than engine of strife. Between the night that the *Dorchester* was attacked and the time Americans read about it, they saw Norman Rockwell's "Freedom to Worship" painting in the *Saturday Evening Post*. Months later, the U.S. Treasury adopted Rockwell's Four Freedoms series to market its 1943 war bond campaign.[69] The sacrifice of the four chaplains and the ability of Americans to apprehend it as heroic depended on both individual decisions and state action. Through the World War II chaplaincy, the military harnessed distinct religious commitments and faith in ecumenical conviction, enlisting clergy to circulate its tri-faith ideal in rhetoric and deed. It was not an unbounded religious worldview. The "four immortal chaplains" represented "interfaith in action" but could never have suggested "integration in action." Indeed, the military could promote its tri-faith American religion precisely because it circumscribed participation in the chaplaincy to a limited population of American clergy.

4

Chaplain Jim Wants You!

PERHAPS THE DELAYS were to be expected. The government needed to thoroughly vet all the passengers, and it would be unwise to fly with a malfunctioning radio receiver. The routine of goodbyes repeated itself once again, the tired passengers reboarded, and finally the Atlantic Clipper took off from New York. It was a short hop to Bermuda, where a pleasant conversation at the governor's mansion with the American Consul and a navy admiral made the afternoon pass quickly; then a long overnight trip to the Azores, with a pause for morning Mass; and finally another nine hours to Lisbon, where the trip really got started. The six-month itinerary was exhausting. After Lisbon came Barcelona, Rome / Vatican City, Seville, Gibraltar, Rabat, Casablanca, London, Glasgow, Dublin, Marrakesh, Oran, Tripoli, Malta, Benghazi, Alexandria, Cairo, Jerusalem, Nazareth, Damascus, Beirut, Aleppo, Ankara, Istanbul, Baghdad, Basra, Tehran, Isfahan, Asmara, Addis Ababa, Khartoum, Kampala, Entebbe, Kisumu, Nairobi, Mombasa, Dar es Salaam, Diego Suarez, Tananarive, Mozambique, Pretoria, and Johannesburg. And that was just the first trip overseas for the military vicar. There would be more, to the Pacific, Australia, and India and back again to Europe, Africa, and the Middle East. With the permission of the president and the military, Archbishop Francis Spellman journeyed far and wide to meet American troops.[1]

The army and navy supported Spellman's trips in the same ways they encouraged comparable trips by Protestant, Jewish, and African American clergy during World War II. They arranged transport, set up meetings, and offered worship opportunities. Prominent clergy giving sermons, the War Department thought, would boost morale among the troops. Celebrity entertainers might have generated more acclaim, but Spellman's trips received quite a bit of attention—not all of it good.[2] The Office of the Chief of Chaplains had to calm a number of concerned citizens who thought the military enabled Catholic proselytizing. To one Mr. Hart, for example, the chief of chaplains stated, "You are advised that Archbishop Spellman has no official position with the armed forces of the United States. He does, by virtue of his ecclesiastical position as Archbishop of New York and Military Vicar in the Catholic Church, exercise spiritual supervision over the Catholic chaplains." In fact, the letter continued, Spellman's role merely paralleled that of Protestant and Jewish leaders in comparable positions. The next year, the War Department repeated the same explanation to Harold Ockenga, a founder of the National Association of Evangelicals. As the army chief of staff wrote, "you appear to be misinformed."[3] For all the benefits of wartime publicity, it also compelled the military to manage perceptions of religion in state spaces and navigate conflict between American faiths.

Spellman, like other religious envoys encouraged by the War Department, contributed to government efforts to inspire religious unity against the Axis. Even as religion buoyed patriotism, national loyalties could rattle religious bonds. It was unsettling, Spellman recorded, to realize that in Rome, "I am an enemy. I am in enemy country. The Italians are my enemies. They are enemies of my country. It all seems so weird and wrong." War separated him from coreligionists, turning his teachers and brothers into rivals. The Vatican still welcomed him as a Catholic, but the experience forced him to consider how combat refashioned friend as foe. As an American, he was committed to the military's religious ideals and observed the world through its lens. In Aleppo, for example, Spellman praised religious coexistence, commenting that it offered the only chance of "counteracting the virus of hatred now flowing in the bloodstreams of men and nations." Aleppo was a notably diverse city, with Muslims, Christians, and Jews sharing space at the end of the Silk Road. Characterizing its population as an exemplar of harmonious living almost certainly concealed the rupture that flooded Aleppo with Christians in the aftermath of the Armenian genocide. Yet Spellman glossed this space in American terms, finding religious cooperation everywhere he went.[4]

Global war connected state power, military force, and religious communities as never before. Between civilian religious leaders like Spellman and the thousands of chaplains flung across the world, the state inserted moral monotheism—in action, if not phrasing—into the lives of its men, their families, and their work. The state's religious project, crafted and tested in the two decades between the wars, went public in World War II. As the armed forces exported religious ideals domestically and globally, the military also learned that once unleashed, ideas, like men, could reverberate in unexpected and sometimes uncomfortable ways. Radio waves carried *Chaplain Jim* into the domestic spaces of the home front, bringing the show's target female audience into the military's religious orbit. At the same time, chaplains tried to use religious and moral suasion to control the sex lives of soldiers and steer marital decisions of servicemen. American religion was on the move—aiding, abetting, and occasionally scuttling military endeavors worldwide. This, in turn, ushered the chaplaincy into the most intimate of spaces, as promoters and protectors of hearth and home.

When Amiela Haznar tuned her radio dial to WBZ on weekday mornings in the summer of 1942, she found an on-air friend, a confidante, a potential savior. Haznar, the mother of a deployed soldier, listened to *Chaplain Jim*, a radio drama that NBC's Blue Network began broadcasting four months after the United States entered World War II.[5] Like the heroes of interwar, golden-age detective fiction, the eponymous Chaplain Jim could solve any problem. From week to week, the clever chaplain addressed practical, emotional, and metaphysical dilemmas in shows ranging from the "Case of the Soldier Who Never Received Mail" and the "Case of the Soldier Who Didn't Believe in Miracles" to the "Case of the Soldier Who (Thought He) Didn't Fit In" and the "Case of the Soldier Who Found God." When *Chaplain Jim* debuted on the week of April 6, 1942, it projected the tri-faith religious program the military had initiated during World War I and continued to hone during the interwar years. To millions of listeners on the American home front, radio carried the gospel of *Chaplain Jim*, the centrality of religion to the warfare state, The storylines infused civilian culture with the military's religious ethos—a commitment to moral monotheism, ecumenism, and interfaith cooperation.[6]

Chaplain Jim illuminated the toll of war and counseled men and women alike on how "The Lord Changes Things." In the original episode draft, however, Chaplain Jim demonstrated how "Christ Changes Things." But a red pencil crossed out "Christ" and substituted "The Lord." The red pencil belonged to William Arnold, who believed that "the fact that CHAPLAIN JIM has not been specifically described as a Protestant, Jewish, or Catholic chaplain has proven to be most helpful to the broadcast." In fact, he continued, "the comments coming from the various religious groups indicat[e] that he is acceptable to all. In view of this I know that you will continue your policy of keeping him anonymous." For the nation's first Catholic chief of chaplains, an anonymous—that is, ecumenical—chaplain was critical to serving the nation and winning the war. Over the run of the show, Arnold deployed his critical eye to ensure that Chaplain Jim remained unmarried (and therefore could be a priest) and never prayed to Christ (so he could be a rabbi). While the composite character was fictional and his globe-trotting adventures invented, Chaplain Jim played a real role in bridging the gap between the military bureaucracy and the home front. Spread by a civilian-generated and military-sanctioned radio show, Chaplain Jim embodied the ideal chaplain, a clergyman who could sublimate sectarian religious interests for the good of the nation. He advanced the military's pragmatic religious outlook and dexterously avoided the religious and racial friction inherent in the tri-faith creed.[7]

Chaplain Jim launched with "The Case of the Soldier Who Never Received Any Mail." The story began with a healthy soldier, one Private Paul Hendricks, attempting to secure a bed in the infirmary. Chaplain Jim set out to investigate why. In the absence of mail from his estranged mother, the private told the other men in his unit that his girlfriend was a famous singer. But the army was bringing her to base to perform, and he knew his friends would discover his lie, so he was trying to hide. Over the next couple of episodes, the radio audience listened as Chaplain Jim caught the soldiers ribbing Paul, plotted with the famous singer, and ultimately addressed the underlying problem by convincing Paul's mother to come visit. As in many later episodes, the setup combined a mildly realistic premise with a few highly unrealistic plot turns. On the one hand, some men undoubtedly failed to get mail and concocted elaborate explanations. Soldiers occasionally felt trapped by their fabrications, and chaplains intervened with men and their families. Famous musicians visited army posts, and men competed to get their attention. On the other hand, chaplains did not typically travel to visit families or negotiate ruses with popular entertainers. But moderate realism sufficed, for the explicit purpose of *Chaplain Jim* was to cultivate sympathy for soldiers, demonstrate men overcoming their foibles, and elevate the chaplain as a multipurpose guidance counselor, moral touchstone, and spiritual advisor. A few embellishments did not hurt.[8]

As part of the scene setting for Paul's woes, the first episode also portrayed a multi-ethnic army unit. During roll call, a sergeant yelled, "McHenry . . . Donetti . . . Jamcoe . . . Kelly . . . Goldberg . . . Riordan . . . Gibbs . . . Hendricks" and then continued, "Maxwell . . . O'Flaherty . . . Adropoupolous . . . Svenson . . . Jackson . . . McDermott . . . Cain." By using the Irish McHenry, the Italian Donetti, the Jewish Goldberg, the Greek Adropoupolous, and the Swedish Svenson alongside less identifiably ethnic names such as Gibbs, Hendricks, Jackson, and Cain, the scriptwriters produced and lauded a diverse American army.[9] The soldiers in Chaplain Jim's unit epitomized the list of races, ethnicities, and religions invoked in the Federal Theater Project's "Ballad for Americans." This folk cantata, made famous by CBS radio's 1939 broadcast of Paul Robeson's performance, anticipated the celebration of diversity in wartime in Frank Sinatra's 1945 film short, *The House I Live In*, and readied readers for Norman Mailer's 1948 bestseller, *The Naked and the Dead*, about racial, ethnic, and religious tension during war. In this way, *Chaplain Jim* adopted a common trope of the era's media productions, the contrived "roster of exotic ethnic surnames" to advance "pan-ethnic Americanism."[10]

The United States' entry into World War II in 1941 coincided with the height of radio's mass media influence. Although *Chaplain Jim* served distinct political and religious purposes, it differed significantly from prototypical forms of political radio, like FDR's "fireside chats," and paradigmatic brands of religious radio, such as the services produced by dramatic evangelist Aimee Semple McPherson.[11] In contrast to the overtly political or religious broadcasts of presidents and preachers, *Chaplain Jim* embedded a politically useful form of religion into the narrative conventions of the soap opera. For three and a half years, in fifteen-minute increments and then hour-long segments, the radio show used religion to boost morale and unite Americans. However, by embedding its views of religion into a collaborative military-civilian radio drama, the state underplayed its own role in inculcating religion in the American war effort. This was intentional, as wartime morale management succeeded when it "obscured the statist foundations of public power while insinuating them into the thoughts and lives of the citizenry."[12]

Although *Chaplain Jim* became part of the Office of War Information's prodigious efforts to promote patriotism during World War II, it not only predated the agency's existence but also originated with a civilian. Louis Cowan, best known as the creator of *The $64,000 Question* and president of CBS radio in the 1950s, initiated *Chaplain Jim* by proposing a religion-oriented wartime show. As a civilian consultant to the War Department's radio branch, he argued that an absorbing drama would assuage parental fears about their sons at war and supersede musical or prayer programs in popularity. With the support of the army, Cowan approached Ed Kovak, the vice president of NBC's Blue Network. Kovak liked Cowan's idea and offered him a short weekday slot. Rather than write the show himself, Cowan deferred to well-known radio serial producers Frank and Anne Hummert. From the New York offices of the Blackett, Sample, and Hummert advertising agency, the husband-and-wife team added another soap opera to their plentiful docket.[13]

In some ways, *Chaplain Jim* resembled the other serials the Hummerts developed. Like other formulaic dramas, the plot built to a suspenseful climax that was resolved at the end of the week. Similarly, it was a national, weekday, daytime show directed at women. Before every episode, radio announcer George Ansbro introduced the show by reminding listeners that "the program was 'dedicated to the mothers, wives, sweethearts, and families of the men who wear the khaki of the United States Army.'"[14] Each episode ended with Chaplain Jim addressing his target female audience in the same way. Just as he asked every soldier whether he had written to his mother, so too did he conclude, "Mothers, wives, and sweethearts are asked this question. 'Have *you* written to your boys in the Army this week? They want mail. They want to hear from you. So write . . . write to them cheerfully and regularly. Keep their spirits up. Don't let them worry about you. Sit down and write today!" The explicit directive to write to their soldiers highlighted that *Chaplain Jim* may have followed narrative conventions of daily soap operas, but it owed its existence to a different and perhaps higher purpose. It represented one of many War Department efforts to improve morale and demonstrate that the military cared for men under its control. Soap operas served as effective carriers of government messages because, as Frank Hummert pronounced, audiences would " 'follow an example, but won't listen to a precept.' " Through its association with the War Department, *Chaplain Jim* diverged from the rest of the Hummert serials in two important ways. First, the Hummerts sent every script for editorial review and approval to two military departments: the Bureau of Public Relations' Radio Branch, which oversaw civilian morale, and the Office of the Army Chief of Chaplains. Second, it incorporated the experience of actual chaplains as well as the worldview of the chief of chaplains into its work. Thus, the narratives often melded fact and fiction, education and entertainment.[15]

The chaplaincy maintained a steady emphasis on nonsectarian ecumenism, and to develop a more accurate portrayal of a chaplain, Arnold wanted the Hummerts to meet real chaplains. He sent them first to Jacob Rothschild, a rabbi who had spent sixteen months in the Southwest Pacific and was briefly based at the New York Port of Embarkation—easily accessible to the Manhattan-based Hummerts. Upon giving Rothschild's contact information to the writers, Arnold clarified, "It is not my intention that a denominational slant should be given to any broadcast. For this reason . . . I should like to recommend other chaplains from time to time so that you might have occasion to meet with chaplains of the Protestant and the Catholic groups."[16] The chief of chaplains reiterated this view to listeners as well. When a Mrs. E. Williams requested that Chaplain Jim "pay tribute to the Salvation Army," Arnold's office acknowledged the suggestion but ducked the plea by asserting, "It would be impossible to do justice to all these organizations" that serve soldiers. Buried in cagey language about the inadvisability of singling out particular groups lay the real reason the Salvation Army would not be mentioned on air: "it would establish an undesired precedent."[17]

Mrs. Williams's request notwithstanding, realities of war played a role in script development. To build a storyline about a chaplain in battle who aided his men while injured, for example, the Hummerts used Chaplain Terence P. Finnegan's (Catholic) experiences in the Pacific. To encourage better race relations and to reach out to African American families, Louis Cowan persuaded the Hummerts to meet with Truman Gibson, a lawyer who advocated for black soldiers as a civilian aide to Secretary of War Henry Stimson. Cowan's effort signaled how civilians could shape the public's encounter with the military. Occasionally, then, the radio show even hinted at the "Protestant-Catholic-Jewish-Negro" taxonomy used by the army chief of chaplains.[18]

Chaplain Jim helped convey this multi-faith—albeit racially segregated—vision to civilians in numerous ways. About thirteen months after the show began, the Hummerts proposed that Chaplain Jim become a transport chaplain. A mobile chaplain could "go to practically all battle fronts and . . . have virtually all the experiences of an Army Chaplain." They suggested several ship-based storylines, including an episode in which "memorial services for all will be conducted—Catholic, Protestant, Jewish services." While Arnold was willing to accept the implausibly portable chaplain, he insisted that the memorial services be changed to "three separate services" rather than a commingled ritual mélange. While joint religious services occasionally occurred, War Department policy provided for separate worship, even if overseen and at times even conducted by a chaplain of a different faith. Therefore, to ensure that Chaplain Jim was not himself associated with a particular service, editorial marks axed lines that enumerated a Chaplain Steiner conducting a Jewish service or a Chaplain Reilly celebrating Mass in favor of banal references to posting schedules of Protestant, Catholic, and Jewish services. Likewise, when Chaplain Jim dispensed a Bible to Paul Hendricks in the second episode of the show, it was merely a Bible—not a King James, a Douay, or a Hebrew Bible. When soldiers worshipped on the show, they simply talked about attending services weekly—exactly what the War Department wanted its soldiers to do—but avoided any reference to what kind of service. What prayers they said were irrelevant; what mattered was that they prayed. When Private Mark Sheldon's girlfriend died in "The Soldier Who Found God," Chaplain Jim told him, "At a time like this, we can always find one consolation . . . if we remember that God is with us." The discussion between the two men centered on a comforting God, a spiritual bulwark in hard times.[19]

As Chaplain Jim's stories moved overseas to combat zones in Europe, religious responses to the violence of war became more prominent. While recovering from minor wounds, the chaplain spent time with other patients at a base hospital in North Africa. There, listeners eavesdropped as he consoled injured men. When a patient died, they heard him murmur, "May the sins of this man have been forgiven"—a less denominationally specific form of the original sentence, "Heavenly Father, forgive this man his sins." In the face of ruthless battles and unmistakable suffering, Chaplain Jim's stance remained the same: stay faithful to God, who is generous, kind, and compassionate. To a private distressed by his brother's death at Anzio, Chaplain Jim relayed his experience of grieving his brother's death during World War I. "I still found comfort in exactly the way I'm asking you to find it, in prayer and in God." The message served a dual purpose: for the radio show, it displayed Chaplain's Jim ongoing ability to aid any soldier, and for the audience at home, it supplied a balm to the torment of daily casualty reports.[20]

Although Chaplain Jim usually conveyed his religious outlook through the show's plotlines, occasionally the character used the show to address his audience directly. In January 1943, a week after President Roosevelt declared his support for the Federal Council of Churches' "Universal Week of Prayer," Chaplain Jim chimed in too. The chaplain agreed with the president's declaration that " 'without spiritual armor we cannot win the war, be worthy of winning it, or be fit to make the peace.' " He then nudged uncertain Americans to participate: "My hope is that many who may have forgotten how to pray were started on this wonderful and consoling path again last week—and that such of you as were, will *continue* with those of us who feel life would neither be possible nor worth living without faith in God and prayer." Tinged with a Protestant emphasis on prayer, belief, and faith, Chaplain Jim urged his followers to act. Join up, he called out; enlist in a community of worshippers and believers—if not also in the military itself.[21]

In matters of race, too, *Chaplain Jim* occasionally provided a lesson alongside a recruiting tool. If Chaplain Jim could mask his religious affiliation, he could not conceal his race. The range of men he served, as denoted by the array of ethnic surnames, meant that he was white because, in the Jim Crow military, black chaplains served only black men. Louis Cowan recalled meeting Judge William Hastie, an African American civilian aide to the secretary of war, who informed him that white Americans "were full of hatred for Negroes in the Army and said they were cowards and ran away every time there was a battle." Yet "it wasn't true . . . and it was an unfair story." After this conversation,

Cowan called the Hummerts and told them since their serials reached millions a day, and because those listeners included "the heart and the backbone of those that have the great prejudices about the Negroes," they had a chance to sway these Americans away from racist thinking.[22]

Similarly, when the army desperately needed African American chaplains, *Chaplain Jim* aired an episode-cum-commercial in an explicit effort to garner more applicants. The episode revolved around a conversation between two Chaplain Jims, the protagonist and the real-life Chaplain James R. C. Pinn (National Baptist), who had recently returned to the United States after serving with the 41st Engineers in Liberia. During the show, the two clergymen discussed Pinn's work on a transport ship, where the character and his namesake shared a 100 percent attendance rate at their weekly worship services for the regiment known as the "Singing Engineers," as well as in West Africa, where the rainy season stymied the construction unit's work but not their spirits. Prompted by Chaplain Jim to reflect on his duties, Chaplain Pinn stated, "I kept telling myself how, I, as a chaplain, must be prepared to take full advantage of every opportunity . . . to inspire constantly . . . men to undaunted faith in God, in their country, in their offices and comrades . . . and in themselves." The emphasis was unswervingly positive, highlighting all the ways black ministers, like their white counterparts, could serve American men. There was no mention, of course, of segregation, discrimination, harassment, or inequitable military justice. Those were not matters for public consumption. The radio recruitment of black chaplains ignored the prominent Double V campaign in the black press—the argument that victory for democracy abroad required victory for full citizenship rights for African Americans at home. The Chaplain Jims concluded with a "shoulder-to-shoulder appeal" for 4,000 more chaplains, even though in reality just 235 spots were reserved for black clergy. The discrimination inherent in opening a mere 5 percent of the chaplain corps to blacks remained inaudible.[23]

Although the show looked past racial injustice, it consistently pushed for capacious religious tolerance. When Chaplain Jim offered condolences to the New York families of servicemen killed in action, the writers placed Frank O'Neill's Catholic mother at the entrance to the apartment of Davy Silverberg's Jewish family. The mothers had bonded as a result of their sons' wartime friendship, and the chaplain commented, "You and Mrs. Silverberg worship God in different ways, perhaps, but you're both Americans, proud of your sons, and glad of the chance to help and understand each other." Religious difference united, rather than divided, Americans. Respect for religious difference traveled overseas, albeit in a more limited form. When Chaplain Jim landed in North Africa, he roamed around Casablanca with his men, where they discovered new foods such as "KOOS-koos" and encountered veiled Muslim women. There, he taught, "these people have different customs, customs that are just as strange to us as ours are to them . . . the Mosque is their *church*. You see, Moslems are just as deeply religious as we are." To avoid accidentally appearing insensitive to or disrespecting Muslims, however, he instructed his teenage American charges to "keep away." Islam could not blend into the American trifecta of Protestantism, Catholicism, and Judaism, but it still deserved deference, at least from a distance.[24]

Despite the efforts to keep Chaplain Jim religiously "anonymous," a discerning ear would have heard a few slips. "The Soldier Who Found God" episodes revealed how the chaplain entered the ministry. Although no denominational information was leaked, the chaplain and his friends used the word "church" and referred to Sunday services. On the one hand, this made Chaplain Jim decidedly Christian. On the other hand, the chaplaincy employed "church" as a stand-in for any place of religious worship, and the War Department encouraged—at times even insisted on—Sunday services for all religious groups. Editorial marks on the manuscripts stressed the capacious use of "church." When Chaplain Jim accompanied soldiers at Normandy, he reflected on the fierce battle he witnessed: "Two hours ago this field was an inferno. Now, it's quiet again and those who have fallen will be buried with all the rites of their church and the sacrament of God." Crossing out the reference to "sacrament"—a religious term frequently used by and associated with Catholicism and Eastern Orthodoxy—helped reduce the particularity of death rites, while preserving "church" allowed a listener to fill in familiar details. If war killed indiscriminately, U.S. military funeral practices still honored the religious affiliation of the serviceman. Indeed, when Chaplain Jim met Davy Silverberg's mother, he assured her that her son was buried "according to Jewish rites" and that "Chaplain Wise, my colleague, conducted the service." Traces of Christian language lingered over 300 scripts, but the bulk of *Chaplain Jim*'s endeavors focused on messages understood as applicable to all Americans, no matter their religious preferences.[25]

Through the editorial work of the chief of chaplains, *Chaplain Jim* promoted moral monotheism and tri-faith cooperation as commensurate with and essential to the state's wartime mission. By eliminating the "folksy" drawl the Hummerts had initially given Chaplain Jim and assiduously correcting syntax, Arnold ensured that the listening public heard a smart, well-spoken clergyman, not a caricature of huckster preachers. The language, actions, and worldview of Chaplain Jim resonated with chaplains who heard the show. Chaplain Alvie McKnight (Southern Baptist) confirmed that the radio protagonist seemed familiar. After listening to a number of episodes after he returned stateside, he judged them "much worth while" and accurate, "quite typical of the Chaplains['] every day experiences out there." He too encouraged families to write to their soldiers with "intimate details of life back home" and even sent the chief of chaplains a script he wrote based on his experiences in the Solomon Islands. Indeed, the bulk of Chaplain Jim's work centered on counseling soldiers on matters of morality, love, and grief. These topics allowed Chaplain Jim to offer advice and comfort without delving too deeply into the specifics of any faith tradition. Yet for listeners like Amiela Haznar, William Arnold and his careful red pencil remained concealed. Radio shrouded his office, his work, and his agenda. From its inception, however, the show represented a civilian-military, commercial-public, Protestant-Catholic-Jewish collaboration while recruiting for and advertising the chaplaincy to Americans. In *Chaplain Jim*, the home front encountered a military dedicated to God, soldier, and country.[26]

Sex exasperated the military and often placed the chaplaincy in an awkward spot. The army approached sexual activity with bait-and-switch maneuvers: publicly protest and privately pardon, or vociferously rebuke but dispense condoms. As an institution charged with promoting morality, the chaplaincy preferred to tout abstinence as a virtue even though it knew that its soldiers were sexually active. With young, unmarried men constituting the bulk of the armed forces, chaplains were responsible for regular lectures on what the military dubbed "sex-morality." Regardless of any religion's view on sex and rather than discussing the values embedded in sexual activity, chaplains counseled chastity. At the same time, sex occurred and venereal disease was real, and the military instructed its medical staff to give "personal hygiene" lectures, operate prophylaxis stations, and treat infections.[27]

While some chaplains accepted this setup as sensible, others resisted. Chaplain Timothy Bowers-Iron (LDS) characterized sexual immorality lectures as fulfilling work, all the while understanding they had little practical effect. A confidential overseas inspection report from future Air Force Chief of Chaplains Charles I. Carpenter (Methodist) critiqued morally laxity. "We appear to have completely given up the fight to maintain ideals and morals, and are simply trying to salvage as much human life as possible from the possible wreckage that can result from lust run wild," he stated. Using drugs to treat infections merely enabled GIs to stray with limited consequences. Figuring out how to handle masses of men devoid of family influence in an environment that venerated the pin-up girl, with its focus "on the feminine form from the purely physical and lust arousing standpoint," in places filled with foreign women stymied even the most dedicated chaplains.[28]

As a Catholic priest, World War II Chief of Chaplains William Arnold had to tread carefully between the teachings of the Church (which required premarital abstinence and forbade contraception) and the goals of the military (which conceded that premarital sex happened and equipped its men with condoms). Internally, Arnold focused his concern on the "indiscriminate distribution" of prophylaxis that, in his opinion, "expose[d] the Army to the very serious charge of actively and directly contributing to the delinquency of youth." He found it troubling that the military would instruct men to obey moral law while granting them the tools to flout it. Publicly, however, Arnold advised his chaplains to hold tight to morality and commended most of the medical corps for offering dignified advice. He acknowledged that occasionally a doctor could act like a "gross-minded smarty" but instructed Chaplain Edward J. Waters (Catholic) to "do what you can to strengthen the character of your boys against the crude methods of men who think that vice is merely a physical danger." Despite Arnold's efforts to placate concerned Catholic priests, they still lamented their inability to curb virile young men, and Catholic leaders were comparably chagrined. Chaplain John Curran (Catholic) informed Bishop John O'Hara, the military vicar, that he stopped medical officers—including a Catholic doctor—from officially supplying condoms. Nevertheless, he felt flummoxed by a secretive contraception supply chain, and O'Hara was nonplussed. He requested a general order prohibiting condom distribution. The reply likely disappointed the Catholic superior, for the War Department held firm to its position that "our efforts to combat venereal disease must be intensely practical" and therefore that "we cannot disregard any effective means of prophylaxis recommended by the medical profession."[29]

The chaplaincy acted on behalf of "the straight state." Although World War II marked the start of Americans "coming out under fire," and despite many gay men serving as chaplain's assistants, the chaplaincy generally understood sexuality as heterosexuality.[30] Chaplain Charles O. Dutton (Methodist) nevertheless became quite cognizant of homosexuality at Fort Bliss, Texas, at least after two men individually approached him, each "claiming that he is homosexual." At a loss for how to respond, he requested assistance from Washington. The response from headquarters cavalierly announced that "'there is one in every hundred,'" adding, "This may not be an accurate statement but sooner or later every chaplain contacts such men and there is a need for a sympathetic and understanding approach." Dismissive but compassionate, the answer lacked much in the way of concrete guidance. Two years later, Chief of Chaplains Arnold responded to a similar query with a far more vituperative stance: the gay soldier should receive an immediate dishonorable discharge because he represented "a virulent danger to the Army. His immorality exerts a vicious influence." The severity of Arnold's opprobrium might have reflected his personal views or offered a more lenient outcome than sending the soldier to court-martial for sodomy.[31] At least two chaplains faced suspicions of homosexuality, one of whom pled guilty to sodomy, for which he was dishonorably discharged and received three years' prison time. Accusations were enough to dislodge a career, as Chief of Chaplains Arnold pointed out: "Entirely aside from one's opinion as to the truth and untruth of the charges of homosexuality . . . where there is so much rumor a chaplain would be under constant suspicion and his usefulness would be marred at every turn." On rare occasions when homosexuality clearly entered the chaplaincy's gaze, consequences fluctuated according to the whims and interpretations of the chaplains involved.[32]

While some chaplains vigorously policed a broad range of tantalizing activity, others defied the military's efforts to regulate their behavior.

At its most extreme, Chaplain Dudley C. Lackey (Methodist) admitted "moral derelictions" after receiving venereal disease treatment. He then confessed to committing adultery and tendered his resignation "for the good of the service." Officially the military frowned upon premarital sex, but Chaplain Bertram Korn (Jewish) was a young, unmarried rabbi when he confided to a fellow chaplain that he was lonely. His "love life, much of an escape as it is, and a rugged one too—has little or no chance of permanency," the future rear admiral wrote. "But the fact that I have someone to make love to, physically and actually, does help." Korn argued his experiences, unusual as they may have been for a chaplain, helped him understand why men he counseled accepted "any kind of marriage that presents itself" and made him "more understanding of the impulses of human beings." Although Korn was atypical in acknowledging his sexual forays, other chaplains also recognized sex as a human desire, albeit one laced imperial complexity. From the Pacific, Chaplain Samuel Silver (Jewish) wryly observed, "Most of the GIs here are fugitives from barren New Guinea GIsles, and the sight of Filipino girls dazzles them. And even more dazzling are the WACs & nurses, here in numbers. . . . I've dug up a few k'subos [marriage contracts], just in case."[33]

Americans seeking sex did not necessarily desire marriage or relationships, and soldiers' behavior ranged from flirtation to rape. In Germany and Japan, wartime propaganda and brutality raised expectations that Americans would act barbarically and rape would be common.[34] The exact number of rapes that occurred during and after the war is unknown, in part because rape was a weapon of war. Between 1942 and 1945, the Judge Advocate General (JAG) handled 904 rape cases in Britain, France, and Germany and convicted 458 men, but rape is chronically underreported and underprosecuted.[35] Rape accusations were not color-blind. Over four and a half months, from D-Day to mid-October 1944, 179 French women lodged rape complaints against American soldiers, with 90 percent asserting that their rapist was black. Of the 100 American soldiers executed for committing rape in France, eighty-six were black, even though African American troops constituted less than 10 percent of the military population in France. In Italy, Private Louis Till was accused, court-martialed, and convicted of rape; the military subsequently executed the father of Emmett Till, the fourteen-year-old kidnapped and lynched for speaking to a white woman in Mississippi in 1955. Jim Crow America made black men's gaze, speech, and gestures suspect, no matter the reality, intention, or geographic location.[36]

These troubling racial demographics led an African American army chaplain to prepare a pamphlet, "Let's Look at Rape!" in the fall of 1944. Despite the jocular exclamation point, the six-page document was deadly serious. It cautioned that "all of these [rape] complaints did not stand up under investigation," but by October 15, a mere seven weeks after the Allies liberated Paris, sixty-four African American men awaited trial for rape, while only eleven white soldiers faced comparable charges. The military determined that one-third of the complaints against black soldiers merited courts-martial (compared to two-thirds of the complaints against white soldiers), but the numbers nevertheless portended "disaster." The inflated statistics of black men accused of rape notwithstanding, "Let's Look at Rape!" insisted that men take responsibility for both their actions and the perception of their actions. Marked "secret," the pamphlet reached the desk of Brigadier General Benjamin O. Davis, the highest-ranking black officer in the European Theater of Operations. It combined declarative sentences, clear infographics, and pert illustrations to make one overarching point: each soldier was responsible for his own behavior. "Women of easy virtue" lingered at the margins, but the pamphlet warned men to be aware of their actions, noting that "drunkenness is never an excuse for YOUR crime." It provided a four-step battle plan for every unit: (1) discuss rape, (2) explicitly instruct men not to rape women, (3) take communal responsibility to thwart inappropriate behavior, and (4) work together to eliminate assault. After reviewing the pamphlet, Davis and Theater Chaplain L. Curtis Tiernan (Catholic) distributed it to all chaplains—black and white—in Europe, advising that the pamphlet was "worthy of the serious consideration of all" and encouraging chaplains to share it with all their troops.[37]

Meanwhile, chaplains stationed in the Pacific encountered state-sanctioned brothels, the Japanese government's response to the expectation that "foreigners would demand sexual gratification." The "comfort facilities" built by entrepreneurs and overseen by local police horrified most chaplains. Financed by government loans, the euphemistically titled Recreation and Amusement Association (RAA) buildings housed women who serviced the erotic fantasies of American soldiers while providing a buffer between soldiers and "good girls." The inexpensive RAA facilities accomplished the goals of the Japanese government: they stemmed rape. They did not, however, achieve the interests of the Occupation Army, which, upon discovering high rates of syphilis and gonorrhea among its troops, disavowed prostitution as a violation of human rights, classified it as undemocratic, and dismantled the RAA centers in 1946. The Japanese Home Ministry responded by asserting that women had the right to work as prostitutes and thus legalized the profession in "red-line" districts. *Panpan* women—or women of the night—became a ubiquitous presence in the streetscapes of postwar Japan.[38]

Chaplain Lawrence L. Lacour (Methodist) found this situation repugnant and, when the navy did little to address his concerns, opted for a more public airing of complaints. From his perch in Tokyo Bay, the navy chaplain mailed a letter to *The Des Moines Register* in which he assailed commanding officers who "refused to do anything to discourage promiscuity." The navy, he argued, needed to "consider the moral aspects of policies governing personnel" and could not rely on naval officers, as some "by example and advice have encouraged immorality among our men." Against the fleet chaplains' protest, he explained, the navy allowed men to frequent houses of prostitution—except for a mandated hiatus when Archbishop Spellman toured the area. Reprinted in local and national publications, the letter entered the *Congressional Record* and led Secretary of the Navy James Forrestal to reaffirm the navy's public policy to suppress prostitution in order to "protect the American ideals of home and family life." The *Navy Department Bulletin* reminded officers that "no action shall be taken that might be construed as encouraging, tacitly approving, or condoning prostitution." But, the memo continued, "commanding officers will not neglect . . . other means of reducing venereal disease in their respective commands but will continue to exert every effort towards this objective." To the likely dismay of Chaplain Lacour, the knots of sexual morality remained twisted as pragmatism countered purity in policy-making.[39]

Alongside the politics of sex, chaplains also grappled with the question of marriage. During his sojourn in North Africa, the fictional Chaplain Jim convinced a young soldier not to wed a French woman he had known for ten days. He enjoyed marrying couples who knew, loved, and respected one another because, he told the home front, marriage was holy. A brief encounter with a foreign woman abroad did not count, a view that underscored the War Department's emphasis on curtailing quick wartime unions. Chaplain Jim provided a short moralizing sermon: "The *war hysteria marriage*, son, between an American boy and girl *or* between an American soldier and foreign girl is just a way of inviting *real trouble* for both parties." For real chaplains, officiating—or dissuading—marriage became a common task as U.S. forces lived in and occupied nations across the globe.[40]

Of the 16 million soldiers and sailors who served in World War II, upwards of 1 million would meet, marry, and bring home war brides from fifty-seven countries between 1942 and 1952. A tiny number of war grooms married WACs, WAVEs, military nurses, and other American women posted overseas. Over 125,000 GI marriages occurred during the war. Most took place in Britain and other English-speaking Allied nations, between white men and white women, while many more sexual liaisons, some of which led to marriage and others of which did not, occurred during postwar deployments.[41] The number of women seeking entry to the United States as the result of wartime relationships led to a flurry of congressional legislation. First, the War Brides Act in December 1945 and then the Fiancées Act in 1946 eased the entry of "alien" partners and children into the United States. These statutes sanctioned war marriages by enabling spouses and children to enter the country without running afoul of either immigration law or national-origin quotas. Yet the legislation was neither total nor neutral: it accounted for only the marriages that resulted from the Occupation Army in Japan and thus did not dismantle the restrictive quotas that limited Japanese immigration.[42] But Japanese war brides existed and their soldier-husbands wanted to return to the United States. In 1947, the Alien Wife Bill, which became the Soldier Brides Act, provided that the "alien spouse" of a citizen-soldier "shall not be considered as inadmissible because of race." However, the law was limited to marriages cemented within thirty days of the Act's passage, thereby restricting its applicability to those who happened to marry within the month—no easy feat due to military regulations. Only in 1952, when the Immigration and Nationality (McCarran-Walter) Act terminated Japanese exclusion by granting nominal immigration quotas to

Japanese nationals—in an act that otherwise retained quotas—could Japanese war brides enter the United States in large numbers.[43]

Against this backdrop, military chaplains played critical roles in negotiating marriage politics. Within the military, marriage had long been the province of chaplains. They were, after all, commissioned clergy deputized by the state to perform marriages. Starting in the Civil War, presiding over and recording marriages—most notably between freed African Americans—became an integral part of chaplains' duties. In the twentieth century, chaplains' marriage work was manifold. Premarital counseling, wedding planning, parental reassurance, ceremony officiation, immigration assistance, and marriage troubleshooting all fell under the chaplains' purview. As the television program *Chaplains in Action* observed, chaplains' work "begins in the chapel, but it doesn't end there."[44]

Although the military assumed all clergy were ready to marry men and women, this role posed difficulties for some chaplains, notably those who were not ordained and unaccustomed to effectuating civil marriage. In particular, LDS and Christian Science chaplains acquired the right and the duty to oversee marriage rites that they did not possess as civilians. The LDS Church sanctioned this role, though framed it as a prerogative from the Church's First Presidency rather than a directive from the state. Nevertheless, the church offered its chaplains a template for a non-Mormon wedding ceremony and model comments to offer the couple. Chaplain Milt Widdison (LDS) recalled being asked to officiate at a wedding, "military formation . . . and all," for which he "borrowed a few ideas from a Methodist friend's book and went along with the program." Despite his unfamiliarity with the ritual, he pronounced it "as valid as a quickie ceremony in a Las Vegas marriage chapel." In the military, as in civilian life, legality could eclipse spirituality. Christian Science leaders found this new power disconcerting and queried the chief of chaplains about its legitimacy, including whether this military function would spill into the civilian realm. The office allayed the Church's concerns, asserting that "because a chaplain holds a commission in the Army, this fact should enable him to qualify in many states to perform marriages," but "if such authority was granted . . . it would cease when they received their discharge from the Army." Presiding over marriages, then, could be both flexible and temporary.[45]

Yet even when the authority to officiate marriages was permanent, the military environment presented unique quandaries. In the arena of marriage, chaplains in uniform occupied the seats of secular county clerks and justices of peace as much as they inhabited their pastoral roles and ministerial robes. In contrast to civilian life, for example, chaplains married men and women who fell outside their faith practices—which could confuse an American public accustomed to marriage ceremonies conducted by clergy only for couples of their religion. When challenged about a Catholic chaplain marrying two Protestants, the Office of the Chief of Chaplains replied, simply, "the marriage was valid." In addition, when stationed abroad, chaplains occasionally encountered nations with rather different legal strictures. Much to the consternation of chaplains accustomed to simultaneously holding ritual and municipal power, in postwar Germany marriage was a civil contract. Chaplain Herman Heuer (Lutheran) learned that when American troops married German nationals, "a clergyman whether he be an indigenous clergyman or a foreign chaplain, may not perform the marriage ceremony." Chaplains retained the right to preside over religious ceremonies, but military regulations insisted that chaplains follow German requirements to ensure that marriages were valid under both international law and U.S. immigration law.[46]

While chaplains presided over military weddings beyond the scope of their roles in civilian religious life, the military toed a careful line between religious dicta and professional duties. A television script written in Chaplain School and revised by Chaplain George H. Birney (Methodist) and Chaplain Wayne L. Hunter (Presbyterian U.S.) highlighted the slippery space of interfaith marriage—allowed by the military but expressly forbidden by some religions.[47] In the show, an officer entered one Chaplain Shain's office and asked him to perform his wedding the next day. The Jewish chaplain was concerned, wondering why the ceremony was hastily arranged, whether the impending partnership was legal, and if the couple was religiously compatible. It turned out the pair had been dating for several years and had acquired a civil license, but the officer was Jewish while his fiancée was not. When the officer made it clear that the chaplain's faith was immaterial to him, Chaplain Shain retorted, "Has it occurred to you that it might make a difference to me?" This perplexed the officer, so the rabbi explained that chaplains "regardless of their denominations still abide by the rules and beliefs of their denominations in their service just as they do in civilian life." He did not perform mixed marriages in civilian life, and he would not do so in uniform. However, rather than block the wedding, Chaplain Shain referred the couple to the local justice of the peace and helped the officer finalize his wedding plans. The scene ended with the officer commending the chaplain for "standing for what you believe to be the right thing to do." Intended to model an appropriate course of action and to provoke discussion among clergy at Chaplain School, the scene exemplified the military's approach to religion and marriage: chaplains retained the right to follow their own doctrine, provided their personal refusal did not prevent personnel from marrying.[48]

Interfaith marriages often strained chaplains' dual commitments to the military and to their faith. The chief of chaplains regularly reminded chaplains that while they had to abide by state laws, civil law did not constrain interfaith marriage. As clergy, chaplains could find interfaith marriage troubling, but "no government agency is in a position to enforce particular religious beliefs and practices." The chaplain himself could elect not to participate in a marriage he found ethically dubious, but as William Arnold recalled, he "once performed 385 marriages in one day, and about half them were between non-Catholics. Some were Protestant, some were Mohammedan, most were pagan." Perhaps exaggerating for effect, the chief of chaplains' position was clear: while clergy could hew to religious doctrine, the needs of couples sometimes occasioned unorthodox situations and commensurate latitude from chaplains. So long as the unconventional was legal, the War Department accepted it.[49]

Parents were less sanguine, however, and often expected chaplains to block interfaith marriages. After her son informed her of his impending marriage to an Englishwoman, Mrs. Cohen implored Chaplain Morris Fierman (Jewish) to intercede. "Needless to say, I was very shocked as we are of the Jewish faith, and she is not," she wrote. "For this reason, I feel that such a marriage would be unsuitable for the problems that will present themselves will be many and great." Although her concerns were more social than theological, Mrs. Cohen saw Chaplain Fierman—much like audiences understood the fictional Chaplain Jim—as her ally. At the very least, she found a confederate. He called her son, and their conversation apparently changed his mind, much to his mother's relief.[50] Nonparent civilians also viewed chaplains as ministerial mediators working on their behalf. From Sioux City, Iowa, Marilyn Penner wrote to the chief of chaplains on behalf of the unmarried women on the home front, pleading with him to "absolutely prohibit marriages between American soldiers and foreign women." She viewed her request as demographic, not xenophobic: "Already thousands of American girls know they face spinsterhood and a life of loneliness and unhappiness" because death and foreign war brides snuffed out too many potential mates. The chaplaincy declined to follow her suggestion, asserting that "relatively few American men will marry foreign girls" and that media reports exaggerated the problem.[51]

Despite opposition from the home front, there were a number of American men who wanted to marry foreign women and sought their chaplain's help in swaying their families. Charlie Lerner was stationed in Calcutta when he fell in love with an Indian Jewish woman named Seemah, but his parents remained skeptical of the match. Over and over again, he reassured them that they had nothing to worry about and hounded them to accept Seemah as his bride. Their concerns were both religious and racial, and he sought to prove that she was "white and Jewish." To make his case to his wary parents, he offered three arguments. First, he reminded his parents that "there are Jews all over the world, yes even in India and [they] are white." Second, he noted that he had a love rival—a Polish Jew who "happens to be some sort of rabbi himself," which led Charlie to point out that "if he's after her for marriage, she must be something *zayer goot* [very good]." Finally, he offered his trump card: he planned to meet with Chaplain David Seligson (Jewish), who, he assured his parents, would provide a "certificate proving her a Jew and white." For his part, Chaplain Seligson affirmed that the couple had talked to him and that Charlie had asked for his endorsement. Although Seligson implicitly indicated that Seemah was Jewish, he ducked an overt declaration of support by suggesting it would be in everyone's best interest for Charlie to return to the United States, establish himself, and then bring Seemah over as his fiancée. When Charlie packed his U.S. Army uniforms to journey halfway across the globe, he brought with him the sensibilities of state, religion, and society. He believed religion could transcend national boundaries, he accepted his family's desire for him to marry a Jewish woman, and he saw the world through ossified American racial categories. Although Chaplain Seligson did not resolve the argument between Charlie and his family, both sides saw the rabbi in uniform as an arbiter of Jewishness and whiteness outside the United States.[52]

At times, chaplains used the military atmosphere as cover for minor violations of religious doctrine. Chaplain John S. Monahan (Catholic) petitioned the archbishop of Baltimore to marry an enlisted couple, a Catholic male officer and a non-Catholic female soldier, in a hotel rather than in a religious venue such as a chapel or church as required by the archdiocese. Monahan knew that "the family of the bride, while greatly prejudiced against the Catholic Church, does not object to having the ceremony performed by a Catholic Army chaplain" but worried that insistence on a chapel wedding "might mean that sufficient pressure would be brought upon the Catholic party to make him weaken and allow the ceremony to be held outside the Church." He further maintained that this situation was unique because it came to his attention after the couple had selected a location, and would not, therefore, set any precedent. As a priest and an officer, Monahan—who served in the chief of chaplains' Washington, DC, office—felt comfortable pushing the Church to accommodate a military predicament. Within the chaplaincy, it was eminently reasonable for a soldier to select the chaplain of his choice to officiate a marriage. When a Catholic chaplain complained that a Protestant chaplain had married a Catholic couple, Monahan replied for the Office of the Chief of Chaplains: unless coercion could be proved, neither the chaplain nor the soldier's actions were problematic.[53]

The exigencies of war could transform regular weddings into grand celebrations. After an American military wedding in the Philippines, Chaplain Samuel Silver (Jewish) declared, "Marriages may be made in heaven, but when [the] fiancé drops in from there, a to-do naturally results." The airman-groom met his WAC bride before "300 people, from colonels to privates," and three Jewish chaplains co-officiated the wedding, leading the groom to comment, "'Back home I could have hardly afforded one rabbi; out here in *dem visten volt* [the desolate world], I have three of them.'" The nuptials occurred in a bamboo chapel with a white parachute draped across poles as the *chuppah* (wedding canopy). After all, Silver wittily noted, "when the bride wears khaki & the groom is in the air force, a parachuppah is the proper touch." The ceremony also included a variety of religious customs, including a Christian choir singing "O Promise Me" and the crowd tossing rice at the newlyweds.[54]

The joy documented by Chaplain Silver did not extend to many of the interracial and binational couples who married overseas. The military's regulation of marriage represented one prong of the state's project to control and discipline racial bodies. Immigration prohibitions and state anti-miscegenation laws hampered interracial relationships that developed abroad (and fueled casual sexual liaisons rather than partnerships). Marriage, as a legal matter, rested on state law. "No Federal statute," the adjutant general reminded a bickering Kentucky court clerk, "empowers an Army chaplain to perform marriage ceremonies in places which are subject to the jurisdiction of the respective states without complying with the laws of the several jurisdictions where such ceremonies are to be performed." Military bases and ships remained an exception, in which marriage was "governed solely by the pertinent provisions of Federal law." The chief of chaplains deflected this leniency, arguing instead that all chaplains must comply with state laws even in military space to avoid "many complicated, unpredictable and undesirable issues insofar as legal rights involved in divorces, inheritances, and other situations arising from marital status are concerned." Hence, regardless of the state laws in effect—residency or age requirements, blood tests, waiting periods, or anti-miscegenation rules—chaplains were "obliged to conform" to them.[55]

No federal law governed marriage, but a passel of regulations engineered nuptial gatekeeping in the military and turned ranking officers into federal marriage policemen. The most significant policy, in place between 1939 and 1996, restricted personnel serving overseas from marrying foreign nationals without the express permission of the region's senior commanding officer. As a result, while chaplains performed marriages abroad, the commanding officer's "subjective assessment of the probable success of marriage" determined whether the ceremony could even occur.[56] In Japan, General Douglas MacArthur refused soldiers permission to marry women who were not allowed to enter the United States according to the rationale that doing so "would be to flaunt the sanctity of the marriage ceremony." MacArthur, who viewed the occupation of Japan as an opportunity for "spiritual recrudescence," infused marriage with religious meaning in order to uphold, rather than criticize, the law. Elsewhere, military officials were more flexible but still considered a range of state and local laws when rendering decisions. By the 1950s, interracial marriages complicated the administration of domestic base assignments, which provided bureau-cratic cover for intransigence in the face of prejudice.[57]

Binational, interracial marriages not only tested American views of miscegenation and cross-cultural exchange but also spurred questions about faith, doctrine, and belief. Chaplain George W. Thompson (American Baptist) served as a staff chaplain with the navy's Military Sea Transport Service (MSTS) from 1949 to 1952. His rotations through the Pacific fleet brought him into close contact with servicemen returning to the United States with Japanese and Korean brides. His 1951 memo, "If I Marry a Foreigner," cautioned men to heed the importance of marriage, to anticipate the ramifications of interracial or binational marriage, and to reckon with the values each individual held. His quiz questions accentuated his white perspective. "Would this person fit into your family and be accepted as an equal, or would the family feel you married beneath your cultural, religious, social, and moral level?" he queried. Then, focusing principally on religion, he created an unambiguous hierarchy between the Christianity he assumed Americans practiced and the other religions—implicitly Buddhism—practiced in Asia. As he articulated it, his concern centered not on the couple but on their anticipated children: "Are you certain that you will be willing for your children to be taught a religion which is contrary to and in a very definite sense has a moral standard below that of the Christian religion?" According to Thompson, it was impossible to reconcile differing belief systems, especially those that encompassed animal or ancestor worship, as "people of other countries worship gods that are strange gods, and gods that require certain loyalties to which we object . . . We cannot believe that sacrifice to heathen gods is right, and it would be difficult for us to compromise on the worship of our God." From his perspective, religious diversity in the world demanded religious exclusion at home.[58]

Chaplain Thompson's efforts to prevent marriages between American Christians and "foreign heathens" through deterrence and conversion did not go unnoticed. The Southern Baptist Convention applauded him and asked the navy chief of chaplains to further his work. They requested that all navy chaplains conduct "Christian Friendliness Surveys" to elicit the religious affiliation of potential immigrants. This was necessary, they argued, because otherwise "they will eventually paganize us instead of our bringing them to Christ."

The Home Mission Board affably volunteered to share this information "among the various denominations and religious bodies of America, based on the religion of these war brides." The denomination also offered to provide instruction classes for Japanese war brides who expressed interest in Christianity, but the navy declined to enact their suggestions.[59]

While the military spurned these evangelization overtures, it allowed chaplains to hold religious classes for war brides on ships—proselytization in form if not name. Baptist, Lutheran, Presbyterian, and Methodist chaplains worked together to develop a curriculum, opining that "since America is a Christian nation, no person is well Americanized until he or she is informed on the teachings of the Christian religion." That the United States was not—at least constitutionally—a Christian nation and that the chaplaincy itself included non-Christians was, to these transport chaplains, unimportant. Chaplain Thompson deemed these classes a forward-thinking, benevolent gesture: "These women are coming to America to become homemakers, mothers, associates, and in time, citizens of this country. . . . Christianity is the predominant religion in America and few of these immigrants will live where Shintoism or Buddhism have temples." Framed as a tool of Americanization and assimilation to middle-class domestic gender norms, these classes became practical rather than evangelical. Ever a teacher and minister, Thompson claimed that exposure to Christianity "can give them a welcome in spite of customs, attitudes, taboos, and racial intolerance." Religion, in its American Christian form, would cloak Japanese war brides from prejudice. The faulty logic ensnared a willful disregard for religious freedom with the perceived need to prepare Japanese women for their new roles as American domestic women. As the tide of war turned in America's favor, the swell fusing nationalism with Christianity began gaining strength.[60]

"What do you do when you meet the pope?"

This was a question on the minds of many American chaplains in Italy after the United States liberated Rome in 1944. How do you show respect without kneeling or kissing his hand, Chaplain Eldin Ricks (Mormon) wondered? Chaplain Harold Saperstein (Jewish) escorted a group of soldiers to meet His Eminence and wanted to know if shaking the pope's hand was sufficient. Whatever worries bedeviled men before encountering the Holy Father, most managed to comport themselves well in person. Chaplain Samuel Faircloth (Baptist) was amazed to watch an Episcopalian chaplain accept the pope's Latin blessing. In contrast, he opted to politely decline the offer from a man he deemed "a rascal, [who] hung out with Nazis . . . Jews went by his window to the gas chambers." More often than not, however, American clergy walked away from their encounters with Pius XII thinking he made a pleasant and gracious impression. In describing the experience in his journal, for example, Chaplain Saperstein concluded that despite not being Catholic, "it was thrilling to think that this man wields power over more human beings than probably any other man on earth and that millions look upon him as the Representative of God on earth." Not to mention, "some Catholic friends at home will probably be tickled to get the mementoes which I will bring home from the occasion."[61]

By the time the chief of chaplains' convoy reached Rome in June 1945, many chaplains had encountered the pope. That did not diminish the excitement for the Protestant and Jewish chaplains who accompanied William Arnold to Vatican City, where he preached Mass on the 37th anniversary of his ordination. Chaplain Aryeh Lev (Jewish) described their session with His Holiness as "quite an experience. I wouldn't have missed it." The head of the Catholic Church was, in Lev's estimation, "very gracious, the graciousness which great men should possess." Lev's European tour roommate, Chaplain Herman Heuer (Lutheran), described the encounter in Vatican City in slightly more detail: "The Chief spent a few minutes with the Pope and then we were ushered in to shake his paw. We found him sitting at his desk. As he greeted us individually he gave us each a memento, thanked us for calling on him, wished us and our families health and happiness, and finally pronounced his blessing." For Lev and Heuer, the tour of Europe with the Chief teemed with visits to religious sites and meetings with clergy and military leaders alike. Like Arnold meeting the pope in Rome, Heuer had a transcendent moment of his own in Germany. "Historic Augsburg!" he exclaimed. "Luther once walked these streets, but what a change since his time!" Lev reconnoitered with his relatives in Palestine, but was even more thrilled in Europe to recognize, "What a break for the Jewish people that we had Jewish chaplains with the Armies of liberation!" For two months, the Arnold-Heuer-Lev trio journeyed together, crisscrossing Europe and the Mediterranean to inspect the work of their American chaplains, most of whom were excited to see them, a few of whom were "obstreperous" in their demands. Along the way, they also called on the dean of Westminster Abbey, marveled at the beautiful bird's-eye view of the French countryside they had expected to be "ravished," discussed plans for postwar Europe with General Eisenhower, indulged in confiscated German champagne to dull their disgust at the "truly diabolical" horrors of the gas chamber at Dachau, drank "thick and sweet" Turkish coffee and visited a mosque in Cairo, and toured holy sites in Jerusalem, which, "like all other things . . . was a revelation." They also watched out for one another's needs, with Heuer dutifully keeping tabs on the daily pork rations in his diary. More than once, he recorded, "Poor Lev is taking a beating at meals."[62]

World War II was a global war, and for Americans sent around the world in the 1940s, war afforded new and unexpected contact with foreigners, sometimes fleeting, sometimes permanent. This contact, in turn, helped craft extended religious networks through which Americans promoted their vision of religion. In letters exchanged and accounts retold, chaplains forged connections between civilians at home and religious groups abroad. As the United States fought for democracy abroad, the military spread pluralism through domestic radio waves and shaped the intimate relationships soldiers brought home. As the United States slipped from combat to reconstruction, the military saw an opportunity to unleash its religious outlook on the world.

5

The Military-Spiritual Complex

Their mission was a secret. The men knew it was important, possibly even significant. They had made it through a rigorous selection process and eight months of preparation. They rehearsed over and over again. Their work was laden with danger and uncertainty. Yet the laughter of their fellow servicemen rang in their ears as they conducted the regular but seemingly irrelevant practice runs. When the men assembled at ten o'clock that night, the briefing felt different. At long last, they knew their charge. When their clocks hit midnight, when Sunday turned to Monday, they met again—to review the assignment, gather equipment, and receive final instructions. And then, before they departed, they prayed. Chaplain William B. Downey (Lutheran) led the group, voicing their wishes in the heat of the dark, humid Pacific night: "Almighty Father . . . guard and protect them. . . . May they, as well as we, know Thy strength and power, and armed with Thy might may they bring this war to a rapid end . . . and once more may we know peace on earth."[1]

Nine hours later, the crew of the *Enola Gay* dropped the atomic bomb on Hiroshima.

As the bomb eviscerated the Japanese supply and shipping depot, the radio relay called back to base: "Mission successful." Blinded by the light of the blast, the men could not see the destruction they had wrought. Nevertheless, Captain Robert Lewis, who maintained a log of the flight, recorded his reaction: "My God!" Colonel Paul W. Tibbets Jr., the pilot of the *Enola Gay*, glimpsed only "a black, boiling nest" below. The bomb's mushroom clouds obscured the obliterated city and the immediate decimation of one-third of Hiroshima's population, but the men understood the gravity of their action. It was a "sobering" moment, Tibbets said, when they experienced the shock waves of devastation before flying back to Tinian Island. Upon their arrival, Downey found his prayers partially answered: all the men flying B-29s on August 6, 1945, returned. His supplication for a rapid end of war—a reflection of the military's calculated attempt to induce unconditional surrender from the Japanese by unleashing nuclear fission—went unheeded.[2]

Three days later, Chaplain Downey prayed again: "Almighty God, Father of all mercies, we pray Thee to be gracious with those who fly this night. Guard and protect those of us who venture out into the darkness of Thy heaven. Uphold them on Thy wings. Keep them safe both in body and soul and bring them back to us. . . . Above all else, our Father, bring peace to Thy world." This time, all the men, including the chaplain, knew what they were doing. This time, the prayer was more ambivalent, seeking God's grace for men who would undoubtedly and distressingly kill. This time, the bomb's early light meant a reckoning with the dark and barbarous underbelly of God's kingdom. Within twelve hours, another crew of American pilots, bombardiers, and navigators found a hole in the cloud cover and detonated a second atomic bomb on Nagasaki. Less than a week later, Japan surrendered, bringing an end to World War II and a chance for the peace for which Downey—and others—prayed and so ardently sought.[3]

Achieving peace would prove more difficult and complicated than ending war—if war had, indeed, stopped. "Wartime" is more fluid than the discrete and temporal markers of outbreak and ending allow. If the American entrance into World War II was clear, its exit was not. Japan's surrender in 1945, President Truman's official pronouncement of the cessation of hostilities in 1946, the formal termination of war against Germany in 1951, or the signing of a peace treaty with Japan in 1952 all represent possible endpoints. In the seven years between dropping atomic bombs and ratifying a peace treaty with Japan, the United States found itself at war again, albeit with new and different enemies. War and peace blurred as the United States entered the ambiguously defined Cold War and then fought and concluded the Korean War. After demobilizing over 10.5 million soldiers between June 1945 and June 1947, the armed forces stood at about 1.5 million personnel. During the same two-year period, military spending shrunk from about 91 billion dollars to 10 billion dollars. Even in this leaner peacetime state, however, the dismantled war machine remained the largest military in the world and more than ten times its size in 1939. For nine years, from the capture of Rome in June 1944 to the signing of the Korean Armistice Agreement in July 1953, the United States occupied and battled across the world.[4]

During this period, the American military underwent significant administrative reorganization. The National Security Act of 1947 separated the air force from the army and unified the army, navy, and air force under the newly created Department of Defense. In 1945, William R. Arnold completed two terms as the army chief of chaplains, after which three men served in quick succession: Luther D. Miller (Episcopalian), Roy H. Parker (Baptist), and Ivan Bennett (Southern Baptist). Similarly, after Robert D. Workman (Presbyterian) oversaw the almost thirty-fold expansion of ministry to sailors and Marines to over 2,900 chaplains, William N. Thomas (Methodist), Stanton W. Salisbury (Presbyterian U.S.), and Edward B. Harp (Reformed) led the Navy Chaplain Corps from the waning days of World War II through the Korean War. When the air force separated from the army, it acquired its own chaplaincy led first by Chief of Chaplains Charles I. Carpenter (Methodist).[5] The newly formed Armed Forces Chaplains Board (AFCB) became responsible for collaboratively addressing military religious needs through programming and policies that supported the military's global reach.

The advent of the Cold War brought with it new conditions, expectations, and concerns stateside and overseas, and the military chaplaincy was part and parcel of these shifts. President Truman and Army Chief of Staff George Marshall pressed for Universal Military Training (UMT) as an alternative to the draft, and they instituted the "Fort Knox Experiment" to test the possibility. Supported by a tri-faith trifecta of local clergy and chaplains, the Fort Knox Experiment picked up where the Civilian Conservation Corps (CCC) Camps left off, reforging the connection between youth, citizenship, and moral training. In 1948, Truman issued Executive Order 9981, which formally desegregated the United States military. The armed forces ambled toward integration, and the implementation process began with a number of presidential commissions, including the President's Committee on Religion and Welfare in the Armed Forces (PCRW).

As the military scrambled to adjust to its new roles in the aftermath of World War II, the place and use of religion within the state's martial enterprise changed as well. Although Truman and Eisenhower did not always agree, the two presidents operated in tandem to build a military-spiritual complex, a religious armory that ideologically structured and crusaded on behalf of the American state. Like the military-industrial complex, the military-spiritual complex contained the seeds of "misplaced power" that, without sufficient temperance, could disrupt the balance between national security and religious liberty. When the military demobilized after 1945, Army Chief of Staff Dwight D. Eisenhower was reluctant to release chaplains. In April 1946, he determined that "the opportunity for service by the Army chaplain is as great, or greater, than it has ever been." A mere seven years later, at the end of the Korean War, President Dwight D. Eisenhower saluted the work of "militant preachers and chaplains" who helped ground the free world in religious faith. "It seems to me," he posited, "no one who is teaching moral standards or spiritual values has any right to do it apologetically. If I have ever had to quarrel with chaplains, it has been because they have been a little bit too diffident where I thought they should have been a little more belligerent." In the wake of Communist threats, maintaining national Providence demanded bellicose, not bashful, clergy.[6]

Little hesitancy or reluctance existed in the chaplaincy during this period. Religion and morality suffused the work of the military. In postwar Europe, chaplains undergirded Jewish renewal in the aftermath of the Holocaust. At home, chaplains fortified morality through character education, which took on new ideological force as an element of national defense during the early Cold War. And in Korea, chaplains not only counseled American forces but also ideologically and materially infused the Korean military with religious fervor.[7] The military-spiritual complex unified the work of chaplains in Europe, the United States, and Asia. As the United States turned to the task of rebuilding a world fractured and broken by war, the chaplaincy offered a state-developed tool for moral and spiritual reconstruction. The best national defense included a robust spiritual offense, and the chaplaincy armored American democracy with a religious mantle. In each setting—postwar Europe, the United States, and Korea—chaplains served as nation-builders, constructing the religious and moral foundations of societies, citizens, and states.

Emperor Hirohito's surrender was a relief. Combat had finally ended. Yet for many chaplains, the meaning of war, the significance of death, and the implications of American intervention abroad were just becoming apparent. Navy chaplain Samuel Sandmel (Jewish) confessed that he felt "strangely inarticulate" upon receiving the news of Japanese capitulation. Army chaplain Morris Frank, the first Jewish chaplain to enter Germany in 1944, expressed a similar reaction to V-E day: "My feelings are mixed—and I find it difficult to write or think. I'm happy that there is an end to the useless killing, but I can't help but think of the some 20 million who have died in this horrible war." Over eleven months, from the liberation of France and invasion of Germany to the defeat of Hitler and the fall of the Rising Sun, American chaplains encountered the tangible reverberations of violence undergirding World War II: bombed-out cities, fractured families, uncertain futures, war crimes, and perhaps most vividly, Nazi atrocities.[8]

The new world, the postwar world, proffered opportunities for peace and peddled fear of future war. Allies quickly become enemies as fragile links between the Soviet Union and the United States broke apart, and vanquished enemies became allies as newly democratized Japan provided a Pacific barrier separating the U.S. from the U.S.S.R and China. Amidst swiftly shifting geopolitics, however, the American Occupation Armies, in Germany and Japan alike, faced tasks both prosaic and extraordinary: how to reestablish everyday life, how to regenerate society, and how to rebuild conquered nations. Through this work, chaplains confronted not only the banality of evil but also the bald immorality that provoked, sustained, and concluded global warfare.

Encounters with refugees, victims, and survivors—the people who would become known as Displaced Persons (DPs) in the immediate aftermath of World War II—began in the middle of the war. From Tehran, in 1943, Chaplain David Rubin (Jewish) reported a swell of Russian and Polish Jews seeking safety, ideally in Palestine. In Rome, in June 1944, Chaplain Morris Kertzer (Jewish) greeted 4,000 Jews gathered at the city's main synagogue, Tempio Israelitico, knowing that the biblical story of liberation was "even more personal" for the congregation of soldiers and survivors who "crowded . . . to raise their voices in prayer and thanksgiving." In Paris, in September 1944, Theater Chaplain Judah Nadich (Jewish) became a liaison between military authorities and French Jewry, while in Reims, Chaplain Isaac Klein (Jewish) organized a religious school and led services for the townspeople. In Germany, in 1945, Chaplain David Max Eichhorn (Jewish) tried to balance the needs of tortured Jewish survivors with the orders of the American military.[9]

Little, however, prepared Americans for the scenes they would find at concentration camps. Hearing about the unfathomable and encountering the inconceivable were not the same. Hitler's plans to decimate world Jewry exceeded the imaginative capacity of most Americans, and even those who knew about death camps could not easily process what they saw. American soldiers discovered Ohrdruf, a labor subcamp of the death camp Buchenwald, by accident on April 4–5, 1945. A week later, Chaplain Edward P. Doyle (Catholic) accompanied the medics of the 104th Infantry Division to Nordhausen, another subcamp of Buchenwald. There, he found "a world difficult to describe," catastrophic conditions that included 700 barely breathing bodies stashed among 3,000 corpses. "I have seen as many as 125 wounded a night in our combat area of Belgium and Holland and assisted in preparing the wounded for surgery and the like, but never have I seen such suffering and anguish," he recalled. A day later, army generals Dwight D. Eisenhower, George Patton, and Omar Bradley toured Ohrdruf, coming face-to-face with Nazi savagery through pyres of corpses, lice-ridden bodies, and torture devices as well as underground bunkers filled with looted art, gold, and jewelry. Eisenhower made publicizing the brutality a priority, entreating the press to visit, to witness, and to broadcast the indescribable scene. He also ordered all units in the vicinity to tour the nightmarish camp. "We are told that the American soldier does not know what he is fighting for," Eisenhower explained. "Now, at least, he will know what he is fighting *against*."[10]

Chaplain Herschel Schacter (Jewish) needed no such reminder. The same day Eisenhower inspected Ohrdruf, the rabbi entered Buchenwald with Patton's Third Army. There he searched for Jews, weaving in and out of the barracks, shouting *"ihr zint frei"* ("You are free"). Survivors were incredulous, some reaching out to touch his chaplain's insignia—the tablets affixed to his uniform—to corroborate the words they heard. His Yiddish language skills allowed him to communicate, and his role as a chaplain let him offer religious solace to the newly liberated. A month later, Signal Corps photographs trumpeted striped-clad survivors joining uniformed American soldiers to celebrate Shavuot, a Jewish holiday commemorating the giving of the Torah at Mount Sinai. Schacter also formed a burial society, drafted lists of survivors to help reunite families, and bent the army postal system to the needs of survivors by mailing letters on their behalf under his name.[11]

While few Jewish men required the motivation of skeletons found at Ohrdruf, Nordhausen, and Buchenwald, they still struggled to comprehend and convey the devastation. When Chaplain Frank wrote to his wife, all he could offer were elliptical phrases: "The stories they tell—the horrors they relate—the brutalities they have undergone— unbelievable—beyond description." For Chaplain Harold Saperstein (Jewish), entering Germany represented an emotional turning point. In contrast to fighting in Italy and France, where he had observed his surroundings with curiosity and even delight, Germany inspired only hatred and vengeance. It was, from his perspective, "a cursed land" where "the indescribable odor of death still pervades the air." After finding thirty-nine boxcars stuffed with "shriveled mummies" and crematoria laden with bones and ash, Chaplain Eichhorn reported, "We cried tears of hate. Combat hardened soldiers, Gentile and Jew, black and white, cried tears of hate." And when Jewish survivors attacked Nazi guards, he and his soldiers stood aside, watching, for "deep anger and hate had temporarily numbed our emotions" and intervention seemed pointless.[12]

The Jewish ritual calendar often provided Jewish chaplains with poignant means to explain their work. Assigned to Southern France, Chaplain Kertzer witnessed the return of the community's rabbi to his congregation. The rabbi, whom the community presumed dead, had been serving with the French Resistance and unexpectedly walked into Friday night services in cavalry boots. As he relayed the scene, Kertzer remarked that it "was a real Shabbat Shuvah." In fact, that night was *Shabbat Shuvah*, the Sabbath of Return that falls between the Jewish High Holy Days of Rosh Hashanah and Yom Kippur and marks the pleas by the prophet Hosea for Israel to return to God. As two rabbis, one French and one American, one liberated and one liberator, led services together, they sanctified the return of French Jewry to their homes and the presence of American Jewry to fill vacant seats. When the

French rabbi wished everyone a "bon Shabbat," a good Sabbath, the American chaplain commented, "Battle-toughened men, men who had lived through Salerno and Anzio, who had driven from Rome to Florence and Pisa, who had come ashore upon the Riviera and helped in the push that drove the Nazis reeling across their own borders—seemed repaid at this moment for all their travail and sacrifice."[13]

For Jewish chaplains stationed in Europe, attachment to the Occupation Army enabled them to serve their country and their religious community. Duty to God and nation took on new import—and novel complications—as American rabbis helped shepherd the "surviving remnant" of European Jewry from the Holocaust to new lives while reporting to military command. By virtue of their military standing and religious roles, chaplains became conduits between army protocol and civilian needs. When Chaplain Eichhorn—who officiated at the first Shabbat service at Dachau after liberation—addressed the survivors in a sermon, he made his multiple identities clear: "Today I come to you in a dual capacity—as a soldier in the American Army and as a representative of the Jewish community of America." As much as it was an honor to represent the military and the Jewish people, however, these "dual capacities," as American chaplain and Jewish rabbi, could also be unnerving. Ten days after the liberation of Paris, Chaplain Frank floundered as he tried to encapsulate how it felt to meet survivors, who "greeted me as a liberator. . . . One would think I was important—or that I had single-handedly liberated the population." Where Frank stressed his small role within a vast military operation, rescued Jews saw the chaplain as a savior.[14]

As American forces captured Nazi territory, the complex administrative work of liberation emerged. The initial experiences with survivors—rescuing men and women from starvation, sickness, and despair, leading religious services, and assailing Nazi atrocities—gave way to the more precarious tasks of sustaining DPs. The responsibility was enormous, and chaplains were bombarded with competing interests. While the needs of Jewish DPs, the intent of the U.S. military, and the goals of aid organizations ostensibly aligned, reality was far less synchronized. The Jewish Welfare Board, for example, explicitly instructed Jewish chaplains to refrain from mentioning relief work in reports—lest it be misconstrued as unsanctioned—and enjoined chaplains to restrict such efforts to personal time. As DPs attempted to start life anew, American chaplains often assisted refugees looking for family members and aided family members seeking their relatives. Fred Oppenheimer was living in Chattanooga, Tennessee, when he received word that his mother, who had been sent to Theresienstadt, had survived. He relied on a trio of Jewish chaplains to communicate with her. Chaplain Morris Frank, who had recently returned to Chattanooga, suggested he write to Chaplain Herman Dicker, a rabbi attached to a medical battalion in Germany, and Chaplain Earl Stone, who was stationed less than 10 miles away, let Oppenheimer borrow his mail privileges to send a package to Germany. Networks of military chaplains enabled civilians to reconnect with far-flung family.[15]

Chaplains helped move supplies from civilian relief organizations through military channels to reach their European brethren. But chaplains worked under the supervision of commanders, which meant that they maneuvered within constraints set by army regulations and the officers enforcing them. The military, moreover, trained men to fight, not to govern, and managing scores of refugees in chaotic environments beset with food scarcity, inadequate shelter, rampant disease, and ethnic tension challenged even the most sympathetic officials. Despite these problems, entrepreneurial Jewish chaplains requisitioned needed food, shelter, and transportation—sometimes through legal purchases and sometimes through illegal borrowing. The havoc of postwar occupation could provide cover for illicit activities. Chaplain Abraham Klausner (Jewish) transferred himself back to Dachau, where he compiled lists of survivors, distributed religious materials, mailed letters on behalf of DPs, and created separate hospitals for Jewish DPs. Chaplain Herbert Friedman (Jewish) similarly engineered commotion to his advantage. At the urging of Gershom Scholem, a German-born scholar of Jewish mysticism at Hebrew University, Friedman forged receipts, commandeered an ambulance, and shipped crates of rare Jewish books and manuscripts to Palestine. Yet the needs of DPs and limited supplies still overwhelmed the chaplains. When Chaplain Aryeh Lev (Jewish) arrived in Europe as part of the chief of chaplains' post-V-E day delegation, he conceded, "A chaplain can do very little."[16]

Despite Lev's concerns, most Jewish chaplains understood their work with Jewish DPs as an ethical imperative derived, in part, from the utterances of daily prayer. Chaplain Morton Fierman traveled to Paris in the winter of 1945, where he first observed the impact of the Nazi regime on European Jewry: their "stories of torture, despair, difficulties threw me off balance . . . the world must be set right." Using the chaplaincy to reset the world transformed prayer from metaphor to reality, from rituals of worship to rituals of service. Every morning, Jewish chaplains chanted prayers praising God for clothing the naked, freeing the imprisoned, and raising the downtrodden. Acting in God's image meant literally doing the same, so much so that several Jewish chaplains extended their commitment to the American military to prioritize their work with DPs over the civilian congregations waiting for them at home. In the summer of 1946, Chaplain Herbert Friedman informed his synagogue president that "legally and theoretically" he could apply for a discharge and return to his civilian pulpit. But, he insisted, "morally and according to the dictates of my conscience, I cannot." Given the ratio of fourteen Jewish chaplains to a quarter million Jewish DPs, Friedman decided "it is simply not right" to leave. He, like several others, saw relief work as a moral calling, and the military accepted, at least temporarily, their drive to devote particular resources (Jewish chaplains) to a particular community (Jewish DPs).[17]

While Friedman and others declared their presence in Europe essential and necessary, not everyone concurred. Rabbi Joseph Lookstein traveled to Europe in the winter of 1946 and reported to Army Chief of Chaplains Luther Miller (Episcopalian) that there were too many chaplains, Jewish and Christian, lingering on the Continent. The number of troops warranted fewer military ministers, and Lookstein recommended rotating chaplains back to the United States, declaring those no longer needed as surplus and releasing those who had fulfilled their terms of service. The Office of the Advisor on Jewish Affairs to the Commander-in-Chief of the European Command nevertheless requested five to ten more Jewish chaplains. As the Occupation Army transitioned to more active oversight of civilian daily life and refugee relief, it created a specialized position because "the Army believes only experienced rabbis in military uniform [could] properly perform" the task. The army wanted clergy familiar with military hierarchy, command, and infrastructure to serve DPs because integrating this work into the operational responsibilities of Jewish chaplains provided an orderly means through which to serve the needs of survivors.[18]

Military investment in religious life and interfaith cooperation impressed and puzzled European Jews more accustomed to hiding their religious practices from state officials. Chaplain Friedman reported that Chaplain Aubrey J. O'Reilly (Catholic) attended the 1946 Passover Seder in Berlin, to the surprise of many DPs. "This Passover had especial significance," Friedman wrote, "since the remnant of the Jewish people, seeking an escape from this land, naturally lean upon the American Army, and appreciate the consideration shown by its leaders." Military officials provided shelter, food, and the possibility of emigration. But they also stimulated religious life, contributing American government resources to help print and distribute religious texts that had been banned and destroyed during war. The negotiations that preceded the publication of the Survivors' Talmud, the compendium of Jewish law, exemplify the military's desire to cultivate religion as well as its squeamishness about religious preferences. When the Occupation Army entered the printing business in postwar Germany, seizing printing presses and securing paper for all sorts of military, scientific, and religious publications, some wondered whether printing the Talmud represented a fair use of scarce supplies. Would dedicating material goods to this project be an "injustice to other Displaced Persons denominations and to the religious groups of German nationals"? In the end, the army set aside its concerns about the limited and particular appeal of the Talmud, and printing began in Heidelberg in 1948.[19]

But the value placed on religious equality often blinded military leaders to the pernicious, if unintended, consequences of uncritically applying it in postwar Europe. The military assumed its logic of religious coexistence could easily transfer to DP camps. Of the 6 million DPs initially recognized on V-E day, the 3 million who remained under American authority originally constituted an undifferentiated lot. By listing people only by nationality and not distinguishing Jews from non-Jews or victims from collaborators, the military allowed tension to fester. Reports and warnings from chaplains, soldiers, journalists, and civilian leaders culminated in President Truman dispatching Anna M. Rosenberg, an expert in manpower and personnel, to examine the circumstances of French Jewry and Earl G. Harrison to study the conditions of German Jewry and Jewish DPs residing in Germany. The Harrison Report detailed the injustices faced by Jewish DPs living alongside former assailants, which engendered the creation of separate camps for Jewish DPs. Chaplain Herman Dicker (Jewish), who served in France and then Germany, later concluded that assigning Jewish chaplains to temporary special duty "eliminate[ed] many of the obstacles caused by lack of mutual understanding" between DPs and American military authorities. Chaplains were supposed to serve all Americans, but sometimes their American values turned outward, to non-Americans, and their religious values swiveled inward, to their coreligionists.[20]

The ethos of postwar reconstruction crossed the Atlantic Ocean and returned home with chaplains. With World War II giving way to the Cold War and communism supplanting Nazism as the primary foe, new responsibilities beckoned. In the words of President Truman, "we must always make spiritual values our main line of defense." In this new world, chaplains' religious guidance and moral suasion shaped the United States into, and ensured it remained, a holy nation. American military chaplains, according to one report, "give our democratic faith a very large measure of its strength" because totalitarian regimes spurned "moral law and individual dignity that is utterly repugnant to any of our religions." No matter the particular faith, the military believed American religion rested on a shared moral code. Military chaplains, representing an array of available religious options, became the federal government's megaphones for individual-centered morality through newly enhanced compulsory character education programs.[21]

The military had long charged chaplains with inculcating morality in its troops, but the armed forces formalized this role in the early postwar years. The postwar Character Guidance program, which tightly and ideologically linked religion and morality with democracy and citizenship, built on the informal and decentralized citizenship and moral training that anchored the chaplaincy's CCC work during the New Deal. Through regular lectures, chaplains instilled—or attempted to—the virtues and values the state viewed as central to its mission. The initial impetus for this program came from Secretary of War Robert Patterson, who sought to use chaplains as a weapon against growing rates of venereal disease and disciplinary cases. Army Chief of Chaplains Luther Miller then shaped the directive into a more expansive series on morality and citizenship, which reflected his leadership of the chaplaincy away from broadening religious access and toward forming model American citizens.[22]

A presidential mandate helped propel the new emphasis on moral training. Truman understood the late 1940s as a period in which the United States "was trying to win the peace . . . and to win that peace we must have these young men as a backlog to secure that peace." Thus, from the Oval Office came the President's Committee on Religion and Welfare in the Armed Forces (PCRW). Led by Frank Weil, an attorney who presided over the Jewish Welfare Board and helped establish the United Service Organization (USO) during World War II, this group included Daniel Poling (a World War I chaplain whose son, Clark Poling, died on the *Dorchester*); Edmund Walsh (an anti-Communist Jesuit who founded Georgetown's School of Foreign Service); Truman Gibson (a Chicago attorney who had served as an advocate for African Americans in the War Department); and Dorothy Enderis (a Milwaukee educator). Truman charged the advisory board with determining how the military could best enact government interests in "the religious, moral, and recreational welfare and character guidance of the persons in the Armed Forces" in order to "enhance the military preparedness and security of the Nation." More than half the drafted servicemen in the postwar military were under twenty-one, and Truman believed the military retained responsibility for fostering morality in impressionable American youth. Truman's charge to the committee not only tied together religion, morality, and welfare, long the province of American military chaplains, but saw them as interrelated concerns. Hence the Weil Committee, as the PCRW was colloquially known, studied a broad set of issues—the chaplaincy, community organizations, housing, and information and education programs—to build the religious underpinnings of national security.[23]

The chaplaincy proved to be the easiest subject for the Weil Committee to investigate, and they generally liked what they discovered: the chaplaincy typified the nonsectarian religious unity undergirding the American elixir of democratic faith and faith in democracy. As a single entity whose decisions rested within a clear chain of command within each branch of the service, the chaplaincy functioned relatively well. No branch met the ideal ratio of chaplain to soldiers, presumed to be about one chaplain per 800 enlistees, which led the PCRW to recommend commissioning a significantly larger pool of chaplains. But according to data compiled in 1949, even the newly formed air force chaplaincy employed one chaplain for 977 soldiers, a rate that far exceeded the previous (unachieved) standard of one chaplain per 1,200 men. In a 1950 letter to Truman, Weil characterized the military's religious programming as "reasonably adequate." Moreover, chaplains "have ample opportunity to function effectively as clergymen within the military service." The final report leveled two concerns about chaplain selection and training: first, whether less desirable men became military ministers, and second, whether the military sufficiently trained its clergy. The committee supplied little evidence that weaker candidates entered the service or that chaplains needed significantly better training. But focusing on these issues allowed the PCRW to reinforce that chaplains needed to "demonstrate the essential unity of all races, faiths, and groups" because as "the servant of God for all, the chaplain cannot cultivate a narrow sectarian spirit." This was neither a new vision nor a novel idea. The army and navy chiefs of chaplains had promoted and, to differing degrees, instilled this pluralistic idea in their chaplains starting in World War I. Few questioned this mission, but reiterating it allowed the committee to declare the chaplaincy's larger purpose: if "we expect our Armed Forces to be physically prepared, we must also expect them to be ideologically prepared." And ideological preparation included religious and moral training.[24]

While the Weil Committee studied the chaplaincy, a trio of chaplains at Fort Knox observed the beliefs and behavior of adolescent American men. In 1946, the War Department designed an experimental unit in which about 800 men would train for one year under Major General John M. Devine. The military expected the trial to prove the efficacy of Universal Military Training (UMT), which would build a rapidly deployable standing army of citizen-soldiers through compulsory military training after high school (or upon turning eighteen). Despite accruing support from about 80 percent of American voters, UMT roused vehement hostility. Whereas advocates heralded UMT as providing cost-efficient national security while teaching men technical skills and morals, critics charged that it was a wasteful, poorly designed, militaristic, and impractical program that contravened individual liberty, stifled freedom, and abrogated rights. Debates over UMT rested on a core divide about the nature of the relationship between the obligations and rights of citizenship in a democracy. Throughout these debates, however, critics never questioned whether the military should contribute to the creation and shaping of "good citizens."[25]

Congress never passed UMT, but Fort Knox operated an experimental moral boot camp. In 1947, 664 young men volunteered for a six-month training session, and the army dispatched chaplains to oversee their religious and moral development. Entrusted to build virtuous Cold Warriors, Chaplains Maury Hundley Jr. (Disciples of Christ), Charles J. Murphy (Catholic), and Morris E. Eson (Jewish) led worship, lectured on ethics, and publicized the value of the program. They met individually with every recruit, compiling reams of data on the religious ideas held by their seventeen- to eighteen-year old congregants. Citizenship and morality lectures were constant and quickly became obligatory for all units at Fort Knox. According to the chaplains, the project succeeded: profanity, alcohol consumption, and venereal infection rates declined and church attendance rose. Of course, the post exchange removed beer from its shelves, trainees lacked regular access to women, and the unit commander made worship all but mandatory—those who elected not to attend chapel faced an hour meeting with a chaplain in its stead. "Father Devine's Heaven," as the Fort Knox regulars referred to the UMT unit, steeped its youth in holy fervor. As Chaplain Murphy insisted, "you are first, last, and always a religious animal, and UMT will not let you forget it."[26]

Since morality was inseparable from religion and both fortified national security, the chaplaincy labored to build a moral sea wall to protect the American people from the looming tides of immoral Communism. Based on the experience at Fort Knox, in the fall of 1947, Army Chief of Chaplains Luther Miller began promoting *The Chaplain's Hour*, a weekly eight-page outline written by Chaplain Martin H. Scharlemann (Missouri Synod Lutheran), which evolved into a serialized, six-volume set of sixty sample talks titled *Duty-Honor-Country*. At once pithy and uncompromising, the original fifty-two lectures— which ranged from "The Meaning of Citizenship" and "Self Control" to "How Free Am I" and "A Fool and His Money"—melded Sunday School lessons, Philosophy 101 classes, and Benjamin Franklin aphorisms into a year's worth of simplistic life lessons adorned with blatant anti-Communism. The military characterized this curriculum, like the less standardized CCC version in the 1930s, as necessary because it thought adolescent men detached from "the normal restraints imposed by the family, the church, [and] the community" were likely to make poor decisions. Moreover, according to Navy Chief of

Chaplains Stanton W. Salisbury, whose service also developed character guidance training, few recruits came from properly religious families. Only half arrived with "at least [a] nominal church relationship" and half started with "no relationship whatever." Of the religiously affiliated, less than half maintained a "strong" church relationship, thus leaving three-quarters of the American navy bereft of civilian spiritual guidance. Although church membership rose significantly in the postwar period, numbers did not necessarily correlate to knowledge. As Salisbury proclaimed, "we are faced with the fact that about 49% of our youngsters are absolutely illiterate in religion and the consequent moral verities."[27]

Character Guidance not only taught servicemen about religion and morality but also portrayed patriotism as religious. While acquiring "a sense of responsibility for the preservation of a free way of life," soldiers would learn that "according to our great American traditions, man is a creature of God and that, therefore, he is both responsible and accountable to the Creator." God the Creator was unassailably ecumenical and, in turn, enabled Character Guidance to seamlessly conflate religion, morality, and patriotism. To be an American was to believe in God, even as the manual distributed to chaplains stated that these "lectures are not sermons" and that "they are not concerned with religion in the technical sense of that word, but only with morality." Chaplains were to teach, not preach, these moral lessons. The logic made a certain military sense: by offering explanations grounded in national tradition and by focusing attention on action rather than causes or processes, the program steered clear of sectarianism. The examples bespoke a different story, however. "Men ought to worship God is a way of expressing the significance of the Ten Commandments," the directions announced, evincing no concern that the Ten Commandments may not be universally accepted or even the same across religious traditions. Despite its religious origin, the Ten Commandments fell under a commonly claimed Judeo-Christian "American inheritance"—a constructed tradition intentionally unrecognized as such. In this way, the state rendered the duty to worship a moral imperative and distinct from the specifics of "how and why God ought to be worshipped," which was religious and denominational.[28]

This view of the United States as a moral and religious nation—a generically monotheistic one, at least—cemented the dichotomy between the United States and the Soviet Union, the free and the fettered, the capitalist and the Communist, the God-fearing and the God-free. As soldiers quickly learned, the world consisted of three kinds of nations: secular, demonic, and covenant. According to this schematic, the secular nation eliminated God from public life, making nontheistic patriotic loyalty its key feature; the demonic nation replaced God with country; and the covenant nation publicly celebrated its relationship with and reliance on divine Providence.[29] Constitutional separation of church and state did not make the United States a secular nation—that designated countries like France. The Soviet Union was, of course, demonic and the United States its holy opponent, not a Christian nation but a Godly one. Subsequent lectures moved easily between the personal and the political, as distinguishing individual rights from wrongs readied recruits to analyze international rights and wrongs, or so the military expected.[30]

These more abstract contemplations gave way to concrete norms as Character Guidance emphasized that membership in a covenant nation obligated military personnel to adhere to certain behavioral standards. Although the military undoubtedly liked thrifty, industrious servicemen, it focused on producing chaste, self-controlled ones. The *Chaplains' Sex Morality Lecture Manual* supplemented the general Character Guidance lectures on abstinence, venereal disease, and family life with six additional outlines for conversations on courtship, clean minds, sexual purity, self-restraint, and appropriate marriages. Not surprisingly, the manual pitched conventional gender norms as natural: "Man by virtue of being the stronger of the two sexes is woman's protector . . . [in] any and all circumstances, her moral as well as her bodily welfare." In the name of mothers, sisters, sweethearts, and daughters, men needed to guard women's honor. The manual did not account for the mid-twentieth century's most cutting-edge sex research, the Kinsey Reports—a move heartily endorsed by the President's Committee on Religion and Welfare, which winced at research "not in accordance with our concept of what the young men in the armed services were." Their young men were, or ought to have been, abstinent, not virile. Venereal disease statistics notwithstanding, the armed forces ignored and rejected Kinsey's findings that Americans engaged in frequent and varied sexual practices. Military morality—which scolded the consumption of liquor and comic books as often as it condemned prostitution and gambling—was often more aspirational than accurate.[31]

Chaplains deemed Character Guidance valuable, efficient, and successful, although occasionally dissenters voiced their objections. From Fort Jackson, South Carolina, Chaplain Lawrence Nelson (Baptist) detailed his chaplains giving 136 lectures to 24,377 men and 94 sex morality lectures to 9,227 men over three months. Meanwhile, in the Philippines Chaplain Loren T. Jenks (Baptist) described his clergy giving 271 lectures to 59,721 American troops and Philippine Scouts. An "irregular and unscientific" survey suggested that the servicemen preferred these lectures to weekly sermons, perhaps, Jenks conjectured, because chaplains combined information and entertainment when addressing large audiences. Jenks cautioned, however, that repetition was becoming a problem. Chaplain Stephen H. Stolz (Catholic) lodged a more direct complaint: "Talking shop, I would pass on to you how many feel about the Citizenship Lectures. Chaplains, officers, and men have told me that they are tired of them, there are too many, that once a week for each organization is too much." He agreed that this grousing was warranted. "There would be no difficulty if I could preach like the military man's Fulton Sheen . . . but I find it difficult to deliver 'Honesty is the Best Policy' on Saturdays with the same zeal as 'Make Friends of the Mammon of Iniquity' on Sunday." He suggested mandatory monthly lectures instead of weekly ones.[32]

This heavy-handed morality could numb as well as motivate, but even amid complaints, the respective chaplaincies remained steadfast in their dedication to Character Guidance. One angry inspector general thought the chaplains were not sufficiently thwarting Communism through character-building, but the AFCB defended its men. The *Chaplain's Hour* and Character Guidance, both of which emphasized the "moral and citizenship responsibilities required in a democracy," accomplished their goals. The inspector remained unsatisfied, seeking some sort of "program involving books and brochures on the subject." Unimpressed by this suggestion, the AFCB countered, "Communism was just one enemy of religious life. Materialism, secularism, fascism, communism, and any other evil philosophy was attacked constantly by chaplains." The group concluded that since the inspector described himself as a "poor Methodist" who "reluctantly admitted" he rarely attended worship, he was incapable of appropriately assessing their anti-Communist work through either religion or morality. They suggested he start attending church "on or off the post."[33]

Other moral ills pecked at American life in the late 1940s, but the chaplaincy elected not to count them as ethical concerns. Just as Character Guidance evaded the moral dilemmas surrounding the atomic bomb by never mentioning it, so too did it studiously avoid what Albert Einstein diagnosed as "the disease of white people"—segregation. Character Guidance's general platitudes to treat people respectfully left racism intact, white supremacy acceptable, and discrimination untouched. Indeed, as the military formalized Chaplain Guidance training, it also honorably discharged Isaac Woodard. In February 1946, the healthy black veteran boarded a bus in Georgia to return to his family. When he resisted the driver's belittling comments, Woodard found himself on the wrong end of a white South Carolina police officer's nightstick. His journey home ended in total darkness, for the uniform did not protect black men from blindness caused by white supremacist violence.[34]

Public outrage over the brutality directed at black veterans forced President Truman to admit "something is radically wrong with the system." In December 1946, he appointed a Presidential Commission on Civil Rights. Their report, *To Secure These Rights*, insisted that the armed forces commit to racial equality because military service stood at the nexus of obligations and rights.[35] On July 26, 1948, President Truman issued Executive Order 9981, which asserted "there shall be equality of treatment and opportunity for all persons in the armed services without regard to race, color, religion, or national origin." Technically, this document instantly overturned more than 150 years of state-sponsored segregation in the military, but the shift was neither sudden nor the implementation swift. The order veered between dictating that discrimination end "as rapidly as possible" and allowing that it would take time to do so "without impairing efficiency or morale."[36]

The reaction to Truman's initiative varied, and the chaplaincy did not always follow general trends. The army, navy, and air force each cleaved to autonomy, leaving James Forrestal, the first secretary of defense, with little capacity to desegregate the military unilaterally. While the army was hostile to change, the army chaplaincy was already integrated, at least administratively. The navy was generally more accepting of integration, but the navy chaplaincy, which defiantly avoided commissioning black chaplains until late in World War II and then promptly dismissed them after the war, remained truculent. When the AFCB discussed integration, the navy representative blanched.

"The employment of negro chaplains" was, "from the Navy viewpoint, purely academic." It would take two and a half more years and the advent of the Korean War for a black chaplain to reappear on the navy's active duty roster. After five years in a civilian pulpit, Chaplain Thomas D. Parham (Presbyterian)—the second of two African American navy chaplains commissioned during World War II—returned to the military, where he spent thirty-one more years. Even so, two months after Parham rejoined the navy, *The Christian Century* reported that "there are still no instances of chaplains being assigned across color lines" and pointed out that, much to their dismay, none of the chaplaincies had "gone on record favoring such exchanges." As the resistance to full inclusion of black clergy demonstrates, the military's moral compass did not register race relations as an ethical imperative. Its commitment to character seemed resolute, but the chaplaincy flinched when it came time to move from personal piety to civil rights.[37]

Just as the chaplaincy did not use Character Guidance to promote better race relations, it also accepted the program's latent religious coercion. Chaplain Martin Poch (Missouri Synod Lutheran) assured the PCRW that nonreligious soldiers were rare, but "we certainly permit him to do as he pleases, and that is his constitutional right." Yet this commitment to moral, rather than religious, character guidance often depended on the individual views of clergy. Chaplain Jim McCollum (Unitarian) rebuked a Catholic chaplain who insisted to soldiers at Fort Leonard Wood, Missouri, that morality depended on accepting Jesus as a savior. The scolding came from a particularly apt source. When the PCRW gathered in the late 1940s, McCollum was a young student at the center of a major Supreme Court case about religion in public schools. His mother, Vashti, a humanist freethinker, challenged the "voluntary" release-time religious instruction in which Protestant, Catholic, and Jewish educators taught half-hour classes for children of their faiths in public school classrooms, much like chaplains instructed teenage soldiers. In an eight-to-one decision, the court struck down the program as unconstitutional. Justice Hugo Black's majority opinion asserted that "the First Amendment rests upon the premise that both religion and government can best work to achieve their lofty aims if each is left free from the other within its respective sphere," while Justice Robert Jackson's concurring opinion cautioned that the Constitution offered little advice on "where the secular ends and the sectarian begins in education."[38]

While public schools could no longer host school-day religious classes, the military retained both religious activities and moral instruction. Chaplains exemplified the mixing of religion and government no longer allowed in schools, but received little guidance on the border between the secular and sectarian. Indeed, the military's moral programming was theistic and, despite the government's assumptions, derivative of particular faith traditions. No matter how strenuously the chaplaincy described Character Guidance as moral rather than religious, it still imposed theologically specific ideas about ethics, relationships, and behaviors on personnel. To teach men that "marriage is a divinely established institution" meant offering a particularly Christian, and primarily Protestant, understanding of matrimony. (Only in 1968, under threat from an American Civil Liberties Union (ACLU) lawsuit, would the military expel "religious dogma," at least in the form of overt "religious references" from the program.)[39]

In the 1940s, however, criticism emerged not from Catholics, Jews, or atheists but from conservative Protestants who bristled at the military's idea of American religion. During one PCRW meeting, an air force representative testified to Protestant-Catholic-Jewish cooperation in military life, noting that there were "22 chaplains on duty at Lackland Air Force Base. This is broken down into a Jewish chaplain, five Catholic, a Christian Scientist, a Mormon, and the rest the normal Protestant denominations." The air force proudly touted its acceptance of minority religions—it boasted Catholics, Jews, Mormons, and Christian Scientists among their corps. But PCRW member Daniel Poling gestured to the problem inherant to this interfaith cooperation. Some churches, the editor of the interdenominational evangelical *Christian Herald* noted, "did not believe it was possible to have a community program on the basis of inter-faith participation and inter-faith responsibility." In other words, the air force chaplaincy did not yet notice the increasing tension between what the military saw as "the normal Protestant denominations" and the growing interest of evangelical and fundamentalist Protestants in the military chaplaincy.[40]

The chaplaincy disregarded the developing cracks in religious unity just as it ignored discrimination against African Americans. The more conservative wing of evangelicals and fundamentalists, whose political prospects rose in the postwar period, rejected the ecumenism of the military. While enticed by the power of the military-spiritual complex and intrigued by the potential to influence so many young Americans via the chaplaincy, many conservative Protestants critiqued its ethos. To them, pluralist religious initiatives merely indicated America's spiraling decline away from its status as a covenant nation into irresponsible secularity and a demonic future. For evangelicals and fundamentalists, the universalizing religio-morality at the core of Character Guidance and the military chaplaincy writ large signaled religious coercion, not freedom. And although neither knew it when the twentieth century hit the halfway mark on New Year's Eve 1950, both evangelicals and African Americans would find opportunities to reshape their relationship to the military after North Korean soldiers crossed the thirty-eighth parallel into South Korea in June.

"Tomorrow we are going into combat," Chaplain Emil Kapaun wrote to his Catholic superior on July 17, 1950. "I have everything in order, all Mass stipends, my will, etc." The Kansas-born priest was wise to ready his spiritual and earthly affairs. Two months after Kapaun landed on the Korean peninsula with the 8th Cavalry, he entered Pyongyang with his unit. As the first snow fell over the hillsides and mountains, the chaplain settled into a daily routine. He led worship, met with soldiers, and wrote letters to the families of hundreds of men killed in combat. Two weeks later, after celebrating four masses on All Saints Day, he dug a foxhole under the full moon and bivouacked in the hills around Unsan with the 3rd Battalion. The mercury hovered around twenty degrees, and the chaplain and his men shivered in their cotton summer uniforms. Loud bursts of rifle fire and grenade blasts woke those who had drifted to sleep. Chinese infantrymen, sent by Beijing to aid their North Korean allies, had surrounded the soldiers. The surprise barrage of attacks decimated the Americans. Only a quarter of the battalion escaped back to the protective cover of the UN lines, and Chaplain Kapaun was not among them. Although he enabled other men to elude capture, the resourceful chaplain found himself marching northward through frozen rivers and over snow-capped mountains. He was a frostbitten prisoner of war (POW).[41]

For six months, the veteran of World War II postings in Burma and India unofficially presided over the imprisoned Americans. While his Chinese captors decided that the chaplain, despite his officer's insignia, scarcely mattered, Kapaun's fellow POWs viewed him as their leader, even their savior. On their overland trek, he carried wounded men, encouraged others to stay strong, and buried the dead, including Chaplain Kenneth Hyslop (Northern Baptist). When the group reached Sambokal, or The Valley—three square miles wedged between mountains, a former farm town turned penal colony—the chaplain secretly prowled for food under the cover of darkness. He also relayed messages between the separately quartered officers and enlisted men and led illicit worship in which the group prayed for freedom—and the deliverance of their guards from Communism. Forced to march again, Kapaun continued to tend to his flock at Camp No. 5 at Pyoktang, a former resort town naturally barricaded by rivers and mountains and politically protected by proximity to the Chinese border. He flummoxed guards, scrounged for food, and offered impromptu hymns to raise flagging spirits. When "the majority of us had turned into animals, fighting for food, irritable, selfish, miserable," Captain Robert E. Burke recalled, "the good priest conducted himself as a human being." And as a human being, Kapaun was fallible, succumbing to a combination of starvation, blood clots, dysentery, and pneumonia on May 23, 1951. Buried in an unmarked mass grave, his congregation honored him with a three-and-a-half-foot handcrafted cross, carved by a Jewish captive who, in the spirit of Kapaun, tricked Communist officials into allowing the men to keep the relic. For his efforts, the chaplain received posthumous military decorations—the Distinguished Service Cross, the Bronze Star, the Legion of Merit medal, the Prisoner of War Medal, and, sixty-two years later, the Medal of Honor.[42]

Chaplain Kapaun understood his courageous service to soldiers as divine work. The fearless POW priest understood the Korean War as a proxy war between the United States and the Soviet Union. He was as committed to anti-Communist ideology as he was to dignifying people—including enemy North Korean soldiers—with proper burials. Months before ministering to men in Korea, he led Easter services in Tokyo, where he reported to a friend, "Here I am in a Mission land, a pagan land, but one which has received exceptional blessings from God and the way it looks (if Russia does not get in here) many of the Japanese are going to receive the true faith." He brought a missionary's mentality with him to war, believing conviction and action would powerfully transform the political regimes and religious systems encountered abroad. And much like Jewish chaplains who encountered Jewish DPs in postwar Europe, when Kapaun found fellow Catholics in Korea, he embraced them. In Ansung, he offered a Thursday Mass for Koreans, the first service celebrated in the town's ransacked church since the Communists had arrived. Although conversations between the chaplain and the townspeople generally required an interpreter, "at the altar [they] had a common language." The following Sunday, Korean civilians and American servicemen worshipped together. For a brief moment, before the Christian soldiers marched on, religion bound together Americans and Koreans, for neither nationality nor vernacular tongue mattered for the Latin prayers. As in Europe, wartime encounters blurred the lines between fellowship and rescue.[43]

The Korean War ended in a stalemate, with the thirty-eighth parallel and the demilitarized zone (DMZ) continuing to divide the Korean peninsula into the Democratic People's Republic of Korea (DPRK) in the North and the Republic of Korea (ROK) in the South. The United States, flanked by UN forces, had entered the civil war in the summer of 1950, after DPRK forces steamrolled into Seoul and South Korea verged on collapse. After stalling the DPRK at the Pusan Perimeter in the peninsula's southeastern corner by early fall, American, South Korean, and British soldiers pushed northward during fall and winter, recapturing Seoul and recrossing the thirty-eighth parallel as the spring sun melted that coldest of winters. For two more years, war slogged on, and casualties mounted—eventually totaling more than 4 million deaths, half military and half civilian. The Korean War represented one of the first hot episodes in the global Cold War, a contest the United States felt compelled to participate in under the banner of maintaining the free world against Soviet and Chinese Communism.[44]

But U.S. interests were tangible too. After Japanese surrender in 1945, the U.S. occupied the island nation as well as its colonial holdings, including Korea. When the U.S. liberated Korea from its fiercest East Asian archenemy, it did so imperiously, with no input from either Koreans or other allied powers. American occupation lasted three years, during which General John Reed Hodge attempted to contain external threats and internal unrest, in part by creating a new Korean military. During this period too, future South Korean president Syngman Rhee returned from exile abroad, guerilla rebellions challenged the fledgling national police, and a combination of political and military forces violently repressed leftist uprisings. While American foreign policy experts debated the value of sending ground forces into Korea in June 1950, the discussions lasted barely a week before General Douglas MacArthur led American combat forces into battle—cavalierly, it turned out—to defend American credibility and prestige. The final military impasse did little to elevate American stature. But the deadlock at the thirty-eighth parallel obfuscated the nature and consequences of the Korean War. It was an "appallingly dirty" war with moral atrocities committed by both sides. It justified containment as the key priority of American foreign policy and, with it, "the enormous foreign military base structure and the domestic military-industrial complex to service it . . . which has come to define the sinews of American global power ever since."[45]

Religion lubricated these sinews of power. As American combat forces labored to a stalemate in 1953, its chaplains endeavored to build more durable links with Korean soldiers and civilians. For Protestant and Catholic clergymen, opportunities to rejuvenate Korean Christianity coexisted with the mandate to serve the religious needs of American servicemen. The military-spiritual complex, initially devised in the ruins of postwar Europe and developed under the looming shadow of Communism at home, sanctioned and encouraged evangelism in Korea. The proselytizing prohibited among Americans acquired a new legitimacy in the ideological and real battlefields of the Korean peninsula. Billy Graham, whose celebrity status was soaring as the Korean War began, spent Christmas 1952 with soldiers on the front. "Koreans," he decided, "are hungry for Christian life," and the evangelist would help feed them. He announced his trip to the American public before receiving permission from the Far East Command, and travel seemed dicey mere days before his projected departure. But he and his staff prayed, and a flurry of Washington meetings saved the evangelist from despair. When he arrived in Asia, he "found the chaplains to be men of God and living lives of radiant testimony for Christ." Graham proclaimed the chaplaincy to be "one of the greatest missionary undertakings a man could ever enter. His opportunities for Christ are unlimited." It was not exactly the message the military wanted to promote about its religious undertaking, but chaplain engagement with local Koreans could benefit the war effort and the military humored the evangelist. Never one to shy away from the stage, Graham preached from a temporary platform in the streets of Pusan to a mostly Korean audience of about 6,000. The cold and wind, for which Graham tried to prepare by layering his heaviest garments, did little to deter his listeners, 300 of whom clawed through the crowd to be born again in the shadow of majestic mountains. The scene repeated itself night after night, with ever-increasing crowds of "GIs and Koreans side by side."[46]

As Graham learned through discussions with military leaders, the chaplaincy needed ministers. When the United States entered the Korean War, it had to rapidly mobilize a larger military force, including chaplains. Army Chief of Chaplains Roy Parker (Southern Baptist) counted only 706 chaplains serving under him in July 1950. With few inactive reserve chaplains eager to volunteer for duty in Korea, the army resorted to involuntary recalls, despite protests from clergy comfortable in their civilian pulpits. By October 1951, the army finally achieved 98.9 percent of its 1,464-chaplain quota, but accumulating losses in Korea hobbled efforts to stay at authorized strength. By 1953, the army chaplaincy mustered only about 1,400 chaplains, 87 percent of the expected 1,618. The navy faced a comparable shortage, made more difficult by the increased allotment of chaplains to the Marines. In World War II, Marine divisions received sixteen navy chaplains; in Korea, the two Marine Divisions required twenty-six chaplains each. Yet in midsummer 1950, the Marines relied on a mere eighteen chaplains dispersed across its units.[47]

Military needs prompted new arrangements from civilian religious groups attempting to supply chaplains to the armed forces. Billy Graham became a recruiter, telling his followers "it is the duty of our young men in seminaries and colleges to volunteer for the chaplaincy." Lest his evangelical flock worry about the constraints of the military environment, he assured them—without any guarantees from the military—that chaplains "are not restricted as to what they may preach. They do not have to pull any punches." Most importantly, he emphasized, "they have great, unparalleled opportunities" and "the chaplaincy is one of the greatest callings of the Church." Likewise, with a paltry outfit of priests in the armed forces, the Military Ordinariate scurried to redress gaps in coverage. The military vicar commended Catholic chaplains for "multipl[ying] themselves in caring for an armed force that was, in the losing days and in the mountainous terrain, just a little above the demoralization point." But stretching the existing Catholic chaplaincy to its limits did not offer a sustainable course of action, and Cardinal Spellman, the military vicar, worried about ecclesiastical disarray amidst intermingled American and Korean troops. The Vatican took the extraordinary step of placing all Catholic chaplains serving under or alongside American troops and her allies under the authority of the American Military Ordinariate "in order to effect some unity and uniformity of jurisdiction and privileges." The Jewish Welfare Board also faced a discrepancy between volunteers and spots available. The flagship seminaries of the three main Jewish movements, Yeshiva University (Orthodox), the Jewish Theological Seminary (Conservative), and the Hebrew Union College–Jewish Institute of Religion (Reform), agreed that each would provide one-third of the Jewish chaplain quota. To accomplish this, the institutions decided to draft rabbis from graduating classes. While the state could not conscript clergy, civilian religious groups could mandate military service.[48]

Meanwhile, in Korea, Bibles and hymnals became a form of religious and imperial currency as Americans built relationships with Korean chaplains, ministers, and civilians. Long a mission field for American Protestants and Catholics, Korea became a mission field for the military as well. The Republic of Korea acquired its chaplaincy—composed of volunteer civilian ministers—in 1951, as a result of coaxing from two American auxiliary chaplains. From the headquarters of the Far East Command, Chaplain Ivan L. Bennett (Southern Baptist) determined that an English-Korean hymnal would be useful for joint American-Korean services during battle. When his office ran into roadblocks acquiring funds for printing, Bennett approached General Douglas MacArthur and asked him to sign the foreword to the hymnal, as FDR had done for the World War II–era American hymnals. MacArthur's signature helped release the necessary funds, and hundreds of Koreans joined Americans at Sunday hilltop, mountainside, or tent services. When Chaplain James Wilson (Methodist) succeeded Bennett as Far East Command chaplain, he maintained the hymnal project. However, he also sought to purchase and distribute 50,000 Korean-language hymnals. Bennett, by then the army chief of chaplains, wondered if the project represented a pressing need given that 175,000 Korean hymnals had shipped overseas, but nevertheless approved the new non-English ones.[49]

Much like the military's printing projects in postwar Germany, religious texts, like religious services, provided a means of contact—and ideally goodwill—with local populations. One Sunday, Andrew Kang decided "for reasons unknown" to attend the ecumenical church service run by Chaplain Sidney Crumpton (United Methodist) in Seoul. When North Korea occupied the capital city in the summer of 1950, his family found themselves behind enemy lines. The regime labeled his parents counterrevolutionaries, murdering his mother and capturing his father. Caught by the North Koreans while hiding with a friend, Kang was on the verge of execution when gunfire lured the soldiers elsewhere. Raised in a Confucian household, he did not accept his Catholic friend's interpretation, that God had rescued them. But he did think about "the very remarkable incident that I was saved." Discovering his mother's tortured corpse in a mass grave three days later did not make him "an instant Christian," but the experience of being unable to recognize her gruesome body and then being compelled to look closer stuck with him as a religious turning point. His chance encounter with Chaplain Crumpton prompted a more extended relationship and, eventually, conversion. Upon realizing that Kang spoke some English and wanted to be a doctor, the minister arranged to send him on full scholarship to his alma mater, Wofford College. The chaplain's intervention changed Kang's life, leading him to a career in medicine in the United States. While this particular outcome was highly unusual, American military chaplains began expanding their work to serving local populations in the postwar years, first in Germany and then in Korea.[50]

American Christian chaplains often aided Korean allies in much the same fashion that American Jewish chaplains had worked with DPs in postwar Europe. One inspection report found that chaplains served as "bridges of understanding between the local citizens" and U.S. military personnel. This role was particularly important because, the report observed, "too frequently the only Koreans our service men see are the camp hangers-on who steal anything and everything, or offer their bodies for sale. Through the chaplain, the service men came to have contact with cultured, intelligent Koreans of character, ideals and achievements equal to or superior to our own, and understanding is born." Laced with socioeconomic, racial, and moral opprobrium, the report nonetheless advocated contact between Americans and Koreans.

Navy chaplain Ross Trower (Lutheran)—later a chief of chaplains—modeled this lauded behavior. When attached to the First Combat Service Group, where he worshipped in the first Quonset hut chapel built by Marines in Korea, he met and prayed with a Korean Methodist minister. He also cosponsored Bible classes with a Korean Catholic priest and taught the Bible to Korean doctors and nurses in a military hospital.[51]

Although worship and Bible study could transcend linguistic and national differences, it nevertheless imposed Western, and specifically Christian, norms on a country immersed in Eastern religions—Taoism, Confucianism, and Buddhism, as well as local animist practices. Protestant and Catholic missionaries introduced Koreans to Christianity beginning in the eighteenth century and successfully converted large percentages of the population by the twentieth century. Yet Korean Christians did not relinquish all ties to more traditional religious practices. This syncretic religion challenged some chaplains. Marine chaplain John Muller (Reformed) observed—somewhat contradictorily—that "the average Korean has no religion, but he probably conforms to many religious practices." This mélange of religious rituals bothered Muller, for Confucianism, he asserted, "is not a religion, but a substitute for religion. Its main belief, ancestor worship, is a real obstacle to the progress of Christianity." Although he countenanced "friendships with the men [that] often crossed religious lines," he could not comprehend or approve of the Asian religions present in the "heathen nation" and hampered by "spiritual poverty." Indeed, he relished transgressing Buddhist space by "preaching Christ in what was once a Buddhist temple" and delighted in reaching out to Korean Christian churches, which he found "live, thriving [and] evangelical." The military chaplaincy's emphasis on pluralism reached a sharp limit in Korea, where Christianity vied for adherents, and many chaplains struggled to escape an American religious logic that equated monotheism with democracy.[52]

Cardinal Spellman had already left for his 1952 Christmas trip to visit American troops in Korea when, a few blocks from St. Patrick's Cathedral, Dwight D. Eisenhower reminded a crowded Waldorf-Astoria ballroom that the battle with Communism was "a struggle for the hearts and souls of men." Three days before Christmas and less than a month before Inauguration Day, the president-elect emphasized that Americans "are a religious people," not simply as individuals but as a nation. In what would become the most famous line of his speech, he argued, "Our form of Government has no sense unless it is founded in a deeply felt religious faith and I don't care what it is." Commentators rushed to explain his statement, parsing the apparent brush-off "and I don't care what it is" as a tribute to ecumenism or an indication of emptiness. What, many wondered, could this "very vague" religion accomplish?[53]

A lot, the nation's thirty-fourth president recognized. His religion was rooted and substantive, albeit nurtured more in the soil of the government than a specific church. The five-star general returned to the United States from his position as Supreme Allied Commander, Europe, of the North Atlantic Treaty Organization, to launch his presidential campaign in June 1952. His thirty-five-year military career, interrupted by a brief stint as the president of Columbia University, had plucked Eisenhower out of Abilene, Kansas, deposited him at West Point, and then sent him around the world. Raised by Mennonites-turned-Jehovah's-Witnesses but untethered to the church's Adventist teachings after he left the Midwest, Eisenhower viewed himself as "deeply religious." His personal faith seemed conspicuously hazy as he worked the campaign trail, but only when assessed apart from the military environment that groomed him for office. As a product of the army, Eisenhower's utterance reflected the success of the modern military chaplaincy's effort to build, teach, and promote moral monotheism as the defining feature of American religion. "I don't care what it is" made manifest the military's emphasis on nondenominational faith—the faith taught to the millions of Americans who had served in World War I, World War II, and the Korean War. And as in the military, this American religion rested on what Eisenhower called "the Judeo-Christian concept." Eisenhower was a son of the armed forces and, as such, "a living embodiment of the nonsectarian ideal."[54]

Profoundly unconcerned with denominational allegiances and deeply committed to religion as a unifying political and social force, the new president joined the ranks of Americans becoming "churched" in February 1953. In 1940, almost half the American population belonged to a church (or synagogue). By 1950, church membership reached 57 percent and, at the end of Eisenhower's presidency, 69 percent of

Americans belonged to organized religious groups. Baptized as a Presbyterian like his wife Mamie, Eisenhower joined the National Presbyterian Church, led by Edward Elson, a World War II army chaplain.[55]
He retained his commitment to broadminded religion, brandishing pluralism as the religious weapon of the Cold War. He had seen the Nazi
death camps, encouraged military chaplains to remain pugnacious in
their work, and negotiated an end to the Korean War. Far from an
empty vessel to be filled by midcentury conservative preachers or Christian businessmen, Eisenhower carried the military's religious ideals
from the Pentagon to the Oval Office and from the Oval Office to
American society. During his two terms in office, "under God" would
be added to the Pledge of Allegiance, currency would proclaim "In God
We Trust," and the National Prayer Breakfast would commence.

To some, these additions highlighted the broad religious tapestry
of American life, a canvas that could stretch to accommodate a growing
number of denominations and faiths. To others, they hailed a reclaiming
of Christian, even Protestant, America. This range of interpretations
represented the military-spiritual complex's substantial strength and
greatest weakness. The conjunction of a relatively capacious religious
vision with the coercive power of the military accommodated a range
of views and made it susceptible—like the military-industrial complex
Eisenhower warned about as he departed the presidency—to "the ac-
quisition of unwarranted influence." What seemed benign or even
beneficial in some contexts, such as deploying clergy and channeling
resources into postwar religious reconstruction, contained the seeds of
"misplaced power" in imperial contexts abroad and among religious
minorities at home. Soaring rhetoric about a religious nation unleashed
heady challenges to the shape and viability of the military-spiritual
complex. The rhetoric of religious pluralism beckoned a broader range
of faiths into the military's orbit while shielding sectarian religious
ideas in plain sight. As the Cold War marched on, the chaplaincy became a political battleground for American faiths pursuing and critiquing state recognition and power.[56]

The chaplaincies expanded numerically and religiously during World War I, in part to help the military manage the millions of young men it drafted. Here a navy chaplain—indicated by the cross on his lapel—distributes newspapers to sailors and Marines, circa 1918. Courtesy of the Naval History and Heritage Command (NH 3027).

In 1918, Jewish soldiers in the American Expeditionary Force attended a Passover Seder sponsored by the Jewish Welfare Board in Paris, France. During World War I, Congress officially opened the chaplaincy to Jews, Mormons, Christian Scientists, the Eastern Orthodox, and the Salvation Army, which enabled more religious minorities to observe their traditions while serving their country. Photo courtesy of the U.S. National Archives and Records Administration, College Park, MD (111-SC-158426).

During World War I, the state mobilized faith to sustain its martial goals. Combat conditions often required chaplains to innovate, including holding outdoor worship services in the ruins of a church in Verdun, France. Photo courtesy of the U.S. National Archives and Records Administration, College Park, MD (111-SC-27518).

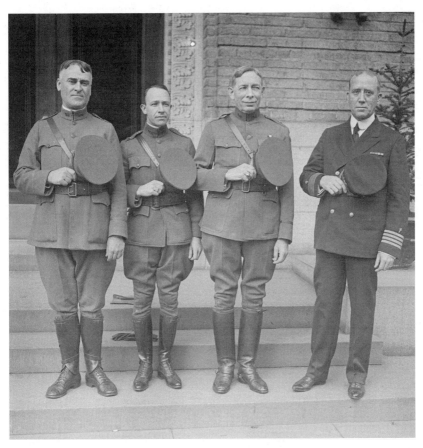

Army Chief of Chaplains John T. Axton (Congregationalist), Chaplain Morris S. Lazaron (Jewish), Right Reverend Charles H. Brent (Episcopalian), and Navy Chief of Chaplains John B. Frazier (Southern Methodist) gather before officiating at the dedication of the Tomb of the Unknown Soldier at Arlington National Cemetery, November 11, 1921. The ceremony heralded the military's new understanding of American religion as a tri-faith enterprise. Photo courtesy of the Harris & Ewing Collection, Library of Congress Prints and Photographs Division, Washington, D.C. (LC-DIG-hec-41638).

Chaplain Anthony J. Morrissey (Catholic) leads a service in a Civilian Conservation Corps camp in 1935. The army chaplaincy ran the religious programming for and oversaw moral education in the CCC, which enabled it to test the tri-faith vision it had articulated in the 1920s. Courtesy of the Library of Congress Prints and Photographs Division, Washington, D.C. (LC-USZ62-41867).

Army Chief of Chaplains William R. Arnold takes the oath of office in 1937. Arnold was the first Catholic to supervise religious ministry in the armed forces and led the army chaplaincy through World War II. Courtesy of the Harris & Ewing Collection, Library of Congress Prints and Photographs Division, Washington, D.C. (LC-DIG-hec-23812).

With battleships in the distance, Chaplain George M. Kemper (Catholic) celebrated Mass for Marines on Guam. War exposed many soldiers to new faiths and unfamiliar rituals, experiences that reshaped Americans' understanding of religion. Courtesy of the Naval History and Heritage Command, Chaplain Corps Collection (UA 17.01).

Chaplain Theodore R. Frierson (United Methodist) chats with African American troops in New Guinea, 1943. The Jim Crow military commissioned African Americans as chaplains but restricted their service to African American units—unlike white chaplains, who could be assigned to any units. Courtesy of the Farm Security Administration–Office of War Information Photograph Collection, Library of Congress Prints and Photographs Division, Washington, D.C. (LC-USE6-D-009132).

Chaplains Fred W. Thissen (Catholic), Ernest F. Pine (Protestant), Samuel A.
Owen (Negro Baptist), and Jacob Rothschild (Jewish) attended Chaplain School
together at Fort Benjamin Harrison, Indiana. Publicly, the army discussed its
chaplaincy as a Protestant-Catholic-Jewish organization, but internally it
operated according to a Protestant-Catholic-Jewish-Negro logic. While
Chaplain School was the first integrated officer training school, race still
eclipsed religion as the defining feature of African American chaplains in the
eyes of the state. Photo by Jack Delano, April 1942. Courtesy of the Farm
Security Administration–Office of War Information Photograph Collection,
Library of Congress Prints and Photographs Division, Washington, D.C.
(LC-USW3-001733-D).

The "Interfaith in Action" postage stamp memorialized the four chaplains who died, arms linked and praying together in English, Latin, and Hebrew, after the sinking of the *Dorchester* in February 1943. Chaplains George L. Fox (Methodist), Clark V. Poling (Reformed Church), John P. Washington (Catholic), and Alexander B. Goode (Jewish) represented white religious pluralism, while tales of their heroic actions masked the role of the state in fashioning a tri-faith nation. United States Postal Service, 1948. Author's collection. Gift of the Four Chaplains Memorial Foundation.

Archbishop Francis Spellman toured bombed ruins in Tunisia with Army Air
Force officers while traveling the world to visit troops during World War II.
Delegations of Protestant, Jewish, and African American clergy made similar
trips, but the Catholic leader's close contact with high-ranking officers attracted
the most scrutiny from the American public. Photo by Nick Parrino, April 1943.
Courtesy of the Farm Security Administration–Office of War Information
Photograph Collection, Library of Congress Prints and Photographs Division,
Washington, D.C. (LC-DIG-fsa-8d31199).

Chaplains' duties included providing sex education and conducting marriages. Because state rather than federal law regulates marriage, regional commanders had to approve marriages performed abroad. Chaplain William T. Green (Baptist) officiated the wedding of Private Florence A. Collins, a WAC of the 6888th Postal Directory Battalion, to Corporal William A. Johnson of the 1696th Labor Supervision Company, in the European Theater of Operations. Courtesy of the U.S. National Archives and Records Administration, College Park, MD (111-SC-210939).

As U.S. servicemen married Japanese and Korean women, several Christian chaplains decided they needed to acculturate war brides to American customs. Chaplain Edwin W. Andrews (Lutheran) developed a manual titled "Orientation Program for Japanese Nationals (Brides)." Assisted by Viola Johnson (left), Mrs. Robert W. Lantz (center), and Betty Waser (right), the chaplain taught a class to women on a transport ship headed to the United States in 1951. U.S. National Archives Photograph. Courtesy of the Naval History and Heritage Command (80-G-438934).

In the aftermath of the Holocaust, Jewish chaplains viewed their contributions to postwar reconstruction as both patriotic and religious. The American military invested in religious life by enabling chaplains to serve Displaced Persons and rescue religious texts. Chaplain Samuel Blinder (Jewish) inspects Torah scrolls found in the basement of the Race Institute in Frankfurt, Germany. Courtesy of the U.S. National Archives and Records Administration, College Park, MD (111-SC-209154).

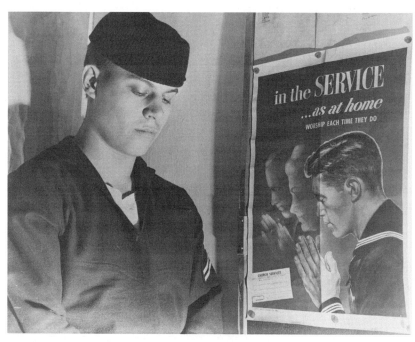

In the early postwar years, chaplains became formally responsible for Character Guidance, a moral education program that tried to avoid religious particularity while encouraging belief in one God and ethical behavior as the core of American religion. The young sailor praying by a poster advertising church services aboard the *USS Wisconsin* exemplified the behavior the military wanted to inculcate in its men. Official U.S. Navy Photograph, now in the collection of the U.S. National Archives. Courtesy of the Naval History and Heritage Command (80-G-443726).

Chaplain Kenny Lynch (Catholic) conducted services in Korea. Christian chaplains led worship for American personnel as well as Korean soldiers and civilians, exporting religion as a central feature of democracy during the Cold War. Courtesy of the U.S. National Archives and Records Administration, College Park, MD (111-SC-378917).

During Operation Passage to Freedom, which transported Vietnamese civilians from North to South in 1954, navy chaplains became key brokers and translators, using religion to encourage the fleeing refugees. A chaplain distributed images of a white Jesus to predominantly Catholic Vietnamese children. U.S. National Archives Photograph. Courtesy of the Naval History and Heritage Command (80-G-65230).

Remember the sabbath day, . . .

They
that go
to sea

EXODUS 20:8

The military sought to encourage Sabbath observance, as this poster for the
Navy's Religious Program commands. However, the military did not always
accommodate a full range of Sabbath beliefs, which led to courts-martial for
members of the Seventh-day Adventist Church who sought to honor their
Saturday Sabbath. Poster designed by Joseph Binder. U.S. Government Printing
Office, 1963. Courtesy of the Library of Congress Prints and Photographs
Division, Washington, D.C. (LC-DIG-ppmsca-42125).

When Chaplain Calvin J. Croston (Episcopalian) offered cloth to a Montagnard woman in Bắc Hội in the Central Vietnamese highlands in 1966, he exemplified the military's use of soft power to try to improve relationships with local communities. In the early 1960s, American military leaders started to recognize that they needed better knowledge of Buddhism and other Vietnamese religious and cultural traditions. Chaplains often became ethnographers, developing pamphlets and curricula to teach soldiers about Vietnam, and served as brokers between U.S. troops and Vietnamese civilians. Photo by Robert W. Dietrich, JOCM, USN, January 1966. Courtesy of the Naval History and Heritage Command (NH 73237).

As Americans protested the Vietnam War as immoral, chaplains struggled to navigate their relationship to God and country. Some clergy decided that their responsibility to drafted men outweighed their objections to war and enlisted to serve conscripted men sent to Vietnam. A Marine atop a tree stood guard while an unarmed Catholic chaplain conducted Mass. Photo courtesy of the U.S. National Archives and Records Administration, College Park, MD (127-N-A193262).

The Jewish seminaries faced fierce battles over the obligation to God, country, and ethics because many rabbinical students rejected the Vietnam War as unjust. The few rabbis who went to Vietnam covered miles of terrain, by jeep and by helicopter. Army Chaplain Ernest Lapp (Jewish), who enlisted to serve the country that sheltered his family when they fled Austria in 1939, led services on the beach in Cam Ranh Bay in 1967. Photo by Thomas L. Larsen, June 1967. David Lapp Collection, courtesy of the National Museum of American Jewish Military History, Washington, D.C. (P990.059.001).

Although President Truman desegregated the armed forces by executive order in 1948, the process of integrating the military took decades. Integration did not beget equality, and racial tensions flared in Vietnam, forcing chaplains to grapple with the relationship between racism and religion. U.S. National Archives Photograph. Courtesy of the Naval History and Heritage Command (K-80354).

A chaplain baptizes a soldier in Vietnam. As liberal religious leaders questioned the Vietnam War, evangelical clergy took advantage of the opportunity to fill spots in the military chaplaincy. The growing evangelical presence deepened rifts about the goals and culture of religion in the military, exposing anew the challenge of crafting a capacious religious institution that could serve all Americans. Photo courtesy of the U.S. Army Chaplain Corps Museum, Fort Jackson, South Carolina.

The military opened the chaplaincies to women in the early 1970s. African American ministers like Stella Sellers, here standing in the chapel in Fort Stewart, Georgia, represented some of the first women to enter the military chaplaincy. Photo courtesy of the U.S. National Archives and Records Administration, College Park, MD (111-SC-680030).

Although Muslim soldiers had long served in the armed forces, it took until 1994 for the military to commission Chaplain Abdul-Rasheed Muhammad as its first Muslim chaplain—seen here leading a field worship service. The expansion of the chaplaincy to include Muslims, followed by Buddhists (2004) and Hindus (2011), required the military to fashion new symbols to identify Islam, Buddhism, and Hinduism on chaplains' uniforms. Despite some resistance, the army chaplaincy altered its regimental insignia, shifting from a cross and tablets to an open book, to portray this growing religious pluralism. Photo courtesy of the U.S. Army Chaplain Corps Museum, Fort Jackson, South Carolina.

6

"Maybe God
Is an American"

IT WAS HOT and muggy as monsoon season crested in the summer of 1954, and hundreds of thousands of Northern Vietnamese refugees descended upon the Red River Delta near Haiphong. They had loaded the things they could carry on their shoulders and walked for days, sidestepping mines and avoiding snipers to reach the space where spongy earth met saltwater. Most were peasants, few spoke French let alone English, and almost all were terrified. Gray vessels larger than most had ever seen loomed on the horizon. Anchored at sea, too big to load from land, the hulking ships could carry 6,000 people south, first to Saigon and then to outlying villages. It took an act of faith to board the watercraft—faith that unfamiliar chunks of steel could spirit people to safe haven, faith in the uniform-clad men who uttered strange words, faith that the unseen city was better than familiar mossy hills, and faith that the vehicles festooned with banners proclaiming "This is your passage to freedom" in English and Vietnamese would fulfill that promise, even for those who could not read.[1]

Latin, it turned out, could serve communication needs effectively, if not always efficiently. In the suffocating late August air, rice farmers temporarily became boat people. And priests, like Chaplain Francis J. Fitzpatrick (Catholic) and his Vietnamese counterparts, accomplished what signs could not. The American, sporting navy-issue white shorts and short-sleeves, and the Vietnamese, clad in long black robes, communicated with one another in Latin. The clergy calmed frightened passengers, convinced them to descend ladders into the below-deck compartments, and explained shipboard procedures. Racing against an advancing Red Curtain and a 300-day limit on border crossing, Operation Exodus—promoted in the United States as Operation Passage to Freedom—ferried over 300,000 people and almost 70,000 tons of cargo from north to south. After a two-month battle, Ho Chi Minh's forces successfully flushed out the colonial French regime from their garrison at Dien Bien Phu in May. The ensuing Geneva Accords divided Vietnam at the seventeenth parallel, with the Viet Minh governing the Democratic Republic of Vietnam in the north and Emperor Bao Dai leading the State (later Republic) of Vietnam in the south. As the French relinquished their hold, Ho Chi Minh established a nationalist-Communist administration in the North while anticommunist Ngo Dinh Diem left an abbey in Bruges, Belgium, and voyaged to Saigon to serve as the new Republic's prime minister. Meanwhile, over the ten months from August 1954 to May 1955, ships accompanied by navy chaplains made 500 three-day trips across the Gulf of Tonkin to the South China Sea as part of the largest civilian evacuation in history.[2]

Passage to Freedom was a humanitarian operation, but it was also a political and military one. Almost a million northern Vietnamese migrated south in 1954–1955, and about two-thirds of the emigrants were Catholic. More than a statistical anomaly in a predominantly Buddhist country, this political calculation "result[ed in] a major reordering of the religious balance of Vietnam." The exodus halved the Catholic population of the north and more than doubled the Catholic population of the south, providing important support to "America's Miracle Man," Ngo Dinh Diem. While refugees moved en masse, their decision was neither automatic nor spontaneous. The United States, through the work of the CIA, the State Department, and the military, facilitated the population transfer. The CIA's propaganda campaign included fabricated tales of Communist brutality, false rumors of forced labor, and fictitious leaflets about nuclear bombs, while the military provided a means of escape. Navy leaders may not have known the extent of CIA deception, but Rear Admiral Lorenzo Sabin, the commanding officer of sea operations for Passage to Freedom, lauded the support of religious networks: "The native Catholic priests are a very determined lot and so far they've been able to get their flocks though the Vietminh lines. And they've got a way of encouraging other natives to join."[3]

Military chaplains, as conduits of information and sources of spiritual sustenance, often represented the last link in this chain of religious encouragement. Even if they "did not think of themselves as instruments of American international policy," they represented the American government and operated in the shadow of its empire. When chaplains celebrated Mass, baptized babies, distributed religious pictures (primarily a white Jesus and Mary), and issued New Testaments to the refugees on their ships, they projected an image of the United States as a Christian nation. Of the sixteen American chaplains who served the Passage to Freedom operation, seven were Catholic and the rest Protestant. For many, Chaplain Spencer J. Palmer's (LDS) sense that "somehow God's flag was the American flag" might have rung true. Safety from communism arrived cloaked in navy blues.[4]

With the Cold War surging in the 1950s, the United States sought to play the role of the world's protector, the global shield against the Soviet Union. Religion served this effort by spiritually insulating democracy, rhetorically framing foreign policy, and substantively undergirding military projects. Religious consensus was, however, more imagined than real. When Chaplain Palmer mused, based on his experiences in Asia in the early 1950s, that many felt "maybe God is an American," he captured a view that the United States wanted to convey to its allies and enemies alike. But if God was an American, it was not clear what American religion God represented, and many vied to be the emblematic faith. The Protestant-Catholic-Jewish moment marked by Will Herberg in 1955 had, in fact, passed by the time stores stocked his book. In its stead stood a more robust and more fragmented American religious mosaic.[5]

As the military became a more powerful institution through postwar campaigns abroad and the concomitant growth of the domestic defense industry at home, the administrative work of governing religion became more daunting. Religious conflict endured, but containing interdenominational squabbling and interfaith disputes had been a signature feat of the military. Since World War I, the armed forces had maintained an imperfectly inclusive but relatively stable religious accord. An assumed compatibility between faith and government sustained the crusade against Communism; the investment in the military-spiritual complex subsequently made the chaplaincy an object of desire and critique, often simultaneously, for those who wanted to shape religion, state, or religion-state interactions. While Catholics and Jews had settled into the military infrastructure as insiders, others jockeyed for legitimation, accommodation, and influence.

A broad range of faiths, from Buddhists and Seventh-day Adventists to Mormons and evangelical Protestants, sought recognition by and more substantial accommodations from the state's religious apparatus. Although these faith groups did not necessarily collaborate—and sometimes antagonized one another—they shared a critique of the military's religious regime as both insufficiently representative and insufficiently sectarian. No matter the battle—over dog tags, Sabbath observance, grooming standards, chapel allocation, or Sunday School curricula—each faith viewed the chaplaincy as a means of authenticating their religion as American. The military's responses ranged from receptive to hostile, depending on the perceived benefit domestically and globally. When, in the mid-1960s, the military deemed understanding Buddhism a priority, it did so for practical reasons—to support operations abroad. Similarly, the decision to brush aside criticism of military regulations that restricted chaplains from appearing in uniform in segregated civilian churches derived from an interest in improving public relations. The motivations were not idealistic, but the consequences mattered. The idea that God might be American fueled marginalized groups—and religious groups that felt marginalized— to pursue state recognition and accommodation while simultaneously coaxing the military to rethink the parameters of pluralism.

When a 1948 petition arrived in Washington, it wrapped a big question in a request for a simple change. Asking the military to add a Buddhist designation on dog tags effectively demanded that the government widen the scope of recognized American religions. The chaplaincy quivered as it considered its options. Mid-twentieth-century American dog tags stamped single letter abbreviations for religious affiliation, and there were only three options: P for Protestant, C for Catholic, and H for Hebrew (Jewish). Soldiers who did not identify as Protestant, Catholic, or Jewish lacked any recourse until approximately 100,000 petitioners, mostly civilians in Hawaii and California, lobbied the military to recognize Buddhism. The organizers, the National Young Buddhists, enlisted the aid of politicians to champion the cause. With large number of Buddhist constituents, the governor of Hawaii, then a U.S. territory, advised, "The faith that is so desired by the service men should be recognized, whether it be Protestant, Catholic, Jewish, Buddhist, Mohammedan or any other faith." California assemblyman Harold Levering (R), most famous for instituting a loyalty oath for state employees, also favored dog tag equity. If Protestants, Catholics, and Jews had letters of their own, so too should Buddhists and others. "To do otherwise," he wrote, "is contrary to the American tradition." The petition therefore made two interrelated claims: first, Buddhism was a religion, and second, it deserved recognition as a valid American choice.[6]

The military remained intransigent, unwilling to recognize Buddhism or widen the spectrum of designated American religious identities. Legislative endorsements notwithstanding, resistance barreled in from across the country. Reserve chaplain Sydney Croft (Episcopalian) vehemently opposed all efforts made by Buddhists to participate religiously in the armed forces. From his perch in Hawaii, he asserted, "Buddhism has degenerated; if it was a religion in the past, it is no longer a religion." Claiming inside information from World War II Japanese American chaplain Hiro Higuchi (Congregationalist), Croft disdained Buddhism while asserting, all too strenuously, that his objections had absolutely no basis in racial discrimination: "I am willingly serving all races of people in my work here, and we live harmoniously together and worship together with sincerity and brotherly devotion." His overly solicitous tone revealed his more sectarian motives. In the Japanese American war experience, he saw Christian religious revival. The postwar return to Buddhism imperiled his church, which had gained members during the war as some Hawaiian *Nisei* took shelter in the protective embrace of American Christianity. Croft stood alone in his shrill denunciation of Buddhism, but his missives joined a chorus of naysayers, unrelenting in their hostility to classifying Buddhists as Buddhists.[7]

Most antagonists objected on supposedly pragmatic grounds. The Red Cross theoretically supported an additional classification—submitting O for Other as an option—but claimed B for Buddhist was impossible because B could also indicate Bahaism. The Armed Forces Chaplains Board extended this logic, alleging that a new religious designation would result in "endless confusion" because "every minute fraction of a percent claiming distinct worship, or even simply belief in

God, would request their own religious symbol. The letter 'B' could be interpreted as Baptist; it could mean 'Believer' for anyone who believes in God; or, under the duress of battle, it understandably could be misread as blood type." Although C could indicate Congregationalist as easily as Catholic, the prospect of misinterpretation did not seem to afflict the existing designations. Outlandish as this concern was, it swayed the military. Chief of Chaplains Luther Miller (Episcopalian) explained the current protocol was satisfactory because religious identification on dog tags was optional. Limiting personnel to three religious classifications reduced confusion, he argued, whereas allowing additional markers of religious affiliation might induce the approximately 250 American denominations to seek letters of their own.[8]

Miller was not entirely wrong; he correctly perceived that other religious groups squirmed under the ill-fitting P and coveted acknowledgment. As the Buddhist campaign for recognition gained momentum in the late 1940s, the Greek Orthodox pled their case too. The "indiscriminate" designation as either Protestant or Catholic was unfair, especially because "the Orthodox Faith is practically as large as the Jewish Faith which is recognized by the proper agency as a principal denomination." If numerical strength mattered, then the Red Cross's suggested O ought to refer to Orthodox, not Other. These efforts to drum up support seemed to go nowhere, as J. Willard Marriott, the hospitality magnate and head of the LDS Military Relations Committee, forecast in 1947. "Even though we do not consider ourselves Protestant, and could convince them of our distinctive position, it would be very difficult for the War Department to separate us from the smaller Christian denominations and put us in a separate category," he apprised Mormon elders. "If they did this for our Church, it would have the same request from Christian Scientists, Southern Baptists, United Brethren and many other minority groups." In trying to contain, rather than splinter, American religion, the military struggled to account for the extant diversity that superseded fictive unity. But advocacy nudged the military. In January 1949, Army Chief of Chaplains Miller recommended a new option, an X for "those soldiers whose religious affiliations does not fit any of the three principal denominations." With an X on a dog tag, a soldier could wear an additional marker of faith, the chief allowed. The X offered an imperfect compromise at best. It conceded the presence of religions outside tri-faith America while refusing to alter the taxonomy of acceptable American religions.[9]

The parallel efforts to challenge military intransigence trucked on, with American Muslims writing to Dwight D. Eisenhower during his presidential run, asking for help designating Islam on dog tags. He demurred, though intimated that as president, he might effect more change. However, when the Romanian Orthodox church asked for an Orthodox notation in 1955, President Eisenhower followed the lead of the military he commanded: "the religious classification letters on identification tags can serve the recognized purpose only if restricted to broad designation categories." That Orthodox was a category as broad and demographically significant as American Judaism, and that plenty of religious groups wanted more than an uninformative X, was immaterial. The president's staff couched the request as trivial, concluding that no letter "would accord the Eastern Orthodox faith any greater recognition than it now enjoys." Yet state endorsement was significant precisely because certifying Eastern Orthodoxy as American would flout the fiction of tri-faith America.[10]

Over time, protest eroded military resolve. First, in 1954, the military acceded to the Jewish request to use J, a religious signifier, rather than H, a racial marker. Then, in 1955, the military permitted soldiers to stamp a "particular religious denomination" on dog tags. The New York Times attributed the development to the Greek Orthodox, reporting that their protest convinced Army Chief of Chaplains Patrick H. Ryan (Catholic) to allow recording "any and all denominations." The Pentecostal Evangel's gleeful announcement, "the name of the Protestant denomination will be shown," reveled in Protestant specificity supplanting general Protestantism and suggested a different explanation for the shift. The Assemblies of God publication rendered the transformation of military identification a victory for Protestants, not for the wide array of non-Protestant groups formerly labeled Protestant. By July 1959, Army Regulations 606–5 formally authorized spelling out religious preferences in eighteen letters, thereby alleviating the problems caused by the initials. Self-selecting religious identities was not radical and it benefited most soldiers. Nevertheless, victory was complicated. Infinite options enabled religious diversity to flourish individually while depriving minority faith groups, such as Buddhists, the validation that accompanied official abbreviations.[11]

Dog tags allowed personnel to convey their religious identities, but many soldiers and sailors wanted to live their faith as well. While both the Constitution and the Uniform Code of Military Justice (UCMJ) protected free exercise of religion, military protocols flustered those whose religious practices fell outside officially recognized norms. As members of more varied faiths entered the armed forces in greater numbers, their willingness to flout standard operating procedures unmasked the assumptions embedded in military religious culture and tested the military's ability to navigate religious difference. The rhetorical emphasis on religion as a weapon against Communism enabled minority faiths to frame ritual needs as protected American practices, though the chaplaincy's effective resolution of conflicts varied.

As a matter of policy, the military supported the biblical commandment to "remember the Sabbath day," but as a ritual practice, regulations often stymied efforts to "keep it holy." One Saturday, a commanding officer instructed a private to stand guard a little after 6 p.m. The soldier refused, citing his religious beliefs. The April Sabbath had not yet ended, and he could not work. Arrested and tried at court-martial under Article 90 of the UCMJ in 1953, Private Gilbert Gonzales argued that his refusal to obey a direct order was legitimate. He was a Seventh-day Adventist (SDA), and one of their fundamental beliefs was the Saturday Sabbath. The military, like most of American society, embraced a de facto ritual calendar in which Christmas was a federal holiday and Sunday the Sabbath. Not all religious Americans followed the same schedule, and the deviation in timing as well as terms of observance challenged military procedures. Even during times of relative peace, an hour-long service was one thing, a full day of rest quite another. An SDA chaplain testified to the authenticity and integrity of Gonzales's beliefs, noting that "when committed to military duties, we ask for the privilege of performing, on the Sabbath, only those duties essential for the preservation of human life or the alleviation of suffering."[17]

Religion arrived in the courtroom when soldiers or commanding officers did not or could not use the chaplaincy to solve problems through administrative channels. The reformation of the military justice system, including the incorporation of due process, created an alternative venue for adjudicating religious conflict. Private Gonzales got lucky: a chaplain's intervention and testimony from several non-SDA officers about Gonzales's character led to a nonguilty verdict. Indeed, it was "the unanimous opinion of this court that this case never should have been brought to trial." Yet statements about the futility of such cases were uncommon; most Seventh-day Adventists charged with disobeying direct orders on the Sabbath were convicted, though their sentences were frequently light.[13]

By the mid-1960s, courts-martial represented a common problem faced by Seventh-day Adventists, in part because their participation in the military accelerated dramatically but SDA ministers were new to the chaplaincy and therefore lacked significant administrative leverage. A mid-nineteenth-century millennialist group formed by prophetess Ellen G. White, the church grew into a denomination and, in the twentieth century, a global church. Longstanding suspicions of government combined with concerns about Sabbath transgressions, the immorality of murder, and the imperative to serve God (not the state) led Seventh-day Adventists to resist war service. They were not pacifists, however, and therefore could not legally acquire conscientious objector status in World War I. The 1918 "Resolutions of Loyalty and Service" articulated a stance of "conscientious cooperation" that promoted patriotic loyalty through noncombatant roles (e.g., medics). But Seventh-day Adventists recoiled at government chaplaincies because they "still involve governmental pay for religious services; still require that this pay for religious services be taken out of general tax funds; still create a class of governmental, or state clergy; still necessitate, unconstitutionally, a religious test for public office." From the SDA perspective, this perilous mingling of church and state, in which the chaplain served as a "morale-builder for our government," damaged both the church and the Constitution. Accepting a military commission bracketed conscience and limited speech so as to avoid a reputation as a " 'huckster of ecclesiastical eccentricities.' " Nevertheless, in the 1930s, Virgil Perry Hulse became the first SDA military chaplain, albeit one endorsed by Baptists, and during World War II, two ministers circumvented the church to become chaplains. The church began to modify its position on chaplaincies due to pressure from both the military and its own membership. Finally, in the 1950s, the General Conference resolved to "place no barrier in the way of Seventh-day Adventist ministers of maturity and high spiritual experience" who felt called to the chaplaincy.[14]

As the SDA church moderated its resistance to the military, its members entered the armed forces in greater numbers, but Sabbath challenges persisted. Carlyle B. Haynes, who monitored complaints on

behalf of the SDA War Service Commission, understood the difficulty. Viewing the Saturday Sabbath as "the seal of God" and the
Sunday Sabbath as "the mark of the beast" would, Haynes knew,
"produce religious contention"—something the church and the
military desperately wanted to avoid. As he informed Private Richard K.
Krieger, accommodations were feasible, but not required: "any privilege of this kind will have to be worked out with a soldier's immediate
superior officer." To avoid such negotiations, some enlisted in Project
Whitecoat, a top-secret biodefense experiment run out of Fort Detrick
that enabled Seventh-day Adventists to serve their country and keep
their Sabbath as noncombatant medical test subjects. Yet not every
church member wanted to serve as a human guinea pig, which left
many men subject to the authority of unsympathetic commanding
officers.[15]

Courts-martial of Seventh-day Adventists accelerated in the postwar
years, and these trials often hinged on disjunctures between religious
dicta and military procedure. Countee Johnson was stationed at Elmen-
dorf Air Force Base in Alaska when a member of the Anchorage SDA
Church convinced him to resume attending services. The lapsed Adventist returned to the church in December 1955, and after two months
of "faithful" participation when possible, the airman refused to bear
arms and requested Saturday leave. He did not get either accommodation, and the base chaplain informed Johnson that as a smoker and
drinker, he did not appear to be a genuine Seventh-day Adventist. His
pastor asserted that Johnson had conquered cigarettes and renounced
liquor, pronouncing him "100% sincere." Despite this testimony, when
charged with violations of Article 90 and 91 of the UCMJ—for refusing
direct, lawful orders to serve on Saturday and to bear arms—Johnson
lacked recourse. The base commander reviewed the file and determined
that "extenuating and mitigating circumstances [were] insufficient" to
drop the charges. Johnson had received the same leave as everyone else,
all of whom were "encouraged to regularly attend church services."
From the perspective of the air force, Johnson's desire for twenty-four
hours of leave, rather than the few necessary for worship, created the
problem since "personnel of all faiths must perform scheduled duty."[16]

The rigorous requirements of SDA Sabbath-keeping stymied the
church's negotiations with the military. In addition to maintaining a
sundown Friday to sundown Saturday Sabbath, the church defined the

day of rest as one in which members "honor God by attending divine services, by ministering to those in need, and by refraining from ordinary pursuits." This doctrine forbid members from partaking in routine work "such as receiving of pay, drills, attendance at inspections, and other services which could be cared for beforehand or postponed." Guard duty and indirect aid to medical staff, such as vehicle maintenance, constituted improper Sabbath work and often precipitated courts-martial. While the military understood its accommodations, like permission to attend church services on Saturday mornings, as adequate, Seventh-day Adventists found these limited adjustments insufficient.[17]

Seventh-day Adventists defined the Sabbath according to precepts more familiar to Jews than Christians, but American Jews rarely faced courts-martial for Sabbath-keeping. Fewer American Jews meticulously adhered to Sabbath regulations, but more importantly, long-established Jewish law elevated *pikuach nefesh* (saving a life) over ritual observance, even mandating violations of the Sabbath to save lives. The Jewish Welfare Board's responsa committee—which settled questions of Jewish law for the armed forces—determined that military needs could fall within this exemption. The committee even instructed rabbis to volunteer for the chaplaincy despite the possibility of desecrating the Sabbath because refusing to serve was "a sin . . . because of the effect such an evasion would have on the Jewish community." Communal standing compelled military service even at the risk of violating religious law. Over time, this strategy enabled access to state power that let Jewish chaplains navigate within the system.[18]

Jewish chaplains thus became an antidote to religious vulnerability, equipping Jews ensconced in the military with the capacity to discreetly resolve religious tension. When, in 1955, a Jewish soldier named John Freeman found himself in the same position as Private Gonzales—on the brink of court-martial for refusing to unload a truck on the Sabbath—he avoided a trial altogether. Much to Freeman's chagrin, an established network of Jewish chaplains integrated into the military command structure assisted him. He was disappointed, for he saw his predicament as "the perfect case, perhaps involving a revision of Army Regulation [and] in any case raising an almighty stink." Freeman wanted his obstinance to trigger policy changes but a Jewish chaplain convinced the staff judge advocate to drop charges and transfer Private Freeman to a different unit where his religious needs posed fewer problems. Aryeh Lev, who came to Freeman's unwanted rescue through his role as the head of the Commission on Jewish Chaplaincy after his wartime stint in the army chief of chaplains office, viewed the intervention as a success. According to him, this maneuvering vindicated Jewish cooperation with the state because the military had accomplished what no civilian organization had done. "The official recognition by the military of the three major faiths as equals, and the promulgation of regulations reflecting that recognition, seep down from the highest echelons of command to the bottom of the military pyramid," he wrote. "Today, as never before, Jews are accepted in America on an equal religious status with Protestants and Catholics." Lev placed his faith in the institutional infrastructure of the military, seeing the state as an agent of Jewish integration into American society.[19]

As a result, within the midcentury military, Jews behaved as American religious insiders, while Seventh-day Adventists retained their separatist sensibilities. They resisted the pragmatic approach taken by Jews, in part because of doctrinal strictures and in part because of lingering misgivings about state authority over religion. Courts-martial represented the cost of religious conviction and a litmus test for constitutional guarantees of church-state separation. The penalties arising out of convictions at court-martial were real, if typically mild. In Countee Johnson's case, the prosecution closed by declaring religion an unacceptable excuse for disobeying orders. "Gentlemen of the court, we are not all Seventh-day Adventists. We are not all even Christians. We have Mohammedans; we have Jews; and we have lots of Christian sects," he declared. "Certain laws govern[] military personnel of the United States . . . there has been no violation of religious scruples." The fact of religious pluralism would not spare Johnson; rather, the mere existence of religious diversity became a tool of exclusion, a rationale for maintaining, not changing, military law. Johnson's defense attorney could do little more than push for mitigation in sentencing, noting that Johnson acted out of genuine religious belief, not "evil purpose." In this he was successful, and Johnson bore a relatively light punishment: confined to base (but not the brig) for forty-five days and a fifty-five-dollar fine.[20]

An impregnable gap between SDA articles of faith and the military's understanding of religious necessity endured through the early Cold

War. In California, in 1951, Marine private Ralph Thomas Clark was court-martialed after refusing to draw his rifle. Found guilty of disobeying a lawful order and undermining good order and discipline, he received clemency due to the "firm and sincere belief of the accused in the faith of the Seventh-day Adventist" and "the clear cut absence of evil motive." In the late 1950s, the navy reasserted the need to limit religious accommodations, arguing that readiness obligations prohibited "fully assur[ing] Seventh-Day Adventists complete freedom for the observance of their Sabbath." In Hawaii, in 1964, Stephen Juhrs was docked forty dollars per month for six months after being convicted of disobeying a direct order to report to work on the Sabbath. After Juhrs's conviction, an SDA representative questioned how "the Navy would call working on a tug within the harbor during peacetime *essential duties* to the extent that they would court-martial a conscientious young man who is trying to be a good citizen of his country." Both church and state appealed to patriotic citizenship, but with the former requesting military accommodation and the latter demanding religious sacrifice, reconciliation appeared unlikely.[21]

If the court-martial pit religious doctrine against military procedure, the stakes were higher for some individuals—not because of their faith, but on account of their race. Trial transcripts indicate that judge advocates tried to impanel nonprejudicial juries by assiduously investigating knowledge of or distrust toward Seventh-day Adventists. Yet when Countee Johnson stood trial in Alaska and when Donald Hayes and Paul Williams did so in New Mexico, the Judge Advocate General (JAG) did not query potential jurors about another form of prejudice: race. In these cases, the Seventh-day Adventists were black men who had returned to the church or recently converted.[22] African Americans composed about 6 percent of the SDA's North American Division at the time, and black membership in and out of the United States was growing. If white church members probed the willingness of the state to accommodate their faith, black Seventh-day Adventists tested both military justice and religious advocacy. Less than a decade after the desegregation of the armed forces and years before racial equality became a military objective, Countee Johnson, Donald Hayes, and Paul Williams felt sufficiently comfortable to assert their religious beliefs and disobey direct orders to adhere to the tenets of Seventh-day Adventism. Whether religion empowered their actions as

racial minorities or their status as religious minorities distracted from
their race in court, their Church and, for at least a brief moment, the
military saw them first and foremost as Seventh-day Adventists.[23]

The burden of explaining unfamiliar religious practices fell on religious minorities, and the military often viewed their rituals as flexible
and subservient to military interests. The draft instigated certain conflicts, as conscripted Americans fought for religious rights to accompany
the obligations of citizenship. When turban-wearing Sikhs requested a
compromise in order to retain their headgear and maintain beards, military leaders disagreed about the proper decision. In 1953, the adjutant
general permitted a Sikh inductee to keep his facial hair but forbid him
from wearing a turban because it did not fit under a military helmet. To
reconcile the problem, the deputy chief of staff instructed the chaplaincy
to determine what, precisely, was mandatory for Sikhs. The chaplains first consulted an attaché at the Embassy of India, who assured
them that turbans were religiously compulsory, though "there is
nothing to prevent an individual Sikh from breaking these tenets of
his religion if he so personally desires." This choice would, however,
entail a cost, as it "would not be well received by his community or religion." At the same time, "under the mistaken impression that Sikhs
were a kind of Islamic sect," the deputy chief of staff's office spoke
with "an Arab official" at a local Ahmadiyya Fazl mosque, who stated
that turbans were "a matter of convenience." To counter this claim,
the army chief of chaplains "was finally able to secure a holographic
statement from a local Sikh" who testified that turbans were "tradition
and custom." Still uncertain about the religious laws governing turbans, the deputy chief of staff deemed them "impractical." Long hair
and beards acquired a different, and somewhat more flexible, standard based on the soldier's status. The enlistee had to conform to the
military's clean-shaven standards regardless of religious requirements,
while the conscript could keep his hair and beard. This distinction
recognized the coercion of the draft while ignoring that the enlisted
soldier might share the same commitments to religious devotion and
patriotism.[24]

The chaplaincy was more attuned to the inherent inequities of
granting religious privileges only to conscripts. In 1960, Muslim soldier Mustafa Yusuf faced a summary court-martial for "willful disobe-
dience of an order to remove his beard." Only after the conviction and

sentencing (fines, a reduction in pay, and a required shave) did the chief of the military justice system wonder if the chief of chaplains could offer any guidance. The ensuing conversation roamed far beyond the particularities of Private Yusuf's case and highlighted the importance of protecting religious minorities. First, the chaplaincy asked whether the order directing Yusuf to shave his beard was even "valid," given that it obstructed his religious commitments. Since draftees could adhere to religious grooming standards, Army Chief of Chaplains Frank Tobey (Baptist) suggested that the same policy could apply to others. Much like the arguments against the Buddhist B on dog tags, supposedly pragmatic prohibitions on facial hair collapsed when accommodations for some, but not all, failed to disrupt discipline. Tobey's memo underscored the importance of considering the spirit of military policies. "A commissioned officer is not expected to blindly follow the letter of regulations as a limitation to judgment. He is expected to use existing regulations as a guide to determine action in similar, though not identical, cases." Standard operating procedure, the chaplain's office proposed, did not excuse officers from considering a range of motivations, some of which might be protected as religious. If belief did not constitute a sufficient defense for refusing a direct order, then religious ignorance ought not support inappropriate commands. Moreover, because the army "extends itself considerably to observe the religious principles and customs of religious minorities," officers "should not ignore the minorities." As a matter of principle, though not necessarily a regular practice, the military could not protect the right to practice rites of majority faiths—including provisions for Jews to access kosher rations, for Catholics to observe fast days, and for Protestants to avoid training on Christmas—without extending the same basic rights to other faiths.[25]

Yet this argument for more expansive religious rights derived as much from political concerns as from first principles. Others had pressed for permission to wear beards, but the shadow of Cold War ambitions made Private Yusuf's predicament especially salient.[26] Tobey concluded that Yusuf's court-martial was "an infringement of his religious rights." The thorough investigation of the case included a discussion of the implications for public relations, especially any sort of letter-writing campaign "to Washington and abroad" that news of the court-martial might instigate. The concern related to distinct Cold War threats: Islam "is the religion of a large part of the world essential to the strength of the anti-Communist nations," and letting loose a flap over a beard could damage foreign policy. Warding off "a propaganda weapon of very great significance" swayed the army to make occasional allowances for religious deviance from military norms.[27]

Here, then, some of the limits of American religion emerged. If God was an American, it was not a God who sanctioned the rituals of all Americans. Global migrations of religious believers diversified American religious practices, which in turn required a reconsideration of standard military protocols. But formal policy changes proceeded unevenly at best. The chaplaincy could inquire and even advocate, thereby bringing unfamiliar religions into closer proximity, but it could not morph unfamiliar and forbidden practices into familiar and accepted rituals. Those changes would take more time.[28]

While Buddhists and the Eastern Orthodox fought to broadcast their religious identities and Seventh-day Adventists, Muslims, and Sikhs battled to practice their religious rituals, white evangelical Protestants began waging a campaign to remap the boundaries of religion in the armed forces. Between 1950 and 1970, the number of chaplains endorsed by the National Association of Evangelicals (NAE) tripled, from 40 to 129. This was intentional. The NAE determined that the chaplaincy's errant ecumenism would only be fixed when evangelicals reached the top of the chaplaincy hierarchy. The NAE represented thirty-five denominations, thousands of churches, millions of church members, and "believe[d] that only a spiritually united church can confront an unbelieving world." After its initial foray into the chaplaincy during World War II, the NAE set its sights on greater access to state power, viewing the military as both a mission field and an opportunity to internally influence government. Despite the NAE's emphasis on Christian unity, the military's capacious definition of Protestant did not meet their standards. In the 1950s and 1960s, the education of chaplains and of children living on military bases became heated arenas of disagreement in which the NAE contested the authority of religious rivals.[29]

Initially, the NAE chafed at the military's insistence on college degrees and graduate training for chaplains, but the organization took a different tack starting in the 1950s. Evangelical investment in education skyrocketed in the postwar years and middling Bible institutes became accredited educational institutions. Once the NAE could more easily supply ministers who met the military's requirements, it embraced those standards. By 1951, the NAE's Chaplains Commission agreed with Navy Chief of Chaplains Stanton Salisbury: "'I want chaplains that are as well-educated as any officer on the ship so that the Admiral, if in need, will feel free to visit the Chaplain for advice.'" The opportunity for a chaplain to advise a ranking superior was appealing. It aligned with Billy Graham's pronouncement of the chaplaincy as "one of the greatest missionary undertakings" and justified rigorous education. More pointedly, the group declared, "Some are of the opinion the educational standards are too high but . . . this Commission feels that the very best we can produce is none too good. At the present time let us take the long range view. Beginning now, students may take enough graduate theological work so that we, within four years, can adequately supply chaplains for this great mission field." Evangelicals would compete with mainline Protestants as educational equals—in organizational capacity if not prestige. With the handful of NAE-endorsed chaplains ballooning to over three dozen by 1950, the education requirements shifted from obstacle to asset, and the chaplaincy confirmed the NAE's place in American life.[30]

Once evangelical ministers could comfortably meet the military's credential requirements, the NAE turned its attention to those who could not. In 1960, the armed forces slightly increased education standards, demanding ninety semester hours of graduate training for all chaplains, no matter the denomination. This shift was immaterial for most faiths because seminary requirements exceeded the military's. For Mormons, however, the change was significant. When World War II ended, J. Willard Marriott, the LDS liaison to the military, convinced Army Chief of Chaplains Luther Miller (Episcopalian) to refine the guidelines for Mormon chaplains. Instead of a college degree and ordination, Marriott negotiated a college degree, a two-year mission, and "a record of continued activity in the organization of our Church." The military remained noncommittal about these concessions until 1950, when the Korean War rejuvenated the need for chaplains. By December 1950, both the army and the navy (but not the air force) had standardized the waiver of seminary training for Mormons and Christian Scientists, allowing them to substitute three years of civilian religious work (e.g., missions or teaching) for seminary study. Never-theless, as Chaplain J. P. Mannion (Catholic) noted, this information was "not stated in the Recruiting Service Instructions or other Re-cruiting Directives . . . for obvious reasons, we do not publish this in-formation in any manner." As with African American clergy during World War II, the military did not advertise its willingness to bend its own rules. By 1965, with the more stringent requirements in place, only five LDS chaplains remained. But escalating tensions in Vietnam meant more Mormons were drafted, and the General LDS Servicemen's Committee issued a "Statement of the Chaplain Problem" detailing the impediments LDS men faced in entering the chaplaincy. To dismantle these hurdles, they proposed that the military recognize their long-standing system of training, informal as it may have seemed, as equiv-alent to other modes of education. Alternatively, they advocated making LDS chaplains responsible for only LDS men. Church representatives approached the chiefs of chaplains, senators, and even the president to request accommodations; failure to enable LDS men to serve as chap-lains, they argued, "seems contrary to the American way."[31]

Not everyone agreed. The General Commission on Chaplains, the successor to the FCC's General Committee on Army and Navy Chap-lains, questioned the Mormon effort to bypass the education require-ments. While acknowledging that education waivers "must have seemed reasonable to the LDS Church," the General Commission noted that it "has created serious problems for other religious bodies. Some church representatives are so disturbed at this erosion of chaplaincy standards and seemingly unfair concession to a single group that they may make a public issue of it." The pre-1960 agreements between Mormons and the military mattered little once the perception of uneven standards flourished. In a letter to President Lyndon B. Johnson, the General Commission alleged that inadequate theological training hampered LDS chaplains and elaborated that even Southern Baptists "uphold these minimal educational standards." Similarly, Christian Scientists, who did not ordain clergy, had adjusted their practices to meet military demands and sent their chaplain candidates to graduate school, which was "beneficial." Marriott deemed the General Commission's letter "snippy" and responded with a religious rejoinder of his own: "The best teachers and most inspirational leaders are not necessarily the ones with the most college degrees . . . neither [Jesus] nor any of his apostles could have met the 90-hour requirement." Since the LDS church recommended only men with college degrees, Marriott averred, they were "not uneducated." This exchange, which allied liberal and conservative Protestants against Mormons, looked like an internecine squabble over formal theological training. But as a battle over government standards for clergy, it also contested who could be a qualified representative of American religion and what role the military should play in these skirmishes—mediator, dictator, or something else altogether?[32]

The NAE perceived Mormons as a great threat to military Protestantism and used the education requirement to pursue their simultaneous aims of evangelical influence and LDS exclusion. For evangelicals who had recently achieved the military's education standards, the absence of professional clergy made Mormons conspicuous targets. The NAE carefully monitored the courtesies extended to their rivals. One 1966 memo disclosed, "Reportedly, on order from higher authority, the Department of Defense has directed that 21 Mormon chaplains be accepted without the requirement of seminary training." The waiver was not new, but as awareness increased, it attracted scrutiny. "The Navy Chief of Chaplains consistently recommends disapproval of any candidate who does not meet the full educational requirements," but, they discovered, "three Mormons with no formal theological training have been approved."[33]

Against this escalation of an education arms race, the Mormon Church also began to adapt its approach to the military. Despite assurances from Army Chief of Chaplains Charles Brown (Methodist) that he would grant education waivers, the LDS Servicemen's Committee began to explore alternatives, notably through graduate education at Brigham Young University (BYU). A committee of BYU faculty who held commissions as reserve chaplains proposed a program of classes focused on religion and counseling. Two years later, in 1971, the LDS Church and the state agreed that coursework in clinical pastoral education would satisfy the military's requirements. While the Church resisted any effort to create a program parallel to seminary training of professional clergy, the military "reminded them that any of their *career* chaplains would be professional clergy and as such should be academically equipped to adequately function and compete with their peers." Despite the emphasis on lay leadership, LDS chaplains operated outside the church and inside the military, where their status as officers and role as professional military clergy demanded education. Satisfied by the Church's "willing spirit to do what they can do within the[ir] doctrinal position," the military ceased issuing education waivers. From 1972 forward, all military chaplains entered the service as college graduates and recipients of graduate training.[34]

For evangelicals, however, education remained a flashpoint of conflict. With the postwar growth of the defense industry, the military encouraged family cohesion by building more extensive family housing. In the air force alone, almost a million children lived on or near military bases by 1954. Similarly, between 1950 and 1960, the number of family members who moved abroad more than quintupled, to almost a half million. As a result, Sunday School attendance increased dramatically, with 85,000 children sitting on the registers of on-base Protestant supplementary schools by the mid-1950s. The chaplains' responsibility for teaching military dependents made a standardized curriculum desirable, for it would allow children to move from installation to installation without interruption. With the approval of the Armed Forces Chaplains Board (AFCB), a military-civilian committee convened to devise what became known as the Unified Protestant Sunday School Curriculum. Much like the chaplaincy itself, the Sunday School program needed to bridge Protestant differences, and rather than craft entirely new materials, the committee opted to mix and match existing materials available from commercial presses. The first prospectus, distributed in 1953, included units on the Bible, the Church, and Jesus from ten different denominations. The army and navy granted chaplains autonomy to choose or reject the prepackaged plans, while the air force compelled compliance through mandatory adoption by 1960. Over time, the military dispensed with variety in favor of a bidding system. In 1962, for example, the Southern Baptists won the contract because it was the most cost-effective. Yet this victory by Southern Baptists did not thrill the NAE because the AFCB still set the requirements. Evangelicals pushed to dislodge the Unified Protestant Sunday School Curriculum precisely because it failed to account for their doctrinal particularity. The Southern Baptists took the lead but still had to craft a sufficiently generic curriculum, which exemplified the NAE's critique of the chaplaincy: it was becoming "more regimented, [with] a greater emphasis . . . on uniformity."[35]

Inclusion in the chaplaincy forced evangelicals to see the state institution for what it was: an interdenominational, interfaith, and pluralistic space. This coercive religious camaraderie riled evangelicals, especially when it revolved around a "morals-centered rather than Christ-centered" theology. Their objection took an ideological turn as well. One correspondent alleged that the Sunday School text *Jesus and the Kingdom of God* "contained statements 'contrary to our United States concept of individual freedom and economic way of life.'" According to these evangelicals, the Cold War demanded a particular strand of anti-Communist Protestantism, a requirement the military's own materials failed to heed. Moreover, while a survey of active-duty chaplains included comments lauding the Sunday School program for "discourage[ing] narrow denominationalism," evangelicals thought the same curriculum ostracized "the 'conservative Evangelical' aspect of the Christian faith."[36]

White evangelicals became increasingly frustrated that the military seemed hell-bent on imposing liberal ideas, whether ecumenism or civil rights, on Americans. Much to the dismay of many conservative religious groups, in 1964 the military informed chaplains that they should not "participate in conferences or speak before audiences where any racial group is segregated or excluded from the meeting or from any of the facilities." Sixteen years after Truman desegregated the armed forces and twelve years after the Supreme Court integrated public schools, religious groups discovered that if God was an American, God did not condone segregated churches. One concerned citizen wondered if a chaplain could attend the (still segregated) Southern Baptist Convention. "Must a chaplain stop at the door of a church to determine that it is an integrated congregation before he may attend or participate or associate himself in any manner with that church?" The army conceded that chaplains could partake of segregated church events as an individual out of uniform but could not signal the imprimatur of the state in discriminatory religious venues.[37]

While few evangelicals were pleased with a spate of court cases that ruled government-backed religion in public schools unconstitutional, the court's reasoning offered evangelicals in the military a glimmer of hope. After the court struck down public-school-sponsored prayer in *Engel v. Vitale* (1962) and then forbid school-sponsored Bible readings in *Abington v. Schempp* (1963), an editorial in *Christianity Today* lambasted the military's Unified Sunday School Curriculum as equally suspect. "Surely it is clear," the magazine argued, "that this is a case in which a religious curriculum is prescribed and religious materials promoted by high military authority." While the goal of consistent curricula was laudable, the publication allowed, such "desirability cannot justify violation of religious freedom." If public school students could not pray aloud or read the Bible with a public school teacher, then military Sunday Schools seemingly violated the law as well. It suggested that the AFCB act only as an information clearinghouse, thereby allowing each chaplain, each Sunday school, and each family the ability to select their preferred ideas. (That the government paid the chaplain and provided the base chapel did not seem to matter.) Representative John B. Anderson (R-IL) entered the editorial into the Congressional Record where he expressed his "concern at this derogation of religious liberty" and requested "the discontinuance of the mandatory prescription" of the curriculum. If Anderson's plea echoed beyond the walls of the chamber, it faded to silence quite quickly.[38]

Had the NAE been willing to consider it, their best ally in pursuit of particularity within religious programming was their perceived antagonist: the LDS Church. Frank C. Kimball, the vice-chairman of the LDS Military Relations Committee, succinctly identified the military's conundrum, the effort "to bring about a suitable philosophy which is acceptable to most people and, they think, offensive to none." Lest chaplains "lose track of any denominational difference and succumb to the pressure for uniformity," he argued, his Church needed to provide ample resources to secure Mormon leadership in the armed forces. Finding space for Mormon worship was tricky, as the president of the New England Mission found when he asked Chaplain Albert Northrop (United Methodist) for use of the chapel at Loring Air Force Base in Maine. Fifty Mormon families lived there, 180 miles away from the closest church in Bangor, and they wanted to hold additional services and school. Framing the request in diminutive terms, the Mormons promised, "If approval is granted to this group, it will be understood that scheduling of services will not interfere with any of the activities of the three major faiths. . . . Supervision and manning of these services will be furnished by the membership, and no special funds or support will be required." Northrop was amenable to their request, in that he knew LDS Sunday services already met in the Chapel Annex, and he acceded to offering space for religious school once a week, "provided it is for a limited time only." He explained the restriction as necessary because a more frequent program "would imply a denominational education program" that was prohibited by policy since "there are well over 200 organized and recognized groups that could claim this privilege." Northrop's reservations anticipated the response Mormon inquiries to the chiefs of chaplains would garner. Deputy Air Force Chief of Chaplains Robert Taylor (Southern Baptist) "was most sympathetic, but he was unable to give us much help" because "the military services are beset with many requests from various religious denominations for the use of chapels on military posts" and regulations capped access to chapel space. If the military understood fine-grained religious distinctions as invidious, so too did many faiths find the erasure of difference deleterious.[39]

Compulsory "General Protestantism" so rankled the Mormon Church that by April 1960, it compiled a nine-point memo alleging religious discrimination. "Data and Documentation Relative to Denial of Religious Freedom to LDS Servicemen" highlighted a range of abuses, from limits on denominational services and prohibition of LDS Sunday schools to curricula and stringent qualifications for chaplains. What had been mere annoyance became a major predicament. The provenance of the problem, the document reiterated, lay in taxonomy. "Latter-day Saints are arbitrarily classified as general Protestants, though our doctrines, practices, and beliefs are wholly at variance with those of all Protestant churches." This echoed a larger point made by a columnist in the *Washington Post*: "The Armed Forces are trying to mold all Protestant churches into one all-embracing religion for American soldiers. Even such non-Protestants as the Orthodox, Mormons, Mohammedans, Buddhists, and Atheists are lumped with the Protestants and sometimes forced to receive 'general Protestant' instruction against their will.'" The NAE surely agreed, but neither those who claimed Protestantism nor those who denied it made much headway with the state's sorting scheme. And rather than working together to find a more satisfactory solution to their conjoined problems, the NAE and the LDS Church fought over and through the chaplaincy. The religious pluralism enshrined in the military chaplaincy for four decades teetered on the brink of collapse, disrupted by discontent believers. While Mormons hankered for recognition through demarcation, evangelicals coveted power through exclusivity.[40]

Frustration over loosely defined Protestantism mounted for the NAE's Chaplains Commission. Not only did the military continue to exclude evangelical literature from Sunday Schools, but chaplains conferences also avoided proclamations in Jesus' name. The NAE pled its case to Air Force Chief of Chaplains Edwin Chess (Catholic), imploring him to recognize that while "the matter has been camouflaged with a great deal of verbiage," an unfair mixing of religion and state remained. "Any system that permits the favoring of one religious literature to the exclusion of all others (even if it is for a very good purpose) can just as easily be employed to discriminate against individuals." Correcting course, the NAE contended in the 1960s, meant eliminating the preference for unified Protestantism. In their eyes, only by moving away from the ecumenism built over the past half century could religious liberty flourish.[41]

Chaplain Meir Engel (Jewish) was nearing the end of his twenty-year military career when he arrived in Southeast Asia in August 1964. The Vietnamese people he encountered dubbed him a curiosity. What, they asked, was a Jewish chaplain? Engel explained that a rabbi was a non-Christian priest, but the mess-hall waitress told him locals assumed "I must be kidding them and therefore this indicates that I am special." From the U.S. military's perspective, Chaplain Engel was special. By late fall, General William C. Westmoreland tapped him to become the American advisor to the Vietnamese military chaplaincy because he could cooperate with Buddhists "without worrying whether they are 'saved' or not." Engel was "non-missionary," "neutral," and removed from the "animosity and suspicion" that characterized the relationship between Buddhists and Christians in Southeast Asia. Yet mere weeks after he began meeting with Vietnamese clergy, Engel finished a late-night letter to his son, walked a painful mile to a military hospital, and collapsed. Felled by a heart attack before he could finish his mission, the Jewish chaplain left the army scrambling to decipher the religious worlds of Vietnam.[42]

A few months later, a 1965 War Games—a training exercise that simulated battle—confirmed what some officers already knew: Americans understood very little about Vietnamese culture and religion. As Marine combat units arrived in Da Nang that same month, Lieutenant General Victor Krulak, commander of the Fleet Marine Force, Pacific, worried that "we can win everything in Vietnam but the people, and suffer an abysmal defeat." The Marine Corps had relied on a combination of local missionary intelligence and the army's *Area Handbook for Vietnam*, a 507-page volume that offered basic background material on social, political, economic, and military conditions. Its anonymous forward asserted that it was neither "official" nor "definitive" and lacked either the "expressed or implicit" approval of the army. Comments and concerns, however, could be directed to the chief of staff for military operations. To better prepare Marines to engage respectfully with foreign populations and avoid alienating local allies, the navy appointed Chaplain Robert L. Mole (SDA) to study "Vietnamese culture, traditions, and religion in order to improve some of the cross-cultural tensions." The decision to deploy a chaplain as an investigator and translator of religious culture in Vietnam was especially important in the wake of the Buddhist revolt that toppled the Diem regime in 1963. The Catholic leader's crackdown on the nation's majority faith made religious knowledge vital as U.S. troops entered Southeast Asia, and Chaplain Mole's task became developing training materials to teach religious and cultural sensitivity to Americans.[43]

Mole was a puckish minister, a chaplain who took pride in his faith and his wit. After a two-year tour at Camp Pendleton as the base's first Seventh-day Adventist chaplain, he celebrated the reduction in courts-martial to zero, attributing the improvement to his counsel and recommending the church support more SDA chaplains as a preventative tonic. A certain jest matched his earnestness. Writing from the South China Sea in 1962, he joked, "I conduct meetings seven days a week—but suppose I ought not broadcast this lest someone accuse me of 'sabbath-breaking.'" At the height of Cold War espionage, he delighted in sending missives in the form of "molegrams" and signing his letters "Friend Mole" or "The Mole." Deployed to Saigon in 1965, Mole left his post at Camp Pendleton to study Vietnam *in situ*. Confident that his language studies (Arabic and Japanese) and missionary experience (in Lebanon and Cyprus) conditioned him to learn about new cultures and handle unexpected challenges, he told a reporter that his "on-site research mission" did not represent an effort to "Americanize the Asians." Rather, he insisted, "We're trying to help them reach their own goals. Of course, religion is the basic value decider of all humanity."[44]

With a clear assumption about the value of religion in place, Mole began his mission. While awaiting clearance to initiate "on-the-spot research" in Vietnam, he moved to Okinawa to read and ready himself for interviews in Southeast Asia. On the last day of August 1966, Mole arrived in Vietnam, excited to consult with chaplains and local missionaries. They took him to "a number of isolated and semi-isolated posts" from which he could study local people. In a late-September molegram, the chaplain reported interviewing 350 missionaries, 225 naval advisors, over a thousand Special Forces personnel, researchers, and civilian government employees to collect basic impressions of Vietnamese culture and religion. Although he never doubted the accuracy or utility of his local Western sources, he quickly deduced that his language skills were not up to par and requested an assignment that would allow him time to acquire new linguistic proficiencies off-duty. French, he determined, would produce more reliable information.[45]

Despite his limited access to local knowledge, Mole dug in. Along with Chaplain Richard McGonigal (United Presbyterian), a minister with a master's degree in sociology, Mole wrote a reference book, *The Religions of Vietnam in Faith and Fact*, that undergirded two lectures, "Religions in Vietnam" and "Religiously Based Customs in Vietnam," given to all pre-deployment personnel. Complete with flip-charts, discussion questions, and model simulations, these materials highlighted the United States' dual approach to operations in Vietnam: hard military force and soft personal engagement. The latter, military leaders hoped, would forestall the former. But to succeed, ground troops had to convince Vietnamese locals that Americans wanted to help, and that demanded respectful encounters with indigenous communities. Just as the Eisenhower-era People-to-People program attempted to promote anti-Communism through the cultural diplomacy of music tours, gardening exchanges, medical missions, and letter-writing campaigns, so too did the military's Personal Response Project (PRP) hope to cultivate "lasting friendship and willing cooperation of the Vietnamese people" by "engender[ing] in Marines a genuine concern and a deep respect for the Vietnamese as our friends, allies, and fellow human beings." As Chaplain Warren Newman (Disciples of Christ) observed, just as Marines "learn the tactical principles of an infantry sweep of an area, they can also be introduced to the principles of courtesy and respect which are appropriate in dealing with Vietnamese village chiefs, elders, and religious officials." Drawing on their experience as character guidance educators, chaplains assumed a new role as mediators between culturally ill-equipped American military personnel and Western-power-weary Vietnamese populations.[46]

These instructional bulletins attempted to depict religious differences and, unlike the *U.S. Army Handbook*, discuss the implications of such differences. Asking, "Do You Know About *Time Concepts in Vietnam?*" one worksheet compared the "circular time" central to Taoism, Confucianism, Hinduism, and Buddhism with a "linear concept of time" endemic to the Judeo-Christian tradition and the "American Way of Life." While the former revolved around a twelve-year repeating calendar that possessed "neither end nor beginning," the latter understood time as "a non repeating straight line with a beginning, an end and fixed important historical events." These explanations contrasted Eastern and Western religious traditions, but the PRP overlaid them with subjective characterizations. Linear time prompted Americans to improve themselves and resulted in a litany of goods ranging from the concrete—abundant food and medicine—to the more nebulous—a "sense of urgency and necessity of immediate productive action." In Vietnam, however, the "endless circle" of time impeded a rush to advancement and progress. Given the spiritual calendar and the adverse material conditions of "insufficient diet, diseases, and climat[e]," the cultural education series editorialized, "it is to the credit of the Vietnamese that this nation has achieved so much."[47]

Not all materials centered on condescending distinctions between the United States and Vietnam; some instructed personnel about holidays and equality across cultures. The PRP taught servicemen that Tet celebrated the new year, was a "special occasion to venerate ancestor spirits," and represented an "opportunity to gather as families." One sign proclaimed, "Respect your Vietnamese friend. Wish him a happy new year!" with appropriate phrasing in Vietnamese and in English transliteration, " 'Chuc Mung Nam Moi' (Chook Mung Nahm Moyee)." To emphasize how Americans should understand the holiday, the document concluded, "TET combines many of the secular features of American holidays and the religious features of Christmas, All Souls' Day, etc., with concepts of animism, Buddhism, Confucianism, and Hinduism. Each may contribute conflicting features and ideas, but all combine to make a valid holiday for our Vietnamese al-lies." Fit into an American religious and patriotic holiday scheme, the PRP attempted to vindicate a festival season and legitimize fraternal activities between servicemen and the Vietnamese.[48]

To improve encounters between soldiers and locals, Marines learned that cultural "booby traps" could be as dangerous as the physical ones planted by the Viet Cong. Because "citizens of the East and West are joined together as partners in a mutual struggle for survival," Ameri-cans needed to understand they shared the same humanity and basic needs as the Vietnamese. The *Unit Leaders Personal Response Handbook* amplified this point in discussion questions centered on interpersonal relationships, friendships, and the fundamental equality of all humans. When a Corporal Smith, for example, declared local villagers to be "animals" because they lived in huts without walls, the sergeant major challenged him, arguing that a closer look showed more signs of simi-larity than difference. Regardless of living conditions, the curriculum taught, both Americans and Vietnamese valued individual liberty and property. A chair hauled twenty miles to a clean hut, a photograph of a child, tools with which to fix the home—all of these symbolized how "everybody likes staying alive and they like being left free to run their own life. In this sense, you bet *your life* we're equal." Free-market capitalism mixed with cross-cultural knowledge to create a potent mo-tivational brew, or so some military leaders hoped.[49]

Impending war encouraged the American state to increase its aware-ness of and sensitivity toward Buddhism, but whether the program accomplished its goal to improve the empathy of American troops was debatable. For Chaplain Robert Radasky (Russian Orthodox), the program's success rested on the chaplain's investment. "After chaplains took steps to learn the culture, they were able to reflect an assurance about the situation which in effect counteracted casual rumor." Radsky confirmed that religion suffused Vietnamese daily life, which made the chaplain into an important resource "even before official action provided him with the tools." Familiarity with religion as a struc-turing agent in everyday circumstances, he argued, proved helpful even without Buddhism-specific knowledge. Chaplain William Asher (American Baptist) discovered plenty of chatter about the PRP, but not all of it positive or persuasive. "The 'Program' meets with varying de-grees of success of acceptance depending upon command attitude, proximity to combat, and an understanding of what the 'Program' is all about. Some Marines discuss it seriously, some with tongue-in-cheek, and some with animosity." Countering rancor was tough, if not impossible, because "some of them are incognito Viet Cong . . . Once a Marine sees a buddy killed by fire from a 'friendly' hamlet, he's not been receptive to the 'Program.' And the unscrupulous 'friendly' Vietnamese makes it difficult to trust any of them." With his Marines' concerns seeping into his evaluation, Chaplain Asher could offer only a mixed review.[50]

Chaplain Ronald L. Hedwall (Lutheran) had even more disappointing news. When he reported, "The program never got off the ground," a reader sarcastically scrawled in the margins "Great! Just Great!!!" The chaplain also underscored missing variables in any "civic action" or humanitarian program: first, "the tool for all of these would be a knowledge of the language," and, second, men have "been highly trained to kill, and not trained at all to assist." Yet while Hedwall identified key weaknesses in program design, he also touted increased compassion for the Vietnamese among his men. Words failed to capture this shift, for "social pressures insist that they be vocally anti-Vietnamese, no matter what their own private attitudes and actions are." But their behavior spoke of another story, of trained killers observing, engaging with, and caring for the Vietnamese they encountered. Elden H. Luffman, a Southern Baptist chaplain assigned to Chu Lai in fall 1967, confirmed the possibility of PRP when he worked with a hospital unit. There he found soldiers open to building cross-cultural relationships by "unselfishly ministering to the sick and wounded bodies of the Vietnamese people." After moving several hours north to a regiment based in Quang Tri, he was pleased to find "a tremendous Personal Response Program going." There, as a result of cooperation with two Vietnamese army chaplains, one Catholic and one Buddhist, the Marines taught English to and played basketball with locals. From this, he concluded that successful "'personal response' must be experienced rather than taught in a classroom." But when the First Marines moved inland, they were cut off from civilian populations and "all Vietnamese became the same—the enemy." The chaplaincy tried to unsettle American views of Vietnamese people and promote them as equals. But the impact of Chaplain Mole's program depended less on religious leadership and more on circumstances. Social pressures and command influence often eclipsed divine work, especially when God seemed to disappear in the jungles of Vietnam.[51]

Chaplain Reeve Brenner (Jewish) was offended. At a 1965 training conference, Chaplain Francis Sampson (Catholic) invoked Jesus at benediction before dinner. In a letter to the priest who would become the army chief of chaplains in two years, Brenner complained, expressing his dismay at sectarian prayer outside of worship and in an interfaith space. Sampson, whose experiences in World War II became the basis for the movie *Saving Private Ryan*, was not offended by Brenner's complaint, but felt his brash, youthful manner was "excessively aggressive, tactless, and over-inclined to take offense from a matter that was obviously not intended to give offense." Moreover, Sampson acknowledged that he tried to avoid infelicitous impressions by dropping Christ from prayers in front of Jews.[52]

Upon further reflection, however, he retracted his compromise because "every non-Christian certainly knows that a Christian has the right to pray publicly or privately (as the Jew or member of any other creed has the same right) according to his beliefs." Analogizing his prayer to the cross he wore on his uniform, Sampson asserted that symbols did not intentionally offend viewers, and the Jewish chaplain— like any other "Jew, Mohammedan, Buddhist, or any non-Christian" ought not infer derogatory meaning from either his insignia or benediction. Chaplain Brenner flinched at this interpretation, asserting that prayer was far more active than glancing at a piece of metal. Casting the senior chaplain as insensitive, Brenner explained, "for the Jew the worship of Jesus is idolatry" and urged Sampson to consider the military context. "Sectarian or denominational phrasing," he alleged, "violates the noble tradition of the Chaplaincy." The NAE's Floyd Robertson disagreed, as he grumbled about "the total absence of any reference to our Christian faith" at an air force chaplains conference in 1968, a situation he chalked up to the presence of Jews even though he alleged "I do not think our Jewish friends expect this type of restraint." Explicit permission for chaplains to offer sectarian prayers in public arenas would be a long and protracted contest, but the clash between religious Americans working side-by-side in the military was brewing.[53]

Floyd Robertson and Reeve Brenner would have agreed on one thing, however: those with religious power could wield it to suit their preferences. What Brenner saw as a personal offense and violation of military pluralism, Robertson viewed as victory for religious specificity and the legitimacy of overt Christianity. Sampson likewise viewed state recognition of Catholics as permission to offer its religious teachings in public prayers in public spaces. Although Chaplain Sampson found Chaplain Brenner's insistent claims unpersuasive, he also stood at remove from Floyd Robertson and other evangelicals' sense of tyranny. After all, Catholics enjoyed their own Sunday School curriculum, dedicated chapel space, demarcated worship times, and a robust chaplain quota. By the mid-1960s, as tensions in Vietnam swelled, the number of men conscripted soared, and anxieties about the morality of war intensified. Cracks in the edifice of a half-century effort to mold an acceptably multi-religious state institution began to show.

7

Moral Objection
and Religious Obligation

IT STARTED WITH a pair, two Vietnamese bodies ablaze in protest. An elderly Buddhist monk, seventy-three years into his life, took his last breaths while burning in lotus position on a busy Saigon boulevard in June 1963, and two months later, a young monk, barely into the third decade of his life, doused himself in kerosene and extinguished his life in Phan Thiet. Then there were three, a trio of Americans who ignited themselves to resist war. In March 1965, flames danced on the body of an eighty-two-year old German-Jewish emigré in Detroit after she took a match to her skin. Eight months later, the sun set as a thirty-one-year-old Quaker torched himself below Robert McNamara's Pentagon window, and a week later, a twenty-two-year-old Catholic Worker followed suit, searing himself as the sun rose at the United Nations' New York plaza.[1]

Thich Quang Duc, the septuagenarian monk, knew what he was doing. As the military's own Personal Response Project explained, the Vietnamese understood these human burnt offerings as " 'murder by oppression.' " His fire, quite literally, spoke. The venerable monk's body bellowed with "courage, frankness, determination, and sincerity," protesting the religious persecution of the American-backed Diem regime. Like the Buddha giving himself to a hungry lion to save her cubs from cannibalism, the monk self-immolated to safeguard Buddhism. Senator Frank Church (D-ID) discerned the message quite well. Reconfigured in terms more resonant with his Presbyterian faith, he viewed the "grisly scenes" of burnt Vietnamese flesh, captured on television and newsprint, as the fate of the Christians who marched into the great stadiums of the Roman Empire. Martyrs of the first and the twentieth centuries, vanquished while struggling to liberate their faith from imperial (and imperially supported) overlords. Norman Morrison, too, understood his suicidal political speech as a form of religious preservation, incinerating himself "'at the cruel edge of [the] five-faced cathedral of violence'" to convey the depth of his Quaker pacifism in the wake of an escalating war. "He was no fanatic," a friend explained. He was "just a religious man." What some clergy classified as errant sin, Morrison believed to be righteous sacrifice.[2]

In those years, the long 1960s, there were other fires to fight as well. In Alabama, Bull Connor's hoses and police dogs attacked African Americans fighting for civil rights. To segregationists, if not the protesters themselves, smoldering activist brush fires were turning quickly into a ferocious forest fire, an inferno water could not contain. In California, flames engulfed Watts as African American residents revolted against prejudiced policing, systemic unemployment, and substandard funding of schools and housing. Washington, DC, ignited as word spread that an assassin's bullet snatched Martin Luther King Jr.'s life, and citizens denied home rule howled through fire. Meanwhile, across an ocean, napalm and Agent Orange consumed Vietnamese villages, indiscriminately targeting civilians and soldiers alike. In response, draft cards burned, set aflame at rallies and set afire by the Catonsville Nine. The fire next time had arrived.

"Do I really *want* to be integrated into a burning house?" asked African American social critic James Baldwin in his 1962 meditation on race, rights, freedom, and faith. He possessed a keen awareness of the complexity of religion and politics: "In the realm of power, Christianity has operated with unmitigated arrogance and cruelty . . . [and] in the realm of morals the role of Christianity has been, at best, ambivalent." God was not dead, but God no longer appeared to be American. Even among those wearing chaplains' insignia on American military uniforms, religion was becoming politicized in new ways. Alert to the growing quagmire in Vietnam, other Americans began to reconsider the relationship between religion and politics. Belief was not enough; religion demanded action.[3] If America was a firescape, crackling with moral questions, religion often presented more questions than answers. The 1960s were a time of rupture, of interconnected domestic and global struggles for freedom, and the Vietnam War riveted and ripped apart the nation. Long and intransigent, the war pillaged American bodies, ravaged Vietnamese soil, and devastated all. In the interest of containing Communism, the United States spent a quarter century, billions of dollars, and thousands of lives chasing Northern Vietnamese soldiers and Viet Cong guerillas through jungles and over mountains.[4] None of these expenditures—of time, capital, or humanity—produced victory. Whether or not the 1973 ceasefire and the 1975 fall of Saigon represented military defeats or diplomatic stalemates, and whether or not the loss of political perspective and moral capital was gradual or immediate, military intervention in Southeast Asia polarized the United States.

But fiery demonstrations were neither the only way to resist state power nor the singular story of the cleavages of the Vietnam War era. Quieter battles, disputed through words, raged over the same issues. Many found older allegiances to God and country no longer harmonized. The pacifist doubts of the 1930s reappeared, with longtime supporters of the chaplaincy suddenly attacking clergy in combat boots, seeing them as an unacceptable entanglement of religion and the federal state and an unprincipled acceptance of imperialism. While new conscientious objectors looked to the courts for approval, many chaplains swiveled between denominational resistance to Vietnam and military requests for service. For military chaplains, moral fracturing was real and religious reckoning constant. Enmeshed in the armed forces and ever cognizant of the protests fulminating around them, clergy in uniform shipped out to Vietnam, where they spent twelve-month tours measuring—and sometimes doubting—their value. Chaplain Leonard L. Ahrnsbrak (Assemblies of God) confided, "As the gigantic footfalls of the Viet Cong mortars stomped their way up the ridge line toward our positions, I had to ask myself why in the name of common sense I was there." As the booming sounds fell away, the minister regained his composure. The voice of a Marine and the words "'Padre, I'm glad you are with us' reaffirmed the necessity of having been there."[5] The lonely soldier on a bombarded traverse occupied a critical place in the narratives about and debates over the chaplaincy in this period.

While some religious leaders rejected the chaplaincy as an instrument of a military involved in an immoral war, others deliberated whether their faith dictated that religious obligation to men superseded moral objection to war. For those chaplains, and for the religious groups supporting them, the central question of the Vietnam War was not whether God and country could align or must diverge, but rather should chaplains occupy a prophetic role or a pastoral one? Vietnam challenged religion in part by changing its meaning: war amplified the political consequences of religious convictions and pushed clergy to distinguish what was owed to God, to the state, and to men conscripted into battle. Chaplains strained to reconcile pure fidelity to God with complex responsibility to man, a struggle that inherently questioned the cozy relationship between religion and state enmeshed in the military-spiritual complex.

The commingling of religion and morality had long defined the chaplaincy, which assumed a clear and easy alignment of ethics and faith with religion and state. Vietnam publicly exposed the fault lines in these presumptions. When war provoked moral turmoil and signaled immorality, were clergy bearing rank and insignia sanctifying profane militarism and absolving the state of unconscionable conduct? As the Vietnam War wracked the nation, the military chaplaincy became a critical arena of conflict, a venue through which religious groups contested American politics, argued about moral priorities, and reconsidered their relationship to the state. At the center of these debates lay claims about the meaning and consequences of conscience—on individual, national, and global scales. With Vietnam dividing the country, chaplains and religious groups questioned the object of religious and ethical imperatives. To whom were chaplains obligated? For what causes or what reasons should clergy serve the military?

By the late 1960s, Chaplain John J. O'Connor (Catholic) found the growing opposition to war disheartening. A navy chaplain since 1952, the Philadelphia-born priest had completed a tour of duty in Vietnam in 1965, where he trucked along dirt roads in open jeeps to reach Marines. His work ethic was legendary, and his grime-caked uniform became an object of pride, a testament to an officer's service among foot soldiers. Once, when summoned to meet a "very spiffy" colonel who queried whether the grubby chaplain had been ministering to men, he lost his patience. " 'No, Colonel,' " he replied, " 'but I have a faithful corporal who takes my uniform out every morning and rolls it around in the dirt so that I can put it on before I come to see you.' " He was not insubordinate by nature, but exasperation could creep into conversations at the end of long days deliberating excruciating choices in Da Nang. "How do you keep close enough to the field hospital, where all casualties are brought, to be of any use to the dying, and at the same time tramp through the hills and valleys to meet the spiritual needs of the living?" he asked. "Do you turn to your all-knowing supervisory chaplain, ensconced virginally in the antiseptic halls of a crystal-palace headquarters? What if you are the supervisory chaplain and you live in a tent in a field hospital?" Present for some of the earliest troop buildups, O'Connor agonized over how to provide religious coverage to the Third Marine Division. As the army had already discovered, fighting in Vietnam did not resemble conventional warfare. Units dispersed over miles of treacherous terrain. Ministering to scattered personnel challenged the chaplains sent to Vietnam who learned, as O'Connor did, that few resources existed to guide them.[6]

As O'Connor meditated on his experiences in Vietnam, the antiwar movement gained strength. In winter 1965, President Lyndon B. Johnson unleashed Operation Rolling Thunder, a torrent of bombing campaigns north of the seventeenth parallel and, in March, sent in the first U.S. ground forces—Chaplain O'Connor's Marines. Although Congress had not declared war, the American public began to view the commitments of resources and people as something rather close to war. Dissent gathered strength on college campuses and spread across the nation. Religious groups joined the fray, and within the year the National Council of Churches (NCC), the American Roman Catholic Bishops, and the Synagogue Council of America, among others, passed resolutions calling for the pursuit of peace through negotiation, not bombs. Protestants, Catholics, and Jews warned American policymakers about "grave danger," understanding that "the present war in Vietnam may, in time, diminish our moral sensitivity to its evils."[7]

Religious leaders viewed themselves as acutely mindful of the moral questions of war, and it was a chaplain—William Sloane Coffin, of Yale—who broadcast the formation of the National Emergency Committee of Clergy Concerned about Vietnam (later, Clergy and Laity Concerned About Vietnam, or CALC) in 1966.[8] A number of Protestant, Catholic, and Jewish clergy gathered to engage cooperatively in the public politics of dissent. The ecumenical organization occupied a middle ground between religious pacifism and radical activism by advocating troop withdrawal from Vietnam and linking the antiwar and

civil rights movements. Above all, CALC thought its "religious, ecumenical, and nonpacifist nature made it more resistant than most antiwar groups to the public's negative attitudes" and thereby legitimized
its dissent as a religious and political necessity. A Protestant, Catholic,
and Jewish trio of CALC theologians published *Vietnam: Crisis of Conscience* in 1967. Presbyterian minister and World War II chaplain
Robert McAfee Brown, rabbi and civil rights activist Abraham Joshua
Heschel, and Catholic philosopher Michael Novak argued for diplomacy, rather than force, as the best moral option for extricating the
United States from Southeast Asia.[9]

The book, which sold 50,000 copies within the year, provoked Chaplain O'Connor, who viewed its antiwar claims as a personal rebuke. He
too understood the conflict as a harrowing moral crisis. But unlike
CALC, he viewed the commitment of ground troops to Vietnam as ra-
tional, humane, and necessary. He wrote his 1968 book, *A Chaplain
Looks At Vietnam*, as a direct retort to *Vietnam: Crisis of Conscience*, a text
he characterized as "misleading." American intervention, he asserted,
reflected "much more justice and sincere concern about the peoples of
Vietnam and all of Asia and all the world than self-aggrandizement, or
arrogance of power . . . much—very much—more anguished determination to achieve a just, enduring peace than to protract war." O'Connor,
who had completed graduate work in ethics at Villanova and was in the
midst of doctoral work in political science at Georgetown, agreed with
his opponents that "war is obviously an evil." But unlike the Catholic
peace activist Berrigan brothers, he did not equate that evil with sin.
As he explained to Navy Chief of Chaplains James Kelly (Southern Baptist) before the rear admiral participated in an event with Heschel, "as
far as I'm concerned, the Rabbi's arguments are strictly emotional. He
wants wars to end. Who doesn't?" O'Connor viewed the war as lawful,
in that it was not, in the parlance of Vatican II, total war or war "aimed
indiscriminately" at the obliteration of land or populations. Likewise,
he separated the morality of engaging in war from the morality of warfare. While he was willing to acknowledge that war tactics could be
inappropriate or disproportionate, he accepted American intervention
in South Vietnam as legitimate and just. War could be bitter, distressing,
horrific, and terrifying without being immoral.[10]

For O'Connor, the moral quandary posed by Vietnam centered on
the question of obligation: moral obligation to what and to whom?

"What binds us," he asked, offering a litany of options to consider: "International laws? Treaties? Pacts? Our word of honor? Private agreements between heads of states? Our real or alleged responsibilities as a world power? Self-interest? Public pledges to 'defend freedom' wherever threatened? A 'moral' obligation to defend the weak from the strong, the oppressed from the oppressor? A divine mission to contain Communism, or to lead the world?" These were the questions he wanted everyone to address, dissenters and proponents alike. His intent, he maintained, was not to disavow conscientious objection (CO) but to plead for all to parse the nuances of obligation. Despite his unwavering public defense of the military in Vietnam, O'Connor conveyed more subtlety when addressing the military hierarchy. Toward the end of 1965, he challenged the very nature of an instructive end-of-tour report. "The night has a thousand eyes. Vietnam has ten thousand faces. Every chaplain sees a different face," he wrote. "To write of 'the war' in Vietnam as viewed by 'the' chaplain, or to write of 'the' chaplain's ministry in the war in Vietnam would be to do a reader a disservice. I can write accurately of only one war in Vietnam, of very few of her faces, and of the way I personally attempt to function." In language lush and contemplative, O'Connor confessed the absence of a singular war that anyone could exalt or denigrate. His experience might be illuminating, but it was unique. When excoriating his antiwar opponents, however, this calm complexity disappeared in favor of obeisance to national leaders.[11]

In his fidelity to the chain of command, O'Connor exemplified his status as both a Catholic priest and a military chaplain, loyal to the hierarchy of the Church and the American state. Bothered by assertions that Lyndon Johnson acted with either "malice or stupidity," he retained confidence in political and military leadership. So long as the president honorably hewed to international law and treaties, there was no reason to doubt the validity of military engagement. "Safe legal grounds," the future navy chief of chaplains conjectured, yielded "reasonably safe moral grounds" from which to operate. Blind to the dubious logic of this claim—slavery, after all, was simultaneously legal and immoral— O'Connor trusted his superiors to relay "the facts" about U.S. intervention in Vietnam accurately. He would later regret publishing "a very bad book . . . a book I should not have written" while critiquing American involvement in Nicaragua and denouncing excessive military spending from his perch as Archbishop of New York in the 1980s. In 1968, however, O'Connor was "convinced that the administration has opted to accept the tragedy of war as the only available road to meaningful peace."[12] In contrast to the skeptical Americans who flagged evidence of the dubious legality of war, O'Connor accepted the administration's goals and information and refrained from airing any concerns publicly. In this way, he echoed the position taken by other ranking chaplains. Gerhardt W. Hyatt (Missouri Synod Lutheran), who became the army's chief of chaplains in August 1971, told a reporter, "A man of discernment has to give his government the benefit of the doubt."[13]

Other religious voices concurred that the Vietnam war was essential and moral, if challenging to reconcile with biblical mandates against murder. The National Association of Evangelicals (NAE) understood intervention against a Communist foe as a war for freedom, and "the price of freedom is always high." Army Chief of Chaplains Francis L. Sampson (Catholic) explained that violence was evil, but so was refusing to protect allies under attack. Even the evangelical periodical *Christianity Today* referenced the tension between violence and faith felt by God-fearing Americans: "Chaplains and lay leaders alike say the major issue raised constantly concerns the morality of war and the killing and maiming that goes on in war. In short," the article asked, "can a serviceman serve God and country?" Interviews revealed that, with a few exceptions, most "searched and struggled deeply" to find answers.[14]

In previous twentieth-century wars, alignment between God and country had kept all but the most committed pacifists at bay. Vietnam raised new questions about individual complicity in state action, and chaplains found themselves in the middle of these debates. Although Chaplain O'Connor latched onto the morality of Vietnam with full fervor, other chaplains expressed less certainty. By the late 1960s, antagonism toward war had so pervaded American society that the navy chief of chaplains—himself an ardent believer in the "God-centered morality" of the war—surveyed his corps to ask if they "consider[ed] American participation in the war in Vietnam to be morally right or wrong." Officially, chaplains repeatedly asserted that Americans in uniform knew why they were fighting. Chaplain Preston Oliver (Presbyterian U.S.) bracketed the festering antiwar movement by declaring "our men in Vietnam are not too much involved with these issues" because "they are busy doing a job, and they do not feel it is their business to second-guess the rationale behind our mission." Moreover, he credited this approach as a manifestation of high morale: Marines "believe what they are doing, hard though it is, is right and necessary." Brutal combat ultimately helped the Vietnamese, Chaplain Loren Lindquist (Congregationalist) insisted. Improving "the future welfare of the Vietnamese gives meaning and purpose" to servicemen, especially because "communist aggression is sinister and real." As a battalion chaplain, Roy Grubbs (Church of God) offered the navy chief of chaplains some grist for a news conference prior to the Tet Offensive in January 1968. Grubbs portrayed Marines as stalwart political saviors, full of respect for the South Vietnamese as "creature[s] of God" harassed by the North Vietnamese army and Viet Cong guerillas who failed to "recognize the essential dignity of each human being." In this Manichean duel, the Marine "is very much aware of this threat to the peace and security of both South Vietnam and the entire free world."[15]

But letters, surveys, and end-of-tour reports furnish a more textured and knotty perspective than a simple fight for freedom over tyranny. At a 1967 nuclear training course for chaplains, the clergy carried on "a free and open—and heated!—debate" about the war. In Vietnam, Chaplain Frederick Arneson (Lutheran) detected complexity among his congregational flock: "The truth is, we may not be unanimous in our motives for being in this country, but we are here—we did not stand idly by and talk." United by a sense of action, the group cohered, but not because they agreed on intentions or purposes. When explaining the necessity of chaplains clambering aside Marines in the field, Chaplain Leonard L. Ahrnsbrak (Assemblies of God) repudiated the image of a lock-step parade of stoic freedom fighters. "The Church is concerned with man's struggle with himself, his fears, life and death," the chaplain commented, "and during operations men do a good amount of struggling in this regard." Neither the mandate to kill nor the prospect of death felt natural, even among those drilled to obey instructions and follow the leader. Chaplain Paul Pearson (United Methodist) speculated that regular encounters with death explained why the troops his unit replaced "seemed to be bitter and hostile." Mines and snipers, not to mention mosquitoes and cobras, tested the resolve of battle-hardened and battle-weary troops. Even when Marines entered Vietnam with clarity of conviction, their tours of duty could snatch it away.[16]

While questions about the role of chaplains in Vietnam percolated, clergy grappled with the anxieties and effects of combat on their psyches. Chaplain John J. Scanlon (Catholic) had an eventful tour chock full of near-death experiences. He acquired an array of practical knowledge: how to steer clear of heavy vehicles in rice paddies, stay hydrated in oppressive heat, avoid being a sitting duck in a Viet Cong shooting gallery, hold counseling sessions during monsoons, continue a service after a chapel collapsed in the gushing rain, and fashion an altar out of used artillery ammo boxes. When reassigned to a medical battalion after nine months in the field, he shuddered and shivered, approaching his new duty with "fear and trembling." His concern was warranted as the relative quiet was a mirage; death interrupted each and every day. Work was hectic and exhausting, for "the dead and dismembered (a highly abstract term), the seriously wounded and the slightly wounded, the neuro-psychiatric cases, dismembered emotionally and mentally—the inevitable product of violent killing, those afflicted by diseases native to this country—all these, as well as the doctors and corpsmen, form the congregation of the Field Hospital Chaplain." The physical exhaustion of combat seemed elementary compared to "the strain of absorbing so much human hurt," a fundamental task of chaplains throughout a century of war.[17]

Although chaplains attempted to alleviate physical and emotional pain with prayer and counsel, many soldiers self-medicated with drugs, finding more solace and comfort through consistent opiate use than regular worship. Addiction and drug-related problems skyrocketed with the easy access to narcotics in Vietnam, but few chaplains possessed any expertise in substance abuse. Chaplain Peter J. Cary (Catholic) admitted as much when he stated "drugs were readily available, according to the hearsay, some of which are exotic varieties not commonly found in the United States." Unable to even identify the type of drugs his Marines inhaled, Cary struggled to reach his men. The uneven application of navy regulations made discipline even more challenging because "the almost universal response of the 'pot-smoker' is that smoking marijuana is no worse than getting drunk, in fact better because there is no hang-over."[18]

Other chaplains developed a deep knowledge of the intricacies of drug manufacturing and trafficking, however. Chaplain Dell F. Stewart (Catholic) learned that Da Nang locals mixed marijuana with opium in extra-long cigarettes. This was a potent mixture, "definitely habit forming because of the opium." A single search-and-seizure operation in one mess hall unveiled a daily haul of more than 7,200 joints, a far cry from the 200 reported by an informant, and easily moved by an informal network of American and Vietnamese food purveyors and garbage collectors. Facing an increasing number of drug-addled men, a trio of Navy chaplains crafted a plan for a Chaplains' Relevance within Emerging Drug Order team, or CREDO as it came to be known (Latin for "I Believe"). To counter the effects of "youth drug culture," the program sought to train chaplains in drug counseling. The larger goal was to build "a supportive, non-threatening place where the drug involved Navyman may make the initial moves toward health through self-initiated inquiry." Assuming that "despair" prompted drug use, the program channeled the spiritual "inner life" to operate as an antidote to narcotics, an effort to recover "the worth and personal dignity of the individual." Whether or not the amalgam of twelve-step programs and therapeutic religion addressed the burgeoning drug issues in Vietnam, CREDO nevertheless expanded the chaplains' portfolio.[19]

Equipping men to handle life in the killing fields similarly required the influence of clergy, according to Chaplain John J. Glynn (Catholic). He arrived in Chu Lai in June 1965 and served with Marine combat and medical battalions where, he asserted, chaplains brandished moral restraint. Over the course of his year in Vietnam, he noticed that the assigned clergyman "is most likely the only voice in his unit who will appeal to his men to show consideration for the native population solely on the basis of charity and human dignity." Without the chaplain's guidance, then, Marines might fail to see the Vietnamese as people, which would hinder "our ultimate goal in Vietnam, the right of people to live as they choose." Drawing on Catholic social teachings that emphasized humans made in God's image as the moral foundation of society, Chaplain Glynn transformed military and political operations into religious and moral work. The political aims of U.S. intervention in Southeast Asia—warding off Communism and implanting democracy, by whatever means necessary—depended on moral conduct. In this rendering, chaplains provided critical instruction. The chaplain reminded his men of "what is often difficult to see in the midst of war—the value of the individual life, Marine or Vietnamese." Men of the cloth might summon what men in fatigues could not: moral courage, the audacity to behave ethically during a nightmare—or so the military and chaplains hoped.[20]

The effectiveness of chaplains as moral vanguards became ever more suspect when atrocities such as the 1968 My Lai massacre became public. On the morning of March 16, 1968, American soldiers mutilated, raped, and murdered upwards of 500 unarmed Vietnamese civilians in the hamlet of My Lai. Despite an American witness, officers covered up the war crimes.[21] When the American public learned that soldiers slaughtered civilians, Robert McAfee Brown cried out, "Where were the chaplains?" As a World War II chaplain, he assumed military clergy stood as moral pillars of American might, restraining the worst of human instincts in war. As a leader in the religious antiwar movement, he expected chaplains to suppress brutality, to insist on moral conduct, even in an immoral war. The state had never commanded chaplains to assess the ethics of killing, but, the theologian's question demanded, what good were chaplains if they did not prevent atrocities? No chaplains participated in or directly witnessed the carnage at My Lai, but Chaplain Carl Creswell (Episcopalian) overheard the plans to "level the village" if necessary. He claimed to have interjected, "I didn't think we made war that way," but said no more. Subsequent investigation revealed that Hugh Thompson, the helicopter pilot who reported the slaughter and tried to stop the massacre, disclosed what he saw to Chaplain Creswell, who informed Division Chaplain Francis Lewis (Methodist) but bypassed other officers in his unit. Chaplains, in other words, could have challenged the cover-up, if not halted the killings. The publication of the Peers Commission report in 1970 made moral culpability impossible to deny, elevating what the *New York Times* dubbed "the perils of serving two masters." What Chaplain Glynn characterized as principled duty to God, country, and men, other religious leaders scorned as warped loyalty. Any support for an immoral war risked elevating mechanical patriotism over prophetic leadership. Yet the dichotomy between obligation and objection was rarely that simple or clear.[22]

More than many other chaplains, veteran Rabbi Roland Gittelsohn (Jewish) understood the plight of conscientious objectors. A former pacifist turned padre in World War II, he knew Judaism did not compel conscientious objection. But when asked by draft boards to "authenticate the assertion by young Jews that Judaism validated their refusal to participate in military activity," he did so easily. As the former Marine chaplain told his Boston congregation in 1970, "Judaism gives even higher priority to responsibly motivated conscience than to government and law." Successful abstention from service in the armed forces depended on government-granted conscientious objector status. But what exactly counted as conscience rattled antiwar activists and draft boards alike. When the United States entered Vietnam, legal conscientious objection required a total rejection of war stemming from an individual's faith in a "Supreme Being." Relatively capacious in its description of religion and categorically strict in its enmity to combat, the Selective Service guidelines became a political and legal battleground as draft calls expanded, inductions soared, and resistance to American militarism surged. World heavyweight boxing champion Muhammad Ali, a convert to the Nation of Islam, declared himself a conscientious objector, but neither his local draft board nor the Department of Justice accepted his claim. Stripped of his crown, banned from the ring for three years, and enmeshed in a protracted lawsuit, Ali surrendered his livelihood for his beliefs. His was one of several conscientious objection cases that reached the Supreme Court in the 1960s, forcing the justices to scrutinize religious ideas about war, the nature of conscience, and the relationship between conscience and religion.[23]

Through Vietnam-era draft cases, the federal judiciary redefined conscience—and with it, religion—by slowly severing ties between conscience and religion to craft a capacious interpretation open to believers, agnostics, and atheists alike. Antiwar convictions and opposition to the draft were time-honored responses to war, but resistance to imperial endeavors took on new urgency in a world ordered by Cold War lenses and colonial frames. Consensus on the morality and legitimacy of the Vietnam War hardly existed within the political elite, much less the citizenry as a whole. Even the NAE's Chaplains Commission, which generally supported American military endeavors, described their men as "appalled at how complex the problems are at all levels."[24] While the American state remained cagey about the soul's role in buffering patriotic obligations, the definition of "conscientious objection" nevertheless evolved over the twentieth century. Initially, conscientious objection required belonging to a historic peace church such as the

Mennonites or Quakers. By World War II, the state cut the tie between conscience and church (or synagogue or mosque) membership and accommodated individual religious objectors by providing two options: noncombatant military service or civilian public service (generally in conservation, prisons, or mental hospitals). Revised again in the postwar period, the law defined religion as "an individual's belief in a relation to a Supreme Being involving duties superior to those arising from any human relation," but explicitly excluded "political, sociological, or philosophical views or a merely personal moral code." In *U.S. v. Seeger* (1965), the court expanded conscientious objection to include those whose beliefs "occup[y] in the life of its possessor a place parallel to that filled by the God of those admittedly qualified for the exemption." Five years later, in *Welsh v. U.S.* (1971), a plurality of the court decided that "deeply held moral, ethical, or religious beliefs" justified conscientious objection, thereby granting nontheistic moral reasons the same status as religious values.[25]

For many Americans, Vietnam represented war-mongering on an unprecedented scale and a quandary that wholesale religious objection could not resolve. American religious groups tended to express distaste for war—it was horrible, unfortunate, and detestable. But with the exception of explicitly pacifist faiths, denominations struggled over the boundaries of acceptable war. There were times, most notably World War II, in which war was necessary and religiously justified. But Vietnam teetered on the narrow edge of a rocky cliff, its grasp on legitimacy far more slippery than earlier military endeavors. The objection was not, as the draft law permitted, to all wars but to this particular war. These believers embraced a position of selective conscientious objection: their conscience, their moral instincts, their ethical scruples stipulated draft resistance, but only sometimes.[26]

Vietnam therefore prompted American religious groups to address their stances on conscientious objection anew. In Jewish communities, rabbinical courts long functioned as authorities on religious dilemmas, ranging from ritual practice to business dealings, while matters of national policy rarely entered their orbit. But as in the rest of American society, "this nightmare of Vietnam" birthed doubt about the ethics of militarism. The Boston *Beit Din*, or rabbinical court, acknowledged that it could not make a "definitive finding" on the morality of Vietnam but still engaged in ten months of study on the question of conscience. What constituted conscientious objection and was it allowed? Given cases like *Seeger* and *Welsh*, "does Judaism make a distinction between religion and morality?" The *Beit Din* deferred to the Supreme Court on the legality of war but insisted that individuals and communities retained the power to question state action. Indeed, for the rabbis, dissent symbolized a robust, secure nation, not a fragile, weak one. They accepted selective conscientious objection as valid while offering a nuanced stance on Vietnam. Biblical sources instructed "do not stand idly by the blood of thy neighbor" (Leviticus 29:16) and "man is his brother's keeper" (Genesis 4:9), thereby defending—at least in theory—some intervention. However, the court also recognized the fallibility of the state, noting that the government's authority to conduct war "is not a mandate to violate the basic principles of justice and morality." As to the relationship between religion and morality, the rabbis concluded they were interdependent, even when the connection to God was faint: moral action, no matter the rationale, expressed religious values. For Judaism, a religion rooted in conduct—ritual, practice, and behavior—this seemingly twisty logic was perfectly straightforward: noble deeds need not originate in religion to be religious.[27]

With approval from religious leaders, conscientious objection began to infiltrate the ranks, much to the dismay of chaplains who had to advise the men that Chaplain Jack Brown (Southern Baptist) deemed "reluctant" soldiers. Regulations stated that personnel seeking discharges on grounds of conscience had to undergo an interview with a chaplain who would evaluate the individual's sincerity and assess "whether the individual's objection to military duty is based on religious beliefs." The shift to acting like a local draft board was often uncomfortable. Chaplain Ronald L. Hedwall (Lutheran) felt ill equipped to address the qualms lodged by an African American soldier who, based on his own inquiries, had "adopted the view that we, as a nation, were wrong in being involved; and that he, as a Negro, had no business being involved." The soldier understood the history of American intervention in Vietnam "in quite an opposite way" than the chaplain did, which left Hedwall "greatly handicapped in my ability to counsel him." And this was not an isolated incident. Although a Presbyterian chaplain maintained that "no chaplain can decide whether the protesting soldier is right or wrong in his decision," Chaplain Brown spared no spite in addressing dissent in his midst. He disapproved of the "negative influence" of the antiwar movement infecting combat-ready units. "I have little patience with men I consider cowards," he wrote in his journal on May 11, 1968. A few months later, all he could do was exclaim: "Gracious! . . . What a demanding ministry" in reference to those who threatened to renounce their citizenship, write to their congressmen, and inhabit a "defector's attitude."[28]

Despite his antagonism toward conscientious objectors, Chaplain Brown also recognized that reconciling deep Christian faith with the violence of war was arduous. Prior to arriving in Vietnam, he wrote "The Question of Jesus and War" to address how Christian Americans could resolve this dilemma. Lessons from the Bible provided a path, if not necessarily a marked trail. Tracing moments of anguish and anger—from Cain's outcry "Am I my brother's keeper?" to Jesus's admonition to aid the downtrodden—Brown found a script justifying military intervention. In contrast to the Boston rabbinical court's interpretation of Cain and Abel, the Southern Baptist minister framed the vexed war as an instance of "defending with whatever means is necessary against those who strike my brother, whoever and wherever my brother might be." Filial protection required confronting the Communist menace. Not only could the United States fight in Vietnam, but it should. With obligation came sacrifice, most often through American lives and bodies, and this sacrifice demanded absolute respect, not protest. Brown made a place for the "patriotic pacifist," the religious believer who refused to bear arms but accepted noncombatant service. For him, this represented responsible pacifism, a position distinct from the reams of draft dodgers, antiwar protesters, and Canada-bound dissidents who engaged in "irresponsible citizenship." Through lenses both religious and political, the chaplain carefully distinguished the righteous from the sinful, the accountable from the culpable, and the patriotic from the traitorous.[29]

Bob Cohoon was one of those men whom Chaplain Brown would have considered a nuisance, if not a full-fledged derelict. Stationed in San Antonio when he realized he could not continue to serve in the military, he requested a discharge for reasons of conscience. When his commanding officer did not release him, he went AWOL. He explained himself to fellow members of the San Antonio Committee for Peace and Freedom, saying that "the Army suppresses anti-war activities" and "I was being denied my rights of free speech and freedom of religion by Army harassment." What Chaplain Brown took to be cowardice and betrayal, many in the antiwar movement saw as strength of spirit. As J. Harold Sherk, a Mennonite peace activist, explained, conscientious objection "may require moral stamina of an unusual kind" because "the service of God and humanity may lead him to unusual hazards."[30]

These hazards extended to chaplains themselves. While clergy chose to enter the service, they too could question the morality of war. Chaplain Harry Schreiner (Jewish) wanted to catalog unmitigated devotion among his fellow clergymen, but exchanges with newly inducted chaplains "reveal[ed] that a minority of the above have serious doubts about our situation in Vietnam. They are disturbed by the 'credibility gap' in govt. circles. . . . They question the moral issues." Indeed, Chaplain Stephen Levinson (Jewish) agonized about how to handle his service obligation in light of his growing ethical aversion to Vietnam. As soon as the Central Conference of American Rabbis validated selective conscientious objection, he requested a discharge because of the "deep, personal distress" the war provoked.[31]

As religiously grounded conscientious objection took root among soldiers and chaplains, the Vietnam War exposed the military chaplaincy's greatest weakness: the potential irreconcilability of religion and state. This threat, silent since the "good war" of World War II overcame the concerns of pacifists in the 1930s, roared back to life. While some Jewish chaplains struggled with the specific dilemmas kindled by Vietnam, Chaplain James R. Forte (Presbyterian U.S.) identified why allegiance to God and country was far more precarious than boosters declared. "Jesus Christ knows no national boundaries. The military establishment knows *only* national boundaries. And the chaplain is part of that establishment."[32] To be an officer in the U.S. military was to obey a human commander-in-chief, and yet God, the ultimate authority, heeded no state loyalties. God might inspire the Geneva Convention but did not obey the boundaries of the demilitarized zone or disperse napalm. As the valence of good—or at least necessary—war slipped away, the military-spiritual complex and its once conjoined dual loyalties to faith and to nation no longer operated quite so smoothly.

The Commission on Jewish Chaplaincy (CJC) was in a bind. It mustered barely 81 percent of the seventy-three-chaplain quota it promised to supply to the military. Already twelve rabbis short, the group knew it would lose an additional fourteen men as they completed their tours of duty in 1966, thus bringing the total of Jewish chaplains owed to the armed forces to twenty-six. With the war in Vietnam escalating, protest proliferated and rabbinical students at Yeshiva University (YU), the Jewish Theological Seminary (JTS), and Hebrew Union College (HUC) more vociferously resisted military service. The men who intended to become American rabbis had no obligation to enlist; they held deferments as students and then exemptions as clergy. The CJC, a subgroup of the Jewish Welfare Board, saw the situation differently. Since 1950, the CJC had operated its own internal draft to provide the military with adequate rabbinical representation, with the seminaries of the three major Jewish movements each furnishing one-third of the military's quota for Jewish chaplains.[33]

Vietnam broke this system. By the mid-1960s, more and more rabbinical students were filing statements of conscientious objection to war and thus refusing to volunteer as noncombatant chaplains. The burden of the chaplaincy fell disproportionately on young, single, fit men—for the CJC's draft followed the contours of the Selective Service in separating men by marital and parental status. Most Orthodox YU students were married and unaffected by the draft, but the very small proportion of affected students became some of the most vocal draft resisters. By winter 1968, YU pulled out of the CJC draft, and the Conservative Movement's Rabbinical Assembly (RA) followed suit. In 1966, the RA had proclaimed, "the American rabbinate cannot shirk its responsibility in providing chaplains." At its annual convention in March 1968, the organization took a radically different position. No longer concerned with "shirking responsibility," it adopted the report of its internal Committee on Chaplaincy, which asserted, "The present system of drafting men into the military chaplaincy is morally untenable." With a mere sixty-six Jewish chaplains in the military and fifteen to be released over the summer, the CJC could rely only on the three campuses of HUC. The Reform movement's reluctance to remove its students from the chaplaincy would, in the words of the RA, produce "a sharp crisis of conscience with which we must reckon."[34]

Although the number of seminarians was small, they were vocal, articulate, passionate, and enmeshed in a much larger, national debate about the ethics of "selective conscientious objection," the tension between objection and obligation, and the meaning of freedom in a democracy. They were at once part of the mainstream and sitting at its periphery. They grappled with collusion in the violence of war as students within a Jewish movement whose political orientation was generally antiwar but whose communal commitments demanded sacrifice. They questioned the role of the military chaplain, wondering if they could accept a position that, for fifty years, the American Jewish community had seen as a badge of American religious legitimacy.

The HUC debate over conscientious objection and the military chaplaincy hinged on the meaning of morality. When announcing new registration procedures in 1965, Nelson Glueck, the president of HUC, had framed the chaplaincy as "a moral obligation for all eligible graduates." Whereas the Conservative movement had initially posited the chaplaincy as a responsibility to American Jewry, the Reform movement's Central Conference of American Rabbis (CCAR) insisted that the chaplaincy represented an ethical imperative. A 1966 memo further elaborated, "We are all mutually obligated to provide sufficient Jewish chaplains for the needs of our men and women in the armed forces. . . . All personal desires must inevitably bow to this obligation and need." Although the military focused on chaplains' ministry to all personnel, the appeal to Jewish need was not vacuous. Marine chaplain Richard Dryer (Jewish) reported traveling extensively over the Da Nang–Chu Lai–Phubai area in order to serve "mobile and widely scattered" Jewish personnel who, despite grueling "combat patrols and similar missions," achieved a 90 percent attendance rate at services. An additional Jewish chaplain, Dryer noted, would not only improve outreach to Jews but also free up the Christian chaplains who had been pitching in. The CCAR's position did not reflect the outlook of rank-and-file Reform rabbis, but it raised the stakes of resistance. The imperative to staff the military chaplaincy stemmed not from patriotic commitment but from moral duty and Jewish communal obligation.[35]

The CCAR's stance echoed that of Protestants embroiled in commensurate disputes about the moral dilemma of the military chaplaincy. World War II chaplain and head of the CCAR's Chaplaincy Committee Bertram Korn informed students, "Chaplains are not propagandists, and they do not give religious sanction to war." Similarly, an editorial from the NCC's General Commission on Army and Navy Chaplains asserted that the role of the military chaplain "does not constitute or imply an endorsement of war in general or of any wars in particular." Rather, it continued, chaplains operated "as morally responsible men" and thus remained "alert and sensitive to conditions of needless inhumanity and unlawful acts of war which might compromise their nation or undermine their own integrity and witness as ministers of the Gospel." Military employment did not sabotage the chaplain's own religious training or moral standards. Rather, the chaplain served watch, guarding the military from itself, from proclivities toward reckless and unnecessary violence that threatened both God and country.[36]

Rabbinical students did not find this line of argument compelling. In 1965, the CCAR Chaplaincy Committee received its first petition "in a number of years" for an exemption on the grounds of conscientious objection (CO). From the LA campus of HUC, Louis Feldman wrote that he was "completely opposed to the use of military force under any circumstance" and that he objected to the chaplaincy because "such noncombatant roles . . . make the combatant soldier possible." Less than a year later, Richard Lavin filed his claim for CO status, noting that his politics and his religion were indivisible, and "paramount in my religious convictions is a belief in the dignity and holiness of human life." As a result, he argued, a chaplain's "presence is a manifestation of the myth of the 'holy war.' His function, as a chaplain, can only serve to perpetuate that myth." Military chaplains, these students asserted, provided moral cover for an immoral military, a role they could neither inhabit nor endorse.[37]

For most rabbinical students, however, the question of conscientious objection to war was more nuanced. Few held absolute pacifist positions, but many regarded American intervention in Vietnam as unethical. As the HUC-NY students stated in February 1968, "many rabbinic students doubt the morality of serving as a chaplain in or during the Viet Nam war or doubt the advisability of having a compulsory chaplaincy system at all." Jerold Levy, a rabbinical student set to graduate in the spring 1968, as the war in Vietnam reached its apex, asserted that HUC's mandatory chaplaincy requirement amounted to nothing less than institutional trampling on individual freedom and conscience. He accused the Chaplaincy Committee of "stifl[ing] our most deeply held—one might say, *religiously* held—convictions against involvement in this immoral war" by forcing rabbis into "the obedient political silence required of officers in the armed forces . . . rather than provide true religious leadership." The particularity of Vietnam, not a universal opposition to war, weakened and then dissolved the Jewish commitment to the chaplaincy. Although American rabbis had eagerly entered the American military chaplaincy since World War I, Vietnam—"this immoral war," in Levy's words—demanded new religious leadership, an obeisance to God not country, and struggling against unyielding military might.[38]

Participating in the chaplaincy, students argued, limited the rabbi's ability to lead through dissent. "Any participation in demonstrations, rallies, meetings, or counseling sessions which were aimed against the policies of the United States Government would be a violation of the oath taken at the time one receives one's commission," they wrote. Air force chaplain Nathan Landman disagreed, arguing, "There is no such thing as 'absolute freedom' of the pulpit." Rather, he asserted, "the preacher has to take into consideration the audience to whom he is preaching. He has to be dedicated to meeting *their* spiritual needs and enlarging *their* spiritual horizons."[39] Where prospective chaplains worried about not protesting war, Chaplain Landman agonized about supporting men at war. Freedom of conscience continued to plague what Rabbi Stephen Passamaneck dubbed the "delicate and explosive" issue of the chaplaincy. He wondered whether the CCAR was "willing to put our morality where our mouth is." Given that "coercion and conscription are indeed anathemas to a group of Rabbis who profess severally and collectively the absolute moral and religious value of personal freedom for all men," Passamaneck continued, how could the organization force its members to enlist?[40]

By the late 1960s, the viability of "selective conscientious objection" wracked the nation, and American rabbis actively contested the implications for the chaplaincy. On the brink of retirement from the Army Reserves, Chaplain David Max Eichhorn (Jewish) rejected selective conscientious objection as ignoble and destructive. Pacifists, he suggested, supported noncombatant chaplains, "while the pseudo-pacifist, the 'selective' COs try to destroy the chaplaincy." In contrast, Bertram Korn, who remained a chaplain in the Naval Reserve, hinted at the impossibility of total conscientious objection. In 1965, when the CCAR received its first petition for CO status from Louis Feldman, Korn responded with several questions. First, he asked, would Feldman resist military service against "the equivalent of Nazis"? Second, he queried,

"If the Arab states were again to attack Israel and you were a resident there, would you refuse to take up arms against them while they made every possible effort to drive the people of Israel into the sea and exterminate them?" In attempting to investigate the veracity of Feldman's convictions, Korn invoked both the recent past and present day. Mixing the rhetoric of Arab nationalism and the biblical language of Pharoah's efforts to extinguish the Israelites in the Red Sea, he pressed the rabbinical student to assess whether his moral objection to war extended to all times and places, to the Holocaust and to the nascent state of Israel, to specifically Jewish causes as well as American ones. Could an American Jewish rabbi really abhor participation in all wars? For Korn, the answer was, undoubtedly, no.[41]

Although the contest over the chaplaincy draft resembled a generational conflict, at its core, the dispute did not reflect a crisis of conscience over Vietnam (which most of the Jewish community agreed was an immoral war). Rather, it signaled a crisis over the value and meaning of the military chaplaincy. For vigorous Jewish advocates of the chaplaincy—most of whom served as chaplains in World War II—the institution did not signal an allegiance to unnecessary force or a commitment to obscene militarism. To those who had placed the tablets insignia on their lapels a quarter century earlier, the chaplaincy represented the military's signal accomplishment for the American Jewish community: granting Judaism "the respected status which it now has in the total American community." Abdicating the chaplaincy to address the problem of Vietnam was, CJC executive director Aryeh Lev argued, "like using a cap gun to explode an iceberg." It would harm only American Jews, not the state. "To remove Jewish chapels and chaplains from that service is to take from the Jewish GI a very important source of comfort, self-expression, and hope," Lev continued, but doing so would not alter government policies in Vietnam. And, as Stephen Passamaneck fretted, a collection of individual decisions to abandon the chaplaincy would turn a pluralist space into a Christian one.[42]

But the late 1960s were a time of "impossible polarization." Appeals to community rarely overtook student opposition to an immoral war. Even chaplains in the field were not immune; some requested discharges to follow their conscience out of uniform. On the question of moral obligation, HUC students and leaders continued to volley back and forth: to individual conscience or to the American Jewish community?

HUC's leadership held on to the chaplaincy draft over and against the "semi-yippy" students who seemed to enter the seminary in greater numbers each year. The CCAR's Chaplaincy Committee rejected the movement's inclination to dissolve the chaplaincy draft, asserting that they would "not be stampeded\ into the rejection of our moral duty." But their verbal recalcitrance could not compete with the ever-increasing moral opprobrium: over the course of 1968 and 1969, petitions for CO status escalated among rabbinical students, and, in 1969, the CCAR extinguished the draft. For Bertram Korn, Aryeh Lev, and the other defenders of the military chaplaincy, there was perhaps one final, if small, victory. In 1969, the HUC student who led the protest against the chaplaincy draft decided, after much "thinking and soul-searching," to accept a commission as a Navy chaplain.[43]

With the CJC draft dismantled, all clergy could selectively conscientiously object to Vietnam—vocally or silently—by refusing to volunteer for the military chaplaincy, but most Americans lacked that option. The NAE reported, somewhat derisively, "the Methodist Church has many church leaders with rather strong pacifist leanings who do not feel ministers should serve in the chaplaincy where the preaching of such doctrine would be restricted." As clergy, chaplains held envious positions from the perspective of other selective conscientious objectors. Freed from the noose of the draft, antiwar ministers, priests, and rabbis could simply choose not to volunteer for military service. Draft-eligible laymen, in contrast, lacked an administrative escape hatch. In *Gillette v. U.S.* (1971), Justice Thurgood Marshall wrote the eight-to-one majority opinion affirming that, regardless of religious or humanist motivation, draft exemptions applied only to those who objected to all war. Plain in its declaration and simple in its meaning, the court stated, "Conscientious scruples relating to war and military service must amount to conscientious opposition to participating personally in any war and all war." In the interest of equity and fairness to all, it was imperative to maintain a system in which "the relevant individual belief is simply objection to all war" lest the "more articulate, better educated, or better counseled" prevail where the less sophisticated, poorly educated, or poorly advised might fail. The very malleability of selective objection voided its legal plausibility as a matter of public policy.[44]

While the court focused on the need to maintain the integrity of the draft and the democratic impulse at the heart of mass conscription, antiwar activists—religious and secular—hewed to selective conscientious objection as an utterly reasonable approach to the exigencies of Vietnam. It remained possible, they felt, that future wars, like some past wars, would meet their moral standards. Justice William Douglas' meditative dissent embraced the religious cause at the heart of Gillette's request: "I had assumed that the welfare of the single human soul was the ultimate test of the vitality of the First Amendment." Although Douglas stood alone, he gestured to the power of selective conscientious objection. In reminding the nation that "freedom to differ is not limited to things that do not matter much . . . the test of its substance is the right to differ as to things that touch the heart of the existing order." The state had long been able to contain conscientious objection by bracketing pacifism because, as an outgrowth of historic peace churches, the categorical refusal to serve in the military made no distinction in the origins, methods, or outcomes of war. But selective conscientious objection operated according to a radically different logic, deriving its legitimacy from parsing, distinguishing, and evaluating war's causes, means, and ends. It thus challenged one of the fundamental domains of the modern state—the ability to wage war. "The existing order" could not remain and the draft was on the verge of extinction, but the military chaplaincy's future remained undetermined.[45]

The angst surrounding the morality of the war and the military chaplaincy reached a fever pitch by the early 1970s. In 1966, the Military Chaplains Association resolved that chaplains who served in Vietnam were "unanimous . . . that our mission is just and that the need of the people there for our support, military, financial, and humanitarian, is real and urgent." However, in response to growing questions about the efficacy and morality of Vietnam, the United Presbyterian Church asked whether the military chaplaincy was "captive or free." Could a church committed to peace and reconciliation sustain military ministry? The unscientific survey offered a telling snapshot of chaplains' concerns. Of the twenty-three who responded, most agreed that they retained freedom of the pulpit in the service—or at least maintained a position as "unfettered" as civilian pastors serving at the will of their congregations "when such questions as conscience versus tact arise." Indeed, Chaplain B, an infantry chaplain in Vietnam, emphasized that he had "preached against the war" without any repercussions from his superiors. Chaplain L similarly insisted that clergy played a pivotal role as patriotic critics. Commanders "worth their salt at all do not want 'yes men' as religious teachers," and in his estimation, his role in the armed forces lent a moral force to military endeavors. He would "raise unholy hell," for example, were he to witness uncontrolled or unscrupulous treatment of prisoners. Whether he would be in a position to observe such action, he did not say.[46]

Several chaplains questioned the Vietnam War without rejecting military service. Chaplain E suggested that limits on a chaplain's freedom of speech were "self-imposed," and military ministers often chose to speak about controversial topics in conversations, not sermons. "My own persuasion is near pacifism, although I believe war is justified under certain conditions," he wrote. "I have presented this view from the pulpit." He saw his intellectual opponents in nuanced terms—as "thoughtful people" who nevertheless condoned American action in Vietnam—and used the contrast between his position and theirs to show that the military allowed heterogeneous points of view. From Chaplain F's perspective, "all war is immoral, but . . . to wish war away does not make reality, incorruptibility, or morality." As a result, he suggested, chaplains serve men "as God's reconciling agent." Here was a new definition of the chaplaincy and of obligation: military clergy stood at the interface between God and country, loyal to God and to soldiers' reckoning with God. If this meant feuding with commanders, so be it, because vulnerability stood at the core of "standing for the gospel."[47]

Not all chaplains found the military so hospitable. Chaplain K sounded a more cautious note, recognizing that the cost of criticism could be one's career: "a man can be given a bad efficiency report because he is not gung-ho about the killing aspects of war." These comments echoed those of Chaplain Samuel Stahl (Jewish), who lamented the army's hostility to his opinions. "We can not freely apply Jewish insights to the Vietnam situation and other crises of equal gravity because we have donned the uniform," he fumed. "I am constantly frustrated by these military limitations on free speech." Among chaplains who found the military restrictive, many sought to change the institution rather than forgo their work. Chaplain H encouraged the United Presbyterian Church to help reform the military chaplaincy. In contrast, Chaplain J minced no words in coaxing the church to consider abolishing the chaplaincy. "Will it be God first or nationalism first?"

he bellowed. Fearing the United States had embraced "American Shinto," a term coined by historian Martin Marty to refer to a form of idolatrous nationalist self-worship, the chaplain wanted his church to intervene to change the chaplaincy or detach itself from the military altogether.[48]

As religious voices questioning the legitimacy of the Vietnam War grew more insistent, the possibility of separating the chaplaincy from the state gained traction. The prospect of state-sanctioned clergy providing moral cover for immoral action propelled interest in a civilian chaplaincy. Colonel Irving Heymont understood that rabbis rejected military pulpits because it was impossible to wear officer stripes without supporting the war—even if "grudging, tacit, or perfunctory." Civilian rabbis, he suggested, could provide an alternate means of meeting servicemen's spiritual needs. As a career military officer who oversaw a Displaced Persons camp in Germany after World War II, Heymont was familiar with the challenges of managing and providing religion. Yet by the advent of Vietnam, he also recognized the moral complexity of deploying clergy in uniform. Most chaplains, like those featured in the Presbyterian survey, were quick to spot the pragmatic obstacles: would churches want this work, would denominations commit the money, would soldiers respect non-uniformed clergy, would civilians be able to function in a military environment? More philosophically, Chaplain A wondered, would an alternative civilian chaplaincy "make for a better, freer, more creative and responsible ministry?" He advocated studying the issue but cautioned that altering internal military structures, identities, and administration might be more productive.[49]

As draft dodging and desertion peaked, a growing public chorus questioned the chaplaincy's existence. Robert McAfee Brown, the chaplain founder of CALC, recommended distancing the chaplaincy from the state. "Surely the time has come," he wrote in a 1971 essay, "for the military chaplaincy to be divested of both the symbolic and actual accouterments that render its ministry ambiguous, so that a genuine chaplaincy to the military can emerge." Chaplains could not lumber along in a military echo chamber, Brown argued. They needed to inhabit a new role as prophets, as the conscience of the nation, who could rage against immorality and scorn depravity carried out in the name of patriotism. His jeremiad attracted company. Sociologist Gordon Zahn argued that military chaplains faced an impossible conundrum: serving two masters, God and country, resulted in an ineluctable "role tension" that constrained clergy in uniform. Had religion in the military remained relegated to the realm of personal morality rather than political morality, the tension might have dissipated. But Vietnam made that distinction untenable, and the chaplaincy had to catch up. Questions of morality during war animated Zahn, who served in Civilian Public Service camps as a Catholic conscientious objector during World War II. In 1969, he used a *Commonweal* article to float the idea of restructuring the chaplaincy, severing it from the military hierarchy and placing it under the jurisdiction of civilian authorities.[50]

Zahn's public critique prompted the FCC, the JWB, and the Military Ordinariate to collaborate on a study of the viability of a civilian chaplaincy. The interfaith committee contemplated the option over two years and published a working paper in a special 1972 issue of *The Chaplain*, the General Commission's quarterly magazine. The study assumed that the chaplaincy could be dismantled for two distinct reasons: first, if challenged in court, the chaplaincy might not pass constitutional muster, and second, ecclesiastical authorities might withdraw their support for the chaplaincy. The group dismissed both possible scenarios as unlikely but predicated its investigation on the latter. Indeed, six years before Zahn published his piece, the two concurring opinions and dissent in *Abington v. Schemmp* (1963) tipped the hand of the court. In contrast to the mandatory Bible readings and Lord's Prayer recitations the justices deemed unconstitutional, federal oversight of military chaplains did not contravene the establishment clause. In fact, Justice William Brennan argued, "hostility, not neutrality, would characterize the refusal to provide chaplains and places of worship for prisoners and soldiers cut off by the State from all civilian opportunities for public communion." The constitutionality of the chaplaincy was judicially, if somewhat obliquely, secure.[51]

Nevertheless a cascade of concerned believers fulminated against the chaplaincy. In June 1971, Catholic laity requested that the Church strip the military of its priests because of "'repeated instances of silence on the part of Catholic chaplains in the face of moral atrocities.'" The critique lodged at the chaplaincy by its most vocal religious critics zeroed in on the oddity of a state-managed religious apparatus dedicated to providing what the military dubbed "religious coverage" and instilling morality. If religious provisioning incensed constitutional critics, responsibility for morality inflamed conscientious objectors. In a trenchant appraisal, the study recognized that "the most vocal antagonists of the military chaplaincy at the present are within the religious bodies of the nation." Even if chaplains maintained freedom of pulpit in the military, antiwar critics surmised that their judgment would become "irremediably faulty" when embedded in military units, living in military barracks and reporting to military commanders. Thus, they contended, "to save the chaplains (and the religious bodies which supply and endorse them) from this almost inevitable moral corrosion[,] the denominations must divorce the chaplaincy from military control altogether." These proponents of a civilian chaplaincy furrowed their collective brow at the likelihood of religious instruments of the state challenging the military apparatus. How could clergy occupy their prophetic mantle if enmeshed in a state project? What Brown, Heschel, and Novak deemed *A Crisis of Conscience* was, when applied to the chaplaincy, a crisis of authority: who controlled religion in the armed forces? Denominational bodies or the military?[52]

Over eighty-eight pages, the study carefully imagined what a civilian chaplaincy would look like. If "quasi-civilian" clergy already pitched in, could their efforts be scaled up? Could these ministers, priests, and rabbis mobilize, and if so, how would they reach military personnel? The thought experiment fared poorly. The interfaith group determined that such a regime would be disastrous and few religious organizations had the capacity to meet the needs of the military. On a financial level alone, the costs would exceed 47,000 dollars per chaplain—a sum few faiths could afford to donate to the government. Logistically, only military posts in or adjacent to major cities could find sufficiently diverse clergy to meet the religious needs of personnel, and navy ships presented a "most acute problem." Whether nonmilitary preachers could connect with men (and a growing number of women) in uniform remained an unsettled question. Potential upsides of a civilian chaplaincy included potentially overcoming the hurdles the military faced in recruiting an adequate supply of clergy. But commanding officers would acquire significant administrative challenges for uncertain benefits.[53]

This parade of pragmatic obstacles doomed the possibility of a civilian chaplaincy. Yet the study's most potent—albeit somewhat buried—critique was historical. The last time civilian clergy played a significant role in military environments was World War I, and that precedent boded poorly. The experience of "auxiliary" chaplains aiding the American Expeditionary Force in France, the study reckoned, "is not reassuring. The system collapsed in all but utter chaos."[54] Indeed, the very pandemonium of uncoordinated and overwhelmed civilian religious services outside the purview of military command led General John Pershing to bring in Charles Brent to redesign the military chaplaincy. Would Vietnam shred that legacy?

If civilianizing the chaplaincy seemed pragmatically impossible, service to returned prisoners of war (POWs) best illustrated why. In 1973, President Richard Nixon fulfilled a 1968 campaign pledge to end the war in Vietnam. After signing the Paris Peace Accords, a ceasefire went into effect on January 28, and that same day, a select group of chaplains reported to Clark Air Force Base. Their assignment, which they learned upon arrival in the Philippines, was to support Operation Homecoming, the negotiated repatriation of 591 POWs. Over two months, flights carrying forty men at a time brought American soldiers back—first to the military, then to their families. The adjustments POWs faced were tremendous. When navy chaplain Edward Roberts (Catholic) led Mass, he did so in English, leading one of the first returnees to exclaim, "'You won't believe it.'" In the years between their capture and return, Vatican II had changed the ritual that had comforted so many men imprisoned at the notorious "Hanoi Hilton" and other North Vietnamese prison camps. The captured Catholic men kept their faith by reciting the prayers they knew in Latin, but the Second Vatican Council authorized prayers in the vernacular. POWs had exemplified the lay participation the Catholic Church sought in its parishes, but their ritual rendition no longer conformed to contemporary practices. As a result, Chaplain Roberts found that he "had to explain the new Mass before Mass." And when he tried to offer a service familiar to his POW parishioners, he found "I couldn't go very far and they came right through with the whole thing in Latin." The initial religious disconnect provoked extensive conversations about faith and worship. It also foreshadowed the challenges of reintegrating into a world that kept spinning while POWs stood still.[55]

The campaign to release American POWs "link[ed] captured men to their families and transform[ed] the POW story into a domestic drama," and chaplains played instrumental roles in the unfolding story.[56]

They were the bearers of the gospel and, often, of bad news too—of deaths, marital troubles, and financial woes.[57] In what became the iconic image of family reunification, fifteen-year-old Lorrie Stirm sprinted toward her father, Lieutenant Colonel Robert L. Stirm, with outstretched arms, the rest of her family in close pursuit. For six years, ever since the air force pilot was shot down, she and her family had wondered if they would see him again. Taken by Associated Press photographer Slava Veder on March 17, 1973, "Burst of Joy" was printed by newspapers across the nation and won the Pulitzer Prize. What the image could not capture, however, were the mixed emotions of the returned POW. With his back to the camera and his uniform representing all repatriated soldiers, his face remained hidden. The photograph could not convey the experience of encountering his wife, from whom he had received a "Dear John" divorce letter upon reentering American territory a mere seventy-two hours prior. A chaplain delivered the note.[58]

Mediating these sorrows fell to chaplains precisely because they operated within the military infrastructure. A waiting wife might have confided in her local pastor, but sending news to her missing or captured husband required working through the military's information channels. The chaplaincy was powerful because, as a state-sanctioned religious institution, it lived within the structure of the military it served. But Vietnam changed the nation and the military with it. The chaplaincy had to adjust as well.

8

Fighting with Faith

CHAPLAIN MATTHEW ZIMMERMAN (National Baptist) felt caught. A handful of men walked into his office in 1971 and asked him to preside over a memorial service for Malcolm X in the chapel the next day. He scurried to get permission from his commander because "that sort of thing wasn't even thought about," much less regularly done. A phone conversation yielded little more than " 'Absolutely not! No way!' "—a reaction that fared poorly among the African Americans he served. Hitching helicopter rides out of Can Tho as the lone chaplain available to troops in the southern part of the Mekong Delta had not prepared Zimmerman for Hanau, Germany, "the worst location with respect to race relations." He witnessed black and white soldiers literally killing one another, bloody encounters between the German police and black soldiers, and personnel self-medicating with addictive drugs. Ultimately, he performed more memorial services for fallen soldiers in Germany than in Vietnam. Perhaps it was not surprising, then, that the soldiers called the third-generation minister " 'Uncle Tom,' and all kinds of unpleasant names" and decided to forge ahead with the memorial service anyway, using the base flagpole as their new location. Zimmerman apprised his superior of the new plan, at which point he was instructed, " 'Be their chaplain.' "[1]

As the *Washington Post* reported in 1970, "race rifts follow the flag," and Zimmerman operated in the shadow of both. He was not even five years into his army career when he received his assignment to Europe, plucked from Fort Hood in the hopes that he could help assuage the military's extensive race problems. Born and raised in South Carolina, Zimmerman was the first black graduate of Duke Divinity

School and ministered to students at Idaho State—"not a place where you found a lot of black folks"—and then Morris College before a friend at Fort Jackson convinced him to volunteer for the chaplaincy. He expected to complete a tour of duty and return to civilian life. Instead, he crisscrossed Europe to teach equal-opportunity courses and conduct racial harmony workshops. While religion could be a salve for weary soldiers, "religious dogma" became a weapon when used to justify racism and inequality. Disarming the religious underpinnings of white supremacy became especially important as chaplains often served as the default equal-opportunity officers.[2]

The young chaplain recognized what senior army brass did not: eradicating overt hostility constituted a mere fraction of the work the military needed to do to engender equality. Midway through the 1970s, "alienation" represented the key finding of a military survey of "the black experience in chapel." The report recommended "demythologize[ing] the 'pure white' interpretation of the Bible" commonly encountered in the military and, instead, preaching justice. But "mercy and love" could not counteract festering inequities. As Chaplain Zimmerman knew, the army frequently "made a lot of not very smart decisions," such as refusing to stock black hair products based on the notion that color-blind policies quelled discrimination. He recognized this flawed logic, understanding that "you never want to say, 'we are colorblind'" because "the objective is not to make me out of a colorless, depersonalized person." Instead, the military had to learn how to respond to specific needs, to build a pluralist ethos out of particularity. And so it was that the Protestant military chaplain led a commemoration service for Malcolm X, the assassinated antiwar black nationalist Muslim leader, attended by "a hundred black soldiers in fatigues and one white lad in a suit who was supposed to be an undercover agent." The uncouth surveillance did not deter the minister. For his men, the service functioned as a release valve, allowing them to express and embrace their racial and religious identities while in uniform. Chaplain Matthew Zimmerman, who within two decades would wear two stars as the nation's first African American chief of chaplains, committed his ministry and career to an institution on the brink of extensive change.[3]

Like the rest of American society, the military was caught in the "age of fracture," flummoxed and flapping about for an appropriate course

228

ENLISTING FAITH

forward after Vietnam and in the midst of raging domestic turmoil over the proper direction of the nation. The racism, sexism, and religious prejudice afflicting American society also plagued the military, and the chaplaincy was not immune. Increasing skepticism toward authority did not help a hierarchical institution during a crisis of legitimacy. In 1974, Army Chief of Chaplains Gerhardt Hyatt (Missouri Synod Lutheran) outlined "a commitment to action rather than reaction." However, like the White House's struggles to restore confidence in government after Watergate, the military lingered in a reactive posture as it endeavored to become all it could be after Vietnam.[4]

It was, therefore, an age of adaptation, and to survive, the chaplaincy—like the military—regrouped. The end of the draft and the rise of the All-Volunteer Force altered recruitment tactics, required new benefits, and yielded significantly more African American and women enlistees. Although the military's religious ministry had always been staffed by volunteers, the space vacated by liberal clergy who morally opposed the Vietnam War created new openings for the evangelicals and fundamentalists who had been itching to gain a foothold in the military since midcentury. Conservative Protestants were not the only ones eying the opportunities the military afforded. In the 1970s and 1980s, the Chaplain Corps diversified in three ways: by recruiting racial minorities, assenting to the inclusion of women, and addressing the needs of more varied faiths. Demographic shifts reinvigorated old questions: Who could serve as a religious leader? What counted—and could be accommodated—as religious practice? These anxieties took on new urgency between the fall of Saigon and the fall of the Berlin Wall. The chaplaincy thus grappled with a set of concerns that hounded American politics and society writ large: Could pluralism include the evangelical and the ecumenical, the sectarian conservative and the progressive pluralist? Could racial, gendered, and religious diversity coexist?[5]

The military wanted its personnel to fight with faith in God and country, but the late-twentieth-century chaplaincy found itself battling faith on multiple fronts. As the composition of the chaplaincy and the military personnel it served shifted, newcomers challenged the pluralist ethos that had guided the chaplaincy through much of the twentieth century. Evangelicals and humanists, African Americans and women, legal agitators and religious minorities like Sikhs and Muslims lobbed different critiques at the chaplaincy. It was too ecumenical and too religious, insufficiently holistic and incongruously preferential, un-constitutionally sound and wretchedly unaware of its limits. Through all of these divergent claims ran the shared experience of values in ten-sion with an institution. The military chaplaincy's well-honed, if lim-ited, worldview assumed unity but had yet to figure out how to serve a broader spectrum of needs and desires.

While liberal Protestant, Catholic, and Jewish clergy debated the mo-rality of accepting commissions as chaplains in the late 1960s, evan-gelical Protestants ministers had few qualms about supporting the war in Vietnam and even fewer about entering the military chaplaincy. Harrowing combat experiences did not dissuade Chaplain John W. Schumacher (Grace Brethren). When he received orders to return to Vietnam in 1969, he recalled his emotions upon leaving Bien Hoa two summers prior. Contemplating the ultimate sacrifice made by so many Americans in uniform, he remembered gazing out the airplane window and "vow[ing] quietly to myself, 'Never again.'" Friends and family suggested he resign his army commission, but Schumacher operated according to a sense of duty, a belief in God and the chain of com-mand, and a single principled stance: "It is right for a clergyman to be with soldiers in time of war." His military career lasted over three de-cades, a period of great evangelical ferment in the armed forces.[6]

Evangelicals viewed the Vietnam and post-Vietnam chaplaincy as a grand opportunity to increase their numbers, find new believers, reach Christians abroad, and relay their faith to a larger American public. By June 1968, at the height of the Vietnam war, the National Association of Evangelicals (NAE) tallied 118 chaplains across the three service branches—forty-three more chaplains than in 1965, more than double the size of 1960, and more than ten times the number allotted to the NAE in World War II. The army's sixty-six NAE chaplains may have represented only 3 percent of the roster, but it reflected an unparalleled two-decade surge. By 1983, evangelical chaplains "populate[d] the corps to a greater degree than ever," thus vindicating the NAE's mid-century decision to invest in seminary infrastructure to meet the mili-tary's education requirements.[7]

As evangelical chaplains seized the chance to flood into the military, they resisted longstanding assumptions about pluralism and imported new sensibilities about particularity. Chaplain Schumacher's choices exemplify the evangelical recalibration of the chaplain's role away from ecumenical collaboration and toward sectarian silos. Assigned to an outpost in Kontum City not far from the Cambodian and Laotian borders, Schumacher led services for Americans and developed a friendship with Father Phan Tan Van, a Vietnamese priest who had once written English propaganda for the Viet Minh. Over meals and prayer, Chaplain Schumacher learned that Father Van "genuinely loved the Lord" and cared for local orphaned children. Despite their budding relationship, Schumacher found "there was little advising [he] could do." He enjoyed regular camaraderie with the neighborhood priest but blanched at enabling the work of Catholics and Buddhists. Whether his refusal to advise these clergy emanated from a sense of religious futility or a position of religious respect is unclear. Elsewhere, he flourished. Successfully converting a drug-addled Marine, for example, constituted victory. "Every assignment," he argued, "presented ministry opportunities in abundance," though not everyone shared his definition of ministry.[8]

In fact, the NAE distinguished the persuasion of evangelism from the coercion of proselytization in order to tiptoe around the state's prohibition on the latter. Many NAE chaplains found "rewarding opportunities in terms of souls won for Christ" within the armed forces and were pleased to provide data that vindicated their successful ministry. At the Naval Training Center in Orlando, Florida, Chaplain Charles E. Dorr (Baptist) counted more than 800 men "indicat[ing] their desire to receive Christ" over eleven months—and those were merely the ones who followed through. Performing baptisms upon request had always been part and parcel of chaplains' work, but treasuring a broad-based evangelical revival through witnessing and conversion was new. As Chaplain Conrad Walker (Lutheran) explained, he baptized hundreds of soldiers at the Fort Benning chapel and in the snake-ridden Chattahoochee River. Lest his efforts seem like proselytizing, he wrote, before every ritual dunking he tried to determine the appropriate family tradition to follow. In the case of a soldier who lacked Christian parents, a "Holy Roller" grandmother offered a charismatic model and, with a Pentecostal and a Catholic as witnesses, the young man committed himself to Christ. This was evangelical military ecumenism in action: baptism of both the new convert and the born-again celebrated by Christians of many denominational communities.[9]

As more and more NAE-endorsed chaplains found a home in the military, the organization became increasingly candid about its view of the armed forces as "one of the world's greatest mission fields" from which they enjoyed amassing "a great harvest of souls." Within an evangelical frame, combat arenas and domestic environments resembled youth ministries: preaching and teaching, studying and witnessing, advising and serving all created moments ripe for personal evangelism which, if carefully conducted, could pass for standard military chaplain activities. A young sergeant visited Chaplain Walker because his wife was acting under the influence of voodoo—and purportedly targeting others with her spells. After a successful parachute jump, the military minister informed the 101st Airborne soldier that "it was time we went to prayer in Jesus' name to wash out, yes, *flush* out, any further influences of voodoo curses and such." Visits and prayers followed, and soon after the jump, the sergeant's wife also restored her faith as a Christian. Similarly, in a report from Vietnam, Chaplain Arthur Guetterman (Conservative Baptist) jotted, "Today I held four services and 10 men trusted Christ." Mission accomplished and missionary success went hand-in-hand.[10]

Becoming born-again in the heat of battle did not necessarily lead to an enduring church commitment, as many chaplains, evangelical and otherwise, discovered. Some victories, like the conversion of West Point graduate John A. Wickham Jr., would pay rich dividends, as the future army chief of staff infused his work—and the military writ large—with evangelical fervor. But for every soldier who found God, there were equal numbers who neither embraced the divine nor expressed any interest in renewed religious fervor. Chaplain Kenneth Gohr (Lutheran) admitted that "there is little evidence of 'Foxhole Religion,'" as those who were not already religious rarely changed their minds. Evangelical chaplains acknowledged this but viewed it as a challenge to overcome rather than a predetermined outcome. In Vietnam, Chaplain Kevin L. Anderson (Southern Baptist) devoted a portion of worship to asking "men to make a definite response or commitment to Jesus Christ." Although he denied using "high pressure or overly emotional appeals," the high stakes environment of combat was not neutral. Nevertheless, the chaplain who considered himself "more Marine green than . . . Navy blue" tempered his passion for Christ with the knowledge of his own weaknesses, recognizing that he had not built a program to sustain new converts. If war dramatized the battle cry for Christianity, it also conspired to corral conversion and baptism as milestones unmoored from day-to-day habits.[11]

The chaplaincy's emphasis on ecumenism nettled many chaplains affiliated with the NAE. When a torrent of rain threatened to wash out tents, an assistant division chaplain cracked that they could deposit "2 Protestants, 2 Catholics, and 2 Jewish chaplains aboard an ark." In stark contrast to this interfaith revelry, the NAE's vigorous objection to tri-faith meetings in the air force occasionally swayed military leaders to abandon their plans. But such clear sectarian victories were scarce. In 1971, the NAE's Floyd Robertson was gratified to report that while the military continued to commend ecumenical services and Sunday schools, the chiefs of chaplains finally allowed clergy to recuse themselves from these events when they deemed participation "'contrary . . . to the tenets of the church he represented or to his own conscience.'" Many of Robertson's evangelical and fundamentalist colleagues tried to push even more sectarian visions into military space. Bill Garman of the Associated Gospel Churches described the nonsectarian Vacation Bible School planned by Chaplain Patrick J. Hessian (Catholic) as reflecting "deplorable un-American, discriminatory conditions in the Army Chaplaincy." Robertson countered that Hessian, a future army chief of chaplains, had every right to act in accordance with his faith. Mutual noninfringement was the best policy, he argued, because it not only safeguarded the chaplaincy from accusations of religious discrimination but also allowed evangelical chaplains to pursue their visions without interference or restrictions.[12]

The dual roles of military responsibility and doctrinal commitment created conflicts for many of the evangelical chaplains who knew that their personal faith collided with the beliefs of the personnel they served. One chaplain, for example, reported declining to marry a couple because the airman's fiancée was a divorcée; he also refused to baptize the dying infant of another soldier. In both cases, the expected religious actions contravened his denomination's principles and his personal precepts. Nevertheless, as a staff officer, he realized his professional role bound him to find another chaplain or, if necessary, civilian minister to perform these rituals. Concerns about diluting the strength of religious messages suffused objections to ecumenical policy. The problem was not denominational—evangelicals were, on the whole, invested in nondenominational Protestantism—but in coddling those who did not share their emphasis on salvation through Christ.[13]

Although evangelical chaplains often felt they were fighting a rising tide of pluralism, they had fellow travelers in their errand into the wilderness. As plans for Campus Crusade for Christ's Explo '72 moved forward, for example, Navy Chief of Chaplains Francis Garrett (United Methodist) promoted it, describing the weeklong evangelical festival aimed at high school and college students as "a springboard for a strategy to help fulfill the Great Commission in this generation." He expected 5,000 or so military personnel to join him in Dallas and encouraged chaplains to use their budgets and chapel funds to sponsor delegations. Chaplain Carl McNally (Baptist) planned to make the 150-mile trip to Dallas from Fort Hood, Texas, with at least 300 men in tow. Evangelicals glowed as the Holy Spirit infused the military—at least the officers and enlisted men, if not yet the chaplaincy itself. By 1972, Bibles and revivals—in Christian coffeehouses, through Jesus rallies, and by touring evangelists—became commonplace, enacted alongside a rhetorical commitment to "'bombing' North Vietnamese villages with the Gospel." A four-star general could proclaim, "The United States is not neutral about God . . . so I have no bashfulness about expressing my convictions for the Lord," and follow through with early morning prayer breakfasts and on-base Bible-study groups.[14]

Rather than hunker down and continue to smuggle in sectarian spiritual care from the bottom up, the NAE initiated a new crusade to overhaul the chaplaincy's worldview from the top down. For every chaplain who extricated himself from an uncomfortably ecumenical situation, others found themselves marginalized. One senior chaplain lamented the paucity of evangelical chaplains in senior leadership positions in the Offices of the Chiefs of Chaplains or as directors of the Armed Forces Chaplains Board (AFCB). According to him, "the chaplaincy climate is completely dominated by the ecumenical philosophy. Those of us who stand for other things are viewed as somewhat 'crack pot' and certainly 'very peculiar.' But you know that. The question is, 'where do we go from here?'" The answer, the chaplain asserted, was to acquire power. "'Since the chaplaincy is such a closed ecclesiastical system I see no remedy, or change of climate, until such time as evangelicals infiltrate the top policy making positions.'"[15] It would take time, but the Vietnam-era exodus of liberal, pluralist clergy who had dominated the chaplaincy for over a half century opened the gates of institutional power to evangelicals. All they had to do was shrewdly pursue it.

Evangelicals were not the only religious group striving to transform the chaplaincy to meet its needs, however. While some religious groups lacked chaplains, they still viewed the chaplaincy as the best venue for pursuing recognition, accommodations, and equality. American adherents of traditional Islam and the Nation of Islam (NOI) increased in the 1970s, and more Muslims sought to practice their faith in uniform. Without Muslim chaplains, the 1970s and 1980s–era chiefs of chaplains scrambled to understand and meet Muslim needs. In 1976, a message arrived in Washington from the *USS Mitscher*, a ship in a destroyer squadron then deployed in the Mediterranean. A practicing Muslim sailor "present[ed] . . . problems aboard ship." Namely, how could the ship accommodate five daily services, Friday noon Sabbath services, dietary needs to abstain from pork "or non-kosher meat," and fasting during Ramadan? The ship's officers announced they would not make special meals but allowed him to buy and store canned tuna in his ship locker. In addition, they authorized daily prayers, "provided there is no interference with assigned military watches/jobs [and] exchange of watches is permitted" and allocated space for private worship.[16]

The accommodations met with approval, granted in bureaucratic language that supported judicious adaptations—sensitive to both religious obligations and the duties of the armed forces. "To the maximum extent permissible," navy leaders affirmed, "a member should be permitted the freedom to adhere to his religious persuasion as long as it does not hinder or restrict the effective fulfillment of the command's and the Navy's mission." The feedback also noted that "diversity of religious persuasions preclude promulgation of general standards," such that the navy needed to tailor responses to individual and military needs. When mission readiness hindered religious practice, the memo suggested, "alternative administrative measures not involving punitive action" were warranted. This leniency did not, however, justify violations of orders, for which judicial proceedings could ensue—as they had for Seventh-day Adventists in previous decades. The resolution deflected possible strife through a rhetorical commitment to religious diversity and offered flexible provisions combined with a reminder that military duties superseded religious obligations.[17]

Much like American Buddhists at midcentury, American Muslims found the military more receptive to learning about Islam when the United States pursued strategic interests in the Middle East and Central Asia. Increasing awareness of Muslim religious rituals produced more accommodations. In 1977, for example, Navy Chief of Chaplains John O'Connor (Catholic) congratulated Chaplain Victor Ivers (Catholic) for "being on the cutting edge of things" by arranging the first Muslim service at Great Lakes Naval Training Center, Illinois. But the shield of faith could easily pivot to American anxiety about the appropriate exercise of the sword of spirit. Thus, American Muslims quickly found themselves on the wrong end of religiously and racially inflected questions of dual loyalty. Like Japanese Americans in World War II, Muslim Americans faced scrutiny about their willingness to fight coreligionists abroad. In the waning days of the Cold War and against the backdrop of the Iran–Iraq War, the military could not stop itself from asking representatives of the American Muslim community, "Is there a conflict for Muslims in carrying out the policies of a non-Muslim state, that is the United States, against any conflict or potential conflict with an Islamic state?"[18]

While evangelicals sought to turn the military into a mission field and Muslims wrestled with minor concessions to their religious needs, another group sought something more basic: recognition. Like their counterparts in the 1920s, atheists and humanists felt rebuffed by the state. In 1979, petty officer Michael Hagen asked the military to create an Armed Forces Atheist Council. In writing to the secretary of defense, he accused the military of "hav[ing] an established Judeo-Christian chaplaincy for I have no figures indicating that Muslims or Buddhists, much less Atheists, have received a commission and acceptance into the Chaplain Corps." The military mandate for chaplains to graduate from seminary meant, he alleged, that all were "indoctrinated" and none had the skills to minister to atheists like him. The navy concurred in principle, but downplayed the ramifications of chaplains not serving atheists. Though it acknowledged "a basic incompatibility" between the chaplaincy and atheists, it was, to their minds, a contradiction that merited no further action.[19]

At least one minister found this response dispiriting. Chaplain Jim Bank (Unitarian Universalist) wanted to make sure that all chaplains understood the depth and range "commitment to religious pluralism in the military requires." As a military chaplain trained in a denomination that included humanists, Bank felt obligated to support all individuals "in achieving religious wholeness as they—not we—see it." Aiding nonbelievers fell within the scope of his duties. In fact, from Bank's perspective, arguments about incompatibility failed because they were predicated on a false premise of bifurcated religious categorization. He anticipated Muslim and Buddhist chaplains entering the corps, and they would be required to minister to "those of Western religious traditions" even as Judaism and Christianity represented "deviating views" theologically. Atheism strained the limits of the chaplaincy, but atheists did not disappear. Rather, they have continued to advocate representation, counseling, and guidance on their terms.[20]

This quarrel over atheists went unresolved, but it highlighted a brief moment in which a broad range of religious and nonreligious voices lodged parallel critiques of religion in the armed forces. Evangelicals, Muslims, and atheists agreed that the success of the military chaplaincy rested on serving a broad spectrum of religions. As the NAE's Floyd Robertson insisted in 1975, "religious liberty is a two-way street. When I defend the right of our chaplains to be evangelical I must at the same time defend the right of those so disposed to be just as liberal as they choose to be."[21] He understood that within the military, religious rights could not be curtailed to satisfy particular theological orientations. At the same time, however, all of these groups felt the chaplaincy did not, or did not fully, represent them. Despite the distinct interests expressed in the evangelical desire for more sectarian military religion, the Muslim requests for appropriate food and worship, and the atheist aspiration to be included, all existed in tension with the ecumenical but not fully representative chaplaincy. As a government institution, the chaplaincy served the state and its citizens, but the goals of each could collide.

While white evangelicals wanted to help soldiers be born-again, another preacher commanded the nation to be born again. From a podium in Atlanta in 1967, Martin Luther King, Jr. pointed out that black men were dying at twice the rate of others while fighting "an unjust, evil war in Vietnam." When King asked, "Where do we go from here," he sought to persuade Americans to leave Vietnam and abandon an unjust imperial war. But for some black clergy, the tempest of the late 1960s and 1970s compelled them to enlist to serve the men dying overseas. Although white evangelicals were the most vocal band of brothers to enter the chaplaincy in large numbers, African American chaplains increased as well. In the army, seventeen active-duty black chaplains in 1963 more than tripled to fifty-five in 1971 and climbed to sixty-five by 1973.[22] As civilians confronted racial oppression in the 1970s, so too did the military, especially as racial tensions spiraled and racial minorities increased in the all-volunteer force. Black chaplains carefully agitated to bend the military toward social justice and sought to use religion to improve conditions faced by communities of color. The black clergy who volunteered for military pulpits rejected the separatism that some black nationalists found appealing, but embraced their militancy. Spiritual resilience, they argued, could not be garrisoned to hour-long worship in chapels and religious leadership could not be cordoned off in an office. The soul, like the mind and the body, needed and was nourished by housing, food, jobs, security, and most of all, equality. Black chaplains thus strove to lead capaciously and serve the whole person in a military rife with racial friction.[23]

Minority personnel rankled at the predominantly white chaplaincy's strict distinction between sacred and secular lives. When Navy Chief of Chaplains O'Connor asked Howard University's School of Religion to assess the chaplaincy's strengths and weaknesses, he may not have expected the critique it lobbed. Black ministry, the scholars explained, applied to the whole person such that "concern for the spiritual aspect of man was not separated from his temporal need for housing, education, employment, and civil and social justice." Without committing to advocacy, chaplains stood at a remove from the reality of black lives and could not satisfy the needs of the African Americans in uniform. Recruiting and promoting more black chaplains, reconceiving Sunday services away from white, middle-class Protestant norms, addressing "the multiplicities within American Black religious experience" in Chaplain School, and fashioning opportunities for black female empowerment would certainly help. But in the end, the report insisted, the problem lay in the structure and ethos of an institution that held "the implicit belief that an understanding and response to the Black religious experience can be realized apart from an understanding of those economic, social, political and psychological forces which impact Black life presently and in the past." State-sanctioned religious leaders could hedge and ignore the structural racism in their midst, but they would do so at their own peril.[24]

The military dawdled in addressing racism and the volatile situations that ensued during the 1960s and 1970s. "Smoldering unrest" abounded, according to Chaplain Peter Cary (Catholic). But, he continued, "the complaints of the Black Marines at the Leadership Council meetings were usually directed to that not so clearly seen or provable area," that is, to obstacles white eyes had trouble seeing. Chaplain Claude Newby (LDS) observed flaring racial tensions as well, though he claimed the environment degraded dramatically between his two tours in Vietnam. In contrast to his experiences in 1966–1967, by 1970 his infantrymen were "succumbing to civilian and rear-area trends, of dividing into us and them." In 1970, the *Pittsburgh Courier*, the African American newspaper that led the Double V campaign in World War II, rebuked the army's resistance to using its coercive power to redress racism. "The army is supposed to be a disciplined body with wide jurisdiction over those who serve under its authority," an editorial lamented. "The army can and must solve the racial problems which are dogging its feet." Racial enmity extended far beyond combat areas, and bigotry knew no geographic borders.[25]

Although the Department of Defense made "eliminating racism and the effects of racism" a command task in the mid-1970s, there were only a few black officers to guide the process, which in turn amplified the role of black chaplains. In 1974, the black officer rates reached 4.2 percent in the army, 2 percent in the air force, 2 percent in the Marine Corps, and 1.1 percent in the navy. Southern whites dominated the officer ranks, placing minority servicemen at the whims and wills of those raised in the Jim Crow South. At Fort Hood, Texas, where black soldiers refused to serve as supplemental riot control for the 1968 Democratic National Convention and racial slurs triggered race riots, several chaplains began offering Sunday morning gospel services. Centered on the hymns and music with which many African American soldiers would have been familiar, the worship services brought the rhythms of the black church into military chapels. Similar services arose at bases in Colorado, Washington, and Germany, often with the help of chaplains like Elvernice Davis (United Methodist), who formed a black gospel choir to support a regular gospel service. These small efforts notwithstanding, most black soldiers and Marines found the military a hostile space, a difficulty the inclusion of a few good chaplains could hardly erase.[26]

Nevertheless, some soldiers identified racially discriminatory religious practices for the military to fight. In 1974, Private Paul R. Armstrong alleged that "the policies of the Mormon institution are racist to an extent that it has an effect on the 'racial harmony' on this post." Mormons did not allow African Americans to hold the priesthood until 1978, and in 1974, Armstrong tried to use the chaplaincy to attack this racist practice. "If the Army does not want to be described as a racist organization," he wrote, "it should not go along with the racist policies that are imbedded in other institutions." In filing a formal complaint, he requested that the military replace Mormon services with "Black Muslim, Buddhist, and other non-western services." Armstrong attempted to use religion as a cudgel against racism. However, the army argued that its hands were tied because it used membership, not leadership, as the standard against which to assess racism. Had the LDS Church forbade black members, rather than restricting African Americans from the priesthood, it would have been in violation of military regulations. But since the army delegated the authority to assess the religious qualifications of chaplains to faith groups, it claimed it could not justify intervention. The army nevertheless continued to ask the LDS Church, like all religious groups, to help supply "minority clergymen," thus exerting a subtle, if unintentional, pressure to open the priesthood to African Americans.[27]

The overarching need to diffuse racial tension led some commanders to request black chaplains, which, in turn, encouraged the military to recruit more black chaplains. Sent to Washington to improve race relations, Chaplain Thomas Parham (United Presbyterian) insisted that the navy learn about the African American community and commit itself to improving housing options for personnel. Parham, only the second black navy chaplain, had served in World War II before the navy forced him to resign during postwar demobilization. In 1951, he re-enlisted, becoming the only black chaplain on active duty and then the first black chaplain to garner sea duty. In 1966, when Parham earned his Captain's bars, he was the first black officer to achieve the rank. But his remained a singular experience; nine years later, in 1975, a mere eleven active-duty black chaplains served in the navy. By 1980, after extensive recruitment and retention efforts, the number stood at thirty-seven.[28]

Direct interventions from the chaplaincy brass induced some change, though rhetoric continued to outpace reality. In March 1974, Army

Chief of Chaplains Gerhardt Hyatt proclaimed that "the Army has set
out to win the battle against racial discrimination" and that the chaplaincy would contribute "the resources of religious faith" to improve
race relations. But it had a ways to go in implementing a truly multicul-
tural ministry. For Hyatt, race relations—including the development of
command-level affirmative-action plans—required "strong moral leadership" of the sort only clergy could provide. With the switch to an
all-volunteer army, the racial composition of the military changed too.
By 1978, African Americans constituted 24 percent of the army, and
other ethnic groups contributed an additional 4.7 percent of personnel. Among the chaplaincy, however, the ninety-two African
American chaplains (including three of five female chaplains) joined
with twenty-two Hispanic, Native American, and Asian American
chaplains to represent a mere 8 percent of the corps. The goal, according
to late-1970s Army Chief of Chaplains Orris E. Kelly (United Methodist) was to reach 15 percent by 1983.[29]

Like Hyatt, John O'Connor, who served as navy chief of chaplains
from 1975 to 1979, played an instrumental role in increasing, promoting,
and supporting African American navy chaplains. When Chaplain J. C.
Williams (Baptist) took the pulpit as the senior chaplain at the Naval
Academy in the summer of 1978, he was the first black minister to occupy that role. Bucking tradition, O'Connor had placed only Williams's
name on the list of candidates forwarded to the superintendent at Annapolis, thereby ensuring cadets would encounter a black chaplain.
Williams could be brash, undaunted in his explicit assessment of the
military he served. The navy, he remarked, "is basically oriented
around the white majority." While the twenty-three black chaplains in
the sea service represented a marked improvement from the four in
uniform when he was commissioned in 1969, he was determined to
recruit a dozen a year. When the corps reached ninety black chaplains,
its demographics would match the racial composition of the navy writ
large. If the optimistic South Carolinian who had led a state NAACP
chapter as a seminary student was outspoken about the needs of African
American midshipmen and sailors, Williams was also confident he had
the backing of his Chief. Six years earlier, O'Connor had been the
first Catholic to serve as the senior chaplain at the Academy. When the
navy contemplated giving the priest smaller living quarters because he
had no family, O'Connor co-opted the language of the civil rights

movement when informing them, "I do not intend to ride in the back of the bus"—the same advice he gave Williams before sending him to the Annapolis, thereby permitting Williams to speak up.[30]

As African American chaplains charted a new course for the chaplaincy, they pursued a more ambitious agenda than the military recognized. Chaplain Willard Bolden (National Baptist) described the O'Connor years as "unprecedented" in the emphasis on recruiting racial and ethnic minorities into the chaplaincy and encouraging white chaplains to attend to "worship needs other than their own." In particular, Bolden explained, the creation of "various cultural workshops . . . to meet the different spiritual needs" of personnel played a vital role. Clergy crafted recommendations to realize equal opportunity in the armed forces with the chief of chaplains or his representative in attendance. The Third Annual Black Chaplains Workshop admonished their fellow military clergy, instructing them "to administer, not just to blacks, but to people." In other words, the group tried to steer the chaplaincy toward a grander vision of ministry, one more in line with the holistic spiritual and political commitments of African Americans. While black clergy garnered the verbal support of a military struggling to address racism, they—like white evangelicals—challenged the armed forces to view religion as more than an ancillary activity. They cajoled military leaders toward a new understanding of religious life, one not limited to lifecycle events or weekly devotion, but also committed to civil rights and social justice. Like white evangelicals, African American chaplains sought to coax the military chaplaincy in new direction; unlike white evangelicals, however, African American chaplains wanted to use the military for racial uplift rather than sectarian religion.[31]

Military religious leadership was on the brink of metamorphosis. If top-down decision-making within the chaplaincy broadened racial diversity, it took the top of the military hierarchy to transform the all-male chaplaincy into a mixed-gender space. At the July 1974 commissioning ceremony for new chaplains, the army distributed the first lieutenant's silver bars and the chaplain's silver cross to Alice M. Henderson (AME). But when the petite twenty-eight-year-old from Atlanta arrived at Fort Hamilton, New York, for Chaplain School, she still needed her army greens. The quartermaster had no clothes for her, as the army had not yet designed and produced uniforms for its newest female officers. The path to the army's first female chaplain traveled through the AME Church. And like many other black women in the 1970s, Henderson had marched for civil rights, protested the war in Vietnam, and questioned the work of second-wave feminists. By the time she arrived on base, war was winding down and she saw no contradiction in entering the military. It provided meaningful employment that helped her support her son. She was no militant feminist, though, as she desisted from joining the women's liberation movement and claimed that she—a single mother—still understood men as heads of households. Even once she had stitched together a uniform that, though intended for a male body, fit her well enough, she remained a curiosity on base. Her novel presence led to lots of attention, and, unlike men, she had to prove herself ready for the responsibilities of being a chaplain—something her commanding officer reported she had done quite well.[32]

Admiral Elmo Zumwalt Jr. became chief of naval operations in 1970, and his policy directives, known as Z-grams, revamped the racial and gender dynamics of the navy.[33] Career military service and progressive social policy confused many onlookers, as Zumwalt himself acknowledged: "There's a good deal of indecision as to whether I am a drooling-fang militarist or a bleeding-heart liberal." In 1970, he required squadrons to appoint a minority servicemember as a special assistant for minority affairs and insisted that the navy fight housing discrimination. Two years later, he issued Z-gram 116, "Equal Opportunities and Rights for Women in the Navy," rescinding restrictions on women serving aboard ships and eliminating discriminatory promotion and assignment patterns. It also ordered the chaplain and civil engineers corps to accept applications from and commission women, "thereby opening all staff corps to women." Just as Truman used an executive order to desegregate the armed forces, so too did Zumwalt use policy prerogatives to integrate women. Eleven months after Zumwalt's Z-gram, Dianna Pohlman (Prebyterian) entered the navy chaplaincy, and Chaplain Henderson followed in the army.[34]

The incorporation of women was not always easy, as Chaplain Pohlman recalled. While she found Catholic chaplains quite supportive, perhaps, she conjectured, because priests were accustomed to working with nuns, Protestants "really had a difficult time with me . . . they had never experienced a woman colleague before." Army Chief of Chaplains Orris Kelly (United Methodist) reported varied responses to the inclusion of women clergy. Rank-and-file troops were "very open" to female religious leadership, but there was "some reluctance by some older, male chaplains to accept women professionally." Military culture, like civilian society, changed slowly, only tentatively accepting women as religious leaders.[35]

Yet improving the gender composition of the chaplaincy corps required more than internal command initiatives; it also needed the assistance of religious groups. Women still had to meet the education requirements of the chaplaincy, and not all faiths groups ordained women, which in turn limited the number of potential female military chaplains. In 1970, women constituted about 3 percent of American clergy, leaving the military with a tiny pool of candidates from which to recruit. Even those denominations that trained women could offer few potential chaplains to the military. The Presbyterian Church allowed women to attend seminary and become full clergy in 1956 but, prior to 1970, never graduated more than nine female ministers a year. In 1972, when the navy chaplaincy opened its doors to women, only the Reform Hebrew Union College and the Reconstructionist Rabbinical College trained women as rabbis. And because nuns are not ordained like priests and are not empowered to celebrate Mass or perform sacraments, the Catholic Church could not endorse any women as chaplains.[36]

By the late 1970s, Navy Chief of Chaplains John J. O'Connor took on the task of finding more women to commission as chaplains. Charged by his country to build a chaplain corps composed of men and women, the Catholic priest implored religious groups to elevate women to positions of leadership and encourage them to enter the officer corps. To John W. Marriott, then the head of the LDS Military Relations Committee, he insisted he was "not being an alarmist" but urged faith groups to "aggressively" recruit women. He appealed to equity—in careers and among religions—noting changing social mores and benefits to religion. "In today's world, equal opportunity without regard to race or sex is a reality quickly coming into sharp focus . . . the implications for ministry under that concept is an opportunity to be grasped; a service to be rendered." Although the Catholic Church would not abide by his request, O'Connor was both priest and chaplain. His loyalties to God and country, pressed to the limit in Vietnam, required him to move deftly between them as the navy's ranking religious officer. His was a role that demanded fidelity to faith and loyalty to the state. In asking religious groups to endorse female candidates to the chaplaincy, he sublimated his religion's doctrine to his country's needs— a move he would later reverse as archbishop of New York, where his positions on women's rights and sexuality fell in line with the Church and attracted controversy. As chief of chaplains, however, O'Connor modeled conscientious deference in setting aside Catholic preferences for the good of the service.[37]

Religious groups could fumble as they tried to meet military needs. Early in her seminary training, Bonnie Koppell noticed a recruiting poster and set her sights on the army chaplaincy. First, she had to convince the Jewish Welfare Board (JWB) to endorse her candidacy, an uncertain proposition given that no Reconstructionist rabbis sat on the committee, Orthodox Jews did not accept women rabbis, and the Conservative movement remained in heady discussions about ordaining women. To her surprise, the JWB supported her candidacy, and Koppell headed to the Chaplain Officer Basic Course. She was one of four Jews and three women in a class of 108—and the only Jewish woman. Nevertheless, she found the 4 a.m. wake-up calls, the marching, and the uniform requirements more challenging than her gender or her religious identity. Yet in 1980, on the verge of accepting her commission as a chaplain in the Army Reserves, Koppell encountered the opposition she had expected several years earlier. What "should have been a pro-forma shuffling of paperwork . . . became a major political battle" between Reform and Orthodox factions of the JWB. All Koppell could do was wait. There was nowhere to march as the limbo stretched on, with the rabbi ticking off days, then weeks, then years wondering what would happen. After seven years of equivocating, the JWB finally signed off on her endorsement, and Koppell became an army chaplain more than ten years after seeing a recruiting poster. Other female rabbis faced the same challenges, much to the dismay of Reform rabbis who felt the "Orthodox Rabbinical Council of America has taken a stand which further polarizes the Jewish community." To the Reform movement, the Orthodox block stank of double standards, in which the "mutual respect and equality" that had long characterized the JWB Chaplaincy Commission evaporated once women ascended the pulpit.[38]

The military's plea for female chaplains split the JWB's Commission on Jewish Chaplaincy and stymied seven decades of American Jewish unity promoted by interaction with the military. Rabbi Louis Bernstein asserted that he and his Orthodox compatriots had little choice, once endorsing Julie Schwartz as a navy chaplain "'was imposed on us,'" for "'Orthodox Judaism cannot accept women rabbis.'" Schwartz understood the situation through a different lens, one familiar to those immersed in the pluralistic environment of the military. From her perspective, "'we were not trying to make them bend their own principles or change their beliefs.'" Rather, she noted, the goal was "a compromise to allow me to have my principles and beliefs." While Schwartz sought a middle ground, the different Jewish movements continued to accuse one another of "shattering" communal consensus—fictive and fragile to be sure, but a consensus that endured until the military sanctioned female clergy. A more measured unity prevailed a few months later, when the commission reorganized as the JWB/Jewish Chaplains Council that was nominally amalgamated but allowed each Jewish movement to approve its own candidates for the chaplaincy, thus removing the impression that the Orthodox would endorse women as rabbis.[39]

Once in the military, female chaplains—like other minorities—found that top-down orders to integrate women moved the process forward but did not counteract resistance on the ground. Chaplain Janet Horton (Christian Science) described her experience as one of the first female army chaplains as being part of "the birth of a new idea" in which there were, inevitably, some "labor pains." For chaplains, she explained, the pushback often emanated from men who felt the American state had controverted or even commandeered religion. While her own denomination long understood women as religious leaders, male chaplains often disagreed, saying, "'God told me you shouldn't be here.'" One day a young man looked at her dress uniform, spilling over with medals for her work, and sputtered, "You can't have possibly deserved those awards," before spitting on her. Although she felt "a lot like a gas grill lighting up" and ready to explode, she turned to Mary Baker Eddy's teaching—"'If you do not handle evil in the very first instance, it will handle you in a second"—before responding calmly.[40]

Others were less sanguine about the work environment. Navy chaplain Carolyn C. Wiggins (CME) encountered women who sought her out "because they feel uncomfortable discussing certain problems with men." But as the first female chaplain at each of her posts—including the Portsmouth Naval Hospital, aboard a submarine tender, and the Naval School of Ordnance Disposal—she had to navigate between pressure to outperform male chaplains and the need to "'downplay being the "first woman.'" Although Wiggins made her career in military ministry, she did so despite a "hostile chaplaincy" filled with men who "have difficulty accepting us as professional colleagues." Changing military culture—like shifting workplace norms across the United States—trudged along.[41] Expanding the gender and racial diversity of religious leadership set new precedents for who could sport the chaplain's insignia. In the 1970s, the cross and the tablets remained the standard emblems of the military chaplaincy. Nevertheless, the religious composition had changed—evangelical ministers and Eastern Orthodox priests increased while priests and rabbis declined. But some wondered whether a state-supported religious institution should exist at all.

Was the military chaplaincy necessary? Or, at the very least, why did the government employ clergy as chaplains? These questions pricked the minds of two Harvard law students while sitting in a constitutional law class, and four years after the fall of Saigon, Joel Katcoff and Allen Wieder decided to do something about it. After a summer's worth of Freedom of Information Act requests yielded valuable military documents, the pair spent the days before Thanksgiving 1979 furiously putting together a legal complaint. The army chaplaincy, they decided, was unconstitutional. It violated the First Amendment's prohibition on government establishment of religion. As taxpayers, they sought relief from the courts, hoping that a judge would bend the military to their will. They wanted the government to cease funding the chaplaincy and thereby dismantle the military's religious programming. Of course, servicemembers had a right to practice their faith—the Constitution also guaranteed them free exercise of religion. But Katcoff and Wieder argued that that could not occur, not fairly at least, with public money financing clergy salaries and chapels, with the military regulating chaplain recruitment and promotion, and with the state recognizing some religions while excluding others. The structured religious environment that the military had built over the twentieth century thus became a constitutional predicament.[42]

Theirs was not the only lawsuit to contest the military chaplaincy, but it was the first to make its way through the federal courts. Katcoff and Wieder undertook what several lawyers for the Department of Defense deemed an "ambitious" effort to decimate the modern military chaplaincy. They hit the military at a vulnerable moment, and their lawsuit gained far more traction than the military had hoped. Chaplain George Evans (Lutheran), who oversaw the Marine Corps chaplaincy, assured the public that religion in the military was on " 'solvent constitutional grounds' because there ha[d] been military chaplains since colonial times."[43] The courts were not enamored with substituting history for constitutionality, however, and instead entertained Katcoff and Wieden's claims. The freshly minted legal duo wanted the courts to apply the "Lemon test," the three-pronged evaluation of interaction between religion and state developed in 1971, to the military chaplaincy. To pass constitutional muster, legislation needed to (1) have a secular purpose, (2) neither advance nor inhibit religion, and (3) avoid "excessive government entanglement" in religion. The army was confident that the military garrisons differed sufficiently from civilian contexts to make the Lemon test moot. But its legal team knew it would need to maneuver carefully to avert a rote application, which the chaplaincy might fail. Army Chief of Chaplains Kermit D. Johnson (United Presbyterian) was unflinching in his appraisal of *Katcoff*: it represented "the single most critical issue facing us at this time. The future of the Chaplaincy rests on the outcome of this case."[44]

The army loathed the lawsuit, but it turned to work, not despair. A shuffling roster of legal and religious manpower from the army and the Department of Justice collaborated to handle the impending trial. On March 7, 1980, the Harvard law graduates met their government antagonists in the courtroom of Judge Jacob Mishler, an efficient and scrupulous arbiter whom lawyers commended for being "down-to-earth." Less than a half year later, the judge issued his ruling. As federal taxpayers, Katcoff and Wieder had standing to sue, and a constitutional question propelled the case forward. When the government's initial effort to dismiss the case failed, Chief of Chaplains Johnson convened a strategy session at Manresa House, a Catholic retreat center on the banks of the Severn River. With a view of the Naval Academy in sight, the army contemplated its options, aided by a designated hitter from the Army Reserves: Chaplain Israel Drazin (Jewish), an Orthodox rabbi, prolific scholar, Chaplain School lecturer, and attorney in private practice. The soft-spoken Drazin impressed the group, and the army recalled him to active duty. The litigation continued through Ronald Reagan's first term as president, first in district court and then in the Court of Appeals.[45]

Katcoff probed the "Olympian generality" of the six words that authorized military religion: "there are Chaplains in the Army." Soon after American television audiences bid farewell to the nation's best-known chaplain, M*A*S*H's Father Mulcahy, the Court of Appeals affirmed that "the primary function of the military chaplain is to engage in activities designed to meet the religious needs of a pluralistic community," a "formidable" challenge in light of the army's size, geographic distribution, and ethnic, racial, and religious diversity. The Court accepted the military's claim that "mobile, deployable" soldiers "uprooted from their home environments" and placed in stressful situations needed support that private civilian programming could not deliver. It was true, the Court conceded, that the chaplaincy would fail the Lemon test, but the chaplaincy did not operate "in a sterile vacuum." Willing to defer to military assessments on matters related to national security but cognizant of the fragility of free exercise, the Court framed "the test of permissibility" as one that weighed options against necessity. Much like the religious groups that studied the chaplaincy in Vietnam, the Court realized that the civilian chaplaincy proposed by the plaintiffs was "so inherently impractical as to border on the frivolous." Although the Appeals Court left room for further litigation, their decision stood: public funds, including the taxes of Joel Katcoff and Allen Wieden, could pay for the military chaplaincy.[46]

The court swatted away existential speculation about the chaplaincy as a state establishment of religion, but not before the litigation unleashed a bevy of scrutiny about the ability of military personnel to fully and freely exercise their religions. While *Katcoff* made its way through the courts, legislators from both parties peered in to inspect religion in the military, initially focusing on the character education program. Questions on other topics, such as the endorsing process, promotions, educational requirements, rules for retired chaplains, denominational recruiting goals, transfers between branches, physical standards, the Chaplain Candidate program (for seminarians), budgets, and religious discrimination in leadership piled on. Congress used its spending power to further evaluate the work of the chaplaincy. The Defense Appropriations Bill of 1985, which was introduced in March 1984 and signed into law by President Reagan on October 19, 1984, included a section that mandated a Department of Defense study group dedicated to "examin[ing] ways to minimize the potential conflict between the interests of members of the Armed Forces in abiding by their religious tenets and the military interest in maintaining discipline." The committee needed to "make the maximum effort to ascertain the views of the broadest spectrum of religious organizations." In particular, Congress demanded that the military look outside the chaplaincy and speak to members of faith groups about their experiences in the armed forces.[47]

Like many of the twentieth-century military's efforts to assess religious toleration or accommodation, the study blended systematic surveying with haphazard investigation. After mailing questionnaires to 179 faith groups, the group received responses from about half and interviewed representatives of a select faiths. Some of the interviewees, like Floyd Robertson of the NAE and Monsignor James Markham of the Military Ordinariate, led organizations that endorsed chaplains. Others, like Edward Elson of the National Presbyterian Church or Mason LaSalle, the manager of the Christian Science Committee on Publication in DC, lived in the area and spent time in uniform. DC connections also led the military to Wali Akbar Muhammed, who was a member of the Nation of Islam and the managing editor of the *American Muslim Journal*, and Guru Sangat Kaur Khalsa, who belonged to the Sikh Dharma's National Affairs Advisors and was also the daughter of former CIA director of counterintelligence, James Angleton. Interviews with Muslims and Sikhs—the religions with which the military was least familiar and lacked chaplains—included military personnel. With all faith groups, the committee elicited feedback about existing accommodations and inquired about religious requirements in the realms of diet, dress, Sabbath observance, and medical practices. Throughout, the committee reported, it tried to ascertain what the military could do rather than what it already did. "While there was great concern over cohesion and unity," the report announced, "there was also a willingness to risk some differentiation if it was 'the right thing to do.'"[48]

At least one member of the interview team came to the project with ideas about what "the right thing" might be. Chaplain Drazin, whose work on *Katcoff* produced a victory for the military chaplaincy, was troubled by the "lack of sensitivity to allowing soldiers their religious freedom." The newly promoted brigadier general (and the first rabbi to hold that rank) questioned the two standards the military used to gauge religious requests: first, was it reasonable, and second, did military necessity allow or preclude deviations from the norm? The problem, as Drazin understood it, was that willingness to bend regulations was "arbitrary" and therefore often "infringe[d] on soldiers' rights." Ever an attorney, he suggested using the Supreme Court's compelling interest standard. Drawn from *Sherbert v. Verner*, a 1963 case about religion and unemployment compensation, this test first assessed whether state action substantially burdened an individual acting on a sincere religious belief and then required the state to demonstrate that it had a "compelling interest" and used the "least restrictive means" to accomplish its goals. Although using the compelling state interest standard required elucidating sincerity, which might require military meddling in matters of belief, Drazin argued that the armed forces already appraised the sincerity of conscientious objectors. Therefore, religious soldiers should and could be treated in a commensurate manner.[49]

The trials of faith experienced by minority religious groups motivated Drazin's work. Seventh-day Adventists represented a particularly acute concern. Even as courts-martial dwindled, Drazin learned there were over 100 cases of soldiers unable to observe their Sabbath. As Seventh-day Adventist Dennis Grier explained, inconsistent interpretations of regulations irritated church members. For over a decade, his commanding officers had accommodated his Saturday Sabbath and then suddenly, a new superior officer spurned even conversations about it, a response he deemed "unjust." He had hoped to find an administrative work-around through the chaplaincy, given his religious inclination "to obey those in authority." But absent assistance, Greer noted, "my faith also teaches me to obey God rather than man when there is a conflict of conscience." For Drazin, resolving this conflict did not demand reinventing free exercise of religion in the military so much as importing its scope from civilian life. "The military," he asserted, "should not adhere to a different standard than the government."[50]

For those faiths most in need of accommodation, however, regulatory exegesis was dangerous. If religious leaders reveled in interpreting faith to their congregations, they were less sanguine about military officials explicating policy to the American faithful. Chaplain Abraham Avreck (Jewish) identified the logical shortcoming that plagued the compelling interest standard: it relied on human authority. Who, after all, determined what counted as a compelling state interest? Asked to consider how he would react to an officer ordering a soldier to violate the Sabbath due to a compelling state interest, the retired chaplain said he would weigh the evidence, ask why it was compelling, and elicit the repercussions of participating or retreating. "If I felt that he had to go, I would tell him to go," the rabbi testified. But if there was no compelling interest or a feasible alternative existed, Avreck insisted, "I would do my utmost to tell him or to try, if I were in a position, to make other arrangements." Despite this imperfect balancing, the compelling interest standard nevertheless resonated with many religious leaders, including those who rarely experienced the collision between religious doctrine and military conformity. For Monsignor Markham, a reasonableness standard yielded "arbitrary" decisions, whereas a compelling interest standard pressured commanders to avoid badgering religious people. Elson, whose parishioners at the National Presbyterian Church had once included FBI Director John Edgar Hoover and President Dwight D. Eisenhower, likewise focused on the problem of command discretion, noting that there are "a lot of unreasonable people in the world."[51]

Interviews created opportunities for the military to engage in religious fact-finding and offered denominations an occasion to distinguish and justify their religious practices. Thus, Christian Scientists explained that, within the military context, their church took a pragmatic approach to matters like vaccinations. They recognized that military needs, particularly rapid deployment to areas with endemic disease, might require vaccines as a public health measure. Former navy pilot Mason LaSalle noted he could understand why "a state of readiness" demanded ensuring that Christian Scientists were "not a hazard." They could be flexible, in other words, and the church affirmed that their religion valued both authority and cooperation. Christian Scientists also used the interview to educate, teaching the American state who they were and who they were not. Specifically, Christian

Scientists distinguished their faith healing from that of Pentecostals, and they wanted the military to appreciate the difference. A memo further clarified that "the Christian Science church does not take an arbitrary, dogmatic position towards doctors characteristic of so many involved in faith healing." Christian Scientists were, their representatives asserted, a reasonable people, ready to collaborate with the military.[52]

The NAE's Floyd Robertson similarly used the interview to discredit allegations of prohibited proselytizing by evangelicals. Although some considered their efforts "to win others to Jesus Christ" a violation of military policy, he insisted on "a distinction between proselytizing and evangelism." Lest this seem like mere word play, he acknowledged the difference was difficult to detect. Evangelism, Robertson explained, relied on persuasion; proselytizing, in contrast, used coercion. A poor grasp of evangelical praxis therefore accounted for the criticism, but that, he insisted, could be rectified without altering regulations. When Monsignor Markham replied that Catholics found the policy reasonable because "Catholics are not proselytizers in the active sense," he obliquely hinted that Robertson's interpretation of both evangelism and military regulations may have been less common than evangelicals presumed (or desired).[53]

The most commonly raised concerns, however, centered on the military's unbending insistence on the appearance of uniform bodies. As in the 1950s, the dress code's prohibition of beards and head coverings, such as religiously mandated turbans (for Sikhs) and yarmulkes (for Jews), remained a point of contention. Although the military experimented with allowing beards in the 1970s, by the early 1980s, it revoked the more liberal policy. In the name of "professionalism," all beards—religiously motivated or not—became verboten. Sikhs found themselves on a roller coaster careening between exemptions that allowed their religious praxis and enforcement that interfered with serving God and country simultaneously. The consequences of erratic accommodation produced a theological problem because, as Guru Sangat Kaur Khalsa remarked, "as American citizens, we believe in our freedom of religion and as Sikhs, we believe in serving our country." In fact, soldiering was itself a longstanding Sikh tradition, and Staff Sergeant Krosen enlisted in the army (instead of the navy) because it appeared to allow men to maintain beards as necessary. His experience in Special Forces demonstrated that beard-wearing Sikhs provided a tactical advantage to the U.S. in the Middle East because they could blend in. Such assurances fell flat, as the military worried that insincere or fake Sikhs might try to take advantage of a more comprehensive grooming exemption. That the American Sikh community could ascertain the difference between genuine and fraudulent community members seemed to mean little, perhaps because a parallel interview with American Muslims offered a more lenient sensibility, one that the military might have preferred to apply to all faiths. Islamic teachings encouraged beards, but the Muslim leaders the military spoke to in the 1980s minimized the importance of facial hair. They classified it as an expression of personal commitment, not a religious requirement—which made sense for clean-shaven members of the NOI. There was no reason, Waki Akbar Muhammed explained, "for us to take a chance on losing credits with the military or disturb, disrupting procedures of the military just to have them accommodate us for the wearing of a beard." He would, of course, prefer that the armed forces allow those who wanted to, but demanding permission was "extreme."[54]

Yet the religious moderate-extreme spectrum was imprecise and thus prone to generating slippery slope concerns. The military prided itself on conformity and uniform cohesiveness, which turbans and yarmulkes seemed to inhibit. Even though yarmulkes were, as Monsignor Markham noted, prevalent and unobtrusive in his home, New York City, and even though Protestants likewise had "no objection to somebody wearing his yarmulke if he wants one with his breakfast," the military still brooded over the head covering as a potential spectacle. Would a camouflage yarmulke suffice? Would a yarmulke emblazoned with the Marine Corps insignia be ok? Chaplain Avreck assured the study group that any aesthetic choice would be fine. For Jews, "a covering is a covering," whether a military-issue hat or a baseball cap. Looking to the broader Jewish world, Avreck reminded American military leaders that the Israeli Defense Forces allowed, but did not require, head coverings without disrupting other dress code requirements. Anticipating the objection that, like a beard exemption for Sikhs, a yarmulke exception for Jews might create a cascade of requests, the JWB's Rabbi David Lapp commented, "a rash of everybody putting on a yarmulke" was unlikely. Instead, he argued for allowing yarmulkes as a statement of goodwill, suggesting that yarmulke-wearing soldiers would appreciate the dispensation because it indicated that they had been "accepted in spite of" their minority faith.[55]

While Drazin and other military leaders focused on the appropriate legal standard for religious accommodations, others were more concerned with equity. Muslims, cognizant of their minority status, requested opportunities for daily worship, alternatives to pork, and recognition of the obligations to fast during Ramadan. But more than any particular provision, they wanted fairness. Specifically, "whatever is allowed for any other group should be allowed for us . . . if members of the Jewish faith are allowed special conditions for their observances or holidays, then we would like the same consideration." It was less Muslim specificity and more religious equality that mattered. For as Wali Akbar Muhammed explained, the military needed to understand that his faith contributed to his national identity. No matter their origin—immigrant or native-born, Islam or the Nation of Islam—Muslims who lived in the United States, he argued, "are part and parcel American Muslims." Muhammed charged the military with wielding its power for the good of the state, religion, and American society. Institutionally accommodating Muslim needs would "give a broader perspective to the private sector" and encourage more religious toleration and equality across American life. The religious needs of the American faithful varied, but a desire for fairness, not neutrality, united their requests.[56]

The resulting report assimilated some recommendations but resisted others. It justified new suggestions on the grounds that "a detailed and inclusive command religious program is a vital element in all military units." The devil, of course, squirmed in the details. Granting time for short periods of religious worship rarely impeded military performance, and most dietary needs could be partially accommodated without significant alteration to regular kitchen procedures. In contrast, permitting exemptions to standard medical procedures would be reckless and allowing deviation from the uniform standards polarizing. Religious conflict was, to some degree, inevitable, but most American religious groups tempered their standards in the military environment. This, from the study's perspective, was laudable and presented the military with a corollary opportunity to resolve discord through administrative mediation instead of legal battles. Most tangibly, the report recommended revising regulations to reflect the acceptability of a non-Sunday Sabbath, exploring the possibility of combat rations that better met a variety of religious diets, and allowing chaplains to wear "religious accouterments with the uniform" while on duty. More amorphously, they suggested that the Department of Defense issue a comprehensive statement about the accommodation of religious practices, create a curriculum that taught personnel and officers about a wider variety of faith traditions, and better inform recruits about the potential tension between religious and military requirements. Despite repeated conversations with a number of faith groups that highlighted the potential benefits of unclenching the tight grip on uniform dress, the committee did not flinch: "visible or otherwise apparent exceptions to military uniform and appearance standards have a significant adverse impact on cohesion, discipline, and military effectiveness."[57]

A few months after the study issued its report, the Department of Defense issued Directive 1300.17. It ordered commanders to approve "requests for accommodation of religious practices . . . when accommodation will not have an adverse impact on military readiness, unit cohesion, standards, or discipline." This wide-ranging instruction attempted to smooth over extraordinarily uneven free-exercise rights in the military as religious pluralism accelerated in the late twentieth century. Yet the emphasis on readiness, cohesion, and discipline provided an easy out. Neither a beard nor a turban nor a yarmulke could pass military muster in 1985, but the renewed struggle to bind religious faith and military duty might have evaded scrutiny had two law students not questioned the constitutionality of the chaplaincy.[58]

As the study group learned, the religious needs of the American military extended far beyond Protestants, Catholics, and Jews, and the chaplaincy began moving away from its tri-faith architecture. A rhetorical shift replaced "three major faith groups" with "four distinctive faith groups" (Protestant, Catholic, Jewish, and Orthodox), thus recognizing—and counting—Orthodox Christians as they had been advocating for decades. "Distinctive" soon took on a life of its own, as a 1987 guide to "denominational issues" defined "distinctive faith groups" as those "desiring to worship separately in denominational services," which enabled numerous evangelical Protestants to separate themselves from the longstanding tradition of "General Protestant" worship.

Nevertheless, in 1987, the Department of Defense set "a historic precedent" by finally recognizing "a group outside the Judeo-Christian tradition" when it designated the Buddhist Churches of America an official endorsing agency. (It would take seventeen years for the navy to commission Jeanette Shin as the military's first Buddhist chaplain.) Around the same time, the chaplaincy abandoned the denominational quotas that had structured chaplain recruitment since World War II—only loosely enforced and often unachieved. Finally, it took almost eighty years to expand religious leadership beyond Christians and Jews, but in 1993, after the military accepted the Islamic Society of North America's endorsement, Imam Abdul-Rasheed Muhammad pinned a crescent to his collar as the nation's first Muslim chaplain.[59]

Unlike in 1917, adding a crescent proved simple and uncontroversial, but commissioning Chaplain Muhammad rendered the Army Chaplain Corps Regimental Crest—which included only a cross and a tablet—incomplete. The army could have appended a crescent and subsequently supplemented it with additional religious symbols. However, Chief of Chaplains Matthew Zimmerman (National Baptist) decided to pursue an alternative option. Two decades after the young Protestant chaplain led a memorial service for Malcolm X and taught race relations workshops in Germany, Zimmerman became the first African American chief of chaplains. The lessons from his early years stuck with him. His time in Europe underscored "the need for diversity in the chaplaincy." As chief of chaplains, he constructed a more capacious and robust vision, one that included Muslims, promoted more women, and increased racial and ethnic diversity. The new corps crest reflected these priorities. It replaced religiously specific emblems with a white dove holding an olive branch atop an open book—a space in which each soldier and each chaplain could place God's word. The NAE was nonplussed, displeased that the chaplaincy's insignia would no longer bear the cross. But to be serious about its recently articulated commitment to "Spiritual Fitness," the military had to expand its worldview to a greater multitude of religions—symbolically and literally. Almost a quarter century after Elmo Zumwalt insisted on equal opportunity in the navy, Chief of Chaplains Zimmerman demanded the army chaplaincy do so as well. "America's Army is ministered to by a chaplaincy that is multi-faith, ethnically and religiously diverse, and supportive of the soldier's right to free exercise of religion.

We must be a model of equal opportunity," he stated, because "the denial of equal opportunity to any one diminishes the worth of the whole Army, and ultimately the Nation." Simultaneously descriptive and aspirational, Zimmerman steered the chaplaincy toward the twenty-first century.[60]

Epilogue

Between God and the American State

THE SUN STREAMED over freshly shorn grass, and the air started to feel heavier as summer advanced upstream over the Potomac River. A few weeks earlier, over Memorial Day weekend in late May, small flags had dotted the landscape, adding splashes of red and blue to the meticulously maintained green grounds. A few months later, after the Vermont stonecutters, polishers, and engravers crafted it from a slab of quarry rock, a regulation headstone would be added to the unceasing rows and columns of memorials to the nation's war dead. The workers who made and installed it might have noticed the emblem etched into the white marble, distinct from most of its neighbors. The star and crescent, stark and black against the cool veiny stone, could not stem the lashing pain of loss, of course, but it could bring comfort to a family. Ghazala Khan's son was buried with full military honors and with the prayers of a Muslim chaplain. There was no mix-up over this burial: his religion, like his service to country, was clear, carved into the monument that bears his name.[1]

Captain Humayun Khan is not the only Muslim buried at Arlington National Ceremony, but he is one of the best known. Like everyone laid to rest there, his grave sits on land that once belonged to Algonquin Indians and now hosts over 4 million visitors a year. The grief of his mother is, more than a decade after his 2004 death, still palpable and, in 2016, became quite public. Khan, many Americans learned through his father's speech at the 2016 Democratic National Convention, was a dedicated soldier who felt compelled to volunteer in his adopted nation's military and combatted coreligionists abroad during Operation Iraqi Freedom. He was, according to those who served alongside him, a "'soldier's officer,'" bridging the distance between the ranks, and "'just your average, all-American kid'" whose heroic dedication saved the lives of others. His story, recounted in newspapers and featured on the nightly news, resounded with many, including those whose footsteps now sink into the grass as they walk through Section 60 to reach Grave 7986. There, visitors pause to deliver notes or leave flowers or simply reflect. The celebration of the life and untimely death of the son of Pakistani immigrants who chose to fulfill an obligation of citizenship— a duty that many native-born Americans no longer complete in the absence of the draft—is compelling. It offers the salve of religious inclusion rather than bigotry, and the balm of multiculturalism rather than xenophobia. It is incomplete, to be sure, eliding the incivility and intolerance that has marked the experience of many Muslim soldiers. But it remains powerful.[2]

Like Private Leonard Shapiro's errant burial sixty years prior, the story of Captain Khan testifies to the state of religion in the armed forces, to the consequences of the decision to enlist faith in support of military endeavors. Because the state waged war, war killed, and death rituals vary by faith, the armed forces needed diverse clergy who could comfort the dying, conduct funerals, and console the living. This demand hardly lessened over the American century, an era defined as much by combat as by living in the shadow of war. For twentieth-century Americans, the passel of people and organizations that mobilized the country for battle often created some of the most tangible and significant encounters with the modern state. The violence of war continues, with 9/11 and the ongoing global War on Terror that followed puncturing any illusion that the twenty-first century would pivot in another direction. For all the differences between Khan and Shapiro, including their religious identities (Muslim and Jew), their military status (officer and enlisted man), and the context of their service (War on Terror and World War II), their respective experiences help mark the ways in which the federal government, through the military chaplaincy, has structured religious encounters, regulated religious identities and practices, and sparked trials of faith in God and country.

A century ago, Congress responded to lobbying pressure from several minority faith groups and opened the chaplaincy to Christian

Scientists, the Eastern Orthodox, Jews, and Mormons. The chaplaincy evolved from a rickety outfit into a sturdy organization more than ten times the size of its 1917 predecessor. Since then, the range of faiths represented in the chaplaincy has multiplied and the effort to adequately assist a broader array of religions intensified. The process of constructing, implementing, and disseminating the modern chaplaincy's worldview has been slow and uneven, with Protestant denominations sliding in far more easily than Islam, Buddhism, Hinduism, and Sikhism. Religious diversity has waxed and waned, but it is, in the end, a fact: American military personnel belong and adhere to a wide variety of faith traditions—and sometimes none at all. Military leaders have spent these last hundred years scrambling to figure out how to handle this heterogeneity and unify the armed forces despite difference. Religious cooperation and racial discrimination frequently coexisted, sometimes reinforcing one another and sometimes contesting one another. The pluralist ethos of the chaplain corps, built intentionally, if imperfectly, since World War I, is a choice inevitably beset with tension. As this sensibility took root, it also generated resistance, both by those who felt the chaplaincy did not uphold its moral claims and by those who rejected its pluralist disposition.

Conflicts recur in part because certain disputes are inherent to the commitment to religious freedom for all—or as many as possible. Take the clash over sectarian prayer in public settings. The epistolary spat between Chaplain Brenner (Jewish) and Chaplain Sampson (Catholic) in 1965 has not disappeared or even dissipated. It has become more common and more virulent. For the most part, it is a conflict over the use of Jesus's name, rather than a more general reference to God, outside designated worship services. Those who want to name Jesus at a premeal benediction or a patriotic ceremony feel prayer is incomplete, even denuded, without it. Those who are offended feel uncomfortable, excluded from the community, and view replacing Jesus with God as an easy, minor fix. The strongest advocates for more sectarian prayer have been evangelical and fundamentalist Protestants who have actively sought to "assume a more effective leadership role in matters that pertain to the Chaplaincy as a whole as well as those which impact on our own chaplains." Framing the military as a mission field meant seeking individual service members and targeting the organization as a whole. Civilian advocacy organizations have added to the fray, with the Chaplain Alliance for Religious Liberty, led by retired chaplains committed to the free exercise of evangelical "orthodox Christian truths," frequently squaring off against the Military Religious Freedom Foundation, which guards against proselytizing and state establishment of religion.[3]

The chaplaincy has long served as a battleground for American faiths and religious Americans looking to influence state and society. The Vietnam War produced some of the deepest and most wrenching challenges, with chaplains engaging in internal debates and facing external attacks over the uncomfortable links between religion and state in an immoral war. But the chaplaincy continues to attract attention for what it is, is not, and could be. Hearing a navy chaplain explain his work on a local Christian radio station upset Peggy Liebe terribly, for example. The chaplain mentioned that "they have to allow Satanists a place to perform their worship rituals." To Liebe, this news was "disturbing" and, frankly, unbelievable. It was, she concluded, a "great tragedy" that the founders lacked the "foresight to state 'Christian religion'" in the First Amendment. After all, "how could they have known of the Eastern cults and demonism that would invade this country?" Navy Chief of Chaplains Alvin D. Koeneman (Lutheran) responded to her 1989 letter, but his answer probably did not satisfy Liebe. He informed her that "Navy policy is to accommodate the doctrinal or traditional observances of the religious faith practiced by individual members when they will not have an adverse impact on military readiness, individual or unit readiness, unit cohesion, health, safety, or discipline." It was possible to forbid any "practice [which] would be detrimental to good order and discipline," but to Liebe's likely dismay, this meant chaplains also retained the discretion to assist members of the military in pursuing their individual practices of faith.[4]

While the case of Satanists was unusual, the issue of American religious boundaries was not. Over the twentieth century, the question of what the state recognized as religion—and what it excluded—endured. As the demographics of the United States shifted as a result of more open and flexible immigration laws and as the population of the military changed in response to the end of the draft, the chaplaincy continued to reevaluate what ministry it provided and how it handled a range of distinct American religions. Yet as the military puzzled its way through a new and fluctuating spiritual landscape, it often acted inconsistently. While it accepted the sacramental use of peyote (provided it was inhaled more than twenty-four hours prior to duty), protected Wiccan religion, and welcomed Muslim, Buddhist, and Hindu clergy into the chaplaincy, it stumbled trying to codify regulations allowing Sikh turbans and Muslim beards, understand the concerns of atheists and humanists, and untangle eruptions of Protestant division. Despite recurring resistance to splintering American religion into ever-smaller categories, in spring 2017, the Department of Defense formally revised and expanded its "faith group codes" to 221 in order to "standardize and better identify religious preferences recognized by the Military Services." The new "Faith and Belief Code" table doubled the religious identification options available to personnel, thereby enabling the military to collect more precise demographic data, create more tailored religious programming, and gauge the need for chaplains from specific traditions more accurately. Since recognition begets accommodation, groups like humanists and heathens celebrated this change, while some others, like Missouri Synod Lutherans, worried about "a heavily secularized military culture" propelled by "atheist activism." Although all of these Americans share a rhetorical commitment to religious freedom, disagreement about its definition and meaning continues to spark conflict.[5]

Nevertheless, regulations have long prompted religious groups to address their own precepts. When asked about Shareda Hosein's effort to become the first female Muslim military chaplain in 2008, Chaplain Richard Pace (Church of God), the director of personnel for the army chaplaincy, replied, "I really don't think the Army needs to be the place for the Muslim community to work out the role of female religious professionals." The military kept its distance, maintaining that Hosein held the requisite graduate degree required for chaplains, but because she was not an imam, she—like Catholic nuns—did not meet the qualification standards. Yet over the past century, the military chaplaincy has often spurred faiths to reconsider their own prerequisites for leadership and, more recently, wrestle with the status of women. In 2001, the Southern Baptist Convention passed a resolution prohibiting local churches from ordaining women as ministers, which in turn prevented them from serving as chaplains. Letters flooded into the offices of the North American Mission Board. While some conveyed their "deep disappointment [and] sense of betrayal," Southern Baptists familiar with the armed forces expressed outrage. The retired Veterans Affairs (VA) Chief of Chaplains, William E. Thompson Jr. (Southern Baptist), castigated his denomination for "such a short sighted position." Pointing out that the then–chief of chaplains for the VA was a Southern Baptist woman, he laid out the long-term consequences: "If Southern Baptist women are not endorsed for chaplaincy, then positions of leadership in all kinds of chaplaincy will *never again* be filled by a Southern Baptist woman." The American state has no jurisdiction over religious leadership, yet for denominations who want their clergy to be able to serve as chaplains, military requirements for chaplains create an incentive for faiths to calibrate their internal standards accordingly.[6]

Religious tension continues to bubble and simmer, with the "culture war in the chaplain corps" testing the resilience of autonomy and self-governance.[7] Some fights have been quite public—witness the controversy over proselytization at the Air Force Academy. There, officers (not chaplains) asserted that religious freedom demanded allowing them to fulfill the mandate of their faith to find converts, while their targets argued that such proselytizing violated the religious freedom of others. Similarly, the end of the military's "Don't Ask, Don't Tell" policy about homosexuality thrilled some chaplains who wanted to marry openly gay servicemembers and vexed others who worried that they would be forced to officiate gay weddings. (This is unlikely, given the military chaplaincy's historic pattern of granting chaplains the autonomy to determine which marriages to perform.) Some battles have taken place in the courtroom. But litigation has rarely proved productive for plaintiffs, because whether challenging the chaplaincy itself, testing the restrictions on religious headgear, or asserting religious bias against evangelical chaplains, the courts have deferred to the military. In contrast, Congressional interventions have shaped the chaplaincy by authorizing chaplain spots for new religious groups, as it did in 1917, and compelling the military to redress inequities related to religious observance, including head coverings, in the late 1980s. The impulse has not always been toward inclusion and pluralism, however. Evangelicals' prolonged effort to alter policy about sectarian prayer found legislative allies who, in 2014, used the Defense Appropriations Bill to allow chaplains to "pray according to the traditions, expressions, and religious exercises of the endorsing faith group." Labeled as a "protection of the religious freedom of military chaplains," the funding bill dictated by statute what internal military policy had resisted for years—on the same religious freedom grounds.[8]

This religious friction is intrinsic—perhaps even endemic—to the military chaplaincy as a constitutionally anomalous institution that manages a tremendous state infrastructure dedicated to serving religious and moral needs. As the current army chaplaincy directives state, "religious support in the Army has no civilian equivalent."[9] Unlike other government spaces, which can bracket off religion as a private matter, no such opportunities for separation exist in the military. When Americans live, fight, and die together, religion does not reside on the margins or evaporate from communal compounds. Instead, the military chaplaincy tries to navigate a careful course that enables religious practice without trampling on the rights of others or establishing a state religion.

In responding to American religious diversity, the military chaplaincy was often at the forefront of recognizing shifting patterns. The armed forces welcomed Catholic and Jewish chaplains much earlier than white Protestant American society viewed Catholics and Jews as their equals. In this, the military was a trendsetter. Engagement with other religious minorities, such as Mormons, Christian Scientists, Eastern Orthodox, Buddhists, Seventh-day Adventists, Muslims, and Sikhs, has often been more fraught. Nevertheless, when the draft conscripted Americans, the chaplaincy had to find ways to meet the needs of a religiously complex population. The tension between conservative and liberal Protestants, a divide expressed in late twentieth- and early twenty-first century political realignment and cultural conflict, began in the military in World War II and persists to the present. While the military ignored the claims of atheists in the 1920s, their voices reverberated more loudly in the late twentieth and early twenty-first century—accompanied by humanists and agnostics who felt ill served by the chaplaincy's theistic limits. Although personnel can officially identify as humanists, their efforts to persuade the military to commission a humanist chaplain have gone unheeded. In contrast, in January 2017, the army settled a decades-long dispute over religious beards and head coverings by updating grooming and appearance regulations to permit religious soldiers to wear hijabs, beards, and turbans.[10]

As an institution, the military chaplaincy responds to a different set of interests and pressures than the political goals of legislators or the constitutional delicacy of judges. In this sense, the military chaplaincy has generally operated out of a sense of pragmatic pluralism, an imperfect yet optimistic sensibility that it is possible to serve a wide array of faiths in the same place. As the navy chaplaincy articulated in 1973, "the chaplains' relationship to their churches, as the source of ecclesiastical credentials, does not exist in isolation from an equally binding relationship to the Navy." Thus, "accepting a Naval commission a member of the clergy acknowledges military command, accepts the principle of command responsibility for the spiritual and moral welfare of naval personnel, and is subject to military regulations and directives and the Uniform Code of Military Justice." In uniform, a chaplain must act in accordance with the dictates of God and the American state. The federal government can proscribe attendance at segregated services, as it did in the 1960s, or proselytizing, as it did for the greater part of the twentieth century. The state can also command chaplains to serve personnel of other faiths, which it enforced among Catholic chaplains even when the Pope resisted interfaith work and it continues to do today. Moreover, changes in policy and culture emerged from the decisions of particular people, so chiefs of chaplains like William Arnold in World War II, John O'Connor in the aftermath of Vietnam, and Matthew Zimmerman in the 1990s shaped the chaplaincy according to their interests in greater religious, racial, ethnic, and gender diversity through savvy command of internal organizational politics. Despite the discursive and policy mandates to serve all, however, the chaplaincy has never been a fully inclusive religious space. Many have felt left out and a good number have succeeded in climbing in. Real gaps remain, and they irk those standing outside.[11]

The chaplaincy yoked religion to the state. Managing religion entailed the creation and oversight of regulations that set the parameters for the chaplaincy's work and built its culture. Often the government has deflected attention away from its role, whether by delegating the responsibility for ecclesiastical endorsement to civilian groups, partnering with private entities to create radio shows like *Chaplain Jim*, or deferring to vague statements about religious freedom without acknowledging the interpretation required to implement them. Nevertheless, over the past century, the chaplaincy has served as a fairly reliable bellwether of the politics of religious toleration and accommodation. If questions about who is included, what counts as American religion, who can be a military chaplain, and what religious practices can be supported are perennial, the chaplaincy has proven resilient and adaptive in response to turbulence—of war, of politics, of social change, of cultural norms, and of religion itself.

Abbreviations

AAAA	American Association for the Advancement of Atheism
ACCC	American Council of Churches of Christ
ACLU	American Civil Liberties Union
AEF	American Expeditionary Force
AFCB	Armed Forces Chaplains Board
AME	African Methodist Episcopalian
AMEZ	African Methodist Episcopalian Zion
BMNA	Buddhist Mission in North America
BYU	Brigham Young University
CALC	Clergy and Laity Concerned About Vietnam
CANRA	Committee on Army and Navy Religious Activities (subgroup of the JWB)
CCAR	Central Conference of American Rabbis (Reform)
CCC	Civilian Conservation Corps
CJC	Commission on Jewish Chaplaincy (replaced CANRA)
CME	Christian (earlier, Colored) Methodist Episcopalian
CO	conscientious objection
CREDO	Chaplains' Relevance within Emerging Drug Order
CRLNC	Committee on Religious Life in the Nation's Capital
CTCA	Commission on Training Camp Activities
DMZ	demilitarized zone (Korea)
DP	Displaced Persons
DPRK	Democratic People's Republic of Korea
FCC	Federal Council of Churches of Christ in America
GHQ	General Headquarters
HUC	Hebrew Union College

JAG	Judge Advocate General
JTS	Jewish Theological Seminary
JWB	Jewish Welfare Board
LDS	Latter-day Saints (Mormon)
MSTS	Military Sea Transport Service
NAE	National Association of Evangelicals
NCCJ	National Conference of Christians and Jews
NCC	National Council of Churches (successor to the FCC)
NOI	Nation of Islam
PCRW	President's Committee on Religion and Welfare in the Armed Forces
POW	prisoner of war
PRP	Personal Response Project
RA	Rabbinical Assembly
RAA	Recreation and Amusement Association
ROK	Republic of Korea
ROTC	Reserve Officer Training Corps
SDA	Seventh-day Adventist
UCMJ	Uniform Code of Military Justice
UMT	Universal Military Training
USO	United Service Organization
VA	Veterans Affairs
WAAC	Women's Auxiliary Army Corps
WACS	Women's Army Corps
WAVES	Women Accepted for Volunteer Emergency Service
YMCA	Young Men's Christian Association
YU	Yeshiva University

Archival Sources

Manuscript Collections

American Catholic Research Center and University Archives, Catholic University of America, Washington, DC

| NCWC | National Catholic War Council Papers |
| ROGS | Records of the Office of the General Secretary—National Catholic Welfare Conference Papers |

American Jewish Archives, Cincinnati, OH

AJA	American Jewish Archives
CCAR	MS 34: Central Conference of American Rabbis
HFP	MS 763: Herbert A. Friedman Papers
HSP	MS 718: Harold Saperstein Papers
MFL	SC 15430: Morris Frank Letters
MFP	MS 170: Morton C. Fierman Papers
MKP	MS 709: Morris Kertzer Papers
PSP	MS 108: Phineas Smoller Papers
RBC	SC 1365: Reeve Brenner Correspondence
RGP	MS 704: Roland Gittelsohn Papers
RHP	MS 675: Richard C. Hertz Papers
SSP	MS 101: Samuel Sandmel Papers

American Jewish Historical Society, New York, NY

| NJWB1 | I-180: National Jewish Welfare Board, Army-Navy Division |
| NJWB2 | I-249: National Jewish Welfare Board Military Chaplaincy Records |

Archives of the Archdiocese of New York, Yonkers, NY
PCH   Patrick Cardinal Hayes Papers
FCS   Francis Cardinal Spellman Papers

Archives of the Billy Graham Center, Wheaton, IL
TMJ   Collection 285: Torrey Maynard Johnson Papers
SDF   Collection 658: Samuel Douglas Faircloth Papers

Church of Jesus Christ of Latter-day Saints Church History Library, Salt Lake City, UT
LDS   LDS Church History Library

Columbia University, New York, NY
CCOH   Columbia Center for Oral History Archives, Rare Book &
                        Manuscript Library

Congregational Library and Archives, Boston, MA
CCCA   RG 4373: Congregational Christian Chaplain Applicant
                        Collection

Dwight D. Eisenhower Presidential Library, Abilene, KS
DDE-AW   Papers as President of the U.S., 1953–61 (Ann Whitman File)
DDE-WH   Papers as President of the U.S., 1953–61 (White House
                        Central Files), General File

General Conference Archives of the Seventh-day Adventist Church, Silver Spring, MD
GCA   General Conference Archives

GLBT Historical Society, San Francisco, CA
GLBT   Allan Berube World War II Project Papers

Harry S. Truman Presidential Library, Independence, MO
HST   RG 220: Records of Temporary Committees, Commissions,
                        and Boards—Records of the President's Committee on
                        Religion and Welfare in the Armed Forces

L. Tom Perry Special Collections, Harold B. Lee Library, Brigham Young University, Provo, UT
ERI   MSS 7752: Oral History Interview with Eldin Ricks,
                        August 2, 1973

| SJP | MSS SC 3000: Spencer J. Palmer Interview, July 30–August 1, 1985 |
| THBI | MSS SC 3190: Timothy Hoyt Bowers-Irons Interview, July 27/August 1/August 8, 1973 |

Library of Congress, Washington, DC

CHB	MSS23564: Charles Henry Brent Collection, Manuscript Division
NBP	MSS11585: Newton D. Baker Papers, Manuscript Division
VHP	Veterans History Project, American Folklife Center

Mary Baker Eddy Library, Boston, MA

| MBEL | Organizational Records of the First Church of Christ, Scientist |

Meir Engel Papers, Private Family Collection

| MEP | Meir Engel Papers |

National Archives and Records Administration I, Washington, DC

| NCCH1 | RG 24, E377: Navy Chaplains Division (General Correspondence, 1916–40) |

National Archives and Records Administration II, College Park, MD

ACCH1	RG 247: Records of the Office of the Army Chief of Chaplains (1920–23)
ACCH2	RG 247: Records of the Office of the Army Chief of Chaplains (1920–75)
ACCH3	RG 247: Records of the Office of the Army Chief of Chaplains (1954–75)
ACCH-SC	RG 247: Records of the Office of the Army Chief of Chaplains (1941–48, Security–Classified)
AEF	RG 247: Records of the Office of the Army Chief of Chaplains (AEF)
NCCH2	RG 24: Navy Chaplains Division (Correspondence, 1941–1959)
NCCH3	RG 24: Navy Chaplains Division (Annual Activity and Trip Reports, 1949–1957)

Navy Chaplains Archive, Fort Jackson, Columbia, SC
CRB   Chaplains Resource Board
FJC   Ft. Jackson scanned material available onsite
RCC   Retired Chiefs of Chaplains
VET   Vietnam End-of-Tour Reports (scanned and available
                       onsite)

Navy History and Heritage Command, Washington Navy Yard, Washington, DC
WL   Collection 201: William Larsen Papers

Presbyterian Historical Society, Philadelphia, PA
FCC   RG 18: Federal Council of Churches of Christ in America
                       Collection

Providence College Library, Special and Archival Collections, Providence, RI
EPD   Edward Paul Doyle, O. P. Collection

Social Welfare History Archives, University of Minnesota, Minneapolis, MN
NCCJ   SW0092: National Conference of Christians and Jews
                       Records

Southern Baptist Historical Library and Archives, Nashville, TN
SBHLA   Southern Baptist Historical Library and Archives

Swarthmore College, Swarthmore, PA
SCPC   Swarthmore College Peace Collection

University of Utah, Salt Lake City, UT
JWM   MS 164: John Willard and Alice Sheets Marriott Papers

U.S. Army Heritage and Education Center, Carlisle, PA
MAZ   Matthew A. Zimmerman Papers

Wheaton College, Wheaton, IL
NAE   SC/113: National Association of Evangelicals Records
                       (1941–2000)

Yale University Archives, New Haven, CT
APS   MS 299: Anson Phelps Stokes Papers

Additional Abbreviations

AC	*The Army Chaplain*
ADW	*Atlanta Daily World*
BAA	*Baltimore Afro-American*
BG	*Boston Globe*
CC	*Christian Century*
CD	*Chicago Defender*
CT	*Christianity Today*
GPO	Government Printing Office, Washington, DC
LAT	*Los Angeles Times*
NPR	National Public Radio
NYT	*New York Times*
OCCH	Office of the (Army) Chief of Chaplains
PC	*Pittsburgh Courier*
PT	*Philadelphia Tribune*
WP	*Washington Post*

Notes

Prologue

1. Kenneth C. Martin to Mrs. Shapiro, October 9, 1944, Box 10, Folder 60, NJWB2.

2. On the cultural significance of Gold Star Mothers, see Rebecca Jo Plant, *Mom: The Transformation of Motherhood in Modern America* (Chicago, 2010).

3. Isaac Toubin to Aryeh Lev, December 5, 1944; William R. Arnold to Kenneth C. Martin, January 9, 1945, Box 10, Folder 60, NJWB2.

4. Lyman C. Berrett Oral History, October 24, 1974, 14, MS-17096, LDS.

5. Charles S. Freedman to Philip S. Bernstein, April 28, 1944, Box 10, Folder 52, NJWB2.

6. William R. Arnold to Kenneth C. Martin, January 9, 1945, Box 10, Folder 60, NJWB2.

7. Mrs. Robert de Yoe to William Larsen, August 1945, Box 1, Series I, Folder: Correspondence with Killed Marines' Families, WL. Many other chaplains also mentioned photographing graves for families.

8. Kenneth C. Martin to William R. Arnold, February 11, 1945, Box 10, Folder 60, NJWB2.

9. Chaplain Roland Gittelsohn (Jewish) estimated that prior to entering the chaplaincy in World War II, 90 percent of his interaction with clergy was with rabbis. Gittelsohn, "Pacifist to Padre," 24, Box 64, Folder 7, RGP.

10. William R. Arnold to Isaac Toubin, March 7, 1945, Box 10, Folder 60, NJWB2.

11. Although First Amendment scholars regularly assess religion-state interaction, historians have rarely paid attention to state engagement with or regulation of religion in the same way they analyze state regulation of race, gender, sexuality, and citizenship. Some exceptions include Sarah Barringer Gordon, *The Spirit of the Law: Religious Voices and the Constitution in Modern America* (Harvard, 2010); Kathleen Holscher, *Religious Lessons: Catholic Sisters and the Captured Schools Crisis in New Mexico* (Oxford, 2012); Axel Shäfer, *Piety and Public Funding: Evangelicals and the State in Modern America* (Penn, 2012); Allison Collis Greene, *No Depression in Heaven: The Great Depression, the New Deal, and the Transformation of Religion in the Delta* (Oxford, 2015). Law and religion scholars often frame state regulation of religion as studies of religious freedom. See Winnifred Sullivan, *The Impossibility*

of Religious Freedom (Princeton, 2005); Tisa Wenger, *We Have a Religion: The 1920s Pueblo Indian Dance Controversy and American Religious Freedom* (UNC, 2009); David Sehat, *The Myth of American Religious Freedom* (Oxford, 2011); Isaac Weiner, *Religion Out Loud: Religious Sound, Public Space, and American Pluralism* (NYU, 2013); Finbarr Curtis, *The Production of American Religious Freedom* (NYU, 2016); Anna Su, *Exporting Freedom: Religious Liberty and American Power* (Harvard, 2016); Tisa Wenger, *Religious Freedom: The Contested History of an American Ideal* (UNC, 2017).

12. Harold B. Lee to Gustave A. Iverson, June 8, 1944, quoted in Joseph Boone, "The Roles of the Church of Jesus Christ of Latter-Day Saints in Relation to the United States Military" (PhD diss., BYU, 1975), 571.

13. Regulations forbid chaplains from proselytizing, but several religious groups still viewed the military as a mission field, ripe with possibility for converting the unchurched.

14. Most scholarship on religion and mobilization for war examines the Cold War. Seth Jacobs, *America's Miracle Man in Vietnam: Ngo Dinh Diem, Religion, Race, and U.S. Intervention in Southeast Asia* (Duke, 2005); David S. Fogelsong, *The American Mission and the "Evil" Empire* (Cambridge, 2007); William Inboden, *Religion and American Foreign Policy, 1945–1960: The Soul of Containment* (Cambridge, 2008); Jeremy Gunn, *Spiritual Weapons: The Cold War and the Forging of an American National Religion* (Praeger, 2009); Jonathan Herzog, *The Spiritual-Industrial Complex: America's Religious Battle against Communism in the Early Cold War* (Oxford, 2011). One exception is Andrew Preston, *Sword of the Spirit, Shield of Faith: Religion in American War and Diplomacy* (Knopf, 2012).

15. Scholarship on religion in twentieth-century America has significantly increased but tends to focus on religious contributions to conservatism or liberalism. On religion and conservatism, see Lisa McGirr, *Suburban Warriors: The Origins of the New American Right* (Princeton, 2002); Donald T. Critchlow, *Phyllis Schlafly and Grassroots Conservatism: A Women's Crusade* (Princeton, 2005); Bethany Moreton, *To Serve God and Wal-Mart: The Making of Christian Free Enterprise* (Harvard, 2009); Daniel Williams, *God's Own Party: The Making of the Christian Right* (Oxford, 2010); Darren Dochuk, *From Bible Belt to Sun Belt: Plain-Folk Religion, Grassroots Politics, and the Rise of Evangelical Conservatism* (Norton, 2012); Kevin Kruse, *One Nation Under God: How Corporate America Invented Christian America* (Basic, 2015); Seth Dowland, *Family Values and the Rise of the Christian Right* (Penn, 2015). On religion and liberalism, see Kevin Schultz, *Tri-faith America: How Catholics and Jews Held Postwar America to Its Protestant Promise* (Oxford, 2011); David R. Swartz, *Moral Minority: The Evangelical Left in an Age of Conservatism* (Penn, 2012); Elesha Coffman, *The Christian Century and the Rise of the Protestant Mainline* (Oxford, 2013); Matthew Hedstrom, *The Rise of Liberal Religion: Book Culture and American Spirituality in the Twentieth Century* (Oxford, 2013); David Hollinger, *After Cloven Tongues of Fire: Protestant Liberalism in Modern American History* (Princeton, 2013); Lila Corwin Berman, *Metropolitan Jews: Politics, Race, and Religion in Postwar Detroit* (Chicago, 2015); David Mislin, *Saving Faith: Making Religious Pluralism an American Value at the Dawn of the Secular Age* (Cornell, 2015); Heather White, *Reforming Sodom: Protestants and the Rise of Gay Rights* (UNC, 2015).

16. Brian Balogh, *The Associational State: American Governance in the Twentieth Century* (Penn, 2015).

17. Winnifred Sullivan, *A Ministry of Presence: Chaplaincy, Spiritual Care, and the Law* (Chicago, 2014); Joshua Dubler, *Down in the Chapel: Religious Life in an American Prison* (Farrar, Straus and Giroux, 2013); Wendy Cadge, *Paging God: Religion in the Halls of Medicine* (Chicago, 2012).

18. Federal authority distinguished the twentieth-century chaplaincy from its antecedents in Christian Republicanism and the moral establishment. On Christian Republicanism, see Mark Noll, *America's God: From Jonathan Edwards to Abraham Lincoln* (Oxford, 2003). On the moral establishment, see Sehat, *The Myth of American Religious Freedom.* On "stealth Protestantism" and the moral establishment, see Janet R. Jakobsen and Ann Pellegrini, *Love the Sin: Sexual Regulation and the Limits of Religious Tolerance* (Beacon, 2003).

19. The military is often considered a total institution, "a place of residence and work where a large number of like-situated individuals cut off from the wider society for an appreciable period of time together lead an enclosed formally administered round of life." Erving Goffman, *Asylums: Essays on the Social Situation of Mental Patients and Other Inmates* (Doubleday, 1961), xxi.

20. Chaplain Martin wrote to Rose Shapiro at 1543 S. Ridgeway, Chicago, IL. In the 1940 census, Rose Shapiro appears at the same address, married to Joe (a tailor), with two daughters and one son. The same family appears on the 1930 census at 1427 S. Lawndale (both in Chicago's North Lawndale neighborhood). Two children's names vary (Victoria/Vivian, Louis/Lewis), while one is consistent (Frieda); the name discrepancies likely resulted from transcription errors and official versus unofficial names. The 1934 HOLC Map of Chicago places these addresses inside a red-lined (or "fourth-grade") section of the city, though immediately adjacent to a yellow (or "third-grade") section. Chicago Residential Security Map, No. 1 Map Section, 1934, available online: http://www.urbanoasis.org/wp-content/uploads/2012/07/NorthChicagoHOLCmapSM.jpg. On Jews in North Lawndale, see Beryl Satter, *Family Properties: How the Struggle over Race and Real Estate Transformed Chicago and Urban America* (Picador, 2010). The 1930 census also indicates that Rose was born in Russia and immigrated in 1914, which means she likely entered the United States through Ellis Island.

21. Randolph Bourne, "Unfinished Fragment on the State (Winter 1918)," in *Untimely Papers* (B. W. Huebsch, 1919), 140–141; Michael Sherry, *In the Shadow of War: The United States since the 1930s* (Yale, 1995).

22. On the vast web of administrative government, see Sophia Z. Lee, *The Workplace Constitution from the New Deal to the New Right* (Cambridge, 2014); Balogh, *The Associational State;* Karen M. Tani, *States of Dependency: Welfare, Rights, and American Governance, 1935–1972* (Cambridge, 2016).

23. Mae Ngai, *Impossible Subjects: Illegal Aliens and the Making of Modern America* (Princeton, 2005); Margot Canady, *The Straight State: Sexuality and Citizenship in Twentieth-Century America* (Princeton, 2009); Kelly Hernandez, *Migra! A History of the U.S. Border Patrol* (California, 2010); Michael Willrich, *Pox: An American Story* (Penguin, 2011); Tani, *States of Dependency;* Gautham Rao, *National Duties: Custom Houses and the Making of the American State* (Chicago, 2016); Jessica Pliley, *Policing Sexuality: The Mann Act and the Making of the FBI* (Harvard, 2015); Risa Goluboff, *The Lost Promise of Civil Rights* (Harvard, 2010); Peggy Pascoe, *What Comes Naturally: Miscegenation Law and the Making of Race in America* (Oxford, 2009).

24. Wendy Wall argued that a coalition of politicians, liberal clergy, intellectuals, corporate managers, and civic leaders "worked to blunt domestic intolerance and to broaden the bounds of national inclusion by promoting both cultural pluralism and a unifying American Way." Wendy Wall, *Inventing the "American Way": The Politics of Consensus from the New Deal to the Civil Rights Movement* (Oxford, 2008), 7.

25. On modern American citizenship, see Gary Gerstle, *American Crucible: Race and Nation on the Twentieth Century* (Princeton, 2001); Alice Kessler-Harris, *In Pursuit of Equity: Women, Men, and the Quest for Economic Citizenship in Twentieth Century America* (Oxford, 2003); Jennifer Klein, *For All These Rights: Business, Labor, and the Shaping of America's Public-Private Welfare State* (Princeton, 2003); Suzanne Mettler, *Soldiers to Citizens: The G.I. Bill and the Making of the Greatest Generation* (Oxford, 2005); Meg Jacobs, *Pocketbook Politics: Economic Citizenship in Twentieth-Century America* (Princeton, 2005); Sarah Igo, *The Averaged American: Surveys, Citizens, and the Making of a Mass Public* (Harvard, 2007).

26. As historians Jon Butler and David Hollinger noted separately in 2004, despite religion's enduring presence in the United States, it has rarely figured rigorously into the historiography of modern America. Kevin Schultz and Paul Harvey have argued that religion remains "everywhere and nowhere," quite remarkable in its "simultaneous presence in American history and absence in recent American historiography." Jon Butler, "Jack-in-the-Box Faith: The Religion Problem in Modern American History," *Journal of American History* 90, no. 4 (March 2004): 1357–1378; David Hollinger, "Jesus Matters in the USA," *Modern Intellectual History* 1, no. 1 (2004): 135–149; Kevin M. Schultz and Paul Harvey, "Everywhere and Nowhere: Recent Trends in American Religious History and Historiography," *Journal of the American Academy of Religion* 78, no. 1 (March 2010): 134.

27. For a historical and sociological overviews of the chaplaincy, see Richard Budd, *Serving Two Masters: The Development of the American Military Chaplaincy, 1860–1920* (Nebraska, 2002); Kim Hansen, *Military Chaplains and Religious Diversity* (Palgrave Macmillan, 2012); Spencer W. McBride, *Pulpit & Nation: Clergymen and the Politics of Religion in Revolutionary America* (Virginia, 2017). For institutional histories of the early chaplaincy, see Clifford Drury, *History of the Chaplain Corps US Navy, 1778–1939, Vol. 1* (GPO, 1948); Roy J. Honeywell, *Chaplains of the United States Army* (GPO, 1958); Parker C. Thompson, *From Its European Antecedents to 1791: The United States Army Chaplaincy*, Vol. 1 (GPO, 1978); Herman A. Norton, *Struggling for Recognition: The United States Army Chaplaincy*, Vol. 2 (GPO, 1977).

28. The state's role in shaping American religion remains underdeveloped, though this is beginning to change. On the history of the American state, see Stephen Skowronek *Building a New American State: The Expansion of National Administrative Capacities, 1877–1920* (Cambridge, 1982); William J. Novak, *The People's Welfare: Law and Regulation in Nineteenth-Century America* (UNC, 1996); Canady, *The Straight State*; James Sparrow, *The Warfare State: World War II Americans and the Age of Big Government* (Oxford, 2011); Joanna L. Grisinger, *The Unwieldy American State: Administrative Politics Since the New Deal* (Cambridge, 2012); Tracy L. Steffes, *School, Society, and State: A New Education to Govern Modern America, 1890–1940* (Chicago, 2012); Michelle L. Dauber, *The Sympathetic State: Disaster Relief and the Origins of the American Welfare State* (Chicago, 2013); Balogh,

The Associational State; Jennifer Mittelstadt, *The Rise of the Military-Welfare State* (Harvard, 2015); Tani, *States of Dependency.*

29. On sight and classification as tools of the state, see James C. Scott, *Seeing Like a State: How Certain Schemes to Improve the Human Condition Have Failed* (Yale, 1998).

30. When historians have examined religion in the military, state administration fades from view. Studies of the military chaplaincy tend to examine either particular religious groups or specific wars. See Donald Crosby, *Battlefield Chaplains: Catholic Priests in World War II* (Kansas, 1994); Anne Loveland, *American Evangelicals and the U.S. Military, 1942–1993* (LSU, 1996); Albert Isaac Slomovitz, *The Fighting Rabbis: Jewish Military Chaplains and American History* (NYU, 1999); Christopher Sterba, *Good Americans: Italian and Jewish Immigrants during the First World War* (Oxford, 2003); Deborah Dash Moore, *G.I. Jews: How World War II Changed a Generation* (Harvard, 2004); Jonathan H. Ebel, *Faith in the Fight: Religion and the American Soldiers in the Great War* (Princeton, 2010); Lyle W. Dorsett, *Serving God and Country: United States Military Chaplains in World War II* (Berkley Books, 2012); Jacqueline E. Whitt, *Bringing God to Men: American Military Chaplains and the Vietnam War* (UNC, 2014).

31. Ann Braude, "Women's History is American Religious History" in *Retelling US Religious History*, ed. Thomas Tweed (California, 1997), 87–107; Robert Orsi, *Thank You, St. Jude: Women's Devotion to the Patron Saint of Hopeless Causes* (Yale, 1996); Judith Weisenfeld, *African American Women and Christian Activism: New York's Black YWCA, 1905–1945* (Harvard, 1998); Karla Goldman, *Beyond the Synagogue Gallery: Finding a Place for Women in American Judaism* (Harvard, 2000).

32. Alva Brasted to William H. Wilson, March 15, 1937, 2–3, Box 6, Folder 000.3 (Religious Ministration, Vol. I), ACCH2.

33. On homosocial spaces, see Susan L. Johnson, *Roaring Camp: The Social World of the California Gold Rush* (Norton, 2000).

34. Morris Lazaron, "Religion for American Manhood," Box 256, Folder 337 (Chaplains' Training Conference 1923), ACCH2.

35. For an overview and history of forms of religious neutrality in law, see Douglas Laycock, "Formal, Substantive, and Disaggregated Neutrality Toward Religion," *De Paul Law Review* 39, no. 4 (Summer 1990): 993–1018.

36. *Abington v. Schempp*, 374 U.S. 203 (1963), at 310.

37. On militarization of everyday life, see Laura McEnaney, *Civil Defense Begins at Home: Militarization Meets Everyday Life in the Fifties* (Princeton, 2000) and Ji-Yeon Yuh, *Beyond the Shadow of Camptown: Korean Military Brides in America* (NYU, 2004).

1 Mobilizing Faith

1. John Dittmer, *Black Georgia in the Progressive Era, 1900–1920* (Illinois, 1977), 12–13, 123–131, 194–197; Nancy Gentile Ford, *Americans All! Foreign-Born Soldiers in World War I* (Texas A&M, 2001), 67–87.

2. Joseph H. Odell, "Making Democracy Safe for the Soldier: An Account of What Atlanta, Georgia Is Doing for a Cantonment," *The Outlook*, November 28, 1917; Joseph H. Odell, *The New Spirit of the New Army: A Message to the "Service-Flag" Homes* (Fleming H. Revell, 1918), 23. *The Outlook* started as *The Christian*

Union, under the editorial leadership of Henry Ward Beecher, in 1870, and became *The Outlook* in 1893. The paper supported military preparedness, which led to conflict with other progressive pacifist organizations.

3. Dittmer, *Black Georgia in the Progressive Era*, 12–13, 123–131, 185–186; Leonard Dinnerstein, *The Leo Frank Case* (Columbia, 1968); Steve Oney, *And the Dead Shall Rise: The Murder of Mary Phagan and the Lynching of Leo Frank* (Pantheon, 2003).

4. Odell, *The New Spirit of the New Army*, 103–105.

5. Lee Levinger, "Christian and Jew at the Front," *The Biblical World* 53, no. 5 (September 1919): 477; John Pershing, *Final Report of General John J. Pershing, Commander-in-Chief, American Expeditionary Forces* (GPO, 1920), 93. On the religious experiences of soldiers, see Jonathan Ebel, *Faith in the Fight: Religion and the American Soldier in the Great War* (Princeton, 2010).

6. Moral monotheism is my term.

7. David Kennedy, *Over Here: The First World War and American Society* (Oxford, 1980), 144–146; Christopher Capozzola, *Uncle Sam Wants You! World War I and the Making of the Modern American Citizen* (Oxford, 2008); Selective Service Regulations (GPO, 1917), 123–148; John Chambers, *To Raise an Army: The Draft Comes to Modern America* (Free Press, 1987), 191.

8. Ford, *Americans All!*; Bruce White, "The American Military and the Melting Pot in World War I," in *War and Society in North America*, ed. J. L. Granatstein and R. D. Cuff (Thomas Nelson, 1971), 37–51. On the contours of white ethnicity in this era, see Matthew Jacobson, *Whiteness of a Different Color: European Immigrants and the Alchemy of Race* (Harvard, 1998).

9. Quoted in Jennifer Keene, *World War I* (Greenwood, 2006), 73; Nancy K. Bristow, *Making Men Moral: Social Engineering during the Great War* (NYU, 1996), 1–4. On efforts to restrain urban vice, see Michael Willrich, *City of Courts: Socializing Justice in Progressive Era Chicago* (Cambridge, 2003). Rural Americans likely knew more about sex than the government assumed; see Gabriel N. Rosenberg, *The 4-H Harvest: Sexuality and the State in Rural America* (Penn, 2016).

10. Ford, *Americans All!*, 13, 102–107.

11. "Chaplains," in *Compilation of General Orders, Circulars, and Bulletins of the War Department, 1881–1915* (GPO, 1916), 38; *Increasing the Number of the Chaplains in the Army: Hearings before the Committee on Military Affairs on S. 2917*, United States Senate, 65th Congress, 1st Session (September 27, 1917), 4; "Modern Army Chaplain Must Be a Regular Fellow," *Baltimore News*, September 18, 1918; John Frazier, *Navy Chaplain's Manual* (1918), 40.

12. Earl Stover, *Up from Handymen: The United States Army Chaplaincy, 1865–1920* (GPO, 1977), 187; Richard Budd, *Serving Two Masters: The Development of American Military Chaplaincy, 1865–1920* (Nebraska, 2002), 121–124; Special Regulations No. 3: Appointment of Chaplains in the Regular Army and the National Army of the United States, 1917, Corrected August 31, 1918 (GPO, 1918), 7–9, Box 2, Folder: Appointment—Choice Candidates, AEF. Chaplains also had to pass the academic exams required of all officers.

13. Budd, *Serving Two Masters*, 112–114. Elihu Root—who would win the Nobel Peace Prize in 1912 and instigated the reform of legal education in the 1920s—began his five-year tenure as secretary of war in the aftermath of the Spanish-

American War. He modernized the army through centralization and education. See Stephen Skowronek, *Building a New American State: The Expansion of National Administrative Capacities, 1877–1920* (Cambridge, 1982), 212–234.

14. In medicine, the 1910 Flexner Report fundamentally altered the training of doctors by consolidating medical schools, increasing admissions standards, intensifying clinical experience, and regulating licensing. Lawyers, who like doctors had long trained through apprenticeship, began learning in accredited classrooms as well. The implantation of the German research university model and its attendant focus on graduate training transformed American higher education. See Kenneth Ludmerer, *Time to Heal: American Medical Education from the Turn of the Century to the Era of Managed Care* (Oxford, 1999); Bruce Kimball, *The Inception of Modern Professional Education: C. C. Langdell, 1826–1906* (UNC, 2009); Frederick Rudolph, *The American College and University: A History* (Knopf, 1962); John Thelin, *A History of American Higher Education* (JHU, 2004).

15. On the history of religion in American higher education, see Julie Reuben, *The Making of the Modern University: Intellectual Transformation and the Marginalization of Morality* (Chicago, 1996). On the tension between theological education and religious studies in the late nineteenth century, see D. G. Hart, *The University Gets Religion: Religious Studies in American Higher Education* (JHU, 1999), 46–66. The late nineteenth century also witnessed the creation of Catholic seminaries and rabbinical schools in the United States, which helped build an American-made, rather than European-imported, priesthood and rabbinate.

16. After World War I, the education requirements would be codified in law through the National Defense Act of 1920 and Army Regulations 605–30. At that point, the prerequisites for chaplains became: (1) men between the ages of twenty-three and thirty-four; (2) a BA and postgraduate degree from an accredited three-year theological seminary program; (3) active employment as a minister; (4) endorsement from a civilian religious organization; and (5) physical exam. The Navy used a lower upper age limit of 31.5 years. Reserve chaplains could be older. See Budd, *Serving Two Masters*, 113; Clifford Drury, *The History of the Chaplain Corps, United States Navy, Vol. I, 1778–1939* (GPO, 1948), 145, 167; Stover, *Up from Handymen.*

17. *Selective Service Regulations* (GPO, 1917), 40. For a discussion of the ideal attributes of chaplain candidates, see the Army and Navy Chaplains Committee Minutes, April 25–26, 1917, Box 70, Folder 8, FCC.

18. Special Regulations No. 3; Reuben, *The Making of the Modern University*, 84; "What the New Army Expects of Its Chaplains," *NYT*, June 17, 1917. On the intellectual foundations and commitments of American liberal Protestantism, see Amy Kittelstrom, *The Religion of Democracy: Seven Liberals and the American Moral Tradition* (Penguin, 2015).

19. Reuben, *The Making of the Modern University*, 88–132.

20. Charles Brent to Raymond Fosdick, July 16, 1918, Box 8, Folder 1, NCWC; James Connolly to Patrick Hayes, July 7, 1918, Box G-49, Folder 3, PCH.

21. *Report of the General War-Time Commission of the Churches* (December 1917), 224, 227. For an internal history of the FCC, see Elias Benjamin Sanford, *Origin and History of the Federal Council of Churches of Christ in America* (S. S. Scranton Company, 1916). On Wilson and religion, see Cara Burnidge, *A Peaceful Conquest: Woodrow Wilson, Religion, and the New World Order* (Chicago, 2016).

22. Committee on Negro Churches Meeting Minutes, October 18, 1917, Box 70, Folder 15, FCC. The question of black officers vexed the black community prior to the war. Du Bois's acceptance of short-term insult for long-term gain enabled the plan to move forward. Chad Williams, *Torchbearers of Democracy: African American Soldiers in the World War I Era* (UNC, 2010), 39–43.

23. Committee on Negro Churches Meeting Minutes; Clyde F. Armitage, "A Memo to Mr. Cavert Concerning Negro Chaplains," June 22, 1918, Box 70, Folder 15, FCC.

24. Charles H, Williams, "A Resume of Conditions Surrounding Negro Troops," August 5, 1918; Armitage, "A Memo to Mr. Cavert," Box 70, Folder 15, FCC.

25. Committee on the Welfare of Negro Troops, Meeting Minutes, February 16, 1918, Box 70, Folder 15, FCC; Armitage, "A Memo to Mr. Cavert."

26. Armitage, "A Memo to Mr. Cavert."

27. Father Dineen to Father Connolly, October 21, 1918, Box G-79, Folder 4, PCH; Armitage, "A Memo to Mr. Cavert." Ultimately, a single black candidate failed out of Chaplain School. Stover, *Up from Handymen*, 216.

28. *Sweatt v. Painter*, 339 U.S. 629 (1950); *McLaurin v. Oklahoma State Regents*, 339 U.S. 637 (1950); Richard Kluger, *Simple Justice: The History of* Brown v. Board of Education *and Black America's Struggle for Equality* (Vintage, 1975, 2004), 137.

29. Isaac Siegel to Cyrus Adler, July 8, 1917, and July 9, 1917, Box 327, Folder: Chaplains—1917, 1919–20, NJWB1. Jewish chaplains had served in the Civil War, generally securing appointments via Congress. Bertram Korn, "Jewish Chaplains during the Civil War," in *Jews and the Civil War: A Reader*, ed. Jonathan Sarna and Adam Mendelsohn (NYU, 2010), 335–352. Jewish chaplains served in other national armies, including Germany, by World War I. See Peter C. Appelbaum, *Loyalty Betrayed: Jewish Chaplains in the German Army during the First World War* (Valentine Mitchell, 2014).

30. John Morris Sheppard, "Chaplains at Large in the Army," Calendar No. 94, Report No. 90 (July 24, 1917); quoted in *Christian Science War Time Activities: A Report to the Board of Directors of the Mother Church* (Christian Science Publishing Society, 1922), 297–298.

31. Joseph Boone, "The Roles of the Church of Jesus Christ of Latter-Day Saints in Relation to the United States Military, 1900–1975," (PhD diss., BYU, 1975), 543–545; Christopher Sterba, *Good Americans: Italian and Jewish Immigrants during the First World War* (Oxford, 2003), 7; Ernest L. Paugh to Cyrus Adler, October 16, 1917, Box 326, Folder: Adler Correspondence 1917; McCain to Harry Cutler, August 3, 1918, Box 328, Folder: Chaplains—1918, NJWB1. While Pershing was amenable to naturalized citizens, Cyrus Adler assumed that the military would be receptive only to American-born rabbis.

32. Isaac Siegel to Cyrus Adler, October 31, 1917, Box 327, Folder: Chaplains—1917, 1919–20, NJWB1; Lee Levinger, *A Jewish Chaplain in France* (Macmillan, 1921), 93. Adler led the committee of Orthodox (David de Sola Pool, Bernard Drachman, M. S. Margolies), Conservative (Elias L. Solomon), and Reform (Louis Grossmna, Maurice Harris, William Rosenau) members. Cyrus Adler to Harry Cutler, October 21, 1917, and Cyrus Adler to the Adjutant General, November 9, 1917, Box 326, Folder: Chaplains—1917, 1919–20, NJWB1. On the state of Jewish seminaries at this time, see Jonathan Sarna, *American Judaism* (Yale,

2004), 192–193. On the intentions and working of the JWB, see Jessica Cooperman, "'A Little Army Discipline Would Improve the Whole House of Israel': The Jewish Welfare Board, State Power and the Shaping of Jewish Identity in World War I America" (PhD diss., NYU, 2010).

33. Jan Shipps argues that Mormonism was not simply an offshoot of Protestantism in *Mormonism: The Story of a New Religious Tradition* (Illinois, 1985), On Mormons and Christian Scientists as religious outsiders, see R. Laurence Moore, *Religious Outsiders and the Making of Americans* (Oxford, 1986), 25–47 and 105–127.

34. Herbert B. Maw Oral History, Interviewed by John R. Sillito, 1975, 18, LDS; *Christian Science War Time Activities*, 296–299.

35. *Christian Science War Time Activities*, 299, 303–304; "Christian Science in the Navy," *The New York World*, February 5, 1918.

36. Quoted in Boone, "The Roles of the Church of Jesus Christ of Latter-Day Saints," 546–547; "New Attack on Polygamy," *Missionary Review of the World* 31 (July 1918): 545; "Is Mormonism Still a Menace?" *Missionary Review of the World* 31 (July 1918): 806.

37. "The Chaplains' Organization in the American Expeditionary Force," October 22, 1918, Box 5, Folder: The Chaplains Organization; "Data Pertaining to Chaplains," Box 4, Folder: Data, AEF.

38. Cooperman, "'A Little Army Discipline.'" Two accounts of the founding of the JWB by insiders offer competing ideas about the organization's purpose and growth but share descriptions of the early challenges. Cyrus Adler, "An Account of the Origin of the Jewish Welfare Board," in *Lectures, Selected Papers, and Addresses* (n.p., 1933); Oscar Janowsky, Louis Kraft, and Bernard Postal, *Change and Challenge: 50 Years of the JWB* (NJWB, 1966). Horace Kallen felt the JWB cared more about itself than Jewish soldiers. See Kallen, "The Soldier and His Jewish Welfare," *The American Jewish Chronicle*, August 23, 1918.

39. Louis Egelson to Cyrus Adler, March 27, 1918, Box 326, Folder: Adler Correspondence, Jan.–Jun. 1918, NJWB1; B. L. Levinthal, "To the Philadelphia Jewish Men of the American Army and Navy," *The Jewish Exponent*, August 31, 1917; Albert Lucas to Harry Cutler, October 5, 1917, Box 334, Folder: Kashrut—1917–19, NJWB1.

40. Harry Cutler to the Paymaster General, August 21, 1917; Theodore Krainin to Bernard Drachman, May 11, 1917; Hyman to Cutler, October 9, 1917, Box 334, Folder: Kashrut—1917–19, NJWB1.

41. Cyrus Adler to Isaac Siegel, January 25, 1918; Harry Davidowitz to Cyrus Adler, February 12, 1918; Cyrus Adler to Harry Davidowitz, February 10, 1918, Box 326, Folder: Chaplains—1918, NJWB1.

42. Albert Slomovitz, *The Fighting Rabbis: Jewish Military Chaplains and American History* (NYU, 1999), 59–61; Report, 1918, Box 327, Folder: Chaplains—1918, NJWB1. The tablets used roman numerals from 1917 to 1980 and then switched to Hebrew letters. Army chaplains adopted this insignia in World War I, while the navy made the change in 1941. Slomovitz, *The Fighting Rabbis*, 59–61. For a more extensive history of the Committee of Six and a slightly different view of the World War I origins of tri-faith America, see David Mislin, "One Nation, Three Faiths: World War I and the Shaping of 'Protestant-Catholic-Jewish' America," *Church History* 84, no. 4 (December 2015): 828–862.

43. Budd, *Serving Two Masters*, 8–10, 121–153; Robert Gushwa, *The Best and Worst of Times: The United States Army Chaplaincy, 1920–1945* (GPO, 1977), 4–5. Technically, the military recognized the chaplains as a corps only in World War II, but it functioned as such before the military named it.

44. Budd, *Serving Two Masters*, 125; John Pershing, *My Experiences in the World War, Vol. 2* (Frederick A. Stokes Company, 1931), 132; H. Allen Griffith to Charles Brent, May 3, 1908, Box 7, Folder: January–February 1908, CHB; Charles H. Brent, "The Wholeness of Holiness," in *The Mount of Vision* (Longmans, Green, and Co., 1918); Eugene Bianchi, "The Ecumenical Thought of Bishop Charles Henry Brent," *Church History* 33, No. 4 (December 1964): 448–461.

45. David Setran, *The College "Y": Student Religion in the Era of Secularization* (Palgrave Macmillan, 2007), 133–134, 147, 249; Brent Diary, January 10, 1918, Box 3, CHB. See also Robert Schneider, "Voice of Many Waters" in *Between the Times: The Travail of the Protestant Establishment in America, 1900–1960*, ed. William Hutchison (Harvard, 1989), 100–111; Clifford Putney, *Muscular Christianity: Manhood and Sports in Protestant America, 1880–1920* (Harvard, 2001).

46. Brent Diary, December 16, 1917, January 10, 1918; Memorandum to the Commanding General Relative to the Organization of the Chaplains, January 10, 1918, quoted in Budd, *Serving Two Masters*, 126, 124–132.

47. "The Chaplains' Organization in the American Expeditionary Force," October 22, 1918, Box 5, Folder: The Chaplains Organization, AEF.

48. John Burke to Minnie Brown, August 21, 1917, Box 10, Folder 104, NCWC.

49. Bishop, Diocese of Alexandria, LA, to John Burke, January 31, 1918, Box 10, Folder 104, NCWC.

50. Lewis O'Hern to John Burke, June 14, 1917; Lewis O'Hern to John Burke, July 13, 1917, Box 10, Folder 104, NCWC.

51. Budd, *Serving Two Masters*, 128–129; Stover, *Up from Handymen*, 192–195; H. C. Stuntz Response, 2, Box 5, Folder: Special Problems in Chaplain's Work, AEF.

52. Charles Brent to John Burke, September 12, 1918, Box 6, Folder 22, NCWC; quoted in Pershing, *My Experiences in the World War*, 133. The lack of respect accorded chaplains due to the absence of clear signals of rank was a common theme in the army's postwar survey of chaplains. See responses in Box 5, Folder: Special Problems in Chaplain's Work, AEF.

53. G. W. Weldon report, January 14, 1919; quoted in Lewis L. Harney to John Axton, June 21, 1919, Box 2, Folder: Activities of Chaplains World War I and Post War, AEF; Alfonso Navarro report to James Gibbons, 2–3, Box 3, Folder 52, NCWC.

54. C. C. Bateman report, 8–9, Box 2, Folder: Activities of Chaplains World War I; S. Arthur Devan, Final Report, Box 5, Folder: Chaplains in Training Areas (Overseas); James M. Howard to Port Chaplain, Hoboken, NJ, May 7, 1919, Folder: Development of Organizations (Overseas), AEF.

55. Arthur C. Whitney to Senior Chaplain, 91st Division, January 31, 1919, Box 14668, Folder 1712, MBEL.

56. Francis B. Doherty to John Burke, June 21, 1918, Box 7, Folder 27; Charles Burke to John Burke, January 18, 1919, Box 6, Folder 22, NCWC.

57. "Priest Serves as Pastor of Three Faiths," *The Rochester Post*, November 1, 1918; Frank Wilson, "Christian and Jew" (emphasis original), undated, Box 4, Folder: Morale and Moral Conditions in European Cities, AEF.

58. National Defense Act of 1920, June 4, 1920, Section 15, 15. The navy's Office of the Chief of Chaplains did not officially exist in law until 1944. Drury, *The History of the Chaplain Corps*, 164. Political scientist Hugh Heclo argues, "Governments not only 'power' . . . they also puzzle." Hugh Heclo, *Modern Social Politics in Britain and Sweden* (Yale, 1974), 305.

2 "Christ Is the Melting Pot for All Our Differences"

1. Samuel Cavert to John Axton, December 8, 1920; John Axton to Samuel Cavert, December 9, 1920, Box 1, Folder 080 (Congregational Christian Churches); John Axton to Cyrus Adler, December 13, 1920, Box 1, Folder 080 (Jewish Welfare Board); John Axton to Clifford Smith, December 14, 1920, Box 1, Folder 080 (Christian Science), ACCH1.

2. Nancy MacLean, *Behind the Mask of Chivalry: The Making of the Second Ku Klux Klan* (Oxford, 1994), 11. For an analysis of the Protestantism of the KKK, see Kelly Baker, *Gospel According to the Klan: The KKK's Appeal to Protestant America, 1915–1930* (Kansas, 2011).

3. Leonard Dinnerstein, *Antisemitism in America* (Oxford, 1995), 78–84.

4. Jerome Karabel, *The Chosen: The Hidden History of Admission and Exclusion at Harvard, Yale, and Princeton* (Houghton Mifflin, 2005), 77–136. On Jewish intellectuals' efforts to rebuff "the Jewish question" and advance ideas about cultural pluralism within the academy, see Daniel Greene, *The Jewish Origins of Cultural Pluralism: The Menorah Association and American Diversity* (Indiana, 2011). Catholics, who had built an array of Catholic universities, did not elicit the same concern or scorn in higher education though they faced similar discrimination in housing and employment.

5. Dinnerstein, *Antisemitism in America*, 78–104; Karabel, *The Chosen*, 77–86.

6. John Higham, *Strangers in the Land: Patterns of American Nativism, 1860–1925* (Rutgers, 1992); Roger Daniels, *Guarding the Golden Door: American Immigration Policy and Immigrants Since 1882* (Hill and Wang, 2004).

7. Martin Marty, *Modern American Religion, Vol. 2: The Noise of Conflict, 1919–1941* (Chicago, 1991), 4. Other historians who identify religious conflict in this period include Sydney Ahlstrom, *A Religious History of the American People* (Yale, 1972); George Marsden, *Fundamentalism and American Culture* (Oxford, 1981, 2006); Alan Brinkley, *Voices of Protest: Huey Long, Father Coughlin, and the Great Depression* (Vintage, 1982); John T. McGreevy, *Parish Boundaries: The Catholic Encounter with Race in the Twentieth-Century Urban North* (Chicago, 1996); Eric Goldstein, *The Price of Whiteness: Jews, Race, and American Identity* (Princeton, 2007).

8. Internal army and navy histories of the respective chaplaincies consider the interwar years a low period tied to the weak fortune of a peacetime military. Robert Gushwa, *The Best and Worst of Times: The United States Army Chaplaincy, 1920–1945* (GPO, 1977); Clifford Drury, *History of the Chaplain Corps US Navy, 1778–1939, Vol. 1* (GPO, 1948).

9. Thomas Washington, "Address," in Appendix Exhibit G to Notes from the Chaplains' Conference; "Program: Conference of US Navy Chaplains, Washington, D.C., May 12–14, 1920," Box 19, Folder: Conference of US Navy Chaplains, NCCH1; James H. Spencer, "General Summary: May 1920," *Climatological Data for the United States by Section*, Vol. 7, Part II (Weather Bureau, 1921), 35.

10. C. Q. Wright, "The Place of Preaching in a Chaplain's Work" (emphasis original), Conference of US Navy Chaplains, Appendix Exhibit C, 1, Box 19, Folder: Conference of US Navy Chaplains, NCCH1.

11. Israel Zangwill's 1908 play *The Melting Pot* and Horace Kallen's three-part series in *The Nation*, "Democracy versus the Melting Pot: A Study in American Nationality," popularized the term and theory of a melting-pot nation. Nineteenth-century thinkers such as Ralph Waldo Emerson, Henry James, and Frederick Jackson Turner used variations of the term, including "smelting pot," "hot pot," and "crucible," but their usage did not penetrate American thought and culture in the same way. Kallen used Zangwill's term in order to critique it; he rejected the assimilatory project of the melting pot and advocated a harmonized orchestra as the metaphor and model of cultural pluralism. See Greene, *The Jewish Origins of Cultural Pluralism*, 76–86.

12. Robert Pierson of the War Department, speaking for the U.S. Army on April 16, 1924, to the Subcommittee of the Committee on Military Affairs, on S. 2532 and H. R. 7038, 68th Congress, 1st Session, "To Increase the Number of Chaplains in the Army," 4–5. Pierson used "Hebrews" and "Jews" interchangeably; his slippage between racial and religious categories in a story about religious accommodation suggests that the government viewed Jews as both insiders and outsiders at a moment that many historians view as the turning point for European ethnic groups becoming white. See Matthew Jacobson, *Whiteness of a Different Color: European Immigrants and the Alchemy of Race* (Harvard, 1998).

13. C. M. Charlton, "The Relation of the Chaplain to His Denomination and to the Church at Large," Conference of US Navy Chaplains, Appendix Exhibit L, Box 19, Folder: Conference of US Navy Chaplains, NCCH1; 1 Corinthians 9:22. See, for example, Chaplain George Waring's comments in "What the New Army Expects of Its Chaplains," *NYT*, June 17, 1917.

14. Julian Yates, "Origins of the Army and Navy Hymnal," 1923; John Axton to Caroline Parker, November 5, 1920, Box 1, Folder 080 (Century Publishing Co.), ACCH1.

15. Caroline Parker to John Axton, July 6, 1921; Caroline Parker to John Frazier, June 29, 1920, Box 1, Folder 080 (Century Publishing Co.), ACCH1; Alice Kessler-Harris, *Out to Work: A History of Wage-Earning Women in the United States* (Oxford, 1982, 2003), 226–227.

16. *The Army and Navy Hymnal* (Century Publishing, 1920), iii. The statistics come from the 1925 Hymn Edition because the layout with lyrics but no music is more straightforward.

17. Yates, "Origins of the Army and Navy Hymnal."

18. Julian Yates, "Report of the Conference on Moral and Religious Work in the Army," 1, Box 256, Folder 337 (Chaplains' Training Conference 1923), ACCH2.

19. Ibid., 1–3.

20. "Services at Tomb Is Heroic as Dead Is Laid Away," *Associated Press*, November 11, 1921. For a cultural reading of the religion of the dedication of the Tomb of the Unknown Soldier, see Jonathan Ebel, *G.I. Messiahs: Soldiering, War, and American Civil Religion* (Yale, 2015), 46–68. On manhood and the military in the preceding quarter-century, see Kristin Hoganson, *Fighting for American Manhood: How Gender Politics Provoked the Spanish-American and Philippine-American Wars* (Yale, 1998) and Gail Bederman, *Manliness and Civilization: A Cul-*

tural History of Gender and Race in the United States, 1880–1917 (Chicago, 1995). On masculinity and American Jewish life, see Sarah Imhoff, *Masculinity and the Making of American Judaism* (Indiana, 2017).

21. Morris Lazaron, "Religion for American Manhood," Box 256, Folder 337 (Chaplains' Training Conference 1923), ACCH2; "The Pittsburgh Platform, 1885," reprinted in Michael Meyer, *Response to Modernity: A History of the Reform Movement in Judaism* (Wayne State, 1995), 387–388. "Protestant, Catholic, Jew" was not yet solidified as the typical order, and multiple speakers used different variations.

22. Lazaron, "Religion for American Manhood." The language of the "God-idea," the conceptualization of religious formality as symbol, and the insistence on responsibility to God as the highest calling of man reflected key platforms of Reform Judaism. Catholics of the era would have disagreed with this statement, for Pope Pius XI dismissed all invitation to participate in pan-Christian movements, much less Christian-Jewish ones. His 1928 encyclical *Mortalium Animos* specifically forbade participation in ecumenical groups as "false Christianity." Conservative Protestants and Orthodox Jews would have been similarly skeptical though perhaps less resistant than Catholics. On the challenges of interfaith cooperation, see Benny Kraut, "A Wary Collaboration: Jews, Catholics, and the Protestant Goodwill Movement," in *Between the Times: The Travail of the Protestant Establishment in America, 1900–1960*, ed. William R. Hutchison (Cambridge, 1989), 193–228.

23. Yates, "Report of the Conference on Moral and Religious Work in the Army," 16–18.

24. Dwight Davis to the President, July 10, 1923; Address of Maj. Gen. John L. Hines; and "Summary of Pronouncements and Findings," in *Report on the Conference on Moral and Religious Work in the Army* (GPO, 1923).

25. U.S. Congress, Joint Hearing before the Subcommittees of the Committee on Military Affairs of the United States Senate and the House of Representatives, *To Increase the Number of Chaplains in the Army*, 68th Congress, 1st session, April 16, 1924, (GPO, 1924), 8–9, 20–21.

26. OCCH, *The Chaplain: His Place and Duties* (GPO, 1926), 4–5.

27. Ibid., 4–6. As a female minister without formal ordination, Aimee Semple McPherson would not have qualified as a chaplain. For more on the popularity and importance of Sister Aimee in the 1920s and 1930s, see Matthew Sutton, *Aimee Semple McPherson and the Resurrection of Christian America* (Harvard, 2009). In many ways, the manual offered a portrait that evoked Max Weber's understanding of charismatic authority in *On Charisma and Institution Building*, ed. S. N. Eisenstadt (Chicago, 1968), 47. On the government's resistance to unruly religion during the New Deal, see Jonathan Ebel, "Re-forming Religion: John Steinbeck, the New Deal, and the Religion of the Wandering Oklahoman," *Journal of Religion* 92, no. 4 (October 2012): 527–535.

28. OCCH, *The Chaplain*, 13–15 (emphasis added).

29. "Report of the Pan-Denominational Conference," May 4–6, 1926, 2, Box 257, Folder 337 (Pan-Denominational Conference), ACCH2.

30. "Report of the Pan-Denominational Conference," 2; Dwight Davis to Charles Smith, April 23, 1926, Charles Smith to Dwight Davis, April 27, 1926, and Memo from John Axton to the Adjutant General and the Secretary of War, April 27, 1926, Box 6, Folder 000.3 (Religious Ministration in the Army, Vol. I), ACCH2; "Court Asked to Oust Army Chaplain Suit," *The Washington Herald*, April 23, 1926.

31. "Report of the Pan-Denominational Conference," 2.

32. Ibid., 2–3, Section XI. On pacifism in this era, see Joseph Kip Kosek, *Acts of Conscience: Christian Nonviolence and Modern American Democracy* (Columbia, 2009); Anne Klejment and Nancy Roberts, eds., *American Catholic Pacifism: The Influence of Dorothy Day and the Catholic Worker Movement* (Praeger, 1996).

33. John Axton to F. A. McCarl, October 1, 1923, Box 2, Folder 080 (YMCA), ACCH2. Thomas died in 1937, and by 1940, three African American chaplains served in the army. In 1940, the Office of the Chief of Chaplains claimed, "there is not any race discrimination against Negro Chaplains, either as to appointment or promotion," but "War Department policy . . . is to assign Negro Chaplains for Negro troops." George Rixey to Ines Cavert, June 10, 1940, Box 66, Folder 080 (Federal Council of Churches of Christ), ACCH2.

34. George J. Waring to Sydney K. Evans, July 15, 1930, and Sydney K. Evans to George J. Waring, July 16, 1930, Box 2, Folder Army + Navy Chaplain Correspondence (Catholic, 1917–1941), NCCH1. When President Woodrow Wilson re-segregated the federal workforce, his administration crafted policy that required photographs with job applications.

35. Meeting Minutes, January 30, 1935; CRLNC, Memorandum, February 25, 1935, Box 12, Folder: Religious Life in the Nation's Capital, NCCH1.

36. Kraut, "A Wary Collaboration," 193–230; Kevin M. Schultz, *Tri-faith America: How Catholics and Jews Held Postwar America to Its Protestant Promise* (Oxford, 2011), 33; Everett Clinchy to Newton Baker, November 5, 1928, Box 168, Folder: NCCJ 1931 & 1928, NBP.

37. Newton Baker to Everett Clinchy, April 21, 1930; Newton D. Baker to Richard F. Nelson, March 1932, Box 168, Folder: NCCJ 1931 & 1928, NBP.

38. Everett Clinchy, John Elliott Ross, and Morris Lazaron, "Story of the First Trio," November 11, 1933, Box 1, Folder: First Trio, NCCJ; Schultz, *Tri-faith America*, 15–67. For responses to NCCJ programs in the military, see Box 32, Folder: Comments, NCCJ.

39. Edward Duff to Anson Phelps Stokes, January 6, 1936; Leonard White to Henry Barden, December 6, 1935, Box 188, Folder 316, APS.

40. William Leuchtenberg, *Franklin D. Roosevelt and the New Deal: 1932–1940* (Harper & Row, 1963); Steve Fraser and Gary Gerstle, eds., *The Rise and Fall of the New Deal Order, 1930–1980* (Princeton, 1990); Alan Brinkley, *The End of Reform: New Deal Liberalism in Recession and War* (Vintage, 1995); David Kennedy, *Freedom from Fear: The American People in Depression and War, 1929–1945* (Oxford, 1999); Anthony Badger, *FDR: The First Hundred Days* (Hill and Wang, 2008); Ira Katznelson, *Fear Itself: The New Deal and the Origins of Our Time* (Norton, 2013); Alison Collis Greene, *No Depression in Heaven: The Great Depression, the New Deal, and the Transformation of Religion in the Delta* (Oxford, 2015).

41. Franklin D. Roosevelt, "Inaugural Address," March 4, 1933, http://www.presidency.ucsb.edu/ws/?pid=14473.

42. Badger, *FDR*, 56; James J. McEntee, *Now They Are Men: The Story of the CCC* (National Home Library Foundation, 1940), 9–12.

43. Margot Canaday, *The Straight State: Sexuality and Citizenship in Twentieth-Century America* (Princeton, 2009), 91–134; quoted in McEntee, *Now They Are Men*, 10.

44. General Committee, "Christian Citizens Challenged" appeal, 1934, Box 69, Folder 080 (General Committee, Volume 1), ACCH2; McEntee, *Now They Are Men*, 28; Greene, *No Depression in Heaven*, 163–193.

45. Julian E. Yates to John F. Leary, July 15, 1933; Alva Brasted to Joseph Sizoo, March 19, 1937, Box 69, Folder 080 (General Committee, Volume 1), ACCH2.

46. Report of the General Committee on Army and Navy Chaplains, September 21, 1933, Box 69, Folder 080 (General Committee, Volume 1), ACCH2.

47. Roy B. Guild to Julian E. Yates, June 16, 1933; Julian E. Yates to Roy Guild, June 19, 1933; Report of the General Committee on Army and Navy Chaplains, September 21, 1933; Gushwa, *The Best and Worst of Times*, 66.

48. David Greenberg, "Recollections of a CCC Chaplain," Box 30, Folder 207, NJWB2; Alva Brasted to Roy B. Guild, April 17, 1934; Edwin Burling to Roy B. Guild, August 4, 1933; Alva Brasted to Roy B. Guild, February 24, 1936, Box 69, Folder 080 (General Committee, Volume 1), ACCH2.

49. Bulletin, December 15, 1934, Box 69, Folder 080 (General Committee, Volume 1), ACCH2; Gushwa, *The Best and Worst of Times*, 61; Richard Braunstien, "The Circuit Rider Returns," *AC* 8, no. 3 (January 1937): 6.

50. David Greenberg, "Recollections of a CCC Chaplain," Box 30, Folder 207, NJWB2; Joseph Sides, "The Functions of the CCC Chaplain," *AC* 5, no. 1 (July 1934): 12. By the late 1930s, articles discussed sermon topics that could apply to all three religious traditions.

51. Report of the General Committee on Army and Navy Chaplains, December 15, 1934, Box 69, Folder 080 (General Committee, Volume 1), ACCH2; Alva Brasted, "A Message from the Chief of Chaplains," *AC* 4, no. 4 (April 1934): 6; Benjamin Franklin, *The Autobiography of Benjamin Franklin*, ed. Charles Eliot (Collier & Son, 1909), 83–85.

52. Alva Brasted, "News from the Office of the Chief of Chaplains," *AC* 5, no. 1 (July 1934): 5; General Committee on Army and Navy Chaplains Bulletin, May 15, 1934, Box 69, Folder 080 (General Committee, Volume 1), ACCH2. Chaplain Charles Conrad (Baptist) created a comparable group known as the "Golden Principle Society." Their membership cards read "In accepting membership in the GOLDEN PRINCIPLE SOCIETY, I will strive each day to mold my life after the pattern of 'THE GREAT TEACHER,' JESUS CHRIST, and to 'DO UNTO THE OTHER FELLOW AS I WOULD HAVE THE OTHER FELLOW DO UNTO ME.' I WILL ALWAYS GIVE MY FELLOW MAN A SQUARE DEAL," thus drawing on biblical and political sources. Charles L. Conrad, "CCC Religious Work," *AC* 5, no. 2 (October 1934): 6.

53. Patrick Clancey, "Conserving the Youth: The Civilian Conservation Corps Experience in the Shenandoah National Park," *The Virginia Magazine of History and Biography* 105, no. 4 (Autumn 1997): 460.

54. Calvin W. Gower, "The Struggle of Blacks for Leadership Positions in the Civilian Conservation Corps: 1933–1942," *Journal of Negro History* 61, no. 2 (April 1976): 130–131, 132–133. Brown's lobbying efforts helped improve the leadership options for African-Americans but earned him the ire of CCC director Robert Fechner, who deemed him a pest. The restriction on black commanders stemmed from the government's interest in sating, rather than baiting, local communities who feared and resisted African American CCC camps.

55. Roy B. Guild to Alva Brasted, October 18, 1934; Department of Race Relations, Federal Council, Reverend Loyd Hickman, Interview with Dr. Haynes, September 14, 1934, Box 69, Folder 080 (General Committee, Volume 1), ACCH2.

56. Alva Brasted to Roy B. Guild, October 24, 1934, Box 69, Folder 080 (General Committee, Volume 1), ACCH2.

57. "Minister Resents 'Slur' on Chaplains," *NYT*, April 16, 1930; "Ainslie on Chaplains," *The Atlanta Constitution*, April 17, 1930.

58. Scott H. Bennett, *Radical Pacifism: The War Resisters League and Gandhian Nonviolence in America, 1915–1963* (Syracuse, 2003), 23–68; Melissa Klapper, *Ballots, Babies, and Banners of Peace: American Jewish Women's Activism, 1890–1940* (NYU, 2013); Joyce Blackwell, *No Peace without Freedom: Race and the Women's International League for Peace and Freedom, 1915–1975* (SIU, 2004); Klejment and Roberts, *American Catholic Pacifism*; Kosek, *Acts of Conscience*, 8–9.

59. Gushwa, *The Best and Worst of Times*, 54; Executive Committee Meeting Minutes, September 28, 1934, Box 1, Folder 18, FCC.

60. Julian E. Yates to Roy B. Guild, July 8, 1933; Alva Brasted to Roy B. Guild, February 24, 1936, Box 69, Folder 080 (General Committee, Volume 1), ACCH2.

61. Alva Brasted to Roy B. Guild, February 24, 1936.

62. Editorial Comment, *AC* 8, no. 1 (July 1937): 1; Cover, *AC* 9, no. 1 (July–August 1938); C. H. Woodward, "True Pacifism," *AC* 8, no. 4 (April 1938): 140–141; Marty, *The Noise of Conflict*, 389; Gushwa, *The Best and Worst of Times*, 51–57; William Hughes, "A Thesis," *AC* 9, no. 2 (October–November 1938): 56–63.

63. Alva Brasted, "In Defense of Chaplains: Plain Philosophy of a Practical Pacifist," *The Lutheran Herald*, (November 5, 1935): 1081–1083. On the history of ELC chaplains, see Lawrence J. Lystig, "The Military Chaplaincy Program of the Evangelical Lutheran Church, 1917–1960," (MA thesis, Luther Theological Seminary, 1977).

64. Joseph Sizoo to Alva Brasted, February 16, 1937; Alva Brasted to Joseph Sizoo, March 19, 1937, Box 69, Folder 080 (General Committee, Volume 1), ACCH2.

65. William Hughes, "A Thesis," *AC* 9, no. 2 (October–November 1938): 56–63.

66. Proceedings of the Conference of Administrative Chaplains, April 2–3, 1941, Box 257, Folder 337 (Conference—Administrative Chaplains, 1941), ACCH2.

3   The Boundaries of Religious Citizenship

1. Board Meeting Minutes, November 5, 1943, and November 12, 1943, Box 259, Folder 337 (Board Meetings, 1943–44), ACCH2.

2. Board Meeting Minutes, November 12, 1943.

3. Robert Gushwa, *The Best and Worst of Times: The United States Army Chaplaincy, 1920–1945* (GPO, 1977), 99.

4. This chapter focuses on the army because most official World War II navy chaplaincy records were destroyed. In addition, the navy was smaller (2,000 chaplains, compared to over 9,000 in the army), more tied to class-based elitism, and more racially segregated. There is a voluminous literature on World War II. For the experience of American Jews in World War II, see Deborah Dash Moore, *GI Jews: How World War II Changed a Generation* (Harvard, 2004). On religion in the

World War II military, see Michael Snape, *God and Uncle Sam: Religion and America's Armed Forces in World War II* (Boydell, 2015).

5. On African American formulations of religio-racial identities in this period, see Judith Weisenfeld, *New World A-Coming: Black Religion and Racial Identity during the Great Migration* (NYU, 2017).

6. On the complexities of black religion as a category, see Barbara Savage, *Your Spirits Walk Beside Us: The Politics of Black Religion* (Harvard, 2008).

7. Moritz Gottlieb to Louis Kraft, November 5, 1943, Box 200, Folder: Australia—Moritz Gottlieb—1943, NJWB1; Francis Spellman to John O'Hara, July 31, 1942, Box S/C-84, Folder 4, FCS; William Larsen to Inga Larsen, December 22, 1944, December 25, 1944, August 9, 1945, Box 1, Folder: Correspondence with Family, WL.

8. News Release, October 6, 1943, Box 18, Folder: Releases Sent, 1943, "B," NCCH1; "Public Relations Material Furnished," July 24, 1945, Correspondence with Chaplains, 1941–59, Box 3, Folder: Sassaman, Robert, NCCH2; OD Foster to William Arnold and John Allan, May 20, 1941, and September 22, 1941, Box 70, Folder 080 (Guardians of America), ACCH2; Army Regulations No. 60–5, February 20, 1941, 3.

9. Philip Bernstein, *Rabbis at War: The CANRA Story* (AJHS, 1971), 9; Reverend George Aki Application, November 17, 1943, Box 1, Folder: Chaplains Aiken-Allenby, CCCA.

10. Gushwa, *The Best and Worst of Times*, 108–111; Roy Honeywell, *Chaplains of the U.S. Army* (GPO, 1958), 247–248; William Arnold to Reed Probst, October 12, 1942 (emphasis original), Box 6, Folder 000.3 (Religious Ministration, Vol. III), ACCH2; Harold Saperstein to parents, July 21, 1943, Box 8, Folder 14, HSP. Roland Gittelsohn (Jewish) characterized his experience at Navy Chaplain School as "most instructive and inspiring. . . . I remember, as some of the most fascinating bull-sessions of my life, several evenings on which I was a lone Jew, sprawled out indelicately in a room with seven or eight Protestants and Catholics . . . the interplay of three major religions in a living democracy was not limited to our personal and informal relationships. It was a conscious and deliberate part of our schooling." Gittelsohn, "Pacifist to Padre," Box 64, Folder 7, RGP.

11. Lyman C. Berrett Oral History, October 24, 1974, 4, 22, MS-17096, LDS.

12. "A Trialogue on National Unity," January 14, 1941; Newport, RI, USO Unit Flier, "Brotherhood Week, February 19–28, 1943"; and Morris Gutstein to William Arnold, March 10, 1943, Box 6, Folder 000.3 (Religious Ministration, Vol. III), ACCH2; Gushwa, *The Best and Worst of Times*, 170. On American Jews and the elision of race and religion, see Eric L. Goldstein, *The Price of Whiteness: Jews, Race, and American Identity* (Princeton, 2006).

13. Gushwa, *The Best and Worst of Times*, 113–115; Scott Hart, "Army Chiefs Open Little Chapel in the Orchard," *WP*, July 28, 1941; William Arnold to Myndert M. Van Patten, March 26, 1943, Box 19, Folder 114, NJWB2; Ralph Vander Pol to William Arnold, February 10, 1943, and Roy J. Honeywell to Ralph Vander Pol, February 17, 1943, Box 6, Folder 000.3 (Religious Ministration, Vol. III), ACCH2. "Holy, holy, holy" comes from Isaiah 6:3 and is found in both Jewish liturgy and Christian hymnody.

14. "Church Services Bulletin for Ft. McClellan, Week of Sunday, February 28, 1943," Box 6, Folder 000.3 (Religious Ministration, Vol. III), ACCH2; Samuel Faircloth, interview by Bob Schuster, May 25, 2011, Tape 2, SDF.

15. Harry Southard to William Arnold, December 11, 1942, Box 6, Folder 000.3 (Religious Ministration, Vol. III), ACCH2; CANRA Meeting Minutes, October 21, 1941, Box 1, Folder: CANRA Meeting Minutes, 1940–45, NJWB2.

16. M. E. Bratcher to William Arnold, April 21, 1943; William Arnold to M. E. Bratcher, April 28, 1943; E. F. Adams to William Arnold, July 15, 1943, Box 58, Folder 080 (Baptist-North, Vol. I), ACCH2.

17. Otho Sullivan to William Arnold, March 8, 1943; William Arnold to Otho Sullivan, March 13, 1943, Box 6, Folder 000.3 (Religious Ministration, Vol III), ACCH2; Francis Spellman, Circular Letter to All Catholic Chaplains, June 8, 1942, Box S/C-84, Folder 2, FCS.

18. Dash Moore, *GI Jews*, 52–58; Phineas Smoller to Laurence Troeger, March 11, 1942, Box 1, Folder 15, PSP; Commission on Jewish Chaplaincy, Responsa Committee, *Responsa in Wartime* (NJWB, 1947). Canned kosher meat was made available for purchase through chaplains or at post exchanges, though that did not satisfy everyone (Box 19, Folders 117–119, NJWB2). The answers later printed in *Responsa in Wartime* are available in Box 21, Folders 129–130, NJWB2.

19. Chief of Chaplains to Commanding General Third Army, January 4, 1943, quoted in Harry Fraser to Hugh Glenn, February 23, 1943, Box 6, Folder 000.3 (Religious Ministration, Vol. IV); Hempstead Lyons to Wilfred B. Wells, August 10, 1942; Roy Honeywell to Frank Bunker, August 31, 1942, Box 62, Folder 080 (Christian Science, Vol. I), ACCH2.

20. Joseph Gredler to William Arnold, March 17, 1943, and Frank Miller to Joseph Gredler, March 24, 1943, Box 6, Folder 000.3 (Religious Ministration, Vol. III), ACCH2.

21. Mary Elizabeth Dibble to the Christian Science Board of Directors, September 30, 1942; Arthur Eckman to Mary Elizabeth Dibble, October 15, 1942, Box 14669, Folder 1476, MBEL.

22. John Telep to William Arnold, October 22, 1942, Box 85, Folder 080 (Russian Orthodox); William Arnold to J. Warren Albinson, November 29, 1943, and Antony Bashir to Franklin D. Roosevelt, April 1, 1942, Box 70, Folder 080 (Greek Orthodox), ACCH2. On the reliability of the Census of Religious Bodies, see Kevin Christiano, "Numbering Israel: The U.S. Census and Religious Organizations," *Social Science History* 8, no. 4 (Autumn 1984): 341–370; Rodney Stark, "The Reliability of Historical United States Census Data on Religion," *Sociological Analysis* 53, no. 1 (Spring 1992): 91–95.

23. William Arnold to Archbishop Athenagoras, February 16, 1943, Box 70, Folder 080 (Greek Orthodox); V. E. Lilikovich to John Lindquist, July 23, 1943, John Telep to William Arnold, July 28, 1943, John Lindquist to William Arnold, August 4, 1943, William Arnold to Ralph Montgomery Arkush, March 17, 1944, and Ralph Montgomery Arkush to William Arnold, March 13, 1944, Box 85, Folder 080 (Russian Orthodox), ACCH2.

24. John G. Lambrides to Families and Friends of the Men of the 407th, March 2, 1943, Box 6, Folder 000.3 (Religious Ministration, Vol. III); Oakley Lee, Article on Yehudi Menuhin visit submitted for publication clearance, May 14, 1943, Box 62, Folder 080 (The Christian Advocate), ACCH2.

25. "The Purest Democracy," MS-704, Box 63, Folder 7, AJA; Roland B. Gittelsohn, "Brothers All?" *The Reconstructionist* 7 (February 1947): 11–12.

26. William Arnold to Alvin Myries, November 12, 1943; Colonel L. G. Fritz, "Memo to All Station Commanders and Personnel of the North Atlantic Wing," November 22, 1943, Box 7, Folder 000.3 (Religious Ministration, Vol. V), ACCH2.

27. Paul L. Benedict to William Arnold, December 30, 1943; Frederick Hagan to Paul L. Benedict, January 4, 1944, Box 7, Folder 000.3 (Religious Ministration, Vol V), ACCH2; Franklin D. Roosevelt, "A Message to Congress on the State of the Union," January 6, 1941, http://www.presidency.ucsb.edu/ws/index.php?pid=16092.

28. C. H. Danielson to the Chief of Chaplains, June 26, 1945, Box 121, Folder 201.2 (Letters of Commendation and Complaints Records, Vol. I), ACCH2.

29. Bishop John Gregg traveled abroad in 1943, Bishop J. J. Wright in 1944, and Reverend William Jernagin followed in 1945, Box 2, Folder 000.3, ACCH2; Gregg, *Of Men and Arms: Chronological Travel Record of Bishop John A. Gregg with Messages of Cheer and Good Will to Negro Soldiers* (AME Sunday School Union Press, 1945); Jernagin, *Christ at the Battlefront: Servicemen Accept the Challenge* (Murray Bros., 1946). For an example of statistics, see Box 260, Folder 337 (July 1944–Dec 1944), ACCH2.

30. When a new chaplain arrived at Fort Clark, Texas, the African American soldiers tested the intransigent seating policy by wading into the right-side seating, theretofore understood as white seating. When told they either had to comply with the standard separate seating or face completely segregated, separate services, the black men and women boycotted services. See HQ of Eighth Service Command, May 2, 1944, Subject: Church Attendance of Negro Personnel, Box 3, Folder 291.2 (Race), ACCH-SC. Policies on mixed-race services were inconsistent, however. When Chaplain Thomas Wright (Catholic) refused to celebrate mass for an interracial congregation, as had been the practice at Fort Bragg, North Carolina, the army chief of chaplains office requested a report and launched an investigation that also asked the Catholic Church to weigh in. Confidential Memo Re: Agitation Caused by Ordering Separate Masses for White & Colored People, Ft. Bragg, NC, April 27, 1945, and Edmund Weber to Chaplain Charles D. Trexler, May 7, 1945, Box 3, Folder 291.2 (Race), ACCH-SC.

31. When a Chinese American pastor wanted to become a chaplain, the Office of the Chief of Chaplains advised, "The only place we could use a Chinese pastor would be with a Chinese unit," but none were planned. Walter Zimmerman to Frederick Fagley, October 15, 1943, Box 64, Folder 080 (Congregational and Christian Churches, Vol II), ACCH2.

32. "The Chaplains and the Negro in the Armed Services" (1944): 5, 7, 11–14, Box 3, Folder 291.2 (Race), ACCH-SC.

33. "The Chaplains and the Negro in the Armed Services," 21, 29.

34. C. Eric Lincoln and Lawrence H. Mamiya argued that the seven denominations of the "Black Church" can be divided into Baptist, Methodist, and Pentecostal traditions. The military worked primarily with Baptists and Methodists due to their general skepticism toward Pentecostal practices. Lincoln and Mamiya, *The Black Church in the African American Experience* (Duke, 1990).

35. William Arnold to C. H. Phillips, January 23, 1943, Box 63, Folder 080 (CME); George Rixey to W. H. Jernagin, July 17, 1943, Box 79, Folder 080 (National

Baptist, Vol. I), ACCH2. The same letter can be found in Box 69, Folder 080 (General Commission, Vol. V), Box 75, Folder 080 (Methodist, Vol II), Box 76, Folder 080 (AME), Box 79, Folder 080 (National Baptist, Vol. I), ACCH2.

36. S. A. Owen to William Arnold, February 7, 1944, Box 79, Folder 080 (National Baptist, Vol. II), ACCH2.

37. E.g., Frederick Fagley to Manager, Charlotte Hotel; Fagley to William Arnold, October 29, 1942, Box 64, Folder 080 (Congregational and Christian Churches, Vol. I), ACCH2.

38. "Preaching No Good to Yanks on Sinking Ship, Chaplain Says"; "Discharged Chaplain May Campaign for Dewey," BAA, September 9, 1944.

39. For a sample letter, see Walter B. Zimmerman to Willard Wickizer, July 21, 1943; Willard Wickizer to Walter Zimmerman, August 5, 1943, Box 64, Folder 080 (Disciples of Christ, Vol. II), ACCH2.

40. "Chaplain's Story of the South Pacific," BAA, April 17, 1943. Without adequate treatment, malaria was a particularly pernicious and indiscriminate killer. Karen M. Masterson, The Malaria Project: The U.S. Government's Secret Mission to Find a Miracle Cure (Penguin, 2014).

41. "Chaplain's Story of the South Pacific."

42. "Chaplain Beats Jim Crow on Dining Car," BAA, September 27, 1941; "Discharge for Chaplain Fuller Recommended by U.S. Army Board," PT, November 20, 1943.

43. "Who Is Chaplain Fuller?" BAA, April 17, 1943; "Discharge for Chaplain Fuller Recommended by U.S. Army Board," PT, November 20, 1943; Interview with Mrs. Margaret J. Wright, American Red Cross, February 2, 1945, Box 3, Folder 291.2 (Race), ACCH-SC.

44. "Treatment of Soldiers Forces Hueston Out of Retirement," BAA, August 7, 1943; "Why Ministers Avoid Chaplain Posts," BAA, June 2, 1945; "Strange Justice Bared in Fuller and Colman Cases," PC, November 20, 1943. The experiences of black chaplains were, of course, varied, but the problem of war ministry exemplifies Eddie Glaude's definition of African American religion as "the encounter between faith, in all its complexity, and white supremacy." Eddie Glaude, African American Religion: A Short Introduction (Oxford, 2014), 6. Abel Meeropol, a Jewish high school teacher and Communist activist, penned the lyrics to "Strange Fruit" in response to a photograph of the lynching of Thomas Shipp and Abram Smith. David Margolick, Strange Fruit: The Biography of a Song (Harper, 2001).

45. "Racial Problems and the Chaplains' Activities," February 14, 1945, Box 3, Folder 291.2 (Race), ACCH-SC.

46. Captain Paul Worden to Officer in Charge, September 26, 1944; John Monahan to Edgar F. Siegfriedt, September 30, 1944, Box 3, Folder 291.2 (Race), ACCH-SC. Throughout the war, the prospect of chaplains "'playing up the equality angle'" was a concern. E.g., Memo Re: U.S. Troops in Australia and New Guinea, August 26, 1944, p. 2, Box 3, Folder 291.2 (Race), ACCH-SC. When black soldiers assaulted white officers at Camp Claiborne, Louisiana, they were often court-martialed on charges of rioting and mutiny. See Adam Fairclough, Race and Democracy: The Civil Rights Struggle in Louisiana, 1915–1972 (Georgia, 1995), 78; Daniel Kryder, Divided Arsenal: Race and the American State during World War II

(Cambridge, 2000), 141–142; Joe Wilson, *The 761st "Black Panther" Tank Battalion in World War II* (McFarland & Company, 1999), 18–19.

47. Confidential Memo from the Chief of Staff to Commanding Generals, July 13, 1943, Box 3, Folder 291.2 (Race), ACCH-SC.

48. Brian Hayashi, *Democratizing the Enemy: The Japanese-American Internment* (Princeton, 2004); Anne M. Blankenship, *Christianity, Social Justice, and the Japanese American Incarceration during World War II* (UNC, 2016).

49. Hayashi, *Democratizing the Enemy*, 139–142, 157–159; Orville Shirey, *Americans: The Story of the 442nd Combat Team* (Infantry Journal Press, 1946), 19–25. On the experience of soldiers in the 100th and 442nd, see Robert Asahina, *Just Americans: How Japanese Americans Won a War at Home and Abroad* (Gotham Books, 2006); Bill Yenne, *Rising Sons: The Japanese American GIs Who Fought for the United States in World War II* (St. Martin's Press, 2007). The prospect of naturalized citizenship accompanied military service, which represented a significant policy change. The U.S. had barred Japanese-born immigrants from citizenship by the Naturalization Act of 1870, *Ozawa v. U.S.*, 260 U.S. 189 (1922), and the Immigration Act of 1924.

50. Israel Yost, *Combat Chaplain: The Personal Story of the World War II Chaplain of the Japanese American 100th Battalion* (Hawaii, 2006), 1–6, 8, 67, 168–170. While Yost found no solace in Buddhism, he reserved judgment for fellow Protestants, writing, for example, that "some Protestant chaplains were weak in theological beliefs and could not understand why Christians such as Episcopalians and Lutherans preferred their own rites as much as Roman Catholics did" (131).

51. William Arnold to William Scobey, June 10, 1943; Harry Lee Virden to Wilfred Munday, December 22, 1942, Box 60, Folder 080 (Buddhist), ACCH2.

52. John Monahan to the Adjutant General, March 26, 1943; William Arnold to Bishop Matsukahe, March 24, 1943, Box 60, Folder 080 (Buddhist), ACCH2. (The correspondence misspelled the name of Bishop Ryotai Matsukage.) Institutionally located in San Francisco, the Buddhist Mission in North America (BMNA) originated as the center of Jodo Shinshu (True Pure Land School) missionary work in the U.S. and remained tied to the headquarters in Kyoto, Japan. In the 1920s, the BMNA began to Anglicize much of its religious terminology, and its religious leaders became known as ministers, priests, and bishops. During World War II, about 55 percent of interned Japanese Americans were Buddhist, the majority of which affiliated with the BMNA; in 1944, a group at the Topaz relocation center suggested changing the religion's name to the Buddhist Church of America to emphasize their Americanness. Richard H. Seager, *Buddhism in America* (Columbia, 1999), 51–59.

53. Masara Kumata to John McCoy, March 30, 1943; William Arnold to Masara Kumata, April 5, 1943; William Arnold to Newton Ishuira, April 10, 1943, Box 60, Folder 080 (Buddhist), ACCH2.

54. "Memorandum for Buddhists for File," April 14, 1943; William Scobey to William Arnold, April 7, 1943; William Arnold to William Scobey, June 10, 1943, Box 60, Folder 080 (Buddhist), ACCH2. Both Mrs. Patterson and Miss Wallihan recommended white Buddhist priests, with the former suggesting Ernest Hunt, who as a British citizen was ineligible, and the latter advising the military to contact Julius Goldwater, an American citizen who lived in Los Angeles. He was the son of German-Jewish immigrants (and first cousin of 1964 Republican Presidential

nominee Barry Goldwater) who had converted to Buddhism and trained in Kyoto as well as Hangzhou, China, in the 1930s.

55. C. S. Reifanider to E. M. Zacharias, June 14, 1943, Box 1, Folder 080 (Societies and Church Organizations), ACCH-SC; William Scobey to William Arnold, June 7, 1943, Box 60, Folder 080 (Buddhist), ACCH2; William Arnold to William Scobey, July 8, 1943, Box 1, Folder 080 (Societies and Church Organizations), ACCH-SC. The role of race, religion, and military service in Americanization was debated inside and outside the community. At least one white chaplain weighed in based on his war service with Japanese Americans. When Senator Thomas Connally (D-TX) asserted that he was a "better American" than Hawaiians because they lacked "American ancestry," Chaplain Thomas E. West (Baptist) protested, writing that he had "nothing but the highest praise and admiration" for Japanese Americans. "Former Chaplain of the 442nd Protests Connally's Remarks," *Pacific Citizen* 34, no. 11 (March 15, 1952).

56. Harry Lee Virden, August 18, 1943, Box 60, Folder 080 (Buddhist), ACCH2.

57. See applications in Boxes 1–6, CCCA; George Aki, "My Thirty Months (1944–46)," 1–3, VHP. George Aki, Hiro Higuchi, Masayoshi Wakai, and Masao Yamada received endorsements, and Higuchi and Yamada went to Europe with the 442nd Battalion. Aki was the first mainland Japanese American to serve as a chaplain. He had been studying at the Pacific School of Religion in Berkeley when he was interned. "Rev. Aki Gets Commission as Combat Team Chaplain," *Pacific Citizen* 18, no. 14 (April 8, 1944). On Japanese American Christian activism, see Stephanie Hinnershitz, *Race, Religion, and Civil Rights: Asian Students on the West Coast, 1900–1968* (Rutgers, 2015).

58. George Rixey to Otis Spurgeon, December 20, 1940; Noble Beall to William Arnold, May 6, 1941; Alfred Carpenter to William Arnold, March 19, 1945, Box 59, Folder 080 (Baptist-South, Vol. III); J. Roswell Flower to William Arnold, January 19, 1942; J. Roswell Flower to William Arnold, July 11, 1942; Walter B. Zimmerman to J. Roswell Flower, May 5, 1943, Box 58, Folder 080 (Assemblies of God, Vol. II), ACCH2. The military differentiated between Pentecostals who practiced glossolalia (speaking in tongues) and those who did not; the former were unacceptable, while the latter, such as male ministers of Aimee Semple McPherson's Four-Square Gospel or the Assemblies of God, were acceptable. William Arnold to Paul Brown, July 24, 1943, Box 44, Folder 032 (Letters to Congress, Vol. II, 1942–43), ACCH2. On the Moody Bible Institute, see Timothy Gloege, *Guaranteed Pure: The Moody Bible Institute, Business, and the Making of Modern Evangelicalism* (UNC, 2015).

59. The annotated census found in military records has a tick mark next to groups with about 100,000 or more members. Because religions count their members in different ways, the government instructed churches to report figures based on their own definition of membership. This fidelity to religious groups' membership policies respected their autonomy but inevitably created a dataset that undercounted adherents of groups with higher thresholds of membership (e.g., adult baptism) relative to others. Department of Commerce, Bureau of the Census, "Census of Religious Bodies: 1936," August 1, 1940, Box 6, Folder 000.3 (Religious Ministration, Vol. I), ACCH2.

60. J. Oliver Buswell, News Release: "How Are Army and Navy Chaplains Appointed?" October 1942, Box 56, Folder 080 (ACCC, Vol. I), ACCH2. On Carl

McIntire's theology and political activism, see Markku Ruotsila, "Carl McIntire and the Fundamentalist Origins of the Christian Right," *Church History* 81, vol. 2 (June 2012): 378–407.

61. Buswell, "How Are Army and Navy Chaplains Appointed?" October 1942; Arthur Williams and J. Oliver Buswell to William Arnold, July 25, 1942; J. Oliver Buswell to William Arnold, October 23, 1942; William Arnold to J. Oliver Buswell, November 3, 1942, Box 56, Folder 080 (ACCC, Vol. I), ACCH2.

62. Harry Lee Virden, "Memorandum," December 19, 1942, Box 56, Folder 080 (ACCC, Vol. I), ACCH2.

63. Board Meeting Minutes, February 5, 1943, Box 259, Folder 337 (Board Meetings, 1943–44), ACCH2. In March, Arnold granted the Independent Fundamentalists ten spots, but because no other constituent group of the ACCC registered even 50,000 members, they did not qualify for chaplains. Whether this slight revision downward reflected aggravation with the group or a shift in the number of chaplains being commissioned is unclear; the ACCC felt it deserved at least double that number. After exhausting Congressional representatives to no avail, Carl McIntire wrote to the president, stating that "another one of our problems has been the chaplaincy" and that neither letters nor meetings with the military had resolved the matter. William Arnold to Commanding General, First Service Command, March 9, 1943; J. Oliver Buswell to William Arnold, April 17, 1943; Carl McIntire to the President, April 1, 1943, Box 56, Folder 080 (ACCC, Vol. I), ACCH2.

64. Carl McIntire to William Arnold, May 10, 1943, RG 247, Box 56, Folder 080 (American Council of Churches of Christ, Vol. I); J. Elwin Wright to William Arnold, March 31, 1943; Leonard E. Smith to William Arnold, January 20, 1944; Sylvia Ruff to William Arnold, January 21, 1944; Bob Jones to William Arnold, January 27, 1944; William Arnold to Frank Stollenwerck, February 3, 1944, Box 79, Folder 080 (NAE), ACCH2.

65. Carl Wilberding, Memo to George Rixey, undated; George Rixey to Colonel Pasco, April 2, 1945, Box 79, Folder 080 (NAE), ACCH2. On the relationship between evangelicals' apocalyptic thinking and their interest in influencing government, see Matthew A. Sutton, *American Apocalypse: A History of Modern Evangelicalism* (Harvard, 2014).

66. "The Saga of the Four Chaplains," The Four Chaplain Memorial Foundation, fourchaplains.org/story; Dan Kurzman, *No Greater Glory: The Four Immortal Chaplains and the Sinking of the Dorchester in World War II* (Random House, 2004), 95–99. Slower Allied ships zigzagged in convoys to stave off the German submarine "wolfpacks" that patrolled the North Atlantic. By February 1943, the British had broken the German naval code and helped ships dodge U-boats. However, the German navy hit almost a hundred more ships between February and May, when they ceded the North Atlantic.

67. "Four More Chaplains Listed as Casualties," *LAT*, March 27, 1943; "Former Rabbi Listed as Missing at Sea, One of Four Chaplain Heroes of Sinking," *NYT*, March 27, 1943; "Four Chaplains Killed in War Honored at 'Back the Attack,'" *WP*, September 16, 1943; Louis Schwimmer, "The Story of the Four Chaplains Stamp," http://www.schwimmer.com/fourchaplains/. By law, commemorative postage stamps are not issued until ten years after the featured individual(s)' death, but Congress waived the rule for the Four Chaplains stamp. Dozens submitted

affidavits testifying to the chaplains' actions, and in 1944, the military awarded each chaplain a Purple Heart and a Distinguished Service Cross (Kurzman, *No Greater Glory*, 221–223). Historians have also noticed and reinforced the symbolic power of the four chaplains. William Hutchinson, *Religious Pluralism in America: The Contentious History of a Founding Ideal* (Yale, 2004), 198–199; Dash Moore, *GI Jews*, 118–123; Schultz, *Tri-Faith America*, 3–7.

68. Kurzman, *No Greater Glory*, 32–3.

69. "Freedom to Worship," *The Saturday Evening Post*, February 27, 1943. Rockwell's initial plan for painting was five men in a barbershop—a Protestant barber, a Catholic priest customer, a Jewish customer, an African American customer, and a white Anglo customer—but early critics deemed it too stereotypical. The final image included seven people, three men and four women, all of whom were praying "according to the dictates of his own conscience." See Colleen McDannell, *Picturing Faith: Photography and the Great Depression* (Yale, 2004), 145.

4 Chaplain Jim Wants You!

1. Francis J. Spellman, *Action This Day: Letters from the Fighting Fronts* (Scribner, 1943).

2. "Abp. Spellman to Cover Africa, India, and China," *BG*, June 6, 1943. Other examples include "Text of Archbishop Spellman's Talk in Africa," March 15, 1943; "Spellman Decides to Visit Ireland," *NYT*, March 24, 1943; "Spellman Returns from Africa; 'Well and Happy' after Long Tour," *NYT*, August 2, 1943.

3. William R. Arnold to Mr. W. W. Hart, January 11, 1944, Box 4, Folder 000.3 (Catholic, January 1944–December 1945); Chief of Staff to H. R. Ockenga, January 3, 1945, Box 79, Folder 080 (NAE), ACCH2.

4. Spellman, *Action This Day*, 31, 130.

5. Amiela Haznar to Chaplain Jim, July 20, 1942, Box 23, Folder 000.77 (Administration Correspondence), ACCH2. A number of mothers wrote directly to Chaplain Jim, assuming he was a real chaplain, not a character. This behavior was consistent with women writing to Betty Crocker, another invented radio personality who gave spirited advice. See Susan Marks, *Finding Betty Crocker* (Simon & Schuster, 2005), 35–82.

6. For a complete list of titles, see scripts located in Boxes 23–28, ACCH2. On detective fiction, see Julian Symons, *Bloody Murder: From the Detective Story to the Crime Novel* (Faber & Faber, 1972). *Chaplain Jim* also followed the conventions of what Larry May has termed the World War II "conversion narrative" in which Americans overcome ethnic divisions at home to defeat the enemy abroad. See May, "Making the American Consensus: The Narrative of Conversion and Subversion in World War II films," in *The War in American Culture, Society, and Consciousness during World War II*, ed. Lewis Erenberg and Susan Hirsch (Chicago, 1996), 71–104.

7. *Chaplain Jim*, Episode 53, May 11, 1942, Box 23, Folder 000.77 (Scripts, Vol. II); William Arnold to Frank and Anne Hummert, March 1, 1944, Box 23, Folder 000.77 (Administrative Correspondence), ACCH2. The chaplaincy consciously cultivated its image. A staff chaplain reminded field officers to hold reports in strict confidence, as the office would "delete or clarify or fit into the military picture such sections of his report as we feel need deleting or doctoring."

John Allan to Paul Moody, May 9, 1941, Box 70, Folder 080 (Guardians of America), ACCH2.

8. *Chaplain Jim*, Episode 1, Number 1, April 6, 1942, Box 23, Folder 000.77 (Scripts, Vol. I), ACCH2.

9. Ibid. As the military remained racially segregated until 1948 and the Hummerts prided themselves on "realism," a racially integrated unit would have been anomalous.

10. David Kennedy, *Freedom from Fear: The United in Depression and War, 1929–45* (Oxford, 1999), 761; Michael Denning, *The Cultural Front: The Laboring of American Culture in the Twentieth Century* (Verso, 1997), 130. For a discussion of the limits of this trope and the latent suspicion toward foreigners it attempted to mask, see Wendy Wall, *Inventing the "American Way": The Politics of Consensus from the New Deal to the Civil Rights Movement* (Oxford, 2008), 138–143.

11. On radio in this period, see Barbara Savage, *Broadcasting Freedom: Radio, War, and the Politics of Race, 1938–1948* (UNC, 1999); Tona J. Hangen, *Redeeming the Dial: Radio, Religion, and Popular Culture in America* (UNC, 2002).

12. James Sparrow, *The Warfare State: World War II Americans and the Age of Big Government* (Oxford, 2011), 49.

13. Reminiscences of Louis Cowan, by Eric Barnouw (1967), CCOH; Howard Blue, *Words at War: World War II Era Radio Drama and the Postwar Broadcasting Industry Blacklist* (Scarecrow Press, 2002), 185–188; "Religion: A Job for Jordan," *TIME*, February 15, 1943.

14. George Ansbro, *I Have a Lady in the Balcony: Memoirs of a Broadcaster in Radio and Television* (McFarland & Company, 2000), 127. Ansbro, who introduced the show on air, claimed that *Chaplain Jim* was not a soap opera, but the narrative structure reflected radio soap operas.

15. *Chaplain Jim*, Episode 1; Jack Gould, "Soap Factory: Something about the Hummerts, Frank and Anne, and 6,000,000 Words a Year," *NYT*, February 14, 1943. The show was publicized nationally in white and black newspapers, e.g., "Radio Today," *NYT*, May 19, 1942, and "Radio Programs," *ADW*, December, 23, 1945.

16. William Arnold to Frank and Anne Hummert, February 14, 1944, Box 23, Folder 000.77 (Administrative Correspondence), ACCH2. After the war, Rothschild accepted a synagogue pulpit in Atlanta, where he denounced segregation and became an outspoken advocate of civil rights. Melissa Fay Greene, *The Temple Bombing* (Addison-Wesley, 1996).

17. Herman H. Heuer to Mrs. E. Williams, March 25, 1944, Box 85, Folder 080 (Salvation Army), ACCH2.

18. Board Meeting Minutes, November 12, 1943, Box 259, Folder 337 (Board Meetings, 1943–44), ACCH2; Reminiscences of Louis Cowan. Finnegan (Catholic) entered the chaplaincy in 1937, where his first assignment was a CCC post. He was in Pearl Harbor on December 7, 1941, and earned a Bronze Star for his work with infantry troops at Guadalcanal in 1942–1943. He became the second Air Force Chief of Chaplains in 1958.

19. Arnold's annotation, Frank and Anne Hummert to E. M. Kirby, May 3 1943, Box 23, Folder 000.77 (Administrative Correspondence); *Chaplain Jim*, Episode 259, June 19, 1945, Box 28, Folder 000.77 (Scripts, 1945); *Chaplain Jim*, Episode 36, May 26, 1942, Box 23, Folder 000.77 (Scripts, Vol. II), ACCH2.

20. *Chaplain Jim*, Episode 153, August 8, 1943, Box 25, Folder 000.77 (Scripts, 138–160); *Chaplain Jim*, Episode 192, May 4, 1944, Box 26, Folder 000.77 (Scripts, 161–173), ACCH2.

21. "President Backs a Week of Prayer," *NYT*, January 3, 1943; *Chaplain Jim*, Episode 123, January 10, 1943 (emphasis original), Box 25, Folder 000.77 (Scripts, 118–137), ACCH2.

22. Reminiscences of Louis Cowan, 62–66.

23. "Chaplain Pinn, Back in States Tells of First U.S. Negro Troops in Africa," *CD*, April 10, 1943; *Chaplain Jim*, Episode 134, March 28, 1943 (ellipses original), Box 25, Folder 000.77 (Scripts, 118–137), ACCH2. On the Double V campaign, see Kimberley L. Phillips, *War! What Is It Good For? Black Freedom Struggles and the U.S. Military from World War II to Iraq* (UNC, 2005), 20–63; Gerald Astor, *The Right to Fight: A History of African Americans in the Military* (Da Capo, 2001).

24. *Chaplain Jim*, Episode 237, March 18, 1945, Box 27, Folder 000.77 (Scripts, 226–250); *Chaplain Jim*, Episode 149, July 11, 1943, Box 27, Folder 000.77 (Scripts, 138–160), ACCH2.

25. *Chaplain Jim*, Episode 36; *Chaplain Jim*, Episode 198, June 18, 1944, Box 27, Folder 000.77 (Scripts, 1944); *Chaplain Jim*, Episode 237. "Wise" would have resonated with American Jewish listeners as the name of Rabbi Stephen Wise, a scion of Reform Judaism and a friend of FDR. On FDR's complicated relationship with American Jewry, see Richard Breitman and Allan J. Lichtman, *FDR and the Jews* (Harvard, 2013).

26. *Chaplain Jim*, Episode 1; "Write Soldier of Details at Home," *News Journal and Guide*, July 3, 1943; Alvie McKnight to Joseph Ensrud, August 22, 1943, Box 23, Folder 000.77 (Administrative Correspondence), ACCH2.

27. In an attempt to provide for their men's sexual needs in a controlled environment, some officers attempted to build brothels—most of which were quickly shuttered by the War Department. Mary Lou Roberts, *What Soldiers Do: Sex and the American GI in World War II France* (Chicago, 2013), 159–162; Bath Bailey and David Farber, *The First Strange Place: The Alchemy of Race and Sex in World War II Hawaii* (Free Press, 1992), 95–132.

28. Timothy Hoyt Bowers-Iron Oral History, 57, 60, THBI; Charles I. Carpenter, Report on Overseas Inspection Trip, January 25, 1944, Box 4, Folder 333.1 (Inspections & Investigations), ACCH-SC.

29. Chief of Chaplains Memo to the Adjutant General, April 21, 1942; William Arnold to Edward J. Waters, March 28, 1941; John O'Hara to William Arnold, December 20, 1940; Army Chief of Staff to John O'Hara, January 22, 1941, Box 195, Folder 250.1 (Conduct and Morals—Misc., Vol. I), ACCH2.

30. Margot Canaday, *The Straight State: Sexuality and Citizenship in Twentieth-Century America* (Princeton, 2009), 55–90, 174–213; Allan Berube, *Coming Out under Fire: The History of Gay Men and Women in World War II* (UNC, 1990), 62.

31. Charles O. Dutton to William Arnold, August 9, 1943; Frederick Hagan to Charles O. Dutton, August 27, 1943, Box 195, Folder 250.1 (Conduct and Morals—Misc., Vol. I), ACCH2; William R. Arnold to William P. Byrnes, January 11, 1945, Box 13, File 10, GLBT. According to a January 10, 1943, memo from the adjutant general, "Sodomy is an act specifically denounced as an offense in violation of Article of War 93 and is punishable by dishonorable discharge, forfeiture of all pay and allowances, and confinement at hard labor in a Federal penitentiary

for five years. The policy of the War Department is that the sexual pervert—the true sodomist—should be promptly tried by general court-martial," barring insufficient evidence or mitigating circumstances (e.g., "mental defect") such that a discharge would best. "Sodomists," Memorandum No. W615-4-43, January 10, 1943, Box 195, Folder 250.1 (Conduct and Morals—Misc., Vol. I), GLBT.

32. *U.S. v. Roderick H. Fitch*, March 16, 1943, Branch Office of the JAG, Southwest Pacific, *Holdings, Opinions and Reviews*, Vol. 1, 105–107; William R. Arnold to Frederick Fagley, October 18, 1943; William R. Arnold to the Ecclesiastical Committee, February 3, 1944, Box 1, Folder 080 (Societies and Church Organizations), ACCH-SC.

33. Milton O. Beebe to Bishop Peele, September 18, 1944, Box 1, Folder 080 (Societies and Church Organizations), ACCH-SC; Bertram Korn to Richard Hertz, January 20, 1945; Samuel Silver to Richard Hertz, February 6, 1945, Box 14, Folder 5, RHP.

34. On the expectation of rape in Germany, see Atina Grossman, "A Question of Silence: The Rape of German Women by Occupation Soldiers," *October* 72 (Spring 1995): 50–53. On Japan, see John Dower, *Embracing Defeat: Japan in the Wake of World War II* (Norton, 1999), 123–127, 211.

35. J. Robert Lilly, *Taken by Force: Rape and American GIs in Europe during World War II* (Palgrave Macmillan, 2007), 11–12. Based on the calculation that only 5 percent of rapes are reported, Lilly estimates that approximately 17,000 rapes by American soldiers occurred in the European Theater of Operations during World War II. The documented rates of rape and sexual assault by Soviet soldiers in Germany were significantly higher. Grossman, "A Question of Silence," 46–47. Rape charges against American soldiers peaked in Germany in April 1945, when 501 soldiers were accused of rape; accusations declined to 241 in May, when Germany surrendered, and decreased to about 45 allegations per month thereafter. The line between rape and sex work was particularly murky in the aftermath of war, and some soldiers saw rape of Germans as revenge. See Petra Goedde, *GIs and Germans: Culture, Gender, and Foreign Relations, 1945–1949* (Yale, 2003), 63–65, 84–85; Anne-Marie Troger, "Between Rape and Prostitution: Survival Strategies and Chances of Emancipation for Berlin Women after World War II," in *Women in Culture and Politics*, ed. Judith Friedlander, Blanche Wiesen Cook, Alice Kessler-Harris, and Carroll Smith-Rosenberg (Indiana, 1986), 97–120.

36. Lilly, *Taken by Force*, 160; Stephen Whitfield, *A Death in the Delta: The Story of Emmett Till* (JHU, 1991), 116–117; John Edgar Wideman, *Writing to Save a Life: The Louis Till File* (Scribner, 2016). These trends held for the Pacific Theater as well. Many of the charges against black men stemmed from general concerns about interracial sex, and white officers played a critical role in pushing trumped-up charges through the system. Michael C. Green, *Black Yanks in the Pacific: Race in the Making of American Military Empire after World War II* (Cornell, 2010), 64, 27.

37. [Unnamed author] "Let's Look at Rape!" Box 12, Folder 2, MKP; L. Curtis Tiernan, Information Sheet No. 6, January 26, 1945, MS 709, Box 12, Folder 2, AJA. The fact that the pamphlet ended up in a Jewish chaplain's papers demonstrates that the army distributed it to black and white chaplains.

38. Dower, *Embracing Defeat*, 121–139; Yuki Tanaka, *Japan's Comfort Women: Sexual Slavery and Prostitution during World War II and the U.S. Occupation* (Routledge, 2002), 133–166.

39. "Charges on Naval Moral Laxity Is Printed in 'Record'; Methodist Chaplain Says Prostitution is Permitted in Japan Occupation," *The [Rockford] Observer*, December 2, 1945; "Sailors and Sex: Prostitution Flourishes in Japan," *Newsweek*, November 12, 1945; "The Navy Provides Social Protection for Servicemen in Japan," *Journal of Social Hygiene* 32, no. 2 (February 1946): 82–89. Sarah Kovner shows that military personnel often inveighed against this interference into their sexual lives. See *Occupying Power: Sex Workers and Servicemen in Postwar Japan* (Stanford, 2012), 28.

40. *Chaplain Jim*, Episode 149.

41. Elfrieda Berthiaume Shukert and Barbara Smith Scibetta, *War Brides of World War II* (Presidio Press, 1988), 1–2; Susan Zeiger, *Entangling Alliances: Foreign War Brides and American Soldiers in the Twentieth Century* (NYU, 2010), 71–72. Shukert and Scibetta compiled this number through a combination of military documents, immigration data, newspaper reports, and regional and local statistics. Zeiger disputes 1 million as a severe overestimate, but provides an estimate for only wartime marriages rather over a decade. See Zeiger, *Entangling Alliances*, 250, note 2.

42. Public Law 271: The War Brides Act (December 28, 1945); Public Law 471: The Fiancees Act (June 29, 1946); Roger Daniels, *Asian America: Chinese and Japanese in the United States Since 1850* (University of Washington, 2015), 149–154. As Mae Ngai has pointed out, the sequential repeal of exclusion for war brides was "particularly significant because [it lay] the basis for Asian family immigration, which had been a near-impossibility under the exclusion laws." Ngai, *Impossible Subjects: Illegal Aliens and the Making of Modern America* (Princeton, 2004), 233.

43. Public Law 213: The Soldier Brides Act (July 22, 1947); Public Law 82–414: The Immigration and Nationality Act (June 27, 1952). Prior to 1952, about 900 Japanese war brides entered the country; during the remainder of the year, over 4,200 Japanese war brides legally entered the United States. See Shukert and Scibetta, *War Brides*, 216.

44. Michael Grossberg, *Governing the Hearth: Law and the Family in Nineteenth-Century America* (UNC, 1985), 76, 94; Nancy Cott, *Public Vows: A History of Marriage and the Nation* (Harvard, 2000), 28, 36, 83; "Chaplains in Action," July 25, 1950, Box 484, Folder 352.11 (TV Course), ACCH2. Ministers occasionally used their power to contravene state law, particularly in the case of interracial marriage. Peggy Pascoe, *What Comes Naturally: Miscegenation Law and the Making of Race in America* (Oxford, 2009), 49, 90. On the nexus of race, religion, and marriage, see Sharon Davies, *Rising Road: A True Tale of Love, Race, and Religion in America* (Oxford, 2010) and Faye Botham, *Almighty God Created the Races: Christianity, Interracial Marriage and American Law* (UNC, 2009).

45. *Servicemen's Committee Instructions to Assistant Co-ordinators, L.D.S. Chaplains, M.I.A. Group Leaders, Mission and Stake Representatives* (LDS Church, 1944), 14; Milt G. Widdison, Unpublished Memoir (2000), 49, MS 17075, LDS; Herbert W. Beck to Herbert E. Rieke, January 26, 1942, ORM, Box 14666, Folder 1609, MBEL. There is no evidence that anyone in the Chief of Chaplains Office consulted any legal authority when rendering this opinion. In 1918, the JAG had asserted the opposite, that a chaplain "has no legal right to perform marriage ceremonies." "Right to Perform Ceremony," May 23, 1918, in *Digest of Opinions of the*

Judge Advocate General of the Army, 1912–1930, Box 197, Folder 291.1 (Marriages, Vol. I), ACCH2.

46. John S. Monahan to John S. Hild, December 18, 1939, Box 197, Folder 291.1 (Marriages, Vol. I); John S. Kelly to Herman Heuer, December 11, 1952, Box 513, Folder 291.1 (Marriage, Vol. XVI), ACCH2.

47. Unlike the military, the Jewish Welfare Board (JWB) argued that "matters of marriage and divorce are not directly connected with military duty" (M-7) and thus forbade Jewish chaplains from officiating or assisting in any form of inter-faith marriage, a policy in accordance with all movements of Judaism at that time. See CANRA Responsa M-1-M-9, Box 21, Folder 130, NJWB2. For a slightly more flexible position on performing mixed marriages—with the caveat that "it is our policy to discourage mixed marriages"—see Philip S. Bernstein to Ephraim Bennett, January 3, 1944, Box 21, Folder 132, NJWB2. Not all Jewish chaplains followed the JWB's policy. Chaplain Samuel Rosen, for example, reported "having solemnized a number of inter-marriages" when he feared the couple would marry anyway, provided the bride (assumed to be the non-Jew) agree to take classes and convert. Excerpt from Monthly January Report Submitted by Chaplain Samuel Rosen, February 15, 1944, Box 21, Folder 132, NJWB2.

48. "Chaplains in Action." Navy Chaplain Francis Garrett (Methodist) relayed a real-life equivalent in which he referred a navy commander to a justice of the peace when Garrett realized the man intended to enter his fourth marriage and he was unable to marry him per church rules. Rear Admiral Francis Leonard Garrett Oral History, interview by H. Lawrence Martin (1984), 24–25, FJC.

49. William R. Arnold to Dominic Ternan, August 28, 1943, Box 197, Folder 291.1 (Marriage, Vol. III), ACCH2.

50. Mrs. Morris Cohen to Morris Fierman, March 5, 1945, MS 170, Box 5, Folder 3, AJA. For comparable letters written by concerned family members and friends, see letters collected in Box 21, Folder 135, NJWB2.

51. Marilyn Penner to the Chief of Chaplains, May 24, 1942; Herman Heuer to Marilyn Penner, May 28, 1942, Box 197, Folder 291.1 (Marriage, Vol. II), ACCH2.

52. Charlie Lerner to Mom, Pop, and Miriam, May 19, 1945; Philip Graubart to David Seligson, May 28, 1945; David J. Seligson to Philip Graubart, June 13, 1945, Box 21, Folder 135, NJWB2. While Seligson avoided the question of race, Seemah likely looked white. The Calcutta Jewish community consisted of a large Baghdadi Jewish merchant class and Charlie emphasized that Seemah had money, which suggests that she was likely a Baghdadi Jew (whom the British classified as European) living in Calcutta. Joan G. Roland, *The Jewish Communities of India: Identity in a Colonial Era* (Transaction, 1998). It is unclear what became of Charlie and Seemah's relationship.

53. John S. Monahan to Reverend Joseph M. Welligan, October 13, 1938, Box 197, Folder 291.1 (Marriages, Vol. I); John S. Monahan to Thomas P. Kelly, May 29, 1942, Box 197, Folder 291.1 (Marriages, Vol. II), ACCH2.

54. Samuel Silver to Richard Hertz, March 4, 1945, MS 675, Box 14, Folder 5, AJA.

55. Adjutant General to C. P. Thiesen, May 10, 1941; Chief of Chaplains to the Adjutant General, April 8, 1941; John S. Monahan to Robert E. McCormick, March 5, 1941, Box 197, Folder 291.1 (Marriages, Vol. I), ACCH2.

56. War Department Circular No. 179 (June 8, 1942). This policy—which expanded AR 600–750 to apply to all personnel rather than just low-ranking enlisted men—held until the 1953 AR 600–240, *Marriage in Overseas Command* issued a more detailed list of rules pertaining to marriages between military personnel and noncitizens. For a brief history of military marriage regulations, see Rose Cuison Villazor, "The Other *Loving:* Uncovering the Federal Regulation of Interracial Marriages," *NYU Law Review* 86 (2011): 1395–1400; Dana Michael Hollywood, "An End to 'Til DEROS Do Us Part': The Army's Regulation of International Marriages in Korea," *Military Law Review* 200 (2009): 164–168. For two critiques of military marriage regulation, see Richard B. Johns, "The Right to Marry: Infringement by the Armed Forces," *Family Law Quarterly* 10, no. 4 (Winter 1977): 357–387; Ross W. Branstetter, "Military Constraints on Marriage of Service Members Overseas; or, If the Army Had Wanted You to Have a Wife . . ." *Military Law Review* 102 (Fall 1983): 5–21.

57. Quoted in Green, *Black Yanks in the Pacific,* 70–71, 81; Rodger Venzke, *Confidence in Battle, Inspiration in Peace: The United States Army Chaplaincy, 1945–75* (GPO, 1977), 1. As Green shows, this policy had particularly pernicious effects on African American soldiers and their Japanese girlfriends, with whom many had children.

58. George W. Thompson, "If I Marry a Foreigner?" (1952), Box 3, Folder: Thompson, George W., NCCH2.

59. C. E. Matthews to Stanton Salisbury, July 17, 1952; Alfred Carpenter to Stanton Salisbury, July 14, 1952; Stanton Salisbury to C. E. Matthews, July 21, 1952; Stanton Salisbury to Alfred Carpenter, July 30, 1952, Box 2, Folder: Baptist (South) 1949–52, NCCH3.

60. George W. Thompson, Press Release: "Navy Chaplains' Concern for Immigrant Dependents of Service Personnel," August 18, 1952; George W. Thompson, "Missionaries at Sea," Box 3, Folder: Thompson, George W., NCCH2. In addressing whether Americans are Christian, the booklet simply states, "Christianity is a way of life. It is not forced upon anyone." The effort to gloss America as Christian was common at midcentury—see Kevin Kruse, *One Nation under God: How Corporate America Invented Christian America* (Basic, 2015). On midcentury domestic ideals and political culture, see Elaine Tyler May, *Homeward Bound: American Families in the Cold War Era* (Basic, 1988).

61. Eldin Ricks Oral History, 32, ERI; Harold Saperstein, "The Eternal City," 1944, Series B, Box 8, Folder 3, HSP; Samuel Faircloth, interviewed by Robert Shuster, Tape 2, SDF.

62. Aryeh Lev Europe 1945 Trip Journal, 26; Herman Heuer Europe 1945 Trip Journal, 66, 34, 9–10, Box 18, Folder 106, NJWB2.

5 The Military-Spiritual Complex

1. Quoted in William Laurence, *Dawn over Zero: The Story of the Atomic Bomb,* 2nd ed. (Greenwood, 1972), 209. In Laurence's text, Downey prays to the Almighty Father. Another version, published in Liam Nolan's history of Japanese Lutheran Kiyoshi Watanabe efforts to help Americans during World War II quotes Downey concluding his prayer in the name of Jesus Christ, but cites no source for the prayer. Liam Nolan, *Small Man of Nanataki* (Peter Davies, 1966), 143.

2. Laurence, *Dawn over Zero*, 212–222; "The Operational History of the 509th Bombardment," in *The Manhattan Project: The Birth of the Atomic Bomb in the Words of Its Creators, Eyewitnesses, and Historians*, ed. Cynthia C. Kelly (Atomic Heritage Foundation, 2007), 330. On the fiftieth anniversary of the bombings, the Smithsonian Museum planned an exhibit of the *Enola Gay*, and a controversy erupted over the portrayal of the decision to use the bomb. See Edward Linenthal and Tom Engelhardt, eds., *History Wars: The* Enola Gay *and Other Battles for the American Past* (Henry Holt, 1996). On the cultural legacies of the atomic bomb, see Paul Boyer, *By the Bomb's Early Light: American Thought and Culture at the Dawn of the Atomic Age* (Random House, 1985).

3. Laurence, *Dawn over Zero*, 229.

4. Mary L. Dudziak, *War Time: An Idea, Its History, Its Consequences* (Oxford, 2012), 3–9, 33–40; Susan L. Carruthers, *The Good Occupation: American Soldiers and the Hazards of Peace* (Harvard, 2016); Robert A. Pollard, *Economic Security and the Origins of the Cold War, 1945–50* (Columbia, 1985), 20–23.

5. Initially, Carpenter was designated as the air force chief of chaplains operating under the army chief of chaplains. However, the chaplaincies split into two separate entities. Reminiscences of Charles I. Carpenter (1971), 45–48, CCOH.

6. Dwight D. Eisenhower, Farewell Address, January 17, 1961, in the *Public Papers of the Presidents of the United States: Dwight D. Eisenhower, 1960–61* (GPO, 1961), 1038; Eisenhower to Dr. Hazen, *The Chaplain* 3, no. 4 (April 1946): front cover; Eisenhower, Speech to the Washington Ministerial Union, May 25, 1953, Speech Series, Box 4, DDE-AW. For two different appraisals of the relationship between Truman and Eisenhower, see Steve Neal, *Harry and Ike: The Partnership That Remade the Postwar World* (Scribner, 2001); William L. Miller, *Two Americans: Truman, Eisenhower, and a Dangerous World* (Vintage, 2012).

7. On the larger context of transmitting American religious ideals abroad in the twentieth century, see Anna Su, *Exporting Freedom: Religious Liberty and American Power* (Harvard, 2016).

8. Samuel Sandmel to Frances Fox Sandmel, August 13, 1945, Box 23, Folder 8, SSP; Morris Frank to Florence Frank, May 7, 1945, MFL.

9. Louis Barish, *Rabbis in Uniform: The Story of the American Jewish Military Chaplain* (Jonathan David, 1962), 21–22; Morris Kertzer, Reflections, and Kertzer, Address at Tempio Israelitico, June 9, 1944, Box 12, Folder 7, MKP; Alex Grobman, *Rekindling the Flame: American Jewish Chaplains and the Survivors of European Jewry, 1944–48* (Wayne State, 1993), 29–33; David Max Eichhorn, May 6, 1945, in *The GI's Rabbi: World War II Letters of David Max Eichhorn*, ed. Greg Palmer and Mark S. Zaid (Kansas, 2004), 182–187.

10. Edward P. Doyle, "I Was There," Address to the International Liberators Conference, 1981, Box 2, Folder 25, EPD; Quoted in Robert Abzug, *Inside the Vicious Heart: Americans and the Liberation of Nazi Concentration Camps* (Oxford, 1985), 30. The descriptions of Ohrdruf and Nordhausen come from Abzug, 21–31.

11. Grobman, *Rekindling the Flame*, 39–40; "Rabbi Herschel Schacter Is Dead at 95; Cried to the Jews of Buchenwald: 'You Are Free,'" *NYT*, March 26, 2013.

12. Morris Frank to Florence Frank, August 28, 1944, MFL; Harold Saperstein, April 11, 1945, Box 8, Folder 1, HSP; Eichhorn, *The GI's Rabbi*, 178.

13. Morris Kertzer to Phil Bernstein, September 24, 1944, Box 12, Folder 7, MKP.

14. Eichhorn, *The GI's Rabbi*, 188; Morris Frank to Florence Frank, August 28, 1944, MFL. Eichhorn planned to hold a Shabbat service on Saturday, May 5, 1945, in Dachau's main square, but threats from non-Jews led to a more limited service in the laundry. Another service was held on Sunday, March 6, in the public square, which was attended by about 2,000 Jews and non-Jews. See *The GI's Rabbi*, 184–188. The public work and private correspondence of chaplains exemplify Hasia Diner's argument that Americans discussed the Holocaust in the early postwar years. Diner, *We Remember with Reverence and Love: American Jews and the Myth of Silence after the Holocaust, 1945–62* (NYU, 2009).

15. Grobman, *Rekindling the Flame*, 24; Fred Oppenheimer to Herman Dicker, July 31, 1945, Abe L. Plotkin Collection, University of Scranton, http://digitalservices.scranton.edu/cdm/singleitem/collection/p9000coll4/id/144/rec/25.

16. Grobman, *Rekindling the Flame*, 43–61; Robert Haeger and Bill Long, "Lost EC Treasure Found in Palestine," *The Stars and Stripes*, December 9, 1947; Aryeh Lev Report, May 31, 1945, Box 200, Folder: William Arnold & Aryeh Lev, 1945—Report, NJWB1.

17. Morton Fierman, "Continental Comments," [1945], Box 5, Folder 5, MFP; Herbert Friedman to Louis Isaacson, July 5, 1946, Box 1, Folder 4, HFP. These prayers come in multiple places in the morning prayers; both the *birchot hashachar* (morning prayers) and the *Amidah* express gratitude for God's role picking up the fallen, healing the sick, and releasing the imprisoned. In the 1960s, Rabbi Abraham Joshua Heschel would similarly argue that when he marched in the civil rights movement his "feet were praying." Shai Held, *Abraham Joshua Heschel: The Call of Transcendence* (Indiana, 2013), 23.

18. CANRA Executive Board Meeting Minutes, March 11, 1946, and October 9, 1947, Box 6, Folder 13; CANRA Annual Report for 1946, December 23, 1946, Box 9, Folder 34, NJWB2. The number of Jewish chaplains requested for this assignment fluctuated between five and ten (up to 25 percent of postwar Jewish army chaplains).

19. Herbert Friedman Monthly Report, April 1946, Box 1, Folder 12, HFP; Quoted in Gerd Korman, "The Survivors' Talmud and the U.S. Army," *American Jewish History* 73, no. 3 (March 1984): 269. Civilian organizations such as the American Bible Society often donated paper, but the military provided all supplies for the first fifty sets of the Talmud.

20. Herman Dicker, "The U.S. Army and Jewish Displaced Persons," *The Chicago Jewish Forum* 19, No. 4 (Summer 1961): 293; Grobman, *Rekindling the Flame*, 70–88. Anna M. Rosenberg would become the first female undersecretary of defense in the Eisenhower Administration. She maintained a strong interest in talking to enlisted personnel to know what was happening on the ground, often to the consternation of high-ranking commanders.

21. "Truman Holds Religion Main Defense Line," *WP*, March 13, 1948; The Military Chaplaincy: A Report to the President by the President's Committee on Religion and Welfare in the Armed Forces, October 1, 1950, 1–2, Box 10, Folder: Chaplaincy Report, HST. This was not a new stance for Truman; as a senator in 1939, he presided over a National Meeting for Moral Re-Armament.

22. Rodger Venzke, *Confidence in Battle, Inspiration in Peace: The United States Army Chaplaincy, 1945–75* (GPO, 1977), 39–46. In *The Spiritual-Industrial Com-*

plex: America's Religious Battle against Communism in the Early Cold War (Oxford, 2011), Jonathan Herzog argues that the chaplaincy's emphasis on character guidance emanated from the PCRW and UMT (118–119); however, this misstates PCRW claims as historical fact. The military's embrace of a formal moral education program represented a federal counterpart to state and local character education that became common in schools during the Depression and was rejuvenated in the late 1940s. On links between sex and character education in public schools, see Jeffrey Moran, *Teaching Sex: The Shaping of Adolescence in the Twentieth Century* (Harvard, 2002); Natalia M. Petrzela, *Classroom Wars: Language, Sex, and the Making of Modern Political Culture* (Oxford, 2015); Clay Howard, "The Closet and the Cul de Sac: Sex, Politics, and Suburbanization in Postwar California" (PhD diss., Michigan, 2010).

23. Harry Truman, "Remarks to the President's Conference on Community Responsibility to Our Peacetime Servicemen and Women," May 25, 1949, printed in *Public Papers of the Presidents of the United States, Harry S. Truman, 1945–1953* (GPO, 1966), 263; Press Release, October 27, 1948, Box 1, Folder 2a: Executive Order 10013, HST. On Walsh, see Patrick H. McNamara, *A Catholic Cold War: Edmund A. Walsh, S. J., and the Politics of American Anticommunism* (Fordham, 2005). On Gibson, see Truman K. Gibson Jr. with Steve Huntley, *Knocking Down Barriers: My Fight for Black America* (Northwestern, 2005).

24. Frank Weil to Harry Truman, November 28, 1950, Box 10, Folder: Chaplaincy Report, HST; The Military Chaplaincy: A Report, 11–12, 2.

25. Michael Hogan, *A Cross of Iron: Harry S. Truman and the Origins of the National Security State, 1945–1954* (Cambridge, 1998), 119–158; John Sager, "Universal Military Training and the Struggle to Define American Identity during the Cold War," *Federal History* 5 (January 2013): 57–74; William A. Taylor, *Every Citizen a Soldier: The Campaign for Universal Military Training after World War II* (Texas A&M, 2014). The anti-UMT lineup included an array of groups and interests that were often more antagonistic than allied: labor unions, educators, some religious leaders, historians, and conservative businessmen. Liberals often claimed it was un-American, while conservatives framed it as wasteful.

26. Matthew H. Imrise, "The Ft. Knox Experiment," *The Army and Navy Chaplain* XVII, no. 4 (April–May 1947): 2–6; "Chaplain Reports Fort Knox Experiment in Training Is Complete Success," *The Milwaukee Sentinel*, January 22, 1948; Hanson W. Baldwin, "Army's Youth Unit Called a Success," *NYT*, May 18, 1947; Quoted in Venzke, *Confidence in Battle*, 42. Initially only Chaplain Hundley and Chaplain Murphy were assigned to Fort Knox, which led Murphy to joke that he "was the Rabbi for the time being." Charles Murphy, "Remarks," August 1947, Box 458, Folder 726 (Hygiene of Diseases, Vol. II), ACCH2.

27. Stanton W. Salisbury, "Navy Chaplains' Religious and Moral Program," April 25, 1951, Box 123, Folder 5214 (Reports to the Secretary of the Navy, 1946–58), CRB; Robert Wuthnow, *The Restructuring of American Religion* (Princeton, 1988), 15–17, 36–37; Stanton W. Salisbury, "This Present Generation," undated (emphasis original), Salisbury, Box 8, Folder: Sermons, RCC.

28. *Chaplains' Character Guidance Manual for Training Divisions and Training Centers*, 1, Box 10, Folder 8, HST. The Ten Commandments are listed differently in Exodus and Deuteronomy, and religious traditions number, translate, and interpret them in distinct ways. On the construction of the "Judeo-Christian tradition,"

see Mark Silk, "Notes on the Judeo-Christian Tradition in America," *American Quarterly* 36, no. 1 (Spring 1984): 65–86. Character Guidance presaged comparable efforts to conjoin and sacralize American history and morality, such as the explicit incorporation of God into currency and the Pledge of Allegiance in the 1950s.

29. *Chaplains' Character Guidance Manual for Training Divisions and Training Centers*, 5–7. The idea of the United States as a covenant nation extends back to John Winthrop's 1630 sermon on the Arbella, "A Model of Christian Charity," in which he pushed his followers to build a "city on a hill." However, as Frank Lambert argues in *The Founding Fathers and the Place of Religion in America* (Princeton, 2003), the Founding Fathers emphasized religious liberty, not Christian state framework of the Puritan Fathers, and the tension between these dueling claims persists.

30. E.g., Lectures—The Chaplain's Hour, Box 481, Folder 330.11 (Character Guidance); *Character Guidance Discussion Topics: Duty-Honor-Country*, Boxes 517–18, Folder 330.11 (Character Guidance), ACCH2. The lectures often resembled nineteenth-century moral advice literature, updated for a new Communist enemy. See, for example, Barbara Reeves-Ellington, Kathryn Kish Sklar, and Connie A. Shemo, eds., *Competing Kingdoms: Women, Mission, Nation, and the American Protestant Empire, 1812–1960* (Duke, 2010); Amy Kaplan, *The Anarchy of Empire in the Making of U.S. Culture* (Harvard, 2002). On the history of moral education writ large, see B. Edward McClellan, *Moral Education in America: Schools and the Shaping of Character since Colonial Times* (Teachers College Press, 1999). McClellan argues that there was a decline in character education during the Cold War, but his focus on schools misses the military as a site of character education.

31. *Chaplains' Sex Morality Lecture Manual* (1948), 12, Box 10, Folder 8; PCRW Morning Meeting, December 20, 1948, 12–13, Box 3, Folder 2B2, HST.

32. Lawrence Nelson to Chief of Chaplains, Fourth Quarter (1947) Report, January 12, 1948, Box 481, Folder 330.11 (Reports on Citizenship & Morality Lectures and VD Control); Loren Jenks to Chief of Chaplains, Quarterly Review of Citizenship and Morality Lecture Program, June 20, 1948; Stephen H. Stolz to James H. O'Neill, July 28, 1948, Box 417, Folder 330.11 (Citizenship & Morality Lectures, Vol. IV), ACCH2. Even the army's internal history deemed the rhetoric of excitement surrounding the program "naïve." See Venzke, *Confidence in Battle*, 43.

33. Inspection of Chaplain Board by Second Army Inspector General, November 30, 1949, Box 482, Folder 334 (Chaplain Board, Vol. II), ACCH2.

34. Fred Jerome and Rodger Taylor, *Einstein on Race and Racism* (Rutgers, 2006), 88; "Southern Schrecklichkeit," *The Crisis* 53, no. 9 (Sept 1946): 276–277.

35. Harry Truman to Ernest W. Roberts, August 18, 1948, quoted in Robert H. Ferrell, ed. *Off the Record: The Private Papers of Harry S. Truman* (Harper & Row, 1980), 146–147; Sheris Mershon and Steven Schlossman, *Foxholes and Color Lines: Desegregating the U.S. Armed Forces* (JHU, 1998), 158–186.

36. Executive Order 9981, July 26, 1948; Christine Knauer, *Let Us Fight as Free Men: Black Soldiers and Civil Rights* (Penn, 2014).

37. Mershon and Schlossman, *Foxholes and Color Lines*, 187–217; AFCB Meeting Minutes Digest, July 6, 1949, Box 1, Folder: AFC Board Agenda and Minutes, NCCH3; H. L. Bergsma, *The Pioneers: A Monograph on the First Two Black Chap-*

lains in the Chaplain Corps of the United States Navy (GPO, 1980), 11–14; "Chaplains Should Practice Nonsegregation, Too," *CC*, March 7, 1951.

38. Jim McCollum, email to author, October 22, 2014; *McCollum v. Board of Education*, 333 U.S. 203 (1948), 213, 238–239. On the humanist history of the McCollum family, see Leigh Eric Schmidt, *Village Atheist: How America's Unbelievers Made Their Way into a Godly Nation* (Princeton, 2016), 267–271.

39. PCRW Morning Meeting, November 4, 1949, 92, Box 5, Folder 2B11; "The Institution of Marriage" in *Chaplains' Sex Morality Lecture Manual* (1948), 27, Box 10, Folder 8, HST; OCCH, *Historical Review 1967–68*, 89–90, and *1968–69*,72–79. For an overview of the ACLU's challenge, see Anne Loveland, *Change and Conflict in the U.S. Army Chaplain Corps Since 1945* (Tennessee, 2014), 31–34. On *McCollum* and other legal challenges by nonbelievers, see Leigh Eric Schmidt, *Village Atheists: How America's Unbelievers Made Their Way in a Godly Nation* (Princeton, 2016), 249–283.

40. PCRW Morning Meeting, January 13, 1950, 82, Box 5, Folder 2B12; PCRW Morning Meeting, November 4, 1949, 131, Box 5, Folder 2B11, HST.

41. Emil Kapaun to Mark Carroll, July 11, 1950, in Arthur Tonne, *The Story of Chaplain Kapaun: Patriot Priest of the Korean Conflict* (Didde Publishers, 1954), 136. Tonne's text reprints many of Kapaun's letters home and forms the basis for William L. Maher's biography, *A Shepherd in Combat Boots: Chaplain Emil Kapaun of the 1st Cavalry Division* (Burd Street, 1997).

42. Robert E. Burke to Arthur Tonne, February 8, 1954, in Tonne, *The Story of Chaplain Kapaun*, 188; Maher, *A Shepherd in Combat Boots*, 116–161; "Medal of Honor Awarded to Korean War Chaplain," *NYT*, April 11, 2013.

43. Maher, *A Shepherd in Combat Boots*, 83, 105; Emil Kapaun to Fred Tuzicka, April 13, 1950, quoted in Maher, 80; Emil Kapaun to Mark Carroll, October 4, 1950, in Tonne, *The Story of Chaplain Kapaun*, 145–146. The archival source base for the chaplaincy in Korea is quite limited. The National Archives has a mere thirty-five boxes from the period (compared to hundreds for the previous decades).

44. Bruce Cumings, *The Korean War: A History* (Random House, 2010), xviii, 35. Using Korean language sources, Cumings wrote several comprehensive volumes on the origins of the Korean War that undergird the shorter Random House volume. He challenged older accounts of the Korean War that emphasized Soviet aggression by showing that internal conflict was central. In *Rethinking the Korean War: A New Diplomatic and Strategic History* (Princeton, 2004), William Stueck argues that both internal and external factors played significant roles in fomenting conflict.

45. Cumings, *The Korean War*, 103–146, 12–15, xviii, 210. In addition to massacres and bombings, the treatment of POWs by both sides raises questions about ethical behavior during war. American POWs testified to the inhumane treatment they received in North Korean and Chinese camps soon after release. Recent scholarship has uncovered the sordid treatment of North Korean POWs by UN forces as well. Monica Kim, "Humanity Interrogated: Empire, Nation, and the Political Subject in U.S. and UN-Controlled POW Camps during the Korean War, 1942–1960" (PhD diss., Michigan, 2011). On the policy of containment, see John Lewis Gaddis, *Strategies of Containment* (Oxford, 1982). On the links between religion and containment, see two slightly different takes:

T. Jeremy Gunn, *The Cold War and the Forging of an American National Religion* (Praeger, 2009) and William Inboden, *Religion and American Foreign Policy, 1945–1960: The Soul of Containment* (Cambridge, 2010).

46. "Billy Graham Plans Trip to Korean Front," *Baltimore Sun*, November 25, 1952; Billy Graham, *I Saw Your Sons at War: The Korean Diary of Billy Graham* (Billy Graham Evangelistic Association, 1953), 12, 18, 24, 26.

47. Venzke, *Confidence in Battle*, 72–3; Clifford Drury, Paul Sanders, and W. Ivan Hoy, *The History of the Chaplain Corps, United States Navy, Vol. VI: During the Korean War* (GPO, 1960), 2.

48. Billy Graham, *I Saw Your Sons at War*, 35; Military Ordinariate Annual Report, November 15, 1950 (includes Segreteria di Stato, N. 6731/50, 27 September 1950), Box 67, Folder 8, ROGS; Remarks of Colonel Aryeh Lev, December 1, 1952, Box 18, Folder 108, NJWB2.

49. Venzke, *Confidence in Battle*, 78, 93–94; Ivan L. Bennett to James T. Wilson, December 3, 1952, Box 526, Folder 461 (Army and Navy Hymnal, Vol. VI), ACCH2.

50. Interview with Dr. Andrew Kang for the Veterans History Project, Center for the Study of War and Society, UT-Knoxville, December 26, 2001, 21–22, http://volweb.utk.edu/~wpcsws/wp-content/uploads/2013/04/2002-Kang-Andrew-1 -transcript.pdf.

51. Richard Raines to Ivan Bennett, November 20, 1952, Box 494, Folder 000.3 (Reports by Religious Consultants, Vol. I), ACCH2; Rear Admiral Ross Henry Trower Oral History, interview by H. Lawrence Martin (Oral History Program, USN, 1985), 42–43.

52. John H. Muller, *Wearing the Cross in Korea* (1954), 27, 16, 62, 29–31.

53. "President-Elect Says Soviet Demoted Zhukov Because of Their Friendship," *NYT*, December 23, 1952; Patrick Henry, "'And I Don't Care What It Is': The Tradition-History of a Civil Religion Proof-Text," *Journal of the American Academy of Religion* 49, no. 1 (March 1981): 35–49; William L. Miller, *Piety along the Potomac: Notes on Politics and Morals in the Fifties* (Houghton Mifflin, 1964), 34.

54. Herzog, *The Spiritual-Industrial Complex*, 96; Gunn, *Spiritual Weapons*, 57. Herzog argues that Eisenhower unexpectedly benefitted from not being closely associated with a particular denomination, whereas Gunn views Eisenhower's profession of religion as an opportunistic move.

55. Stephen Whitfield, *The Culture of the Cold War*, 2nd ed. (JHU, 1996), 83.

56. Kevin Kruse, *One Nation under God: How Corporate America Invented Christian America* (Basic, 2015); Eisenhower, Farewell Address.

6   "Maybe God Is an American"

1. Withers M. Moore, *Navy Chaplains in Vietnam, 1954–1964* (GPO, 1968), 5–54.

2. Ibid., 142–152. For an extended and celebratory account of the operation, see Ronald B. Frankum, *Operation Passage to Freedom: The United States Navy in Vietnam, 1954–1955* (Texas Tech, 2007). For more critical appraisals, see T. Jeremy Gunn, *Spiritual Weapons: The Cold War and the Forging of an American National Religion* (Praeger, 2009), 155–175; Seth Jacobs, *America's Miracle Man in Vietnam: Ngo Dinh Diem, Religion, Race, and U.S. Intervention in Southeast Asia* (Duke, 2005), 127–170.

3. Frederik Logevall, *Embers of War: The Fall of an Empire and the Making of America's Vietnam* (Random House, 2012), 666; Jacobs, *America's Miracle Man*, 131–132; Gunn, *Spiritual Weapons*, 167–175. Rear Admiral Lorenzo Sabin to Admiral F. B. Stump (CINCPAC), August 24, 1954, Virtual Vietnam Archive, Texas Tech University. By May 1955, the Catholic population of Saigon exceeded that of Paris or Rome.

4. Moore, *Navy Chaplains in Vietnam*, 3, 27–29, 138; Spencer J. Palmer Oral History, 13, SJP.

5. Spencer J. Palmer Oral History, 13. On religion and the Cold War more generally, see Andrew Preston, *Sword of the Spirit, Shield of Faith: Religion in American War and Diplomacy* (Knopf, 2012), 411–496; Jonathan Herzog, *The Spiritual-Industrial Complex: America's Religious Battle against Communism in the Early Cold War* (Oxford, 2011); Jacobs, *America's Miracle Man;* William Inboden, *Religion and American Foreign Policy, 1945–1960: The Soul of Containment* (Cambridge, 2008); David S. Fogelsong, *The American Mission and the "Evil" Empire* (Cambridge, 2007); Gunn, *Spiritual Weapons*.

6. Ingram Stainbeck to Ralph Honda, Kenji Onodera, Shiro Kashiwa, October 26, 1948; John L. E. Collier to Ryu Munekata, November 8, 1948; Harold Levering to National Young Buddhists, December 3, 1948, Box 466, ACCH2. On the Civil War origins of American military dog tags, see David McCormick, "Inventing Military Dog Tags," *America's Civil War* 25, no. 2 (May 2012): 56–59. State documents use letters to mark numerous identities—religion, race, gender, sexuality, etc.—and state acceptance or rejection of individual choices is significant in other realms as well. Gayle Salamon, *Assuming a Body: Transgender and Rhetorics of Materiality* (Columbia, 2010), 171–193.

7. Sydney Croft to Luther D. Miller, November 20, 1948; Sydney Croft to James Forrestal, September 21, 1948, Box 384, 080 (Buddhist), ACCH2.

8. Ruth Blakey to Mike Iwatsubo, November 17, 1948, Box 466; Chaplain Board to the Office of the Chief of Chaplains, October 22, 1948; Luther D. Miller to Leonard Bloom, September 28, 1948, Box 384, Folder 080 (Buddhist), ACCH2. Depending on his source of information, Miller's concern was either accurate or exaggerated. The 1936 Census of Religious Bodies in the United States identified 256 denominations—forty-three more than had been noted in 1926—and the number probably grew. In 1945, the Secretary of War set chaplaincy quotas that encompassed thirty-eight religious groups (with at least 100,000 adherents) and an additional thirty-two denominations classified as "miscellaneous" (whose numbers did not reach 100,000 members) for a total of seventy recognized religious entities. "Religious Bodies: 1936, Volume I, Summary and Detailed Tables," (GPO, 1941); "Data Sheet: Quotas for Chaplains," May 1, 1945, Box 8, Folder 3a, HST.

9. Peter Chumbris to Luther D. Miller, January 8, 1948, Box 471, 080 (Greek Orthodox), ACCH2; J. Willard Marriott to Harold B. Lee and Mark E. Petersen, April 23, 1947, quoted in Joseph Boone, "The Roles of the Church of Jesus Christ of Latter-Day Saints in Relation to the United States Military" (PhD diss., BYU, 1975); "Chief Chaplain Asks 'X' Designation on Army's 'Dog Tags,'" *Chicago Tribune*, January 7, 1949.

10. Abdallah Ingram to Dwight D. Eisenhower, July 29, 1952, Box 619, Folder OF 144B-4; Assistant to the President to the Bishop of the Romanian Orthodox Episcopate of America, June 2, 1955, Box 691, Folder OF 118G, DDE-WH. Three decades later, the Orthodox were still petitioning "to be considered and listed as

a fourth major religious body," at which point the AFCB recommended "the word 'distinctive' instead of the word 'major' when addressing the matter of religious bodies or faith groups. It was noted that 'distinctive' could be used with all faith groups." See AFCB Minutes, June 4, 1975, in AFCB Minutes 1974–76, FJC.

11. Deborah Dash Moore, "Jewish GIs and the Creation of the Judeo-Christian Tradition," *Religion and American Culture* 8, no. 1 (Winter 2008): 52, note 39; "Army 'Dog Tags' to List G.I.'s Choice of Religion," *NYT*, July 28, 1955; "New Ruling on 'Dog Tags,'" *The Pentecostal Evangel*, August 28, 1955; Frank A. Tobey Circular Letter, August 14, 1959, Box 561, Folder 312.1 (Monthly Letters, 1959), ACCH2.

12. Verbatim Record of Trial of US 54 074 019 by General Court Martial, May 15, 1953, 15, Box 10475, GCA. Christmas became a federal holiday in 1870. Nineteenth-century efforts notwithstanding, the post office granted Sunday as a holiday to mail carriers, and many states retained "blue laws" that forbid the sale of alcohol on Sundays. In 1961, the Supreme Court deemed Sunday laws permissible on the grounds that there could be a secular purpose to a common day of rest. See *McGowan v. Maryland* (366 U.S. 420); *Two Guys v. McGinley* (366 U.S. 582); *Braunfield v. Brown* (366 U.S. 599); *Gallagher v. Crown Kosher* (366 U.S. 617).

13. Elizabeth Hillman, *Defending America: Military Culture and the Cold War Court Martial* (Princeton, 2005); Verbatim Record of Trial of US 54 074 019, 25, 34.

14. "Why Seventh-day Adventists Cannot Engage in War," *The Review and Herald*, March 7, 1865; Robert Mole, *God Also Loves Military People: A Brief Story of the Seventh-Day Adventist Church and the American Military Chaplaincy, 1860–1976* (General Conference of Seventh-day Adventists, 1977), 27–29, 38–40; Carlyle B. Haynes, "Shall We Recommend Our Ministers for Military Chaplaincies?" (1941), 2–4, 6–7; "General Conference Committee Actions regarding Chaplaincies," (n.d.), Box 10519, Folder: Material from Carlyle B. Haynes Files on Chaplains, GCA; Mole, *God Also Loves Military People*, 43–62. On tension between American SDA and the military, see Ronald Lawson, "Onward Christian Soldiers: Seventh-Day Adventists and the Issue of Military Service," *Review of Religious Research* 37, no. 3 (March 1966): 193–218. Some Southern Baptists echoed the SDA concern about tax dollars paying for chaplains, given the denomination's historic wariness toward church-state intermingling, but few ministers cared as Southern Baptists were often overrepresented in the chaplaincy. Samuel McCrea Cavert, General Commission Dinner Remarks, 1957, AR 631–18, SBHLA.

15. Haynes, "Shall We Recommend Our Ministers," 6–7; Carlyle B. Haynes to Richard K. Kreiger, November 27, 1945, Box 10473, Folder 3, GCA; J. R. Nelson, "SDA Military Enlistments Bring Problems," *Columbia Union Visitor* 69, no. 29 (July 16, 1964). The church recommended that men wait to be drafted into the army to secure noncombatant status and limit Sabbath conflicts. Project Whitecoat ran from 1955 to 1974 and included about 2,300 Adventist volunteers. The emphasis on biological warfare later led members to scrutinize the ethics of this noncombatant military service. See Jonathan D. Moreno, *Undue Risk: Secret State Experiments on Humans* (Routledge, 2001), 258–262; Douglas Morgan, *Adventism and the American Republic: The Public Involvement of a Major Apocalyptic Movement* (Tennessee, 2001), 157.

16. Merle W. Smith letter "to whom it may concern," April 3, 1956; Merle Smith to George W. Chambers, March 16, 1956; Commander, 5039th Air Base Wing to Commander AAC, Box 10473, Folder: Johnson Court Martial, GCA.

17. "Belief and Practice of Seventh-day Adventists regarding Sabbath Keeping in the Armed Forces," War Service Commission of Seventh-day Adventist General Conference, May 1, 1955, Box 12522, Folder: General Letters—Chaplains, GCA; Summarized Record of Trial, Special Court Martial of Brian M. Bennett, Virgil E. Jones, and George C. Myers, October 11, 1955, Box 10474, Folder: Bennett/Jones/Myers Court Martial, GCA. On Friday night, the three men—who were part of the Medical Detachment of the 723rd Tank Battalion—refused to transport medics to the field; they were convicted and sentenced to reduction to the lowest grade of enlisted men and a reduction in pay.

18. Responsa on "Volunteering for the Military Chaplaincy," December 13, 1950, Box 7, Folder 17; form letter used to excuse Shomer Shabbat men from duty, February 15, 1960, Box 20, Folder 120, NJWB2. As enunciated in the Babylonian Talmud (Yoma 84b), one may fight fires, break walls, and swim (all prohibited on the Sabbath) to save a life. The rabbis derived this principle from Leviticus 18:5, which instructs the Israelites to "live by" God's laws. While the exact latitude of saving lives on the Sabbath has been debated, it offered a viable foundation for flexibility in the military.

19. John Freeman to Harry, December 14, 1955; Jack Ostrovsky to Rabbi B. Borchardt, December 22, 1955, Box 21, Folder 136; CJC Director's Report, November 2, 1960, Box 4, Folder: CJC Minutes, 1959–71, NJWB2. Freeman also contacted Rabbi Boruch Borchardt, the head of the Orthodox Agudat Israel's Youth Division, who wrote to George W. Chambers, the head of the Seventh-day Adventist War Service Commission, who was resigned to less than desirable outcomes. G. W. Chambers to Rabbi B. Borchardt, December 21, 1955, Box 21, Folder 136, NJWB2.

20. Verbatim Record of Trial, Special Court Martial of Countee Johnson (AF 15 297 907), April 17, 1956, 69, 77, Box 10473, Folder: Johnson Court Martial, GCA.

21. Trial by General Court Martial of Ralph Thomas Clark, March 22–23, 1951, 30, Box 10473, Folder: Clark Court Martial; Richard Johnson to George Chambers, January 7, 1958, Box 12522, Folder: Simonetti Letters; Lavern Peterson to Secretary of the Navy, July 17, 1964 (emphasis original), Box 10473, Folder: Hawaii—Special—Juhrs' Case and Others, GCA.

22. Special Court Martial of Countee Johnson, 6; F. H. Hewitt to George Chambers, March 18, 1957, and March 29, 1957, Box 10474, Folder: Court-Martial—Air Force—Williams and Hayes, GCA. Neither the Johnson trial record nor the correspondence about the court-martial note Johnson's race; however, a *Cleveland Plain Dealer* obituary (February 14, 2012) indicates that he was African American.

23. Henry E. Felder, "Black Seventh-Day Adventists and Church Economics," in *Perspectives: Black Seventh-day Adventists Face the Twenty-First Century*, ed. Calvin B. Rock (Review and Herald, 1996), 63. Ascertaining the role of race in military accommodations for Seventh-day Adventists is challenging because there is no complete record of when, how many, and how they resolved religious conflicts administratively or judicially. Available records of court-martial do not demonstrate a difference in conviction or sentencing rates, but they are incomplete. On race and military justice more generally, see Hillman, *Defending America*, 92–108.

24. Military and Naval Attache, Embassy of India, quoted in "Summary of Major Events and Problems, FY 1961," 131; "Summary of Major Events and Problems, FY 1961," 131–132, Box 561, Folder 314.7 (1961), ACCH2. The Ahmadiyya movement originated in India (in the area that became Pakistan after partition) in 1889 and arrived in the United States in 1920. The group's headquarters moved to Washington, DC, in 1950, further enabling contact with government officials. Jane I. Smith, *Islam in America* (Columbia, 1999), 73–75. The issue of turbans gained traction in the 1960s, as the Sikh American community grew and more Sikhs sought assistance. The prohibition on turbans created disincentives to Sikh enlistment that continued until a 2017 policy change allowed beards and turbans for religious reasons. "[The recruit] can't show up at basic training without shaving his beard, cutting his hair and taking off his turban, in violation of his religion." David Alexander, "U.S. Lawmakers Urge Pentagon to Allow Sikhs Leeway in Military Attire," *Reuters*, March 10, 2014.

25. Peter C. Manson, Memo for the Record, January 26, 1960; Army Chief of Chaplains response, Memo for the Record, January 29, 1960, Box 544, Folder 000.3 (Religious Ministrations, 1960), ACCH2. One possible outcome, the memo suggested, was an administrative discharge that would enable the soldier to return to civilian life without a blemish on his record.

26. Jews faced similar problems, and the army rejected Aryeh Lev's request to accommodate a beard-wearing seminary student who wanted to volunteer as a chaplain. Aryeh Lev to Ellis H. Zirkind, August 18, 1953; Abraham Simon to Aryeh Lev, February 21, 1967; A. E. Michelson to Abraham Simon, February 21, 1967, Box 12, Folder 72, NJWB2. The appeal to Cold War politics resembles arguments about race. See Mary Dudziak, *Cold War Civil Rights: Race and the Image of American Democracy* (Princeton, 2001).

27. Infringement of Religious Rights in the Case of Private Mustapha Yusuf, January 29, 1960; Hajj I. Sassman to Commanding General, Fifth Army HQ, January 19, 1960, Box 544, Folder 000.3 (Religious Ministrations, 1960), ACCH2. Imam Hajj I. Sammsan, of the Universal Muslim Brotherhood of Islam in Detroit, confirmed that wearing a beard was a religious duty for observant Muslims. He also highlighted the need for the military to grapple with Islamic practices because "if the religion of Islam is repugnant to the Army, seemingly Congress would be the proper power to come forth with a repudiation." Beards continued to trouble the military, but as part of a strategy to boost recruitment during Vietnam, the navy loosened grooming restrictions in the 1970s. By the early 1980s, a push for "professionalism" banned beards again and renewed fights for religious accommodations. Only in 2017 did policy change to enable religious exemptions (see Epilogue). "Beards Banned by the Navy, But Rank Still Has Privileges," *WP*, July 4, 1981; "Navy Decides Sailors May Not Have Beards," *NYT*, December 15, 1984.

28. The Immigration and Nationality Act of 1965 altered the religious composition of the United States. Diana Eck, *A New Religious America: How A "Christian Country" Has Become the World's Most Religiously Diverse Nation* (HarperCollins, 2001); Peggy Levitt, *God Needs No Passport: Immigrants and the Changing American Religious Landscape* (New Press, 2007). Beards would remain vexing to the military (see Chapter 8) and other state institutions such as the police (e.g., *Police v. City of Newark*, 170 F.3d 359 (1999)).

29. Floyd Robertson to Bill Lanpher, December 8, 1981, Box 152, Folder: Commission on Chaplains; Report, September 16, 1970, Box 171, Folder: Commission on Chaplains; "Declaration on Ecumenical Councils and Christian Unity," October 9, 1962, Box 147, Folder: Ecumenicity, NAE. On broader evangelical efforts to influence American state and society in the postwar period, see Axel R. Schafer, *Piety and Public Funding: Evangelicals and the State in Modern America* (Penn, 2012); Daniel K. Williams, *God's Own Party: The Making of the Christian Right* (Oxford, 2012); Frances FitzGerald, *The Evangelicals: The Struggle to Shape America* (Simon and Schuster, 2017).

30. Floyd Robertson to Bill Lanpher, December 8, 1981; Report of the Chaplains Commission to the NAE Board, October 11–12, 1951, Box 44, Folder 7, TMJ; Billy Graham, *I Saw Your Sons at War: The Korean Diary* (Billy Graham Evangelistic Association, 1953). On the development of evangelical and fundamentalist educational institutions and networks, see Joel Carpenter, *Revive Us Again: The Reawakening of American Fundamentalism* (Oxford, 1997). Accreditation also allowed veterans to use their GI benefits.

31. J. W. Marriott to Luther Miller, October 2, 1945, Box 73, Folder 080 (LDS), ACCH2; J. P. Mannion to P. B. Wintersteen, November 2, 1954, Box 9, Folder: Ninth Naval District, 1954, NCCH3; LDS Servicemen's Committee, "Statement of the Chaplain Problem," February 1965, quoted in Boone, "The Roles of the Church of Jesus Christ of Latter-Day Saints," 622–630.

32. Ray Appelquist to J. Willard Marriott, October 23, 1966; Edward Brubaker to the President, November 4, 1966; J. Willard Marriott to Ray Appelquist, November 28, 1966, Box 85, Folder 2, JWM. This dispute went public in the Christian media. See "President Debases Chaplaincy Standards," *CC*, November 30, 1966, and "Mormon Waiver Watched," *CT*, April 28, 1967. On clashes and cooperation between Mormons and evangelicals, see Neil J. Young, *We Gather Together: The Religious Right and the Problem of Interfaith Politics* (Oxford, 2015).

33. Report: Commission on Chaplains and Service to Military Personnel, September 28, 1966, Box 152, Folder: Commission on Chaplains, NAE.

34. William Goldie, Memo about J. Willard Marriott Visit, November 30, 1971, Box 85, Folder 7, JWM. BYU eventually created a pastoral counseling master's program for an array of chaplaincy settings, from the military and prisons to hospitals and industry.

35. Anni Baker, *Life in the U.S. Armed Forces: (Not) Just Another Job* (Praeger, 2008), 73–74; Jorgenson, *Air Force Chaplains*, Vol. 2, 230–240; Donna Alvah, *Unofficial Ambassadors: American Military Families Overseas and the Cold War, 1946–1965* (NYU, 2007), 32–36; OCCH Staff Meeting Minutes, May 9, 1962, Box 577, Folder 337 (Minutes of the Staff Meetings, 1962), ACCH2; Report from the Commission on Chaplains and Service to Military Personnel to the National Association of Evangelicals' Board of Administration, October 11, 1965, Box 75, Folder C-1965, NAE. The military also requested Catholic and Jewish Supplementary School curricula from the Military Ordinariate and the Jewish Welfare Board. The emphasis on the nuclear family within the military echoed the cultivation of white middle-class domesticity in Cold War America. See Elaine Tyler May, *Homeward Bound: American Families in the Cold War Era* (Basic, 1988).

36. "Summary of Major Events and Problems, FY 1961," 78–79; Letter 67, Committee on Program for Service Personnel of the Board of Christian Education,

1957, AR 631–18, Folder: Ackiss, E. L., SBHLA. On conservative Protestants and public schools, see Seth Dowland, *Family Values and the Rise of the Christian Right* (Penn, 2015).

37. "Guidelines," July 14, 1964; Sam Walter to *The Alabama Baptist*, July 22, 1964; William Moran to Chief, Office of Legislative Liaison, November 4, 1964, Box 4, Folder: Chaplains and Segregated Meetings, ACCH3.

38. "Religious Liberty and the Armed Forces Sunday Schools," *CT*, July 17, 1964; *Congressional Record*, July 27, 1964, Box 152, Folder: Commission on Chaplains, NAE. On conservative Protestants and public schools, see Seth Dowland, *Family Values and the Rise of the Christian Right* (Penn, 2015).

39. Frank C. Kimball to J. Willard Marriott, March 18, 1960, Box 73, Folder 3; Edgar B. Brossard to Albert Northrop, September 19, 1959; Albert Northrop to Edgar Brossard, October 2, 1959; Frank Kimball to Bruce McConkie, December 8, 1959, Box 73, Folder 2, JWM. Taylor, a World War II POW who survived the Bataan Death March and three and a half years in Japanese camps, became Air Force Chief of Chaplains in 1962. See Richard Roper, *Brothers of Paul: Activities of Prisoner of War Chaplains in the Philippines during World War II* (Revere, 2003). The chapel space problem existed across the air force, including at the newly constructed Air Force Academy.

40. "Data and Documentation Relative to Denial of Religious Freedom to LDS Servicemen," April 1960, Box 73, Folder 6, JWM; Drew Pearson, "One Church for Protestant GIs?" *WP*, July 14, 1957.

41. Floyd Robertson to Edwin Chess, October 22, 1968, Box 152, Folder: Commission on Chaplains, NAE. According to Robertson, "Dr. Haggai appeared to go out of his way to offend the evangelicals who were present. It may be that some Christians fit his grotesque description of evangelical . . . Dr. Haggai's remarks bring into bold relief the controversy over the exclusion of certain types of evangelical Sunday School literature from military Sunday Schools."

42. Meir Engel to David Engel, #338, #339; General W. C. Westmoreland to Chaplain Brown, December 16, 1964; Meir Engel to Myra Engel, #286, #262, #260, #345, #336; Meir Engel to David Engel, #341, MEP; CJC Director's Report, May 10, 1965, Box 4, NJWB2; "Chaplain Meir Engel Dies on Duty in Vietnam; Was Born in Israel," *Jewish Telegraphic Agency*, December 17, 1964.

43. V. H. Krulak, Foreword, *Understanding the Vietnamese: Personal Response Project Resource Material*, 1966, FJC; George L. Harris et al., *U.S. Army Area Handbook for Vietnam* (GPO, 1962), iv; Moore, *Navy Chaplains in Vietnam, 1954–1964*, 130; Bergsma, *Chaplains with Marines in Vietnam, 1962–1971*, 100; Jacobs, *America's Miracle Man*, 267–270. On the military's use of ethnography more generally, see David H. Price, *Anthropological Intelligence: The Deployment and Neglect of American Anthropology in the Second World War* (Duke, 2008).

44. Robert Mole, "Resume of Seventh-day Adventist Chaplain Tour of Duty at Camp Pendleton," May 24, 1965; Robert Mole to W. F. Bradley, March 20, 1962, Box 10599, Folder: Robert L. Mole; "The Mole" to Mrs. White, December 5, 1967, Box 10445, Folder: Robert L. Mole; Robert Mole to J. R. Nelson, September 20, 1961, Box 10599, Folder: Robert L. Mole, GCA; "Chaplain Is Conducting On-Site Research Study," *The Free Lance-Star*, September 10, 1965.

45. Robert Mole, "First Progress Report of Southeast Asian Religious Research Project," September 30, 1965; Robert Mole to John Crave (Force Chaplain, Fleet

Marine Force, Pacific), September 29, 1965, FJC. On the role of missionaries in shaping American ideals and diplomacy, see David Hollinger, *Protestants Abroad: How Missionaries Tried to Change the World but Changed America* (Princeton, 2017).

46. Lt. General H. W. Buse, "Foreword, October 12, 1967," in *Unit Leaders Personal Response Handbook* (NAVMC 2616), 1967; Warren Newman, "The Personal Response Project—A Communications Perspective," 1968, VET. On the People-to-People Program, see Christina Klein, *Cold War Orientalism: Asia in the Middle-brow Imagination, 1945–61* (California, 2003), 49–56. On the larger Combined Action Programs of which the PRP was a part, see Richard Hunt, *Pacification: The American Struggle for Vietnam's Hearts and Minds* (Westview, 1995); Michael Peterson, *The Combined Action Platoons: The U.S. Marines' Other War in Vietnam* (Praeger, 1989).

47. "Do You Know about *Time Concepts in Vietnam?*" U.S. Navy Personal Response Project, Series A-6, Box 10445, Folder: Robert L. Mole, GCA.

48. "Tet," U.S. Navy Personal Response Project, Series A-6, Box 10445, Folder: Robert L. Mole, GCA.

49. "Cross-Cultural Understanding Can Bridge the Geographical Distance," U.S. Navy Personal Response Project, Series A-15, Box 10445, Folder: Robert L. Mole, GCA; *Unit Leaders Personal Response Handbook*, 71–72.

50. Robert M. Radasky, End of Tour Report, August 22, 1966, 2, quoted in Bergsma, *Chaplains with Marines in Vietnam*, 124; William Asher, Personal Narrative Report, 1966–1967, 3–4, VET.

51. Ronald L. Hedwall, "Experiences and Observations in Vietnam," 2, 3, 10, 9, August 22, 1967, VET; Elden H. Luffman, "Experiences and Observations in Vietnam," 1968, 1–4, VET. Hedwall's impressions correlate with Nick Turse's argument that the military pushed men to kill. *Kill Anything That Moves: The Real American War in Vietnam* (Picador, 2013).

52. Francis Sampson to Reeve Brenner, March 16, 1965; Reeve Brenner to Francis Sampson, March 31, 1965, RBC.

53. Ibid.; Floyd Robertson to Edwin Chess, October 22, 1968, Box 152, Folder: Commission on Chaplains, NAE. It was not until the 2014 Defense Appropriations Bill that, in the name of religious freedom, chaplains received permission to use "the traditions, expressions, and religious exercises of the endorsing faith group." See 2014 National Defense Authorization Act, Section 529.

7   Moral Objection and Religious Obligation

1. "Fire Suicide Proves Point," *BG*, June 12, 1963; "2d Buddhist Sets Fire to Himself, Dies: Viet Monk Protests Religious Bias," *Chicago Tribune*, August 5, 1963; "Woman, 82, Sets Herself Afire in Street as Protest on Vietnam," *NYT*, March 18, 1965; "Hate of War Led to Fiery Death," *BG*, November 4, 1965; "Torch Suicides: Sinful at Worst, Futile at Best," *WP*, November 15, 1965.

2. Robert Mole, "Vietnamese Self-Sacrifice Customs," 18–19, FJC; Tad Szulc, "Kennedy Warns the Diem Regime U.S. Will Oppose All Divisive Actions," *NYT*, September 13, 1963; "Hate of War Led to Fiery Death," *BG*, November 4, 1965; "Torch Suicides: Sinful at Worst, Futile at Best," *WP*, November 15, 1965.

3. James Baldwin, "Down at the Cross: Letter from a Region in My Mind," in *The Fire Next Time* (1962; reprint First Vintage International Edition, 1993), 94, 45–46 (emphasis original); "Is God Dead?" *TIME*, April 8, 1966, front cover.

4. Vietnamese casualty estimates vary, but military and civilian deaths combined to total approximately 3.8 million people. Christian Appy, *Working Class War: American Combat Soldiers and Vietnam* (UNC, 1993), 16.

5. Leonard L. Ahrnsbrak, End of Tour Report, 1966, FJC.

6. Joe Klein, "Abortion and the Archbishop," *New York Magazine*, October 1, 1984, 40; Herbert L. Bergsma, *Chaplains with Marines in Vietnam, 1962–1971* (GPO, 1985), 9, 19–20; John J. O'Connor, "A Point of View in Vietnam" (1965; emphasis original), FJC.

7. "Statement of the American Roman Catholic Bishops, Meeting in Washington DC, November 1966, in Appendix, Robert McAfee Brown, Abraham Joshua Heschel, and Michael Novak, *Vietnam: Crisis of Conscience* (Association Press, 1967), 117. On the demographics, nature, reach, and development of the antiwar movement, see Melvin Small, *Antiwarriors: The Vietnam War and the Battle for America's Hearts and Minds* (SR Books, 2002). On the impact on liberal Protestants, see Jill Gill, *Embattled Ecumenism: The National Council of Churches, the Vietnam War, and the Trials of the Protestant Left* (NIU, 2011).

8. The name of the organization underwent multiple changes, from Clergy Concerned to Clergy and Laymen Concerned and finally to Clergy and Laity Concerned. A 1972 resolution by the local Ann Arbor, Michigan, affiliate helped instigate the latter change to avoid sexism. Mollie Babize to CALC Field Staff, August 11, 1972, DG 120, Series I, Box 1, Folder: CALC Steering Committee, 1972, Files of Trudi Young, SCPC.

9. Mitchell K. Hall, *Because of Their Faith: CALCAV and Religious Opposition to War* (Columbia, 1990), 175–176, 47; Brown, Heschel, and Novak, *Vietnam: Crisis of Conscience*.

10. John J. O'Connor, *A Chaplain Looks at Vietnam* (World Publishing Company, 1968), 235, xvi, 7–8; John J. O'Connor to James W. Kelly, January 2, 1968, Box 123, Folder 2, CRB. O'Connor's intuition about CALC was apt; the organization helped publish a 1971 volume that decried the chaplaincy as corrupted by the military. Harvey Cox, ed., *Military Chaplains: From a Religious Military to a Military Religion* (American Report Press, 1971).

11. O'Connor, *A Chaplain Looks at Vietnam*, 13; O'Connor, "A Point of View in Vietnam."

12. O'Connor, *A Chaplain Looks at Vietnam*, 16, 225, 12–13, 4; Nat Hentoff, *John Cardinal O'Connor: At the Storm Center of a Changing American Catholic Church* (Scribner, 1988), 4, 51; "Meet Cardinal O'Connor: With Gold Braid or Red Hat, with John O'Connor 'Loyalty Is First,'" *National Catholic Reporter*, May 3, 1985, 22; "Cardinal O'Connor, 80, Dies; Forceful Voice for Vatican," *NYT*, May 3, 2000.

13. Quoted in Ralph Blumenthal, "Chaplains' Role Questioned Because They Support War," *NYT*, June 22, 1971.

14. Floyd Robertson, "Report: Commission on Chaplains and Service to Military Personnel," April 19, 1966, Box 171, Folder: Commission on Chaplains, NAE; Blumenthal, "Chaplains' Role Questioned Because They Support War"; "Bibles in the Barracks—God and the Military," *CT*, March 31, 1972.

15. Preston C. Oliver to James Kelly, January 2, 1967; Loren M. Lindquist to Chief of Chaplains, December 29, 1967; Roy D. Grubbs to James Kelly, December 19, 1967, Box 123, Folder 2, CRB.

16. Chaplain P in the United Presbyterian Church, "The Military Chaplaincy: Captive or Free?" 1968, xi, Box 15, Folder 93, NJWB2; Frederick Arneson, End of Tour Report, September 10, 1968, FJC; Leonard L. Ahrnsbrak, End of Tour Report, 1965–1966, FJC; Paul W. Pearson, End of Tour Report, 3, 1966, FJC.

17. John J. Scanlon, End of Tour Report, August 1966, 8–9, FJC. Whether Scanlon's use of "fear and trembling" intentionally referenced philosopher Soren Kierkegaard's work by the same name or Philippians 2:12 or Psalms 55:6 is unclear.

18. Peter J. Cary, End of Tour Report, 1969, 3, FJC. On the use and abuse of heroin in Vietnam, see Eric C. Schneider, *Smack: Heroin and the American City* (Penn, 2008), 159–181. Schneider argues that the dramatic decline in heroin use among returning veterans suggests that social needs and availability, rather than addiction, explains the rates of drug use. Although the acceleration of drug use was documented in the early 1970s, chaplains briefed Navy Chief of Chaplains James Kelly on marijuana, heroin, and opium during his 1967 Christmas visit to Vietnam. Ralph W. Below, "Narrative Report on the Chief of Chaplain's Christmas 1967 Visit to III Marine Amphibious Force, RVN," February 5, 1968, FJC.

19. Dell F. Stewart, End of Tour Report, September 15, 1970, 3, FJC; "CREDO Program Proposal," February 19, 1971, Box 193, Folder 3, CRB. CREDO endured beyond the war and evolved into a larger pastoral counseling program in which the acronym stood for Chaplains Religious Enrichment Development Operation. See "Chaplains Celebrate 40 Years of Special Services to Sailors," *Navy News Service*, April 7, 2011.

20. J. J. Glynn, Report of Chaplain's Experiences and Observations in Vietnam, 1966, 1, FJC.

21. There is an extensive literature on My Lai. See Joseph Goldstein, Burke Marshall, and Jack Schwartz, *The My Lai Massacre and Its Cover-Up: Beyond the Reach of the Law? The Peers Commission Report* (Free Press, 1976); James S. Olson and Randy Roberts, *My Lai: A Brief History with Documents* (Bedford / St. Martins, 1998); William T. Allison, *My Lai: An American Atrocity in the Vietnam War* (JHU, 2012); Michael Bilton and Kevin Sim, *Four Hours in My Lai* (Penguin, 1993). For an expose of American war crimes in Vietnam that highlights how the military encouraged immoral behavior, see Nick Turso, *Kill Anything That Moves: The Real American War in Vietnam* (Metropolitan, 2013).

22. Robert McAfee Brown, "Military Chaplaincy as Ministry," in *Military Chaplains: From Religious Military to Military Religion*, ed. Harvey G. Cox (American Report Press, 1971), 144–145; "Calley's Defense—Destroy My Lai Was Ordered; Soldiers Obey," *Hartford Courant*, December 20, 1970; Goldstein et al., *The My Lai Massacre and Its Cover-Up;* "The Perils of Serving Two Masters," *NYT*, January 30, 1972.

23. Roland B. Gittelsohn, *Here I Am—Harnessed to Hope* (Vantage Press, 1988), 96, 99; *Clay v. U.S.*, 403 U.S. 698 (1971). Like Gittelsohn, former air force chaplain Arthur Hertzberg (Jewish) felt his military experiences bolstered his antiwar credentials, making it easier to be "a dove on Vietnam." George Dugan, "Chaplains Urged to Doff Uniforms," *NYT*, June 4, 1970.

24. Floyd Robertson, "Report: Commission on Chaplains and Service to Military Personnel," April 19, 1966, Box 171, Folder: Commission on Chaplains, NAE.

25. Selective Training and Service Act of 1940, Public Law 76–783 (September 16, 1940); Selective Service Act of 1948, Public Law 1759 (June 24, 1948); *U.S. v. Seeger*, 380 US 163; *Welsh v. U.S.*, 398 US 333 (1970). On citizenship, the draft, and conscientious objection, see Christopher Capozzola, *Uncle Sam Wants You: World War I and the Making of the Modern American Citizen* (Oxford, 2008), 55–82; Jeremy Kessler, *Fortress of Liberty: The Rise and Fall of the Draft and the Remaking of American Law* (Harvard, forthcoming).

26. Catholic just war doctrine (*jus ad bellum*) focuses on seven related criteria: rightful cause; proper authority; comparative justice; peaceful intent; last resort; likelihood of success; and proportionality. Just war theory also sets parameters for behavior during war (*jus in bello*): discrimination; proportionality; minimum necessary force; fair treatment of prisoners of war; no evil means (rape, nuclear weapons, etc.). Jean Bethke Elshtain, ed., *Just War Theory* (NYU, 1991).

27. Samuel I. Korff, "A Responsum on Questions of Conscience," January 14, 1970, 10–11, 2, 4, 21–22, 38–9, 35, 53: http://www.utzedek.org/files/Boston%20Beit%20Din,%20Conscientious%20Objection%20Responsa.pdf. For other religious arguments supporting selective conscientious objection, see James Finn, ed., *A Conflict of Loyalties: The Case for Selective Conscientious Objection* (Pegasus, 1968); John A. Rohr, *Prophets Without Honor: Public Policy and the Selective Conscientious Objector* (Abingdon, 1971).

28. Jack Brown, *Another Side of Combat: A Chaplain Remembers Vietnam* (Cold Tree Press, 2006), 65–67; Army Regulations 635–20, January 5, 1966; OCCH, *Historical Review*, July 1965–December 1966," 43; Ronald L. Hedwall, Experiences and Observations in Vietnam, August 22, 1967, 2, FJC; Chaplain H in "The Military Chaplaincy: Captive or Free?" xii.

29. Jack Brown, "The Question of Jesus and War," *The Link* 26, no. 1 (January 1968): 16–19. From Brown's perspective, the Southern Vietnamese were brothers.

30. J. Harold Sherk (Mennonite), "What Is a Conscientious Objector?" (1964), DG 025, Part II, Series A, Box 7, Folder: Correspondence (Mss article), SCPC.

31. Harry Schreiner to Aryeh Lev, March 24, 1967, Box 28, Folder 196, NJWB2; Stephen Levinson to Bertram Korn, June 20, 1968, Box 24, Folder 5, CCAR.

32. "The Military Chaplaincy: Captive or Free?" iii.

33. Report of the Committee on Chaplaincy to the CCAR, June 8, 1966, Box 23, Folder 2, CCAR.

34. RA, "Report of the Chaplaincy Study Committee" (1966), Box 23, Folder 4, CCAR; RA Report of Committee on Chaplaincy, March 25, 1968, 3, Box 15, Folder 93, NJWB2; "Chaplain 'Draft' Ended by Rabbis," *NYT*, March 27, 1968.

35. Nelson Glueck Memo to 1st and 2nd Year Students, February 11, 1965, Box 22, Folder 1, CCAR; Chaplaincy Coordinating Committee of HUC-JIR and CCAR to Members of the Classes of 1967, 1968, 1969, 1970, and thereafter, March 21, 1966, Box 22, Folder 13, CCAR; Richard E. Dryer to Aryeh Lev, July 23, 1965, Box 22, Folder 3, CCAR. The distinctions made by each movement followed existing ideological affiliations, in which Conservative Judaism emphasized Jewish peoplehood and Reform Judaism foregrounded Jewish ethics.

36. Report of the Committee on the Chaplaincy of the Student Rabbinic Association of HUC-NY, February 29, 1968, 7, Box 24, Folder 2, CCAR; "Editor's Note: Dissent over Vietnam," *The Chaplain* (June 1968).

37. Bertram Korn to CCAR Chaplaincy Committee, November 1965; Louis Feldman to Sylvan Schwartzman, November 8, 1965, Box 22, Folder 3; Richard Lavin to Chaplaincy Coordinating Committee of HUC-JIR and CCAR, October 9, 1966, Box 23, Folder 3, CCAR.

38. Report of the Committee on the Chaplaincy of the Student Rabbinic Association of HUC-NY; Jerold Levy, letter to the editor of *The Reconstructionist*, April 17, 1968 (emphasis original). The personnel strength of the U.S. military in Vietnam reached its height (543,400) in April 1968. Henry F. Ackermann, *He Was Always There: U.S. Army Chaplain Ministry in the Vietnam Conflict* (GPO, 1989), 198.

39. Nathan Landman to Samuel Karff, May 38, 1968 (emphasis original), Box 24, Folder 5, CCAR. Landman's position echoed that of a Presbyterian chaplain surveyed for the church's query about the chaplaincy. In asking whether the chaplaincy was "captive or free," one Chaplain M responded, "I am at least as unfettered as a pastor in his civilian parish when such questions as conscience versus tact arise." See "The Military Chaplaincy: Captive or Free?" Aryeh Lev also wrote an impassioned defense of the chaplaincy, "The Function and Freedom of the Military Chaplaincy," Box 25, Folder 93, NJWB2.

40. Stephen Passamaneck to Al Akselrod, August 5, 1968, Box 24, Folder 6, CCAR.

41. David Max Eichhorn note appended to Jerold Levy letter to the editor, April 17, 1968, Box 15, Folder 93, NJWB2; Bertram Korn to Louis Feldman, December 22, 1965, Box 22, Folder 3, CCAR.

42. Aryeh Lev to Mark Goldman, February 24, 1969, Box 25, Folder 4, CCAR; Stephen Passamaneck to Al Akselrod, August 5, 1968.

43. Sylvan Schwartzman to Bertram Korn, May 1, 1968, Box 24, Folder 3; Stephen Levinson to Bertram Korn, June 20, 1968, Box 24, Folder 5; Bertram Korn to CCAR Executive Board, May 19, 1969, Box 25, Folder 6; Sylvan Schwartzman to Bertram Korn, October 18, 1968, Box 24, Folder 7, CCAR; Peter Rubinstein to Sylvan Schwartzman, January 15, 1969, Box 25, Folder 4, CCAR. Petitions requesting selective conscientious objector status are in Boxes 24 and 25, CCAR.

44. Floyd Robertson, "Report: Commission on Chaplains and Service to Military Personnel, National Association of Evangelicals," September 20, 1967, Box 171, Folder: Commission on Chaplains, NAE; *Gillette v. U.S.* 401 U.S. 437 (1971), 444, 455, 458. The rhetoric of fairness echoed the 1967 Selective Service report, *In Pursuit of Equity: Who Serves When Not All Serve?* (GPO, 1967). The data on enlisted men during Vietnam clearly demonstrate that the "more articulate, better educated, or better counseled" avoided the military altogether or, at the very least, escaped deployment in Vietnam. See Appy, *Working Class War*.

45. *Gillette v. U.S.*, 470–471; Beth Bailey, *America's Army: Making the All-Volunteer Force* (Harvard, 2009).

46. "1966 Convention Resolutions," *The Chaplain* 39, no. 3 (May–June 1966): 24; Chaplain M in "The Military Chaplaincy: Captive or Free?" vii–viii. The Church anonymized the participating chaplains in the results but listed the names and rank elsewhere. They came from the active and reserve army, navy, and air

force, and they ranged from new lieutenants to Army Majors, Air Force Colonels, and retired Navy Captains. Some referenced their location, others did not.

47. "The Military Chaplaincy: Captive or Free?" x, xii.

48. "The Military Chaplaincy: Captive or Free?" x, xii, vi; Samuel Stahl to Aryeh Lev, October 29, 1968, Box 24, Folder 8, CCAR; Martin Marty, *Second Chance for American Protestants* (Harper, 1963), 72. (Chaplain Stahl is of no relation to me.)

49. Irving Heymont, letter to the editor of *The Reconstructionist*, October 11, 1968; "Irving Heymont, 90, Commanded Displaced Persons Camp after WWII," *WP*, April 8, 2009; "The Military Chaplaincy: Captive or Free?" xiii–xvi.

50. Appy, *Working-Class War*, 95, 112; Robert McAfee Brown, "Military Chaplaincy as Ministry," in *Military Chaplains: From Religious Military to a Military Religion*, ed. Harvey Cox (American Report Press, 1971), 147; Gordon Zahn, "What Did You Do during the War, Father? The Chaplain's Role: Serving Morale or Morality?" *Commonweal* (May 2, 1969): 195–199.

51. "Armed Forces Chaplains: *All* Civilians? (A Feasibility Study)," *The Chaplain* 29, no. 1 (May 1972): 2–3; *Abington v. Schempp* 374 U.S. 203 (1963), at 300. The Southern New Jersey branch of the ACLU had raised questions about the constitutionality of the chaplaincy in the early 1960s, but in 1964 the national ACLU's annual report disclaimed the legal action taken by the NJ chapter. However, the Church and State Committee of the ACLU inquired about the chaplaincy in 1963, though it did not express any intent to challenge the institution. See Charles Crabbe Thomas to Robert McNamara, September 7, 1963; John I. Rhea, "Memorandum for the Chief of Chaplains, March 23, 1965; John deJ. Pemberton to Chaplain Taylor, December 10, 1963, Box 4, Folder: Constitutionality of the Chaplaincy, ACCH3.

52. Quoted in Ralph Blumenthal, "Chaplains' Role Questioned Because They Support War," *NYT*, June 22, 1971; "Armed Forces Chaplains: *All* Civilians?" 10, 9. As early as 1962, Martin Siegel—a rabbi who served a two-year stint as a navy chaplain—began lobbying to civilianize the chaplaincy. Martin Siegel, "Revamping the Military Chaplaincy," *CC*, August 8, 1962: 959–960; "Whither the Military Chaplaincy," *CC*, September 19, 1962: 1119–1120.

53. Harry C. Wood, former navy chaplain and head of the United Presbyterian Church's chaplaincy program, said it would be impossible for his church to fund chaplains. "Chaplains Urged to Doff Uniforms."

54. "Armed Forces Chaplains: *All* Civilians?" 70, 27, 49–50, 20.

55. Edward Roberts, Report 1, February 16, 1973, in "Operation Homecoming: The Navy Chaplains' Report—A Transcript of the Taped Situation Reports to the Chief of Chaplains Rear Admiral Francis L. Garrett," 1973, 14–15, FJC.

56. Natasha Zaretsky, *No Direction Home: The American Family and the Fear of National Decline, 1968–1980* (UNC, 2007), 27. On POW/MIA soldiers challenging patriotism and national unity, see Michael J. Allen, *Until the Last Man Comes Home: POWs, MIAs, and the Unending Vietnam War* (UNC, 2009).

57. Ross Trower, Report 1, February 16, 1973, in "Operation Homecoming: The Navy Chaplains' Report," 2. Trower estimated that they had to divulge bad news between a quarter and a third of the time, most often relating to divorce.

58. Carolyn Kleiner Butler, "Coming Home," *Smithsonian Magazine* (January 2005).

8 Fighting with Faith

1. Oral History of Major General Matthew Zimmerman (Ret.), 1997, 32–37, Box 1, MAZ; "Race Rifts Follow the Flag: Blacks Focus on Dissent," *WP*, September 27, 1970; John Brinsfield, *Encouraging Faith, Supporting Soldiers: The Army Chaplaincy, 1975–1995* (GPO, 1997), 5–6. Many soldiers in Germany had served tours in Vietnam, which suggests that racial problems moved with the troops. James Westheider has argued that combat produced better rapport between whites and blacks, but that camaraderie was fleeting. James E. Westheider, *Fighting on Two Fronts: African Americans and the Vietnam War* (NYU, 1997). On Malcolm X, see Manning Marable, *Malcolm X: A Life of Reinvention* (Penguin, 2011).

2. Zimmerman Oral History, 7, 34–35.

3. John C. Pearson, "The Black Experience in the Military Chapel," *Military Chaplains Review* (Winter 1975), 23; Zimmerman Oral History, 39, 43, 37. Zimmerman served as the Army Chief of Chaplains from 1990 to 1994. The navy's first African American Chief of Chaplains was Barry Black (SDA), who served from 2000–2003.

4. Daniel T. Rodgers, *Age of Fracture* (Harvard, 2011); Brinsfield, *Encouraging Faith*, 29.

5. On the composition of the post-1973 military, see Beth Bailey, *America's Army: Making the All-Volunteer Force* (Harvard, 2009). On the new benefits, see Jennifer Mittelstadt, *The Rise of the Military-Welfare State* (Harvard, 2015). On the evangelical-ecumenical spectrum, see David Hollinger, *After Cloven Tongues of Fire: Protestant Liberalism in Modern American History* (Princeton, 2013).

6. Andrew Preston, *Sword of the Spirit, Shield of Faith: Religion in American War and Diplomacy* (Anchor Books, 2012), 530–536; John W. Schumacher, *A Soldier of God Remembers: Memoir Highlights of a Career Army Chaplain* (Grace Brethren, 2000), 95, 299.

7. Floyd Robertson to Bill Lanpher, December 8, 1981, Box 152, Folder: Commission on Chaplains; "Report," October 7, 1968, Box 171, Folder: Commission on Chaplains, NAE; Beth Spring, "Are Military Chaplains Illegal?" *CT*, February 18, 1983.

8. Schumacher, *A Soldier of God Remembers*, 103–104, 112.

9. Floyd Robertson, "Report," April 8, 1970, Box 171, Folder: Commission on Chaplains, NAE; Conrad N. Walker and J. Walker Winslow, *The Leapin' Deacon: The Soldier's Chaplain* (Langmarc, 2004), 139–140.

10. Floyd Robertson, "Report," September 16, 1970, and April 3, 1967, Box 171, Folder: Commission on Chaplains, NAE; Walker and Winslow, *The Leapin' Deacon*, 87 (emphasis original); Floyd Robertson, "Report," October 7, 1968, Box 171, Folder: Commission on Chaplains, NAE.

11. Mittelstadt, *The Rise of the Military-Welfare State*, 148–170; Kenneth Gohr, "Information for Chief of Chaplains News Conferences," n.d., Box 123, Folder 2, CRB; Kevin L. Anderson, End of Tour Report 1968, 2, VET; Kevin Anderson, interview by Paul Zarbock, March 15, 2007, UNCW Military Chaplain Interview Project, http://library.uncw.edu/web/collections./oralhistories/transcripts /649.html.

12. Connell J. Maguire, End of Tour Report 1966, 2, VET; Robertson, "Report," April 3, 1967; Floyd Robertson, "Report," April 20, 1971, Box 171, Folder:

Commission on Chaplains; Bill Garman to Bob Jones, Jr., May 7, 1975; Floyd Robertson to James C. Lont, October 26, 1977, Box 147, Folder: Commission on Chaplains—Permanent File, NAE. Garman was frequently disgruntled with the chaplaincy. He lambasted an optional chaplains conference for allowing dancing, ecumenical prayer, and discussion of topics like masturbation. Russell Shive to Billy Melvin, June 12, 1975, Box 147, Folder: Commission on Chaplains—Permanent File, NAE

13. Floyd Robertson, "Report," April 8, 1970, Box 171, Folder: Commission on Chaplains, NAE. Scholars frequently characterize evangelicalism as a four-pronged religious movement: conversion (being "born-again"); active proselytizing; belief in biblical inerrancy and authority; and salvation through Christ. In the military, the NAE tended to emphasize conversion and salvation.

14. Floyd Robertson to the Membership of the Christian Servicemen's Fellowship, April 1972, Box 171, Folder: Commission on Chaplains, NAE; Anne Loveland, *American Evangelicals and the U.S. Military, 1942–1993* (LSU, 1996); General Ralph E. Haines Jr., quoted in "Bibles in the Barracks—God and the Military," *CT*, March 31, 1972. For more on Explo '72, see John G. Turner, *Bill Bright and Campus Crusade for Christ: The Renewal of Evangelicalism in Postwar America* (UNC, 2008).

15. Floyd Robertson, "Report," September 16, 1970, Box 171, Folder: Commission on Chaplains, NAE.

16. "Army Admits First Muslim Chaplain," *CC*, January 19, 1994; "A Nation Challenged: The Clergy; Military Clerics Balance Arms and Allah," *NYT*, October 7, 2001; "Chaplain Recalls Path to Making History," *The Fort Jackson Leader*, June 12, 2009; COMDESRON TWO to CHNAVPERS, September 19, 1976, Box 79, Folder 1736/7 (Islam + Related Religions), CRB. Muslims eat halal meat, which, like kosher meat, comes only from certain animals and must be ritually slaughtered.

17. CHNAVPERS to COMDESRON TWO, September 21, 1976, Box 79, Folder 1736/7 (Islam + Related Religions), CRB.

18. John J. O'Connor to Victor J. Ivers, March 22, 1977, Box 79, Folder 1736/7 (Islamic Worship), CRB; Interview with Wali Akbar Mohammed, Mazhar Hussain, Robert Farug, and Lt. Ayesha Muhammed, USN, January 14, 1985, 14–22, Box 79, Folder 1736/7 (Muslims), CRB.

19. Michael Dean Hagen to Secretary of Defense, August 29, 1979; "Considerations of the Proposal for the Establishment of an Armed Forces Atheist Council," September 27, 1979, Box 82, Folder 1736/8 (Proposal of an Armed Forces Atheist Council), CRB. Hagen also sent a letter to President Jimmy Carter in which he volunteered to coordinate an Atheist Council.

20. Jim Bank to Ross Trower, August 17, 1980, Box 82, Folder 1736/8 (Proposal of an Armed Forces Atheist Council), CRB. In 2013, Jason Heap applied to be a humanist chaplain, which elicited a fiery response from those who thought the chaplaincy ought to be theistic. "Should Military Chaplains Have to Believe in God?" NPR, July 31, 2013.

21. Floyd Robertson to Billy Melvin, July 21, 1975, Box 152, Folder: Commission on Chaplains—Current Files, NAE.

22. Martin Luther King Jr., "Where Do We Go From Here?" August 16, 1967; Henry F. Ackermann, *He Was Always There: The U.S. Army Chaplain Ministry in the Vietnam Conflict* (GPO, 1989), 206; John W. Brinsfield, *Encouraging Faith*, 7.

The sixty-five black chaplains in 1973 consisted of 3 percent of the chaplaincy corps, well below the 15 percent the Army sought. There are very few references to African American chaplains in archival sources from Vietnam. Jacqueline Whitt suggests that black chaplains from historically African American denominations received fewer overseas assignments. Whitt, *Bringing God to Men: American Military Chaplains and the Vietnam War* (UNC, 2014), 245, note 90.

23. Bailey, *America's Army*, 108–130; John D. Sherwood, *White Sailor, Black Navy: Racial Unrest in the Fleet during the Vietnam War Era* (NYU, 2007). The literature on the black power movement is extensive. For an overview, see Peniel Joseph, *Waiting 'til the Midnight Hour: A Narrative History of Black Power in America* (Henry Holt, 2007).

24. Howard University School of Religion, "Report of the Navy Chaplaincy Program," November 20, 1978, 3–4, 9, Box 60, Folder 1731 / 193 (African Americans), CRB.

25. Peter J. Cary, End of Tour Report 1969, 4, VET; Claude Newby, *It Took Heroes: A Cavalry Chaplain's Memoir of Vietnam* (Ballantine Books, 2003), 521; "Racism in the Army," *PC*, February 7, 1970.

26. "Army Chiefs Asked to End Racism," *BAA*, September 27, 1975; David Cortright, *Soldiers in Revolt: GI Resistance during the Vietnam War* (Haymarket, 1975, 2005), 205–209; "60 Negroes Balk at Possible Riot Control," *LAT*, August 25, 1968; Brinsfield, *Encouraging Faith*, 7; "Song Service Due," *The Fort Hood Sentinel*, November 15, 1974.

27. Equal Opportunity Complaints Information Work Sheet, 1974; Information Paper, "Racial Discrimination Complaint against the LDS Church," May 28, 1974, Box 85, Folder 9; Kenneth P. Edwards to J. Willard Marriott, August 7, 1975, Box 85, Folder 10, JWM. The Army's argument was somewhat disingenuous since the LDS priesthood was open to all white males, thus blurring the lines between membership and leadership. On race relations in the LDS Church, see Armand L. Mauss, *All Abraham's Children: Changing Mormon Conceptions of Race and Lineage* (Illinois, 2003).

28. H. L. Bergsma, "The Pioneers: A Monograph on the First Two Black Chaplains in the Chaplain Corps of the United States Navy" (GPO, 1981), 11–23; "Black Chaplain End Strength, 1975–1980," Box 32A, Folder 1540/42 (Black Chaplains Workshop), CRB.

29. OCCH, *Historical Review* (1973–1974): 37–39; OCCH, *Historical Review* (1972–1973): 66; "Army Seeks More Black Chaplains," *Los Angeles Sentinel*, February 23, 1978.

30. "Black Chaplain Spreads Good Word at U.S. Naval Academy," *New Journal and Guide*, July 28, 1978; "Augusta Man Recalls Cardinal O'Connor," *The Augusta Chronicle*, May 5, 2000. Mandatory chapel services ended in 1973, but the senior chaplain was still a prime (and visible) posting. "3 Academies Drop Mandatory Chapel," *WP*, January 6, 1973.

31. Willard B. Bolden to Merle L. Metcalf, February 16, 1984, Box 59, Folder 1731 / 193, CRB; "Black Navy Chaplains Meet; to Work with King Center, ITC," *ADW*, April 27, 1978.

32. "Chaplaincy Ready; Quartermaster Isn't, as Woman Signs Up," *NYT*, August 14, 1974; "AME Minister, Rev. Alice M. Henderson, Blazes Trail for Women Clerics in the Army," *Ebony* (October 1975): 44–52.

33. "Elmo R. Zumwalt, Admiral Who Modernized the Navy, Is Dead at 79," *NYT*, January 3, 2000. Zumwalt's actions in Vietnam were mixed. On the one hand, he opposed the war in the early 1960s. On the other, he ordered the spraying of Agent Orange in the Mekong Delta, which devastated not only Vietnamese land and people but also his own son, who later died from cancer resulting from exposure to the toxin. Larry Berman, *Zumwalt: The Life and Times of Admiral Elmo Russell "Bud" Zumwalt, Jr.* (HarperCollins, 2012).

34. "Playboy Interview: Admiral Elmo Zumwalt," *Playboy* (July 1974): 73; Z-gram #116, "Equal Rights and Opportunities for Women," August 7, 1972, available online: http://www.history.navy.mil/faqs/faq93-116.htm.

35. Dianna Pohlman Bell, interview by Margaret G. Kibbin, 1994, Oral History Program Chaplain Corps USN, 14, FJC; "Army Seeks More Black Chaplains."

36. Mark Chaves, "The Symbolic Significance of Women's Ordination," *The Journal of Religion* 77, no. 1 (1997): 87–114; Bonnie Koppell, "Female Rabbis in the Military: A View from the Trenches," *Army Chaplaincy* (Winter–Spring 2000), 54. On Protestant women becoming ministers, see Virginia Lieson Brereton and Christa Ressmeyer Klein, "American Women in Ministry: A History of Protestant Beginning Points," in *Women in American Religion*, ed. Janet Wilson James (Penn, 1980), 171–190; Cynthia Grant Tucker, *Prophetic Sisterhood: Liberal Women Ministers of the Frontier, 1880–1930* (Indiana, 1990); Catherine Wessinger, ed., *Religious Institutions and Women's Leadership: New Roles Inside the Mainstream* (South Carolina, 1996); Carl Schneider and Dorothy Schneider, *In Their Own Right: The History of American Clergywomen* (Crossroad, 1997).

37. John O'Connor to J. W. Marriott, December 5, 1977, Box 85, Folder 13, JWM. O'Connor's resistance to LGBT rights during the early years of the HIV/AIDS crisis was particularly controversial. See Tamar Carroll, *Mobilizing New York: AIDS, Antipoverty, and Feminist Activism* (UNC, 2015), 131–161; Anthony Petro, *After the Wrath of God: AIDS, Sexuality, and American Religion* (Oxford, 2015), 137–185.

38. "Female Enters Chaplain Program," *The American Israelite*, October 25, 1979; Koppell, "Female Rabbis in the Military," 54; "Woman Navy Chaplain Irks Orthodox," *Jewish Advocate*, July 3, 1986.

39. "Issue of Women as Rabbis Breaks Up Jewish Unit," *NYT*, June 18, 1986; "3 Wings of Judaism Reach Compromise," *LAT*, August 16, 1986. For a more extended discussion, see Albert Slomovitz, *The Fighting Rabbis: Jewish Military Chaplains and American History* (NYU, 1998), 124–127. While the JWB tried to delicately handle the division over women rabbis, other American religions were also struggling to handle competing views about women clergy in general and in the military. The Southern Baptist Convention, for example, ejected churches that selected female pastors.

40. Janet Horton in "Our Highest Selfhood, Women in Leadership," available online: http://www.marybakereddylibrary.org/project/women-in-military-ministry-with-janet-horton/.

41. "Young Female Finds Niche in Ministry," *Norfolk Journal and Guide*, February 1, 1980; "Chaplain Serves with Boom," *BAA*, January 1, 1985; Carolyn C. Wiggins, "Personal Reflections on Women in Naval Chaplaincy," *Navy Chaplain*

1 (Winter 1987): 4. On diversity in the workplace, see Nancy MacLean, *Freedom Is Not Enough: The Opening of the American Workplace* (Harvard, 2006).

42. *Katcoff v. Marsh*, 755 F2d 223 (1985); *Katcoff v. Marsh*, 582 F. Supp. 463 (E.D.N.Y. 1984). They focused on the army as the largest branch of the military and because the army, unlike the navy, fulfilled their Freedom of Information Act requests without advanced payment required. For extensive background on *Katcoff v. Marsh*, albeit from the perspective of the military's legal team, see Israel Drazin and Cecil B. Currey, *For God and Country: The History of a Constitutional Challenge to the Army Chaplaincy* (KTAV, 1995).

43. Drazin and Currey, *For God and Country*, 1; "Law Students Challenge Military Chaplain Programs," *WP*, May 2, 1980. Katcoff was viable because the Supreme Court had granted taxpayers standing to sue the government in Establishment Clause cases in *Flast v. Cohen* (1968). Prior to that, cases against the chaplaincy such as *Elliott v. White*, 23 F2nd 997 (1928), brought by an atheist against the U.S. Treasury for funding government chaplains, were dismissed for lack of standing.

44. *Lemon v. Kurtzman*, 403 U.S. 602 (1971); Kermit D. Johnson to Manresa Conference, January 16, 1981, quoted in John Brinsfield, *Encouraging Faith*, 126. The 8–0 decision in *Lemon* determined that public reimbursement of parochial schools for salaries and materials used for secular subjects was unconstitutional. The military clearly used public funds to pay for clergy and religious materials, making it even more vulnerable on its face.

45. "Jacob Mishler, Old-Fashioned Judge 'Who Understands Real Life,'" *NYT*, October 17, 1993; Brinsfield, *Encouraging Faith*, 125. Drazin was promoted to brigadier-general for his work on this case.

46. *Katcoff v. Marsh*, 582 F. Supp. 463 (E.D.N.Y. 1984), at 466; *Katcoff v. Marsh*, 755 F2d 223 (1985); "M*A*S*H Farewells Mix Fun and Nostalgia," *NYT*, March 1, 1983. On judicial deference to the military, see David Rudenstine, *The Age of Deference: The Supreme Court, National Security, and the Constitutional Order* (Oxford, 2016).

47. Drazin and Currey, *For God and Country*, 110–113; *Department of Defense Authorization Act, 1985*, Public Law 98–525, Section 554, *U.S. Statutes at Large* 98 (1984): 2532–2533.

48. "Study Methods" and "Report on the Joint Study Group on Religious Practice" (March 1985), x, Box 55, Folder 1730/8, CRB. The Military Ordinariate became the Archdiocese for Military Service in 1985. Archival sources do not indicate why the military chose to interview only members of the Nation of Islam. However, given the Nation's work in federal prisons, the military may have relied on existing federal connections. Sarah Barringer Gordon, *The Spirit of the Law: Religious Voices and the Constitution in Modern America* (Harvard, 2010), 96–132.

49. *Sherbert v. Verner*, 374 U.S. 398 (1963); "One-man war; Army is insensitive to religious freedom, chaplain says," *New York Jewish Week*, October 26, 1984.

50. Dennis Grier to Commander, Company B, September 6, 1984, and Dennis Grier to Chief of Starr through Division Chaplain, September 16, 1984, Box 55, Folder 1730/8, CRB.

51. Interview with Rabbi Avreck, January 23, 1985, 40, Box 78, Folder 1736/6; Interview with Floyd Robertson, Monsignor James Markham, and Dr. Elson, January 22, 1985, 19–21, Box 76, Folder 1735, CRB.

52. Interview with Mr. Mason LaSalle and Mr. David Williams, Christian Science, 5, 13, 18–19, 37, 5–6; "Notes on the Differences between Christian Science and Fundamentalist Faith Healing Groups," Box 77, Folder 1735/895, CRB.

53. Interview with Robertson, Markham, and Elson, 1–2, 11–12.

54. Interview with Mrs. Guru Sangat Kaur Khalsa and SSgt Kroesen, December 19, 1984, 2, 37, Box 78, Folder 1736; Interview with Wali Akbar Mohammed, Mazhar Hussain, Robert Farug, and Lt. Ayesha Muhammed, USN, January 14, 1985, 38, Box 79, Folder 1736/7, CRB.

55. Interview with Robertson, Markham, and Elson, 3; Interview with Rabbi Avreck, 12–16; Interview with Rabbi Lapp (JWB), January 15, 1985, 57, Box 78, Folder 1736/6, CRB. The military transcript misspelled Avrech's name.

56. Interview with Mohammed, Hussain, Farug, and Muhammed, 34, 24, 53.

57. "Report on the Joint Study Group on Religious Practice" (March 1985), Box 55, Folder 1730/8, CRB. The issue of beard exemptions for Sikhs has been unrelenting. "Sikh Soldier Allowed to Keep His Beard in Rare Army Exception," *NYT*, December 13, 2015.

58. Department of Defense Directive 1300.17, "Accommodation of Religious Practices within the Military Services," June 18, 1985. In 1987, the Supreme Court would hear and decide a case about an air force psychologist who wanted to wear a yarmulke (and had, undetected, for years). In a 5–4 decision, the majority deferred to the military's "considered" reasoning, while the dissent lambasted the notion that a regulation written from the perspective of Christians could be neutral. *Goldman v. Weinberger*, 475 U.S. 503. Congress then passed a law approving "neat and conservative" headgear, which helped Jews but left the status of Sikh turbans unclear. See "The Religious Apparel Amendment," *Congressional Record* 133, no. 75 (May 11, 1987); "Religious Garb in Military Advances," *WP*, September 26, 1987.

59. Quoted in Brinsfield, *Encouraging Faith*, 246; "Military Opens Chaplains Ranks to Buddhists," *LAT*, October 27, 1987; "Chaplain Recalls Path to Making History," *Fort Jackson Leader*, June 12, 2009.

60. Zimmerman Oral History, 43; Brinsfield, *Encouraging Faith*, 331, 338. Many understand the dove with an olive branch to symbolize peace and God's messenger, based on the story of Noah in the Hebrew Bible (with a parallel in the Epic of Gilgamesh). In the New Testament, the dove also represents the Holy Spirit. While it does not have the same resonance in all religious traditions, the dove is more pluralistic than crosses, tablets, crescents, etc.

Epilogue

1. "Barre Marble Cutters Prepare Headstones for Soldiers," *Vermont Public Radio*, May 30, 2005; "Carved in Stone: Monument Workers Shape Nation's History," *Hartford Courant*, May 31, 2004; "Trump Criticized My Silence; He Knows Nothing about True Sacrifice," *WP*, July 31, 2016.

2. "A 'Peacemaker' Is Laid to Rest," *WP*, June 16, 2004; "Capt. Humayun Khan, whose grieving parents have been criticized by Trump, was 'a soldier's officer,'" *WP*, August 2, 2016; "A New Gathering Spot at Arlington: Capt. Humayun Khan's Grave," *NYT*, September 12, 2016; "Muslims in the Military: The Few, the Proud, the Welcome," *NYT*, August 2, 2016; Robin Wright, "Humuyan Khan Isn't

the Only Muslim American Hero," *The New Yorker*, August 15, 2016, http://www
.newyorker.com/news/news-desk/humayun-khan-isnt-the-only-muslim
-american-hero.

3. Floyd Robertson, Semi-Annual Report of the Commission on Chaplains,
October 4, 1988, Box 85, Folder: Chaplains Committee Pre-1992, NAE; Chap-
lain Alliance for Religious Liberty, "Purpose Statement," http://chaplainalliance
.org/about-us/purpose-statement/; Military Religious Freedom Foundation,
"Our Mission," https://www.militaryreligiousfreedom.org/about/our-mission/.
On the inherent tension embedded in religious freedom, see Elizabeth Shakman
Hurd, *Beyond Religious Freedom: The New Global Politics of Religion* (Princeton,
2015).

4. Peggy Liebe to President Bush, 1989; Alvin B. Koeneman to Peggy Liebe,
October 17, 1989, Box 78, Folder 1736 (Other Religions + Comparative Religion),
CRB.

5. Memorandum, "Sacramental Use of Peyote by Native American Service
Members," May 21, 1997 and J. R. McNamara to Chaplains, August 13, 1987, Box
81, Folder: Native Americans; S. J. Linehan to Sarah M. Pike, July 20, 1999, Box
82, Folder 1736/9 (Wicca), CRB; "Military Opens Chaplain Ranks to Buddhists,"
LAT, October 27, 1987; "Serving Country, Serving Allah," *On Being*, May 26, 2005,
http://www.onbeing.org/program/abdul-rasheed-muhammad-serving-country
-serving-allah/transcript/6945; Office of the Assistant Secretary of Defense, Memo
on Faith and Belief Codes for the Reporting Personnel Data of Service Members,
March 27, 2017, http://americanhumanist.org/wp-content/uploads/2017/04/Faith
-and-Belief-Codes-for-Reporting-Personnel-Data-of-Service-Members.pdf;
"Defense Department Expands Its List of Recognized Religions," *Religious
News Service*, April 21, 2017; "Synod, Other Advocates Speak for Religious Liberty
in Secularized Military," April 10, 2017, https://blogs.lcms.org/2017/religious
-liberty-in-secularized-military.

6. "Soldier of Faith," *WP*, January 20, 2008; Charles McGuire to the Chairman,
North American Mission Board, March 11, 2001; William E. Thompson Jr., to
Ken Alford, Chair, NAMB, February 20, 2002, AR 631–18, Folder: Endorsing Or-
dained Women Chaplains—Response to SBC Resolution, 2001–2, SBHLA.

7. Kim Hansen, *Military Chaplains and Religious Diversity* (Palgrave MacMillan,
2012), 165–202; Anne Loveland, *Change and Conflict in the U.S. Army Chaplin Corps
since 1945* (Tennessee, 2014), 169–248. Hansen's study demonstrates that chaplains
disagree about the degree to which evangelicals had or lacked power in the military. Charges of evangelical takeovers grew in the 1990s, in part because of
evangelical officers who were not chaplains.

8. "Air Force Chaplain Tells of Academy Proselytizing, *NYT*, May 12, 2005;
"Air Force Academy Staff Found Promoting Religion," *NYT*, June 23, 2005;
"The Unlikely Story of America's First Gay Military Wedding," *Slate*, July 17,
2012; National Defense Authorization Act for Fiscal Year 2014, HR 1960, 113th
Congress, 1st Session, July 8, 2013, https://www.govtrack.us/congress/bills/113
/hr1960/text. Michael Weinstein, who founded the Military Religious Freedom
Foundation, was the major force behind publicizing the evangelical tenor of
the Air Force Academy. Michael Weinstein and Davin Seay, *With God on Our
Side: One Man's War against an Evangelical Coup in America's Military* (Thomas
Dunne, 2006).

9. Army Field Manual 1–05: *Religious Support*, October 5, 2012, 1–1, available online: http://armypubs.army.mil/doctrine/DR_pubs/dr_a/pdf/fm1_05.pdf.

10. "Secular Group Protests Navy's Rejection of Humanist Chaplain," *WP*, June 17, 2014; "New Army Policy Oks Soldiers to Wear Hijabs, Turbans, and Religious Beards," *Army Times*, January 5, 2017.

11. *Navy Chaplain's Manual* (OPNAVINST 1730.1), Section 1203.1 (1973).

Acknowledgments

ONE OF THE great joys of finishing a book is getting to name and thank the many people who made it possible. Like most histories, this book has multiple origin points, but substantively, the research and writing began at the University of Michigan. There is no greater mentor or advocate than Deborah Dash Moore. She knows exactly how to frame feedback at every stage of a project, and she has read, commented on, and discussed more versions of each chapter than anyone else. Each iteration received her meticulous attention to detail and her incredible ability to sculpt the big picture. Most importantly, however, Deborah invests in her students as people, and I am grateful for her wide-ranging and always thoughtful advice.

Matt Lassiter has always taken seriously my claims about the importance of religion in modern America and pushed me to refine my ideas to reach the broad audiences. He too read a number of drafts, and his invaluable advice not only addressed what I needed to do but suggested various ways to do it. Sue Juster waded into the twentieth century with me, asking potent questions about the long history of the relationship between religion and state in America. Bill Novak exudes joy in the life of the mind, and he made tackling intellectual challenges bracing and fun. At Michigan, Howard Brick, Matthew Countryman, Todd Endelman, Karla Goldman, Martha Jones, Mary Kelley, Julian Levinson, Anita Norich, Marty Pernick, and Leslie Pincus all encouraged my work at various points along the way. Finally, Lorna Alstetter, Diana Denney, and Kathleen King took care of all the administrative details of graduate school.

Numerous scholars provided valuable feedback at conferences, workshops, and talks. Margot Canaday expressed interest in my project when I was a graduate student and more recently responded to a lecture with wit, wisdom, and an extraordinarily useful set of questions. The Center for the Study of Force and Diplomacy at Temple University allowed me to present ideas to numerous military historians. I thank Kate Moran and the Cultures of American Religion group at St. Louis University; Jessica Levy, Rebecca Stoil-Shimoni, and the Twentieth-Century Seminar at Johns Hopkins University; and Sally Gordon, Sophia Lee, Serena Mayeri, and the rest of the Legal History Writer's Bloc at Penn for energizing workshops. Over the years, I have presented parts of this book at numerous conferences, including those run by the American Academy of Religion, the American Historical Association, the Association for Jewish Studies, the Biennial Scholars' Conference on American Jewish History, the History of Education Society, the Law and Society Association, the Organization of American Historians, *Journal of Policy History* / Institute for Political History, and the Society for the History of American Foreign Relations. Colleagues, friends, and other scholars from those orbits have generously helped me frame ideas and clarify points large and small. I am especially thankful for advice and comments from Jessica Chapman, Jonathan Ebel, Healan Gaston, Kathleen Holscher, Jeremy Kessler, Kip Kosek, Marian Mollin, Robert Self, Tom Sugrue, Matthew Sutton, Barbara Welke, Tisa Wenger, and Jonathan Zimmerman.

Many colleagues and friends offered challenging and insightful feedback. I am indebted to Darren Dochuk, Liz Harmon, Nora Krinitsky, Cyrus O'Brien, Sarah Robey, and G. Kurt Piehler for generously reading and commenting on drafts of the entire manuscript. Rabia Belt, Angus Burgin, Allison Collis Greene, Aston Gonzales, Clay Howard, Bob Lockhart, Lerone Martin, Katie Rosenblatt, Leigh Schmidt, and Lauren Turek offered incisive comments on individual chapters. Toward the end, Joe Cialdella, Katie Lennard, Liz Papp-Kamali, Ashley Rockenbach, and Lauren Thompson reviewed chapters speedily.

I am fortunate to have dwelled in many academic communities filled with generous and smart colleagues. At the Danforth Center on Religion and Politics at Washington University in St. Louis, colloquia sessions and engaging conversation with faculty, including Darren Dochuk, Andrea Friedman, Marie Griffith, John Inazu, Laurie Maffly-Kipp, Lerone Martin, Leigh Schmidt, and Mark Valeri, propelled my work forward. Maryam Kashani and Rachel Lindsey, Stephanie Gaskill, Scott Gibson, Lauren Turek, and Stephanie Wolfe, offered sustenance along with feedback. Debra Kennard and Sheri Pena made sure everything ran smoothly. More recently, at the University of Pennsylvania, the faculty and staff of the Department of Medical Ethics and Health Policy warmly welcomed a historian, while my co-fellows—Bege Dauda, Grace Lee, Matt McCoy, Jessica Martucci, and Jessica Mozersky—encouraged me to get the book finished. Lila Corwin Berman, Anthea Butler, Sally Gordon, and Beth Wenger enthusiastically welcomed me to Philadelphia as I completed the book.

Research and writing require money as well as time, and I am grateful to a number of institutions for the generous financial support that undergirds this project. At its earliest stages, the Department of History, the Frankel Center for Judaic Studies, the Eisenberg Institute for Historical Studies, and the Rackham Graduate School at the University of Michigan funded research and writing. A Charlotte W. Newcombe Fellowship gave me a full year to focus on writing the first draft. Grants from the American Jewish Archives, the Eisenhower Presidential Library, the Feinstein Center for American Jewish History at Temple University, the Mary Baker Eddy Library, and the Truman Presidential Library enabled me to do extensive archival work. I began revisions as a research associate at the John C. Danforth Center on Religion and Politics at Washington University in St. Louis and completed the book as a fellow in the Department of Medical Ethics and Health Policy at the University of Pennsylvania. Both institutions funded research and conference travel, provided protected writing time, and gave me access to wonderful colleagues who asked smart questions.

Archivists and research librarians made traveling to many institutions in many states pleasant and productive. I am indebted to the library and ILL staff at the University of Michigan, Washington University in St. Louis, and the University of Pennsylvania. At the National Archives, patient archivists explained to me how military records work and alerted me to relevant material over my many months in Washington, DC, and College Park, Maryland. Historian John Sherwood at the Naval History and Heritage Command helped me track down key navy chaplaincy material, and Chaplain (Ret.) Randy Cash welcomed me at Fort Jackson, where he not only opened the archives but also introduced me to a number of thoughtful and thought-provoking Navy chaplains. Many thanks as well to Kevin Profitt and Dana Herman at the American Jewish Archives; Melanie Meyers at the American Jewish Historical Society; Father Michael Morris at the Archives of the Archdiocese of New York; W. John Sheppard at the Catholic University of America Archives; the late Herb Pankratz at the Eisenhower Presidential Library; David Trim, Peter Chiomenti, Ashlee Chism, and Gary Councell at the General Conference Archives of Seventh-day Adventists; Marjorie Bryer at the GLBT Historical Society; Richard McCulley at the Legislative Archives of the National Archives; Kurt Morris at the Mary Baker Eddy Library; Lisa Jacobson at the Presbyterian Historical Society; Linnea Anderson and Ryan Bean at the Social Welfare Archives at the University of Minnesota; Bill Sumners and Taffey Halls at the Southern Baptist Historical Library and Archives; Wendy Chmielewski at the Swarthmore College Peace Collection; David Clark at the Truman Presidential Library; and Bob Shuster at the Wheaton College Archives. As I conducted research across the country, friends and family housed and fed me. For this hospitality, I thank Emily and Leslie Atwood, Dara Cohen and Barry Wohl, Amanda Hendrix-Komoto, Sarah Kummerfeld and Matt Pellow, Jonathan Lerner, Jessica Ohly, Tamar Rabinowitz, and Jonathan and Jordan Stahl.

My first exposure to the delights of thinking like a historian came in high school, under the watchful eye and careful tutelage of Carole S. Powers. There, too, K. Gill Cook and Susan Zuckerman taught me how to write. At Williams College, Regina Kunzel, Karen Merrill, and Frank Oakley all pushed me to seek out good stories and ask hard questions. At Stanford University's School of Education, David Labaree promoted clear writing and Larry Cuban reminded me why I love history. A brief stop at the University of Wisconsin gave me the chance to learn from Charles L. Cohen, Jennifer Ratner-Rosenhagen, and Bill Reese.

I have spent many years in academic settings, and in that time, many colleagues have become friends. In Madison, I was fortunate to meet John Coakley, Robbie Gross, Doria Dee Johnson, Ethan Katz, Cam Scribner, and Britt Tevis. In Ann Arbor, Marie Stango—roommate, friend, and colleague—turned an apartment into a home over meals, conversation, and general amusement at my tendency to pace. On campus, Jacqueline Antonovich, Rabia Belt, Millington Bergeson-Lockwood, Gene Cassidy, Aaron Cavin, Chelsea del Rio, Laura Ferguson, Kara French, Aston Gonzalez, Sarah Hamilton, Amanda Hendrix-Komoto, Sophie Hunt, Emily Klancher Merchant, Trevor Kilgore, Nora Krinitsky, Sara Lampert, Suzi Linsley, Elspeth Martini, Austin McCoy, Alice Mishkin, Josh Mound, Minayo Nasiali, Cyrus O'Brien, Angela Parker, Patrick Parker, Lissy Reiman, David Schlitt, Kate Silbert, Colleen Woods, and Cookie Woolner formed various overlapping circles of intellectual and social camaraderie. Michigan connections enabled productive conversations with Tamar Carroll, Nathan Connolly, Lily Geismer, Andrew Highsmith, and Lauren Hirschberg. Elsewhere in Ann Arbor, Jenna Brand, Rae Hoekstra, Rossie Hutchinson, Karen LePage, and Brenda Ratliff welcomed me into their sewing and quilting worlds, giving me a wonderful creative outlet away from my computer. Over the course of writing this book, many friends have checked in and offered unflagging support. I especially thank Claire Adida and Jen Burney, Mark Axelrod and Marissa Miller, Jenny and Matt Brinkmeier, Dina Danon and Eliav Bock, Rachel Deblinger, Chavi Kahn and Rafi Pristoop, Mike Gross and Anna Kneitel, Liora Halperin and Sasha Senderovich, Peter and Elizabeth Maer, Beth Maer Magden, Jenny Meyer and Jeremy White, Sibyl Siegfried, Rebecca Stoil-Shimoni, Claire Sufrin and Michael Simon, Shayna Weiss, and Roberta and Henry Wulf.

At Harvard University Press, Joyce Seltzer took on this project with enthusiasm, immediately posed tough questions, and expertly shaped the narrative. Brian Distelberg initially reached out to me, and Kathleen Drummy smoothly guided the review and production process. Rachel Keith expertly copyedited the manuscript and Kimberly Giambattisto shepherded it through the production process. I am grateful to the two anonymous readers who offered trenchant comments while prodding me to think bigger and raise the stakes of the argument.

This book exists because four friends flung across the country made sure I finished it. Torie Gorges let me brainstorm wildly into her ear, excised (some) writing tics, and never let me forget the value of my work. A conversation with Sivan Zakai helped me find my argument, but even more importantly, she prioritized friendship and conversation in frenetically busy times. Joel Creswell not only convinced me that scientists (or at least one) will read this book but also nerded out over federal agency rules. On the day the final manuscript was due, he sent pep talks along with photos of his new daughter (whose birthday I won't forget!). Katie Rosenblatt has been a selfless pillar of support, sage confidante, fearless thinker, and the best of friends over many years and many drafts (of this project and beer).

My parents, Sharyn and Richard Stahl, were my first teachers, modeling how to read, think, create, and most importantly, ask questions. Danielle Stahl Rummel and Jonathan and Jordan Stahl have offered enthusiastic encouragement over the course of this project— even when they admitted they had no idea what I was doing or how I spent my time. My mother is, as many have said about their chaplains, "always there." Her steadfast and unwavering support allayed stress and propelled me forward.

On November 24, 2013, my father died suddenly. Until then, he was my most constant intellectual interlocutor, especially in matters related to law, politics, and religion. During the Vietnam War, he had a low draft number and entered the Army Reserves. After completing basic training at Fort Jackson (no love lost there—he cringed when I told him I would be going there to do research), he finished his service through weekend duty. On Saturdays, he told me, he would check in and then attend Shabbat morning services. On Sundays, he would go in and take church call, at which point he nabbed a few more hours of sleep. I don't think his capacious religious practice was quite what the military had in mind, but his ecumenical approach—and keen sense of administrative loopholes—nevertheless animate this project. I only wish he were here to read it.

Index

339